TRANSATLANTIC 2020

A Tale of Four Futures

Daniel Hamilton and Kurt Volker, eds.

Center for Transatlantic Relations
Paul H. Nitze School of Advanced International Studies
Johns Hopkins University

Hamilton, Daniel S. and Volker, Kurt, *Transatlantic 2020: A Tale of Four Futures*
Washington, DC: Center for Transatlantic Relations, 2011.
© Center for Transatlantic Relations, 2011

Center for Transatlantic Relations
The Paul H. Nitze School of Advanced International Studies
The Johns Hopkins University
1717 Massachusetts Ave., NW, Suite 525
Washington, DC 20036
Tel: (202) 663-5880
Fax (202) 663-5879
Email: transatlantic@jhu.edu
http://transatlantic.sais-jhu.edu

ISBN 978-0-9841341-5-1
ISBN 0-9841341-5-8

Front cover: Patrol boat photo courtesy of NATO.

Table of Contents

Section IV: Human Mobility

Section V: Questions of Energy Sustainability

Section VI: The Future of the Knowledge Economy

Section VII: New and Traditional Dimensions of Security

Preface and Acknowledgements

This book offers possible futures for the relationship between America and Europe in a rapidly changing world. We do not try to predict the future; rather we take trends rooted in the present and paint a picture of different futures.

We want to thank the Unit for Policy Planning and Research of the Finnish Ministry for Foreign Affairs and the Heinrich Böll Stiftung for their support of this project. Colleagues from many other research institutions, universities, governments and think tanks participated and contributed in interactive sessions we conducted with the Transatlantic Academy in Washington, DC; with the European Commission's Bureau of European Policy Advisors in Brussels; and with the Finnish Ministry for Foreign Affairs and the Heinrich Böll Stiftung in Helsinki and in Berlin. We thank them all for their engagement and encouragement.

We would also like to thank our colleagues at the Center for Transatlantic Relations for their help and good cheer throughout this project, and Peggy Irvine for working with us on the many details related to the production of the book.

Our authors express their own views, and the future scenarios do not necessarily reflect views of any contributor, any institution or any government.

Daniel Hamilton
Kurt Volker

Introduction

A Tale of Four Futures

Daniel Hamilton and Kurt Volker

This is a tale of four futures. Each examines a plausible look at the world in the year 2020. Each is an exaggeration—an over-amplification of a potential model in order to put its contours in sharp relief. These futures are not predictions; they are narratives of how trends evident today could interact and evolve to shape the world we live in tomorrow. Each tale is vastly different from the next, and each provides profoundly different results for Europe, America, and the transatlantic partnership. Nonetheless, as different as they may be, each of these scenarios offers lessons for policy choices today—and in many cases, the same lessons.

The tales are told in the form of readable memos—from policy expert to political leader. Although the leaders change—the head of the 'Atlantic Basin Network;' a U.S. president and a U.S. presidential candidate; the Chancellor of Germany about to attend a 'Euro-mark Summit'—the style is intended to be policy-relevant and constructive.

The scenarios are shaped by the interplay between a few key variables—does Europe emerge from its current crisis stronger than before, or weak and divided? Does the United States emerge as a re-invented and stronger global player, or as a weaker and still declining great power? Does the developing world take off on its own, leaving the transatlantic community in its wake? Or do globalization, widespread economic development and innovation bring the rest of the world and the transatlantic community into a closer alignment?[1]

---

[1] For other scenarios and discussions of scenario-building, see U.S. National Intelligence Council, *Global Trends 2025: A Transformed World* (Washington, DC, 2008);European Commission, *The World in 2025: Rising Asia and Socio-Ecological Transition* (Brussels, 2009); and the Worldwatch Institute's annual *State of the World* series; James Canton, *The Extreme Future: The Top Trends that Will Reshape the World in the*

1

Answering these questions in different ways produces dramatically different results. Yet the forces that shape each scenario are present in real-world politics and economics today. The combination of developments in the developing world and choices made by leaders and publics in the United States and Europe will determine which forces are likely to dominate, producing vastly different outcomes. In each case, we ask whether these changes mean that Europeans and Americans will need each other more or need each other less, and whether they will drive us together or drive us apart.

- **Come Together** represents an optimistic, positive future. The newly developed countries have prospered—but they have done so in parallel with adaptation and continued strength in the older developed world as well. The story takes the form of a memorandum from an African deputy to the Brazilian head of the Atlantic Basin Network—a new and vibrant grouping that links the four continents of Africa, Latin America, Europe and North America around a set of shared political and economic interests across the North and South Atlantic. The rising South Atlantic, having grown to some degree in defiance of North Atlantic nations, is realizing its own interest in closer integration and collaboration with older developed economies in the world, just as Europeans and North Americans have come to appreciate that they must redefine 'Atlanticism' in a globalizing world.

- **Hello Goodbye** portrays a United States that has gone into steep decline, while the rest of the world has moved forward—including both Europe and the developing world. Here, domestic political gridlock in the U.S. precipitated a massive budgetary and economic meltdown, which in turn brought to power a largely reactionary and isolationist gov-

---

Next 20 Years (New York: Penguin, 2007); Daniel Benjamin, ed., *Europe 2030* (Washington, DC: Brookings Institution Press, 2010); Eamonn Kelly, *Powerful Times: Rising to the Challenge of Our Uncertain World* (Upper Saddle River, NJ: Pearson, 2006); Peter Schwartz, *The Art of the Long View* (New York: Doubleday, 1991); European Union Institute for Security Studies and National Intelligence Council, *Global Governance 2025: At a Critical Juncture* (Paris: EUISS, 2010); Neyla Arnas, ed., *Fighting Chance: Global Trends and Shocks in the National Security Environment* (Washington, DC: National Defense University, 2009).

ernment. With a looming Presidential election, 2020 is a fresh opportunity to change course in the United States, and the story takes the form of a memorandum from a campaign advisor to a leading presidential candidate as the primary season gets underway.

- **Live and Let Die** is the opposite scenario: whereas Europe has descended into geriatric decline, the United States—thanks in no small measure to continued immigration and population growth—has managed its fiscal problems and become more closely tied to a growing developing world. The transatlantic relationship has become largely irrelevant, and Europe is faced with previously unthinkable choices about reversing key elements of European integration as competitive parts of the continent scramble to connect to dynamic markets elsewhere in a very different world order. The rise of the 'Global South' has rendered the 'European South' unsustainable within the old EU framework.

- **With a Little Help From My Friends** shows both Europe and the United States having declined, with neither one having come to grips with its fiscal imbalances, changing demographic pyramid, and high-cost, uncompetitive economic structures. Meanwhile, the relatively unregulated, low-cost, and often state-led economies of the newly developed world have boomed, turning the transatlantic relationship into a sideshow. The focus of global development and competition is now among players in the South, rather than in the interplay of North and South. This has left the transatlantic community with the choice of continued erosion in a losing global competition, or erecting higher barriers around a more integrated transatlantic marketplace in a (perhaps futile) effort to preserve liberal economics and high living standards in the developed North.

Underlying Forces

As different as these scenarios are, the forces that shaped them are real and identifiable even today. The question is how these forces are harnessed or managed—if they can be—over the decade ahead. The authors in this volume discuss these forces, and recommend ways the U.S. and Europe can best address them. Some of the most important of these forces include:

- **Deficits and Debt:** One of the most obvious underlying factors is whether Americans and Europeans are able to get control of their fiscal imbalances while the rest of the world moves ahead. While each side of the Atlantic faces its own particular set of economic challenges, at their core both crises are essentially political. Each side of the Atlantic is paying a high economic price for evading hard political choices. In this regard, the twin crisis of deficits and debt could be a watershed moment: either the political spur to more competitive economies in the U.S. and Europe, or the time when each began to lose out to more vigorous powers.

- **Demographics:** Intimately tied to the question of fiscal management is the question of demographic change. Reiner Klingholz and Carl Haub explain that while the situation on each continent is considerably different, both continents face the challenge of aging populations. With low birth rates, low immigration, and longer average life spans, the population pyramid can flatten out or even reverse, with a smaller young population supporting a larger retired population. To the extent the demographic challenge is mitigated by larger immigration and/or birth rates, the challenges becomes more manageable. Yet such immigration and birth rate change would have significant social consequences—and with more significant consequences in Europe than in the United States. In fact, Theo Veenkamp suggests that the rise of anti-immigrant populism represents an early warning signal for a serious systemic crisis emerging in Europe.

- **Human Mobility:** International migration is larger and more diverse than at any time in history. Demetrios G. Papademetriou and Madeleine Sumption explain how it touches upon highly sensitive questions of economic prosperity, national identity, social cohesion, and in some cases, national security. Although the global economic crisis has cast uncertainty over migration projections for the next ten years, such factors as economic growth, talent and geographical mismatches, persistently below-replacement fertility, and the rising cost of labor will continue to drive flows of people to traditional immigrant destinations, but also, increasingly, to emerging economies. At the same time, the notion of "mobility" will increasingly compete with "migration" as the core concept around which human movements are understood and examined, challenging countries to incorporate greater flexibility into their immigration systems and complicating issues of immigrant integration.

- **The Rise of Other Powers:** Rising powers clearly seek influence commensurate with their growing presence in their respective regions and on the global stage. Will these powers challenge the prevailing order or accommodate themselves within it? Hanns Maull and James Dobbins argue that they seek greater say and better status within the current international order, but not any fundamental revolutionary reconstitution of that order—although they acknowledge that at the regional level, for example in the Persian Gulf and East Asia, some do challenge existing arrangements. In contrast, Michael F. Oppenheimer argues that rising states will pose a severe challenge to the liberal order: they were not 'present at the creation;' many pursue illiberal economic and political policies; and they are ready to assert their growing power in the face of an uncertain and divided West. Bruce Jentleson, Giovanni Grevi and Richard Youngs add that what had been a sense of global convergence around such Western norms as rule-based institutions of collaboration, open non-discriminatory trading rules, the 'democratic peace,' and the 'Washington consensus' on development has given way to a broader and more complex global competition of ideas over such issues as multilateralism, the use of force, the rights and responsibilities of state sovereignty, international justice, and alternative models for domestic governance, particularly the relationship between state and market.

- **State-led Economics:** The effect of state-driven economics within developing countries can also be significant, though its long-term implications can cut both ways. On the one hand, state-driven development provides an opportunity to assign resources more strategically, to prioritize infrastructure development, and to negotiate long-term access to energy and other raw materials. It can allow for directly negotiated deals for inputs that undercut global competition. This model appears successful today in cases such as China, even while past models of state-led development elsewhere have failed. Yet we know from experience that large, state-led enterprises over time can tend toward inefficiency, waste and corruption. In addition, Bengt-Åke Lundvall demonstrates that despite China's remarkable investment in academic knowledge, its indigenous innovation capacity remains limited. Whether state-led economics proves sustainable in the medium and long term will have a substantial determinative effect on the nature of the global market we encounter a decade from now.

- **Regulation, Innovation and Competition:** A related current is the interplay between older, highly regulated economies in the United States and Europe, and far less regulated developing economies in the Global South. In everything from environmental standards to safety to labor market protections, relatively less regulated developing markets enjoy a built-in cost advantage. This is reinforced by generally lower wage expectations of populations emerging from poverty, as compared with those having become accustomed to long-term prosperity. The presence of relatively easier regulatory conditions also contributes to attracting new investment and fostering innovation, increasing further the potential competitiveness of developing economies over time. The effect of these advantages has long been mitigated by relatively lower levels of education and middle-class purchasing power within the developing world. But as these factors change—more widespread education and growing purchasing power—the competitive advantages of less regulated economies could become more pronounced, unless the U.S. and Europe take advantage of such strengths as innovation, services and high-end manufacturing.

- **Energy:** Within the overall question of the rise of state-driven economies, energy continues to stand out as perhaps the most important challenge for developing and developed countries alike. Global energy and climate trends are unsustainable, as Christof van Agt, Alexander Ochs and Shakuntala Makhijani all demonstrate. On the one hand, a resource-scarce environment can favor state-driven economies that have the ability to produce and consume on a massive scale, and to negotiate long-term, privileged contracts to assure a reliable energy supply at the lowest cost possible. The imposition of costs tied to emissions reductions in developed economies can further add to the relative advantage newly developing countries enjoy in the energy sphere. On the other hand, a growing energy supply that outpaces growing global demand—for example, through new oil discoveries, Arctic exploitation, shale gas, and falling costs of renewables—could diminish the short-term advantages of state-led economics and even redistribute global market power away from the handful of major oil producing nations, although in some cases at significant environmental cost. How the energy sector develops—and is managed within developed countries—will be one of the most important factors in determining the contours of the world we will face in 2020. If the world truly is to break the link between the production of wealth and the consumption of resources, and thus move to a new model of economic development, the developed countries must chart a path forward.

- **Security Challenges:** Notably, while security challenges do not disappear over the coming decade—and arguably could become worse—they do not present themselves as the drivers of change. Grevi and Youngs, James Dobbins and Andrew Mack all question the rise of a multipolar, zero-sum world; they argue that deepening interdependence has entered the strategic calculus of all major powers, increasing their stakes in the stability of an open international system and tilting the balance away from confrontation. Terrorism and extremism, regional security competition, fragile states and proliferation of agents of mass destruction are likely to continue and indeed require active policy responses. But the other economic and structural forces our authors describe are likely to be much more significant in determining the shape of the world we will inhabit in 2020, and in fact are generating other security challenges. Growing interdependence among the critical—and vulnerable—transboundary arteries carrying energy, people, money, data, goods and services upon which our societies rely is making 'societal resilience' a key aspect of security in a rapidly connecting world.

Lessons for Transatlantic Policymakers Today

The question of how best to address these underlying forces helps to establish an agenda for policymaking in the United States and Europe today. While trends outside the control of any government may do the most to determine how the real world evolves by 2020, government policy can still be mindful of, and in some cases even shape, these trends. Key areas of attention should include:

- **Sound Fiscal Management and Higher Productivity Amidst a Changing Demographic Pyramid**: Clearly—and no surprise to anyone following the daily news cycle—gaining a handle on the structural deficit and debt problems besetting Europe and the United States will be essential if governments are to have the means to influence other long-term economic trends. We share Hanns Maull's assertion that without fiscal solvency, economic growth and job creation, sustained transatlantic leadership is implausible, for the normative appeal and continued relevance of the U.S. and European models for others depends heavily on how well they work for their own people. This is a challenge based not merely on fixing this year's or next year's balance sheets, but on boosting innovation and productivity while redesigning the structures of government expense and income given long-term changes in the shape of our respective demographics: fewer young people and workers, and an older population living longer. Either the work force is increased through higher birth rates and immigration, and also made more productive through innovation, or expenses need to be reduced. Reiner Klingholz argues that Europe in particular must make a virtue out of necessity; since European societies are aging ahead of others, Europeans can—and must—pioneer new lifestyle models for shrinking, aging societies before other continents, which will all join Europe sooner or later. Bengt-Åke Lundvall and Theo Veenkamp join him in contending that this requires a fresh burst of social innovation. Yet while a few individual European countries have tackled these changes successfully for now, overall there is no Europe-wide, nor American, solution in sight, and overall the challenges loom larger for Europe.

- **Active Defense of—and Adherence to—the Liberal International Economic Order:** If the short-term success of state-led economic development and managed trade relationships continues, it could increasingly disadvantage Europe and the United States. An urgent priority for the transatlantic partners, therefore is to reinforce the international liberal economic order. In the short-term, this may mean more economic conflict, rather than less. There may need to be greater push-back on rapidly developing economies through established trade and regulatory mechanisms in order to increase the incentives for these countries to become true "responsible stakeholders" in the global economic system. But the goal of such push-back must clearly be to strengthen the global system itself, not to engage in cheap protectionism for short-term political expediency. It should be possible to develop a transatlantic dialogue about how to avoid destructive competition for emerging markets while enhancing our collective leverage for liberal principles. As Grevi and Youngs point out, in a world of relative power the normative posture of the EU and the U.S. constitutes a comparative advantage at a time when the normative identity of many of their partners is in flux. Yet if they want others to join and support the liberal order, they must be more consistent in supporting it themselves.

- **Realistic Regulatory Policies:** The United States and Europe will need to look carefully at the self-imposed costs of extensive regulatory practices in their internal markets. By creating long-term structural differences in costs between the developed transatlantic economies and the rapidly developing economies of the Global South, they have contributed to a long-term trend of job loss and low-cost external competition. Addressing this challenge can come in a combination of two approaches: reducing unnecessary regulations internally, while imposing regulations on trading partners as part of the price of access to what are still the world's largest pan-continental markets. For example, greenhouse gas standards may need to be more aspirational than mandatory for some time within already developed economies, as it is impossible to force developing economies to adopt equivalent standards. On the other hand, stronger enforcement of existing regulations on quality and product safety can—at admittedly higher cost—reinforce domestic industries and impose a cost on developing nation industries that fail to meet such standards.

- **Leadership in Global Energy Transformation:** As energy will continue to play a dominant role in shaping the global future, Europe and the United States have a keen interest in helping ensure that energy markets provide abundant, affordable, diversified supply. The transatlantic community should provide global leadership in all areas: supporting transparent and non-discriminatory energy market rules; developing new sources of traditional fuels; bringing non-traditional fuels (such as shale gas) into the mainstream while accounting for potential environmental concerns; overcoming distribution and refining bottlenecks to create more flexible markets; investing in technologies to make renewable fuels more cost effective, and investing in cost-effective technologies aimed at reducing energy consumption, and thereby keeping energy prices down and reducing overall costs of energy consumption within the economy.

- **Security Management:** There is a paradoxical lesson on security. While investment in national and global security clearly remains essential, this needs to be kept in proportion with the importance of security issues within this overall global economic environment. Operations such as those in Afghanistan, while vital to combating terrorism and preventing greater regional instability, have also been extremely costly. In the context of meeting the challenges of massive global economic change, investment in such security operations, and in homeland security measures in our own countries, also needs to be as efficient and cost-effective as possible. Even so, James Dobbins underscores an important reality: as the world's predominant power for another generation at least the United States will continue to assume leadership responsibilities for protecting the global commons, including freedom of the seas, space and cyberspace, even as it seeks to share that responsibility more broadly. Security for the global commons also means ensuring the resilience of transboundary arteries carrying energy, people, money, data, goods and services, a task which is also essential to Europe's future.

The Asymmetrical Impact of Change on Europe and America

Each of our tales, and all of our authors, underscore that the trends discussed in this book are likely to affect Europe and America in different ways, highlighting the asymmetrical nature of the transatlantic relationship.

- **Power:** Although the U.S. is apt to be less dominant than it has been over past decades, it is likely to remain the world's principal power for another generation, whereas Europe appears to be waning faster as others rise. Grevi and Youngs highlight the difference: whereas the U.S. is a superpower able to switch through different modes of interaction, from occasional bargains and coalition-building to balance of power and coercion, the EU is unequipped institutionally and politically to do so.

- **Principle:** Differences in relative power can account for differences in the application of principles. For superpower America, multilateral engagement remains a choice. As a result the U.S. has been and continues to be simultaneously a guardian of international norms; a norm entrepreneur challenging prevailing norms as insufficient; a norm externalizer when it tries to advance norms for others that it is reluctant to apply to itself; and a norm blocker when it comes to issues that may threaten its position, or that exacerbate divisions among conflicting currents of American politics. On balance (and despite exceptions), the U.S. has sought to manage this normative-hegemonic interplay by accepting some limits on its power in exchange for greater legitimacy and acceptance of its leadership by others. The unresolved question today is whether the U.S. and other key players are prepared to stick with this bargain.[2] Grevi and Youngs underscore that for the EU, in contrast, multilateralism it is not a matter of convenience but one of essence, as it goes to the heart of the European project. The growing normative assertiveness of rising powers will arguably test the EU's role as a leading normative entrepreneur more than that of the U.S.

• **Mobility/Migration:** The EU and U.S. face similar migration pressures, ranging from publics often skeptical about migration's benefits; strong underlying pressures for migration from neighboring developing countries; the need to manage porous borders effectively; and concerns about immigrant integration. Here again, however, asymmetries emerge, in part due to different social models and the degree to which demographics will drive immigration policies. The most worrisome trend for Europe, however, is that the EU has become a magnet for the unskilled, and lacks pan-European strategies to attract and integrate the highly skilled, whereas the U.S. continues to attract highly skilled migrants, even while struggling to take full advantage of its migrant population as a generator of growth.

• **Demographic Change:** Reiner Klingholz and Carl Haub point to another factor that will affect the transatlantic partners unevenly—demographic change. Whereas both sides of the Atlantic face the prospect of aging societies, Europe is arriving there first. America's demographic situation is different, characterized by a relatively robust population growth rate and youthful population by European standards. It will also have to deal with the aging issue, but the experience is likely to be less severe. But the U.S. will need to face the fact that close allies facing aging, shrinking populations may be less able to support their militaries or provide foreign aid, per-

---

[2] See Daniel S. Hamilton, "The United States: A Normative Power?" in Nathalie Tocci, ed., *Who is a Normative Foreign Policy Actor?* (Brussels: Center for European Policy Studies, 2008), pp. 76-155.

haps contributing to extra stress on U.S. resources.

- **Innovation:** Bengt-Åke Lundvall underscores some key differences in U.S. and European models of innovation. The U.S. competitive advantage, he argues, is an innovation model that combines strong technological capacity with entrepreneurial initiative, managerial competence and advanced markets for services. He contends that parts of Europe, not least the egalitarian welfare states in Scandinavia, have a unique potential when it comes to mobilizing employees in processes of change and engaging consumers as advanced users. He argues for the need to pay more attention in innovation systems to organizational learning, not just scientific knowledge, and the role of employees in the innovation process—areas in which parts of Europe may have some comparative advantage. Both Europeans and Americans, however, share an interest in incorporating the rising powers into a stronger international rule-based regime for governing the sharing and protection of knowledge.

- **Military Capability:** Even though U.S. power has declined relative to other rising powers, the United States military remains highly capable, whereas Europe's military capabilities continue to decline. Even though Europeans took the political lead in the 2011 Libya intervention, they remained reliant on critical American assets that European militaries simply do not have. As James Dobbins notes, Europe thus remains fully as dependent on American military capabilities today is it did sixteen years ago in the Balkans, despite all of the intervening rhetoric and institutional innovation designed to strengthen Europe's capacity for independent expeditionary warfare. And despite consistent and highly public American admonishment, there seems to be little prospect that European governments will halt the decline in their military capabilities or narrow their differences over the use of armed force as an instrument of policy. National decision-making is likely to remain decisive, with EU military expeditions limited to the least demanding of cases.

Taken together, these trends suggest a transatlantic relationship that, while still necessary, is no longer sufficient to tackle the most critical challenges facing each partner or the world; a relationship that remains important for both sides, but one that requires tending and that cannot be taken for granted. As Bruce Jentleson suggests, the relationship "needs to be valued for what it can, and needs to, be in the 21st century: the partnership of the world's most stable democracies who have established a security community among themselves and who seek not just to advance their own interests but to promote broad international cooperation and foster a greater sense of global community." Europe and America may no longer represent 'the' Free World, but at their best they can still be an anchor in a far freer and more fluid world. Their influence is likely to rest on their socio-economic performance at home; their normative consistency at home and abroad; and their ability to work together to engage others in support of the liberal order.

It is of course impossible to predict what the real world will look like in 2020—or even next week. But the exercise of extrapolating existing long-term trends in a variety of scenarios is instructive. By challenging current assumptions and conventional wisdom, it can evoke imagination, provoke deeper reflection, and open the door to new insights. It can clarify our understanding of the bigger issues when they can be lost amid the complexity and competing demands of the day-to-day. By focusing on potential outcomes in the future, it is possible to sharpen our understanding of the present. That, at least, is what the tales of the future we present in this volume are intended to achieve.

Come Together

January 15, 2020

To: *Anna Soares, President, Atlantic Basin Network*
From: *Gregory Ngwenya, Secretary-General*
Subject: *The First Atlantic Basin Summit: How We Got Here and Why It*
Matters

The first summit of the new Atlantic Basin Network promises to advance a number of key goals of our many countries along the Atlantic rim. The peoples of the North and South Atlantic are interacting in a whole host of ways that present both opportunities and challenges. In fact, the most striking development of the past decade has been the new dynamic encompassing the peoples on all four continents of the Atlantic Basin.

As we consider our specific goals for this new initiative, it is perhaps useful to reflect on developments that have spawned the Atlantic Basin Network and given it such relevance. The simple fact is that globalization has generated more connections across the four continents of the Atlantic than perhaps ever before. The well-being of people across this vast region is increasingly influenced by interrelated flows of people, money and weapons, goods and services, technology, toxins and terror, drugs and disease. Not only have the peoples of the Atlantic gained greater access to each other's markets, resources, and ideas, we are also confronting challenges that require us to erase the invisible dividing line that has separated the North and South Atlantic for so long.

In retrospect, it is strange that until now there has been no framework for Atlantic nations to address the issues they face together, even though there are many such efforts in the Asia-Pacific region. But of course we know that globalization is not confined to one region of the world, and the new Atlantic dynamic is really quite striking. You will want the government, business and NGO leaders to focus their attention on this new Atlantic dynamic, and to consider ways to work more effectively together. There a number of reasons why.

The Energy Renaissance is perhaps the most exciting development of recent years—not only because of the transformation of both

Gazprom and OPEC, but because new energy sources are now coming on stream, and a host of new technological advances truly offer the prospect that we can break the link between the production of wealth and the consumption of resources. It's good that this has happened, because the prospect of 9 billion people basing their future growth on extensive use of oil and gas, as well as other resources, is simply untenable. Breaking the link is an historic challenge—but also an opportunity to move toward entirely different patterns of consumption and competitiveness. Cooperation and innovation across the Atlantic Basin could lead the way.

Of course, your own country of Brazil is quickly emerging as a major oil exporter now that the Santos Basin fields are fully on stream; oil now accounts for more than 10% of Brazilian GDP. High oil prices will continue to benefit oil exporters such as Brazil, but the extension of oil production beyond OPEC to the BRINKs and the inability of this more diverse group of producers to agree on pricing has blunted the full impact of China's conversion to a consumer society. It has also made other alternatives more feasible and economical. In retrospect, OPEC simply wasn't prepared for the BRINK countries (Brazil, Russia, Iraq, Nigeria, Kazakhstan), which have added more than 7 million barrels a day of new crude oil capacity over the past decade. Even so, other developments are accelerating the world's transition from oil.

Perhaps the most significant transformation of energy markets has come from full-scale development of what used to be called "unconventional" gas resources. With unconventional gas deposits discovered in significant quantities on every continent, and with technology improvements to mitigate the environmental cost of fracking, together with breakthroughs in gas-to-liquid technologies, energy markets have been reshaped. The United States has become a major gas producer and exporter, while European production facilities in Poland, Ukraine and elsewhere are already producing 100 bcm of unconventional gas and are likely to double their production in the next five years. The EU's new Green Strategy accelerated the continent's shift from coal to gas, stimulated renewables R&D investment, and facilitated the introduction of a carbon tax. The EU also finally took concrete steps to enhance transparency and competition in energy markets and cross-border investments by enforcing the Treaty of Rome's Article 28 competition and antitrust rules in EU energy markets, charging Russian companies Transneft and Gazprom with the same anti-monopoly violations as they did to American companies Microsoft and Intel a decade earlier. Taken together, these developments have stimulated competition and lowered prices. Even Gazprom, though still under state control, has moved toward a business model that is more efficient and has even introduced competition. Russia is exploiting its own shale gas resources, which are close to its existing pipeline infrastructure and cheaper to develop than its Arctic Shtokman or Siberian Yamal gas fields.

Alternative energy technologies have become profitable that previously had been considered commercially unviable. The Energy Renaissance is being facilitated by such advancements in improved energy storage technologies as battery materials, ultracapacitors and hydrogen storage materials for fuel cells, which have literally jumpstarted the prospects for hydrogen-based energy systems; as well as by a host of renewable energy sources such as wind, solar, and low-emission transport vehicles. The ability to generate hydrogen for automotive fuel cells from electricity in a homeowner's garage has helped us avoid the need to develop complex hydrogen transportation infrastructure. As connection technologies and renewable energies merge to create the powerful new "energy internet," the potential for millions of individuals and businesses to produce and share renewable energy will be transformative.

Markets for renewable energy are growing across the Atlantic Basin and elsewhere around the world. Clean coal advances have raised prospects for eliminating greenhouse gas emissions from coal plants. Emerging biofuels technologies that avoid significant land-use changes are already reducing net CO_2 emissions to the atmosphere.

Traditional terms of trade are also shifting, as technological and scientific innovation spreads across the Atlantic Basin. A series of innovations have not only unleashed new economic growth but transformed the very nature of our economies. The Internet of Things has made ubiquitous computing now a mainstay of daily life, boosted economic dynamism and growth first in the U.S. and then in Europe and Asia, and is generating considerable market potential for companies in Africa and South America. But the Faber Revolution—3D custom printing of goods and even living human cells from digital designs—

has truly transformed manufacturing. Now people can download real products, just like they used to download music, at home or at a local 3D production center. The Faber Revolution has reduced waste, sparked innovation, and revived manufacturing in the developed world, while introducing new possibilities to companies on your continent and mine.

Related innovations in service robotics and human cognitive augmentation technologies, including wearable and implantable devices, are improving vision, hearing, and even memory. Bio and information technologies have enhanced human mental performance at every life stage, and "biogerontology" advances have extended average human life by another five years. Manual workers are able to perform what were once thought to be superhuman tasks. Manufacturing and services productivity have been boosted, and the creative industries are enjoying mega-growth.

Taken together, these new technologies are already radically accelerating a range of enhanced efficiencies, streamlining supply chains, and generating cost and efficiency savings. They have helped some key economies cope with aging and shrinking populations.

We have entered a world driven by mass collaboration. Real-time, borderless, digitally-enabled collaboration has become the dominant paradigm of human activity at any scale, worldwide. The Cloud, the past decade's innovative business model, is already being incorporated into a much broader, seamless software platform as purpose-driven online collaboration generates economic growth and improves lives. The rapid and continuous development and operation of such smart systems, which have become critical to every major economic and social sector, is driving new growth and employment.

Of course, we cannot deny that the transition has been wrenching as workers adjust and education systems are challenged. Unskilled labor markets and immigration patterns have been disrupted. While convulsions in job markets have been mitigated by the recent wave of social services innovations, structural unemployment afflicts many countries accustomed to a different division of labor, highlighting the need for viable mechanisms to skill and re-skill workers over the course of their working lives. And we continue to grapple with different approaches to privacy, security and even more profoundly, e-identity. While this is not exclusively an issue for the peoples of the Atlantic, it is useful for discuss.

The invention of lithium air has not only transformed the electric car industry, it underscores an important trend: the Western lead in technology is no longer as predominant as it once was. Although a Japanese company claims credit, the real breakthroughs came from Chinese scientists at the company's research facility in Guangzhou. This innovation has the potential to again transform the way our economies work and our societies are organized. Moreover, the recent breakthrough in India of a nano-plastic membrane capable of converting saltwater into freshwater will transform the challenge of clean water. Cost constraints could still hamper large-scale adaptation, but the potential is huge—with initial advantage going to the Indian consortium that invented it.

Nonetheless, the economic revival of the North Atlantic has contributed to a staggering increase in the volume of Atlantic commerce. Despite the rise of the Pacific, more trade and investment continues to flow across the Atlantic than any other part of the world. Never have so many workers and consumers entered the Atlantic economy as quickly or as suddenly as in the past fifteen years. The global middle class has doubled over the past decade and now accounts for roughly 40 percent of the world's population—and a healthy percentage lives in Atlantic nations. While in the past rapidly developing Atlantic countries were best known for the inexpensive goods and commodities they supplied to the rest of the world, today our consumers are have become a major engine of the global economy. Moreover, the 2015 financial crisis finally convinced companies to consolidate their increasingly global—and increasingly vulnerable—supply chains of products and tasks toward more inner-regional production chains. Although Chinese financing for Columbia's grand Dry Canal Project—a 220 km rail line linking Columbia's Atlantic and Pacific coasts—has been a showcase for China's stepped-up lending to the developing world, overall leaders in both Latin America and Africa have become more wary of Chinese aims.

These developments, positive and negative, have prompted a new approach by both the U.S. and Europe to their neighborhoods and a new view of their role as we begin the third decade of the 21st century.

Both the U.S. and Europe are repositioning and re-energizing their partnership for these new times—in ways that we, as Atlantic nations, can profit from.

The United States has become one of your most important supporters as the new U.S. President works to position her country as a full Atlantic and Pacific power. She acted quickly to prompt the U.S. Senate to ratify the Law of the Sea Treaty, removing an important irritant in relations with your country as well as others. The U.S.-Brazils renewable energy alliance has shown remarkable progress in promoting ethanol as a globally traded commodity and promoting the development, distribution and commercialization of other renewables. The Atlantic Basin Network's private-public Energy Cooperation Forum, instigated by the two countries, has been the most visible and concrete manifestation of the new Atlantic networks now being forged in a variety of areas. A starting point for this new relationship was agreement between Washington and Brasilia to guard against Chinese currency manipulation, as Brazil struggled with a flood of cheap Chinese goods and a surging Brazilian real. Ultimately, it was the ability of the U.S. to put together a new coalition—EU, Japan, Brazil, Mexico, India, South Africa and Korea—that made the difference. This new type of coalition-building is now much more characteristic of American approaches than in the past, and affords critical countries on each of our continents new opportunities for influence.

We have such potential for influence in part because the U.S. President has recognized that in a world of diffuse influence the U.S. can still play a singular role as a pivotal power, able to profit simultaneously from its position in the Atlantic Hemisphere and from its deep ties in the Asian Hemisphere. She has maintained close relations with traditional allies in Europe and Asia, but her trademark initiatives have all sought to encourage more effective and inclusive networks with other countries, including our own. The revival of the U.S. economy has facilitated her efforts; after struggles with recession and war there is a new consensus in the U.S. that Americans must band together with others if they are to advance their values, protect their interests, and extend their influence, and that without the engagement of other partners, Americans alone would pay the costs, in lives and treasure, of maintaining global stability.

Europe, too, is better positioned than it was a decade ago. In retrospect, the Great Recession and the lingering turmoil over the euro through 2013 served as the spur to a more competitive Union. The European Stability Mechanism, the innovation of "Maastricht bonds" and credible austerity measures have given the eurozone a scale and market depth only slightly below that of the U.S. treasury market. Although the EU failed again to achieve all of its Europe 2020 goals, it has recorded some notable achievements, particularly serious progress towards completion of its Single Market and related Digital Single Market, which have given EU companies new possibilities to restructure their activities on a pan-European scale and narrowed the gap among disparate EU economies. The Europeans are leading the world in terms of energy efficiency and use of renewables. They also seem to have understood earlier than most that the manufacturing and services industries were becoming increasingly intertwined, and have been able to make greater progress than anticipated in capitalizing on their advantages in each area. Innovations in the delivery of social services have restored some luster to the "European model" and improved the EU's attractiveness as place to invest, work and study. The EU also has demonstrated that economic strength can go hand in hand with high standards of welfare, despite intense competitive pressures. European flexicurity schemes, which help workers adjust as jobs come and go and develop skills over the course of their working lives, are being studied and emulated in many countries. European birth rates are again on the rise and the EU's pan-European talent strategy combining free flow of labor, skills training and integration of migrants has helped to address the challenges of an aging and shrinking population.

Europe's internal transformation has had profound external consequences. The EU remains the world's largest exporting entity, largest source and destination of foreign direct investment, largest donor of foreign aid, and a critical source of capital for many other world regions. The EU has maintained its share of world exports despite the rise of other trading powers, and is a more significant trading partner for both the BRICs and the BRINKs than either the U.S. or Japan. Rapidly emerging economies continue to register high demand in the types of products in which many European exporters specialize.

By 2015 the Europeans realized that an EU that could move only in lock-step integration would be an EU unlikely to progress at all. Once a new consensus was forged around the premise that EU countries could only solve their debilitating focus on institutional processes through "variable geometry"—allowing some members to move toward deeper integration while others did not—the EU has become much more outward looking and flexible. Ukraine's suddenly positive prospects, boosted by its own reformist government's recent efforts, have prompted the EU to offer to begin accession negotiations. The prospect of Ukrainian membership in 2030, preceded by Turkish membership in 2025, promises to address Europe's growth challenges and enable European companies to make use of a bigger Single Market to extend their production networks and thus to compete more effectively. Turkish membership will strengthen the EU in terms of energy links, economic growth, military capability, geopolitical reach, and will enable the EU to demonstrate that Western democracy and Islam are compatible.

Europe is preoccupied, as usual, but now with historic opportunities: the Arab Renaissance and the uneven rise of open societies across the Arab world; the revived Union for the Mediterranean; the Desertec Solar Initiative linking Europe and North Africa in an expansive solar grid; and the possibilities ensuing from the resolution of the Arab-Israeli conflict. Europe's Modernization Partnership with a reformist Russia holds considerable promise.

Despite the many positive changes to have affected the U.S. and Europe, it is interesting to see how such innovative societies, each more similar to each other than either would care to admit, always manage to embroil themselves in such tendentious transatlantic spats. The Transatlantic Forward Technologies Council created in 2016 to align regulations and standards governing new innovations has yet to demonstrate its effectiveness. The EU's decision to ban human RFID implants until it can sort out not only the legal implications but the potential consequences for human development itself has triggered a major transatlantic row, even as both sides continue to their decade-long fight over appropriate legal systems to protect privacy. The dispute has spilled over into NATO, where a fierce but largely abstract debate rages over whether NATO would ever allow use of "drone armies" to fight human enemies on the battlefield.

Nonetheless, as Europeans and Americans reposition their own economies and societies for the new global economy, they share a keen interest in integrating others into mechanisms of global good governance and building the societal resilience of other nations. While there are some reasons to remain skeptical of Western intentions, it is an opportunity we in the South Atlantic should seize.

Most countries along the Atlantic rim take our budding cooperation seriously and see it as essential to their own development. As we look to future challenges, an Atlantic Basin Initiative has the potential for us all to address opportunities and challenges particular to the Atlantic while positioning Atlantic nations for a very different world as we look to 2030.

Your own country of Brazil has become a strong and influential regional and global player, not only in agriculture and energy, but as a burgeoning services and manufacturing power and a healthy multi-ethnic democracy. Brazilian leadership of the World Bank has been an important signal of the growing influence of rising powers. At home, progress over the past decade to lower crime, reduce poverty and advance the rule of law has been significant. Investment in Brazil has far outpaced that in China, India or Russia.

Brazil's progress has been matched by steady economic growth and positive political developments elsewhere on your continent. Nonetheless, South America has yet to meet its potential. The economic competitiveness of South America continues to lag behind Asia and some other fast growing areas. Some parts of the continent continue to be among the most violent in the world, due to the activities of drug trafficking organizations, transnational criminal cartels, and persistent weaknesses in governance and the rule of law. Those connections are not only flowing south-north through the Americas, they are increasingly flowing west-east as well, encompassing the entire Atlantic Hemisphere.

If South Americans intend to play a larger role on the world stage, they must seek opportunities to address together these broader challenges. The Atlantic Basin Network offers one such frame—it is not exclusive, nor does it compete with other organizations. In fact, its innovation is that it is premised on the notion of public-private networks rather than state-based hierarchies. The new attitude shown the region by the U.S. and Europe offer a potentially interesting new window for South Americans to step up their international profile while dealing in practical terms with issues they face together with other Atlantic partners. It is time to set aside the zero-sum formulas of the past and seek a genuine partnership with the North Atlantic.

Although the situation on my home continent of Africa is in many ways different, we Africans face many similar opportunities and challenges. Parts of Africa are among the fastest growing regions of the world and Africa is a major global supplier of oil, gas and other commodities. It is now viewed widely across the Atlantic Basin and around the world as an opportunity to be grasped, rather than a burden to be carried. The false dawns of the past have given way to prospects for real progress for the future. Market liberalization, improved public management of finances, the continuing boom in Africa's commodities trade, and rapid expansion of consumer spending as well as banking, telecommunications and other services have created a new virtuous cycle for our continent. Africa is increasingly attractive as a base for low-cost manufacturing and offshoring, now that labor prices have risen so much in China and even in India.

At the same time, my continent remains vulnerable to HIV/AIDS, economic disruption, population stresses, civil conflict, corruption and failed governance. Many states lack the capacity to break up terror cells, thwart trafficking in arms, drugs or people, or provide domestic security. The stability of some regions of West Africa is being undermined by drugs coming from Latin America. Up to 250 million Africans could face starvation and malnutrition due to lack of fresh water supplies, lower crop yields, and drought. The dramatic crisis in Nigeria, which only came to what we can only hope will be a peaceful resolution last year, was a wake-up call to the need for Africans to tackle their internal challenges. Integrating Nigeria via the Atlantic Basin Network offers an opportunity.

Our four continents are being bound together in new ways. The opportunities we share are vast; the challenges we face are daunting. Even as the growing latticework of interdependencies across the Atlantic Basin has spawned new opportunities, it has also generated new vulnerabilities along the interconnected arteries and nodes that support the movement of people, goods, services, capital, ideas, and technology upon which our societies depend. As our interconnections widen and deepen, our mutual vulnerability to breaks in these flows has increased, requiring mutual efforts to enhance the resilience of these networks and the critical functions of societies across the Atlantic space. A key goal for the Summit is to get both the leaders and the private and NGO stakeholders who will be attending to agree that together we are called to protect our connectedness, not just our territorial security. These developments call for close interactions between governments, the private sector, the scientific community, and non-governmental organizations. The very networks that have enabled globalization bring these dangers closer and make our societies more vulnerable to disruption. The networks themselves are prone to catastrophic disruption, either through aggressive action or because of the sheer complexity of the technology. Yet, these networks remain essential sinews of the global economy and of daily communications. As a result, they require protection. Just as governments used to protect their territories, so they must now protect the networks that connect them and their citizens with the rest of the world. Any truly transformative definition of security must go beyond territorial integrity to include protecting society's critical functions, the networks that sustain them, and the connections those networks bring with other societies.

Natural changes have made this effort even more urgent. The accelerated melt of Greenland's ice cap, together with major changes in the Antarctic ice shelf have given all Atlantic nations reasons to band together to address the consequences. The tragic hurricanes that hit England have galvanized the Europeans into action, and Hurricane Lois destroyed in two days what it took the people of New Orleans a decade to rebuild.

That is why the Summit's headline project—the creation of the public-private Atlantic Movement Management Initiative (AMMI)—is so relevant. AMMI promises to align security and resilience with commercial imperatives in Atlantic movement systems, including shipping, air transport, even the internet. It will improve cooperation among public and private stakeholders and could serve as the core for a more ambitious global governance framework.

AMMI is a prominent example of how the Atlantic Basin Network can serve as midwife for the new Atlantic system that is emerging under globalization. The Atlantic Hemisphere is characterized by new interdependencies, the rise of new actors, a new technological and ecological environment, and new power relationships. Concerted efforts are required to enhance and protect the global economic, political, technological and human flows on which the globalized Atlantic system depends; and to ensure that societies along the Atlantic Basin are resilient enough to capitalize on the opportunities and deal with the potential disruptions they may face. In our increasingly interconnected region, capacity is derived from connectivity. This should prompt Atlantic leaders to strengthen connections to solve shared problems.

The Atlantic Basin Network agenda is ambitious: advancing cooperation on resource and energy connections; promoting trade and investment; coping with migration and integration; building resilient societies; enhancing good governance; investing in health and human development; and fighting organized crime, drugs and other transnational challenges. If the Summit is successful, there is a good chance that this initiative can avoid becoming just another acronym in the alphabet soup of new multilateral groups. In fact, its key strength is its role as an international **non**-organization—a network of networks that can facilitate robust functional linkages among the Atlantic continents organized around the principle of open regionalism.

I know that our history in dealing with our North Atlantic neighbors could give us pause when contemplating a new initiative bringing us closer together. But as I have outlined here, a host of developments suggest that broad, interwoven, multi-directional hemispheric cooperation is possible. I look forward to working with you to make this first Summit a success.

Reference Notes

p. 15, ... erase the invisible dividing line that has separated the North and South Atlantic for so long ... Anne-Marie Slaughter, former Director of the U.S. State Department's Policy Planning Staff, has drawn attention to the possibilities: "The leading countries of the Atlantic hemisphere are more peaceful, stable and economically diversified that those in the Asian hemisphere ... It is quite a promising neighborhood, home to a wealth of human, economic, material and natural resources." She pointed to the enormous potential for further integration of the Hemisphere, underscoring that Canadian oil sands and Brazilian sugar cane are more promising than depending on Russian pipelines, and that markets for renewable energy—such as from biomass, wind, geothermal technology and other sources—are growing in Latin America. See Anne-Marie Slaughter, "America's Edge: Power in the Networked Century," *Foreign Affairs*, January/February 2009, pp. 94-113.

p. 16, ... break the link between the production of wealth and the consumption of resources ... See "We Can't Get There From Here," *Newsweek*, March 13, 2009, http://www.newsweek.com/2009/03/13/we-can-t-get-there-from-here.html; Rob Atkinson, Michael Shellenberger, Ted Nordhaus, Devon Swezey, Teryn Norris, Jesse Jenkins, Leigh Ewbank, Johanna Peace and Yael Borofsky, *Rising Tigers, Sleeping Giant* (Washington, DC: Breakthrough Institute and Information Technology and Innovation Foundation, 2009); Matt Hourihan, "UN Climate Negotiations and the Race to the Top (of the Clean Energy Heap)," http://www.innovationpolicy.org/33932291 The United Nations produces a series of reports on this topic; see for instance the report by the UN Department of Economic and Social Affairs, Division for Sustainable Development, *Trends in Sustainable Development—Towards Sustainable Consumption and Production* 2010-2011, available at http://www.un.org/esa/dsd/resources/res_publtrends_2010_scp.shtml. For a security perspective on growing resource needs, see Christine Parthemore with Will Rogers, "Sustaining Security: How Natural Resources Influence National Security," Center for a New American Security, June 2010.

p. 16, ... wasn't prepared for the BRINK countries ... ..The term appears to have been coined by PFC Energy. See 'Evolving Structures of the Global Oil and Gas Industry,' Prepared for New America, Fareed Mohamedi, Partner and Head of Markets and Country Strategies, PFC Energy, March 2011. For more on the energy potential of the Atlantic Basin, see Amy Myers Jaffe, "The Americas, Not the Middle East, will be the World Capital of Energy," *Foreign Policy*, September/October 2011.

p. 16, ... are likely to double their production in the next five years ... See Roderick Kefferpütz, "Shale Fever: Replicating the US gas revolution in the EU?" (Brussels: Centre for European Policy Studies, 2010)," http://www.ceps.eu/book/shale-fever-replicating-us-gas-revolution-eu.

p. 17, ... the potential for millions of individuals and businesses to produce and share renewable energy will be transformative ... Richard Smalley's phrase 'energy internet,' was picked up by *The Economist* and then by other authors, including Jeremy Rifkin and Thomas Friedman. See http://econlog.econlib.org/archives/2004/07/an_energy_inter.html; http://www.economist.com/research/articlesBySubject/dis-

playStory.cfm?EMAILAUTH=&REFRESH=0&SUBJECTID=348909&STORY_I
D=2476988; Gunjan Sinha, "Energy internet," *The Smart Techie*, April 2009,
http://www.thesmarttechie.com/magazine_articles/Energy_Internet_id_FMJA29108
0186_2009.html; Jeremy Rifkin, "Only an 'energy internet' can ward off disaster,"
Financial Times, May 11, 2011; Thomas Friedman, *Hot, Flat, and Crowded* (Farrar,
Straus and Giroux, New York, 2008).

*p. 17, ... Markets for renewable energy are growing across the Atlantic Basin and
elsewhere around the world ... .*See World Economic Forum, "Green Investing:
Toward a Clean Energy Infrastructure" (Geneva, Switzerland: WEF, January 2009),
http://www.weforum.org/pdf/climate/Green.pdf; a recent opportunity estimate for
China alone predicted a maximum market opportunity of $500 billion to $1 trillion
by 2013. China Green Tech Initiative, "The China Greentech Report 2009" (Sep-
tember 10, 2009), http://www.china-greentech.com/report; Hourihan, op. cit.;
Miguel Carriquiry, Fengxia Dong, Xiaodong Du, Amani Elobeid, Jacinto F. Fabiosa,
Ed Chavez, and Suwen Pan, "World Market Impacts of High Biofuel Use in the
European Union," *Working Paper 10-WP 508* (Ames, IA: Center for Agricultural and
Rural Development, Iowa State University, July 2010); International Energy Agency
(IEA), *World Energy Outlook 2009;* OECD, *Economic Assessment of Biofuel Support Poli-
cies.* Directorate for Trade and Agriculture, OECD.

p. 17, ... The Internet of Things ... See Kevin Ashton, "That 'Internet of Things'
Thing," in *RFID Journal,* July 22, 2009; "Top 10 Internet of Things Developments of
2010", Readwriteweb.com, http://www.readwriteweb.com/archives/top_10_inter-
net_of_ things_developments_of_2010.php; Commission of the European Communities, "Internet of Things — An action plan for Europe" (Brussels, June 2009); U.S.
National Intelligence Council, *Global Trends 2025: A Transformed World* (Washington,
DC, 2008), which discusses the term as the wholesale tagging and networking of
mundane objects, such as food packages, furniture, room sensors, and paper documents. Such items will be located and identified, monitored, and remotely controlled
through enabling technologies—including Radio Frequency Identifications, sensor
networks, tiny embedded servers, and energy harvesters—connected via the next-
generation Internet using abundant, low cost, and high-power computing.

p. 18, ... the Faber Revolution ... has truly transformed manufacturing ... Fabricators,
or "fabers," also known as 3D printing/additive manufacturing, offer the potential for
custom manufacturing of goods at the price of mass manufacturing of goods, and
thus to cut costs, boost efficiencies, reduce waste, allow for customization, lower
entry barriers to manufacturing, spur innovation, reinforce the movement toward
mass collaboration, and potentially to return manufacturing to developed countries.
See *The Economist*, "The printed world," February 12, 2011; Bonnie Berkowitz, "Living body parts, hot off the printer," *The Washington Post*, May 10, 2011.

*p. 18, ... Related innovations in service robotics and human cognitive augmentation
technologies ... Global Trends 2025*, op.cit.—Human cognitive augmentation technologies include drugs, implants, virtual learning environments, and wearable devices
to enhance human cognitive abilities. Biomechanical devices promise to restore capabilities for many disabled persons while greatly improving labor productivity by
reducing the number of humans needed for a task or increasing the amount of work a

single human can accomplish. Biogerontechnology improvements include biosensors for real-time monitoring of human health, robust information technology, ubiquitous DNA sequencing and DNA-specific medicine, and fully targeted drug delivery mechanisms, which are prolonging life. See also E. S. Boyden, "In Pursuit of Human Augmentation." Ed Boyden's Blog. *Technology Review*, September 17, 2007 (http://www.technologyreview.com/blog/boyden/21839/); James Canton, *The Extreme Future: The Top Trends that Will Reshape the World in the Next 20 Years* (New York: Penguin, 2007).

p. 18, ... We have entered a world driven by mass collaboration ... *Global Trends 2025*, op. cit.; European Internet Foundation, *The World in 2025: Indicators for European Action* (Brussels: September 2009); Robert Huggins and Hiro Izushi, *Competing for Knowledge: Creating, Connecting, and Growing* (London: Routledge, 2009), p. 1; W. M. Cohen and D. A. Levinthal, "Absorptive Capacity: A New Perspective on Learning and Innovation," *Administrative Science Quarterly* 35(1): 128-152, 1990.

p. 19, ... we continue to grapple with different approaches to privacy, security and even more profoundly, e-identity ... See European Internet Foundation, *The World in 2025*, op. cit.; William Dutton, Gerardo A. Guerra, Daniel J. Zizzo, Malcolm Peltu, "The cyber trust tension in E-government: Balancing identity, privacy, security," *Information Polity - Public Administration in the Information Society: Essays in Risk and Trust*, Volume 10, Issue 1,2, April 2005.

p. 19, ... the Western lead in technology is no longer as predominant as it once was ... See Steve Levin, "The Great Battery Race," *Foreign Policy*, November 2010, pp. 90-95; "Innovation futures in Europe: A foresight exercise on emerging patterns of innovation. Visions, scenarios and implications for policy and practice," European Research Area, Socio-Economic Sciences and Humanities Research Policy Brief, October 2010; OECD, *OECD Science, Technology and Industry Scoreboard* (Paris: Organization for Economic Cooperation and Development, 2009); OECD, *Indicators of Innovation and Transfer in Environmentally Sound Technologies: Methodological Issues* (Paris: Organization for Economic Cooperation and Development, 2009). Rob Atkinson, Michael Shellenberger, Ted Nordhaus, Devon Swezey, Teryn Norris, Jesse Jenkins, Leigh Ewbank, Johanna Peace and Yael Borofsky, *Rising Tigers, Sleeping Giant* (Washington, DC: Breakthrough Institute and Information Technology and Innovation Foundation, 2009); Charles Leadbeater and James Wilsdon, *How Asian innovation can benefit us all* (London: Demos, 2007); http://www.iomjapan.org/archives/Presentation_ProfCastles.pdf; OECD, http:// masetto.sourceoecd.org / vl=4322866 / cl=19 / nw=1 / rpsv / sti2007 / b-6.htm.

p. 19, ... more trade and investment continues to flow across the Atlantic than any other part of the world ... See Daniel S. Hamilton and Joseph P. Quinlan, *The Transatlantic Economy 2011* (Washington, DC: Center for Transatlantic Relations, 2011); Daniel S. Hamilton, *Europe 2020: Competitive or Complacent* (Washington, DC: Center for Transatlantic Relations, 2011); David Brooks, "Relax, We'll Be Fine," *New York Times*, April 6, 2010; Stephen J. Rose, *Rebound: Why America Will Emerge Stronger from the Financial Crisis;* Joseph Quinlan, "The Shape of the Future: The Transatlantic Economy by 2025," *Policy Brief*, German Marshall Fund of the U.S., 2011.

p. 20 ... a new consensus in the U.S. that Americans must band together with others if they are to advance their values, protect their interests, and extend their influence ... See Joseph S. Nye, Jr., "The Future of American Power," *Foreign Affairs*, November/December 2010; G. John Ikenberry, "Liberal Internationalism 3.0: America and the Dilemmas of Liberal World Order," *Perspectives on Politics* 7(1): 71-87, 2009; G. John Ikenberry, "The Future of the Liberal World Order," *Foreign Affairs*, May/June 2011; Thomas Wright, "On Reforming the International Order," policy analysis brief, The Stanley Foundation, February 2009; Bruce Jones, Carlos Pascual and Stephen Stedman, *Power and Responsibility. Building International Order in An Era of Transnational Threats* (Washington, DC: Brookings Institution Press, 2009), pp 8-15.

p. 21, ... have given the eurozone a scale and market depth only slightly below that of the U.S. treasury market ... See Jacob Funk Kirkegaard, "In Defense of Europe's Grand Bargain," Policy Brief, June 2010 (Washington, DC: Peterson Institute for International Economics, 2010).

p. 21, ... improved the EU's attractiveness as place to invest, work and study ... Completing, deepening and making full use of the EU Single Market would potentially produce growth of about 4% of GDP over the next ten years. A more complete and vibrant Single Market would provide countries and companies with a stronger geo-economic base in a world of continental-sized players. See Hamilton, *Europe 2020*, op. cit.; Mario Monti, *A New Strategy for the Single Market At the Service of Europe's Economy and Society*, http://ec.europa.eu/bepa/pdf/monti_report_final_10_05_2010_en.pdf; André Sapir, "Globalisation and the Reform of European Social Models," Background document for the presentation at ECOFIN Informal Meeting in Manchester, September 9, 2005 (Brussels: Bruegel, 2005), http://ddata.over-blog.com/xxxyyy/0/28/07/62/sapir/sapirpaper080905.pdf.

p. 21 ... the EU's pan-European talent strategy ... A pan-European talent strategy would attract skilled foreign labor; ensure the free movement of people among member states; facilitate better links between business and education; improve access to and harmonize key features of the labor market; promote higher education and training in key enabling technologies; and boost overall skills training and re-skilling across the EU. See Hamilton, *Europe 2020*, op. cit.; *European Competitiveness Report 2010*, p. 12.

p.22, ... European flexicurity schemes ... are being studied and emulated in many countries ... See T. Andersen and M. Svarer, "Flexicurity—the Danish labour market model," MIT working paper; K. Madsen, "The Danish model of "Flexicurity"—a paradise with some snakes," European Foundation for the Improvement of Living and Working Conditions, 2002.

p. 22, ... The EU remains the world's largest exporting entity, largest source and destination of foreign direct investment, largest donor of foreign aid, and a critical source of capital for many other world regions ... see Hamilton, *Europe 2020*, op. cit.

p. 22, ... Turkish membership will strengthen the EU ... See "Turkey 2020," *CGA Scenarios*, Spring 2011; Henri Barkey, "Turkey's Moment of Inflection," *Survival*, June-July 2010; "Ukraine 2020," *CGA Scenarios*, Spring 2011.

p. 22, ... the Desertec Solar Initiative linking Europe and North Africa in an expansive solar grid ... The Desertec Initiative is being advanced by the Desertec Foundation, a coalition of various European companies and institutions. It seeks to cover 15% of European energy needs by 2050. See Isabelle Werenfels and Kirsten Westphal, "Solarstrom aus Nordafrika: Rahmenbedingungen und Perspektiven," *SWP-Studie*, February 2010 (Berlin: Stiftung Wissenschaft und Politik, 2010); the Mediterranean Solar Plan is led by Germany, France, Italy and Spain, together with the European Solar Thermal Electricity Association (ESTELA). ESTELA, *Solar Power from the Sun Belt* (Brussels, June 2009). See also Daniel Schäfer, "Solarthermie, Physik und Technik der Solarthermie in Afrika," *Spiegel der Forschung*, 2, December 2008, pp. 11-15, available at http://geb.uni-giessen.de/geb/volltexte/2009/6731/pdf/SdF_2008-02-11-15.pdf.

p. 23, ... South America has yet to meet its potential ... For views, see Russell Crandall, "The Post-American Hemisphere," *Foreign Affairs*, May/June 2011; Council on Foreign Relations, *Global Brazil and U.S.-Brazil Relations*, July 2011; Riordan Roett, *The New Brazil* (Washington, DC: Brookings Institution Press, June 2009); Mauricio Cardenas and Eduardo Levy-Yeyati, with Camila Henao, *Brookings Latin America Economic Perspectives* (Washington, DC: Brookings Institution Press, September 2010).

p. 24, ... Africa is increasingly attractive ... now that labor prices have risen so much in China and even in India ... William Wallis, Andrew England and Katrina Manson, "Ripe for reappraisal," *Financial Times*, May 19, 2011; Acha Leke, Susan Lund, Charles Roxburgh, and Arend van Wamelen, "What's driving Africa's growth," *McKinsey Quarterly*, June 2010; Jakkie Cilliers, Barry Hughes, and Jonathan Moyer, *African Futures 2050: The Next Forty Years* (Pretoria: Institute for Security Studies, January 2011).

p. 25, ... the creation of the public-private Atlantic Movement Management Initiative ... This idea is drawn from a report by IBM Global Business Services, "Global Movement Management: Commerce, Security, and Resilience in Today's Networked World," and a 2005 paper entitled "Global Movement Management: Security the Global Economy," available through www.ibm.com/gbs/government. For more on the international aspects of resilient networks, see Bengt Sundelius, "Beyond Anti-Terrorism: Ensuring Free and Resilient Societies," in Daniel S. Hamilton, ed., *Shoulder to Shoulder: Forging a Strategic U.S.-EU Partnership* (Washington, DC: Center for Transatlantic Relations, 2010); Esther Brimmer and Daniel S. Hamilton, "Introduction: Five Dimensions of Homeland and International Security," in Esther Brimmer, ed., *Five Dimensions of Homeland and International Security* (Washington, DC: Center for Transatlantic Relations, 2008); David Omand, "The International Aspects of Societal Resilience: Framing the Issues," in Brimmer, op. cit.; Heiko Borchert and Karina Forster, "Homeland Security and the Protection of Critical Energy Infrastructures: A European Perspective," in Brimmer, op . cit.; "Mobilizing Information to Prevent Terrorism," Third Report of the Markle Foundation Task Force, July 2006; Arjen Boin,"Enhancing Societal Security in the Face of Transboundary Crises: Pointers for Transatlantic Cooperation," unpublished paper prepared for the Center for Transatlantic Relations/PACER, January 2009; Bob Whalley, "Improving the International Coordination and Co-Operation on Homeland Security/Societal Security and Resilience Issues," unpublished paper prepared for Center for Transatlantic Relations/PACER, January 2009; Jonathan M. Winer, "An Initial International Cooperation Agenda on High Consequence Events for the Obama Administration," unpublished paper prepared for the Center for Transatlantic Relations/PACER, January 2009.

p. 26, ... organized around the principle of open regionalism ... The notion of an Atlantic Hemisphere is spurred in part by Kishore Mahbubani's assertion that there is something called an 'Asian' Hemisphere. See Kishore Mahbubani, *The New Asian Hemisphere: The Irresistible Shift of Global Power to the East* (New York: PublicAffairs, 2008). For a different view, see Joshua Kurlantzick, "The Asian Century? Not Quite Yet," *Current History*, January 2011.

Hello Goodbye

January 23, 2020

To: Governor Gifford
From: Your National Security Adviser
Subject: Charting a New Foreign Policy for the 2020 Campaign

The President has staked his Presidency on a reticent America. While that posture fit the national mood in 2016, when the Great Crash forced the country to retrench and resulted in his surprise election, America is in need of the new vision you can provide for the country. Your other campaign memos have focused on domestic policy. This memo reviews the dramatic changes in U.S. foreign policy in recent years and recommends a course of action for you to win the foreign policy debate and ultimately the Presidency.

America's dramatic retrenchment over the past four years resulted not from overstretch overseas but from fiscal, economic and political problems at home. While wars in Iraq, Afghanistan and North Africa certainly helped to dilute the U.S. position in the world, in the end the country's failure to tackle its own domestic challenges proved decisive.

A decade ago, America was burdened by a historically unprecedented and ultimately unsustainable national debt; high, persistent unemployment; creaking infrastructure; and declining competitiveness—all exacerbated by polarized politics that blocked the country from tackling any of these challenges effectively. If the situation had been allowed to continue, America's federal, state and local debt to GDP rate today would have been more than 120 percent. We would have become Greece.

But we never reached that point. When debt hit 100 percent of GDP at the end of 2015, confidence in Washington's ability to control its debt evaporated, triggering a dollar crisis in global financial markets. China's announcement that it was cutting back its dollar holdings imposed tremendous pressure on the dollar. The Fed was forced to raise interest rates sharply and President Obama had to revoke his own budget in his last year in office. U.S. authority and influence were badly tarnished, and the appeal of the American model of market-based capitalism was considerably weakened.

Obama's successor rode into office on a wave of anger at profligate government and the country's dependence on foreign entanglements. The old center of American politics vanished as chastened Democrats pledged to narrow their focus on those most hurt by the crisis and the Republican party all but collapsed into the Tea Party, its leaders vowing to take a hatchet to the federal budget. It was an ugly and punitive time. No category of federal spending was spared, including entitlements and defense. Each side realized that they had to compromise on some fundamental points. Deficits were cut sharply through a combination of big spending cuts, tax increases and re-imposed budget rules. Despite their very different starting points, both political camps rallied to a new consensus centered on a far more circumspect and reticent America. In short, America's diminished role was not due to the rise of other powers or external threats; it was a conscious decision by the American people.

Americans have not lost their sense of exceptionalism. But in the 2016 election the American people made it clear that they believed the best way to restore U.S. vigor and strength was to focus on problems at home, not engage in adventures abroad. In this sense the new national mood is more evocative of America's Jeffersonian tradition, which has always prioritized building a model society that others might emulate, rather than the Wilsonian notion that the U.S. has both a moral duty and a practical need to spread democracy to the ends of the earth. America's "new normal" consensus is that U.S. attempts to foster regime change abroad have on balance weakened American security, cast whole regions of the world into upheaval, and created whirlpools of instability from which undreamed-of threats later arise. The President himself is a reborn Jeffersonian who never tires of saying that his job is not to spread democracy abroad but to safeguard it at home. He likes to evoke Jefferson's admonishment to make America "a standing monument for the aim and imitation by other countries." He has been effective in capitalizing on the widespread belief that the 20th century legacy of protecting Europe and Asia had become outdated and only left America weaker and less competitive.

What has given the President's message real force, however, has been the Jacksonian storm that swept both houses of Congress. The Jacksonian majority in the House is characterized by antiestablishment populism, strong aversion to government debt, cuts to any defense programs not clearly focused on the American homeland; skepticism that free trade with low-wage countries benefits Americans; and rejection of the scientific consensus on climate change. These tenets are all energized by a firm belief in America's "manifest destiny" yet fueled by deep skepticism about America's ability to create a liberal world order. Born-again Jacksonians believe that the U.S. government should focus like a laser beam on the physical security and narrow economic self-interests of the American people. They are unlikely to support any U.S. military intervention in the name of human rights or any limited aims other than retribution for an attack on the United States. They are prepared to do whatever it takes to defend the country, but they do not believe that U.S. interests are best served by a liberal world order.

This historically unusual amalgam of Jeffersonian and Jacksonian traditions is reflected in the rather solid popular consensus that such global phenomena as outsourcing and offshoring have not only destroyed the viability of low-skill, high-wage manufacturing jobs, but have also displaced many high-skill service activities as well. As a result of this convergence of views, American political leaders are inclined to resist any "entangling" institutional commitments and obligations, and the U.S. Senate is unlikely to ratify any of the pending treaties gathering dust in its subcommittee chambers. The country has turned against the easy rhetoric of free trade and the benefits of international engagement. Popular support for an expansive foreign policy has shriveled; there is little to no support for expensive state-building interventions leading to state-building exercises, such as those in Afghanistan and Iraq. Nor is there any support for the kind of humanitarian interventions to rescue people under assault from their own governments that we've seen over the past decade, like Syria, Yemen, or Libya.

This new national consensus gave the President a clear mandate in his first term to reduce America's footprint abroad and to focus, in his words, on "restoring America's promise at home." With support in the Congress, he is engaged in a massive burden-shedding exercise— shedding the burden of defending countries able to defend themselves, abandoning efforts to fix failed states, and focusing on those security challenges that he believes pose the greatest threat to America. Defense spending has been cut dramatically, and the current

BRAC exercise is slated to recommend the complete elimination of the U.S. forward presence in Europe, Japan, and the Middle East, with only a small force in the Strait of Hormuz and a token presence in South Korea.

If the President is re-elected, the changes are likely to be even more dramatic. The President's goal is to transform America's security posture from one premised on forward presence to one based on offshore balancing. His key argument is that the most vital U.S. interests are to prevent an attack on the American homeland; to prevent the emergence of any dominant power in Eurasia; and to forestall the emergence of a regional ("oil") hegemon in the Middle East. The U.S. should not become embroiled in the conflicts of other regions, but should instead promote regional balances of power to thwart any states with hegemonic aspirations. The President has argued that such a strategic shift will not only reduce conflict and make the U.S. safer, it will allow him to reshape the U.S. military to suit this more modest set of objectives, at a price that American taxpayers can swallow. This is the rationale behind his interest in withdrawing U.S. ground forces from Europe and Eurasia (including the Middle East) and assuming an over-the-horizon military posture. He has stated repeatedly that the U.S. should reinsert troops into Eurasia only if regional power balances crumbled.

He has matched these efforts by picking up the pace on nuclear disarmament and really starting to zero. He has ordered unilateral reductions of the U.S. nuclear arsenal that do not depend on Russia or on the Congress, going even beyond the provisions of the 2017 START Reduction Treaty—which is languishing in the Senate—to cut the active U.S. arsenal to 800 weapons and removing all remaining U.S. nuclear bombs in Europe.

The sole area where the President has boosted spending is in homeland security, to protect American soil from terrorist attacks and nuclear threats. His ambitious proposals to create "America's Shield" has invited great criticism from other countries and generated considerable controversy within his own party. But he is determined to shift the historic calculus governing America's deterrence strategy from offense to defense.

The President has been effective in arguing that his policy accommodates the rise of emerging powers; shifts the responsibility of defending Euro-Asian powers onto themselves; is unlikely to embroil the U.S. in other countries' disputes; and is thus both more efficient and effective in defending vital American interests than those wedded to the past. His strategy seeks to turn the emergence of other powers to U.S. advantage. It relies on a balance among many states to maintain U.S. security. All the other great powers are in neighborhoods populated by other would-be powers or dangerous regional foes. In contrast to a world of forward-deployed U.S. forces, which he believes only served to embroil America in others' disputes and made the U.S. a magnet for others' resentments, he believes that his approach to a multipolar world has deflected others' attention toward threats nearer to home, and that self-imposed U.S. restraints have further negated others' incentives to balance against American power. His approach is based on burden shifting, not burden sharing. It has transformed the U.S. from a regional stabilizer into a balancer of last resort by passing to others the primary responsibility for maintaining regional power balances and stabilizing Europe, East Asia and the Middle East. He argues that encouraging other countries to provide more for their own security, rather than relying on the United States, is a fundamental U.S. interest. Rather than identifying himself with Harry Truman's admonition that "the buck stops here," he has essentially passed the buck to other powers to take on the burdens of pacifying their regions, because their security and economic interests are greater. Better them than us, he always says.

The President believes that America is not in the business of solving other peoples' problems, and can afford to be a bystander in the opening stages of regional conflicts. In most cases, he argues, regional powers will be able to deal with trouble-making neighbors. And in the few instances where they cannot, the U.S., as offshore balancer, can always step in to defeat an aggressor.

Global Impact

The President's approach, supported by the Jacksonian-Jeffersonian majority in the Congress, has enjoyed some reasonable popular support. Faced with an overstretched military, massive government debt, popular disenchantment with foreign wars, and mounting challenges at home, Americans have indeed lost their appetite for fixing other people's problems.

Yet America's new stance has had various repercussions overseas. Allies who had alternately relied on and recoiled from U.S. global leadership are finding it hard to adjust to America's retrenchment. The current drawdown and likely full withdrawal of U.S. ground forces from Europe has unnerved governments across the continent. Europeans were particularly surprised when the U.S. failed to join them to address the renewed violence in the Balkans. NATO's 70th anniversary summit was more funeral than birthday. The message the allies took away from that disaster is that Europe cannot rely on the United States. The effect has been to galvanize European cooperation in some ways, while adding to Europe's internal disagreements in others. Moreover, some of our relationships, even among some former close allies, have become more selective and situational, so that it has become harder to classify European countries as either allies or adversaries; they cooperate on some issues and resist on others.

Japan, South Korea and Taiwan have also been confused by U.S. retrenchment from its high-profile position in the Asia-Pacific region. They do not want to trade traditional U.S. security support for any collective regional security arrangement. Nonetheless, American reticence and new Asian dynamics point to more intra-Asian, and less Asian-American cooperation. The Administration's neglect of Taiwan, coupled with the continued rise of Chinese military power, means that the U.S. is no longer able to defend Taiwan from Chinese attack, a reality that could be tested in the near future.

Even as our traditional bonds with Europe and Japan have weakened, many countries have been attracted by China's alternative development model. Moreover, China is increasingly becoming the epicenter of an increasingly interlinked Asian hemisphere. In fact, greater Asian integration oriented around China is slowly filling the vacuum left by the weakening multilateral order, further undermining that order in the process. The creation of an Asian basket of currencies was perhaps the most visible recent effort by Asians to insulate themselves from financial contagion from volatile Western financial markets; reduce their overreliance on the United States; and facilitate regional economic integration.

Maritime security concerns are providing a rationale for naval buildups and modernization efforts, such as China's and India's development of blue-water naval capabilities. India and China can now project naval power to European shores far more easily than European powers can project power to the Pacific. The buildup of regional naval capabilities could lead to increased tensions, rivalries, and counterbalancing moves, but it also will create opportunities for multinational cooperation in protecting critical sea lanes.

Advances by others in science and technology, expanded adoption of irregular warfare tactics by both state and non-state actors, proliferation of long-range precision weapons, and growing use of cyber warfare tactics will increasingly constrict U.S. freedom of action. The multiplicity of influential actors and distrust of vast power means less room for the U.S. to call the shots without the support of strong partnerships.

These trends, of course, are uneven—although China and India compete, they are also rising together. The invention of the next generation of Internet by a joint Chinese-Indian team of scientists should prod us to understand the need to make equally important connections. Early and significant adoption of these technologies is already providing considerable economic advantage to those countries.

Perhaps the greatest impact of a more reticent America, however, has been in the Middle East. Lacking consensus behind a military solution to Iranian development of nuclear-weapons capability, and now faced with a nuclear Iran, the United States declared that it could live with a nuclear-armed Iran—just as it did with China in the 1960s, when China was seen as far more dangerous a rogue state than Iran was at the time. The President has declared that while a nuclear-armed Iran hardly is desirable, neither is it "intolerable," because it can be contained and deterred successfully by the United States. His explicit extension of the U.S. deterrence umbrella to Israel, Saudi Arabia and the Gulf states, together with Iran's dual declaration that it would not attack Israel and not supply such weapons to terrorists, have dampened the possibility of a proliferation snowball in the Middle East. Nonetheless, politically the President has distanced himself from Israel, where—as elsewhere in the region—there is consternation about his assertion that America's new deterrence strategy for the

Middle East did not require an on-the-ground American military presence in the region, and that offshore U.S. air and naval power would provide sufficient deterrent power. Regional fears about a nuclear armed Iran could still trigger an arms race and greater militarization. States in the region worried about Iran and feeling abandoned by the U.S. are developing new security arrangements with external powers, acquiring additional weapons, and some are pursuing their own nuclear ambitions. Episodes of low-intensity conflict taking place under a nuclear umbrella could lead to an unintended escalation and broader conflict if clear red lines between those states involved are not well established.

America's diminished presence in the Middle East has only accelerated deeper economic ties between that region and Asia. Some two-thirds of Mideast oil exports go to Asia, and some 70 percent of Asian imports are from the Middle East. This pattern is likely to intensify. The U.S. unwillingness to maintain open seas has prompted concern over oil supply routes and is now leading to a China-India naval arms race. Japan, alarmed at the prospect of its oil supplies being disrupted, is engaged in a furious domestic debate about whether to revitalize its naval projection power.

The President's offshore balancing strategy means that the United States has abandoned any pretense of promoting democratic transformation in the Middle East. Faced with the rise of the Muslim Brotherhood in Egypt, and confronted tribal conflicts resulting in a radical Libyan regime following Gaddafi's ouster, the United States simply opted out, arguing that it could not successfully pick and chose winners in the region's politics, and decided to avoid the double risk of becoming entrapped in potential domestic upheavals and thereby giving additional stimulus to radical Islamic terrorists who want to target the United States.

All told, this Administration's foreign policy is hastening the emergence of an apolar world, as other states rise, globalization quickens, and non-state actors play increasingly influential roles. The relatively predictable relationships and structures of the past have given way to fluid patterns of simultaneous cooperation and competition among the major powers—the U.S., China, the still-fitful EU, Russia, India and Brazil—as each seeks to obtain the best economic and political advantage for itself while cooperating on issues of common concern. A whole other tier of emerging powers—from Turkey and South Africa to Indonesia and Egypt—are gaming the system, asserting their voice without necessarily buying into international rules or norms of behavior. This pattern is producing unexpected accommodations and temporary alliances. It has generated tensions and made it far harder to build collective responses and to make institutions work. The Brasilia Round of global trade talks—following on the heels of the Doha Round's failure—itself proved to be stillborn, as other countries have followed the U.S. call to "take care of their own."

As a result, U.S. influence is not what it once was. Both Beijing and Moscow diluted international efforts to pressure the government in Nigeria to end its tragic conflict. The joint EU-Chinese peacekeeping operation in Africa foundered. Resource nationalism has reappeared as countries scramble to secure supplies of raw materials, food, water and energy.

This is not a world conducive to American interests. Apolarity has increased the number and nature of threats and vulnerabilities facing the United States. These threats can take the form of rogue states, terrorist groups, energy producers that choose to reduce their output, or central banks whose action or inaction can create conditions that affect the role and strength of the U.S. dollar.

Your challenge in the coming campaign will be to convince the American people that a world without America is a dangerous world for Americans. The government may be broke, but America is not poor. To advance American interests and values, the United States must reinvest and reengage. It is time to embark on a new course.

Winning Back the Presidency—and America

For the moment, the traditional internationalist alliance between those who believe that open commerce and an activist U.S. political and military presence are the best means to ensure American prosperity and security is on the defensive. America's Wilsonian impulse—the notion that the United States has both a moral obligation and an important national interest in spreading American democratic and social values throughout the world, creating a peaceful international community that accepts the rule of law— has been muted.

But the President was wounded in his own party's early primaries by Senator Cartwright's charge that his extreme policies had sacrificed our allies and our interests. Similarly, your initial statements challenging your primary opponents, most of whom still cling to the rhetoric of retrenchment, have resonated with an activist core of supporters. If you are to win the foreign policy debate and with it not only our party's nomination but the election, your challenge will be to unite this internationalist core, which straddles both parties as well as independent voters.

The President's improbable election was due to a unique moment in American political life when economic crisis coincided with a surge of populist political energy and a significant loss of popular confidence in establishment institutions, ranging from mainstream media and the foreign policy and defense and intellectual establishments to the financial and corporate leadership and the government itself. The failure of political leaders of the time to break out of their petty bickering and to tackle the mounting pressures on America's position at home and abroad unleashed a populist backlash of striking proportions. Yet this constellation is uneasy, unsustainable, and vulnerable to change.

You should have no illusions—your call for a revival of America's internationalist impulse will be difficult. If done right, however, your message could resonate with the forgotten mainstream. In retrospect these past four years have perhaps been an inevitable corrective, a necessary interlude, a painful *intermezzo* of realigning ends and means. But the President has made mistakes, the country is on the rebound, and there is a growing realization—which you can capture—that America cannot simply retreat from the world. Voters are turning away from the President's message of sullen retrenchment and are receptive to a new message of progress. This is your opportunity.

Your opponent's call to "take care of our own" is resonant in America today. Indeed, the need for domestic renewal is self-evident. But how do we "take care of our own" in a world where it takes seconds to transfer wealth, minutes to flash news, or hours to transmit diseases from one continent to another? An apolar world of disparate itinerant and diffident powers will not help us cope with new diseases, civilian disasters, conflicts over resources or the breakdown of world trade. America's domestic renewal requires America's active engagement abroad. The affairs of the world have become too deeply integrated into the fabric of our lives for us simply to ignore the rest of the globe while we concentrate on our domestic priorities. Foreign policy must be founded on a renewal of our domestic strength; yet we cannot rebuild our domestic strength in opposition to an active foreign policy.

America cannot sustain an effective foreign policy unless the American people are confident that our actions abroad serve our interests at home. America still has greater capacity over more dimensions of power than any other country, and traditionally has been better connected to all other countries than they have been to each other. The problem is that in our decade of retrenchment we have allowed all of this to atrophy. We have cut ourselves off from a critical source of American strength—the openness of our country and our people. You have the opportunity to challenge the prevailing consensus and to build a new domestic coalition to reestablish American vigor at home and abroad.

You must be clear that the need for constructive engagement is not a call for a new unilateralism. It is an effort to reconcile our domestic needs with our international challenges. What is required is a fusion of our values and our interests. As the next American President, you have the opportunity to break the cycle of expansive idealism alternating with narrow self-interest—both, at heart, forms of unilateralism. It is time to build a consensus on new priorities.

Today's apolar world is an increasingly difficult and dangerous one for America. That is why you have a chance to change the terms of debate—to emerge from our decade of retrenchment to encourage a greater degree of global integration, establish a core group of governments and others committed to cooperative multilateralism to help manage apolarity and increase the odds that the international system will not deteriorate or disintegrate. To win the Presidency, you must tackle this mood head-on and energize a new coalition of internationalists; free-trade pragmatists; and value-centered voters.

You must make the case that there is no substitute for American leadership, but in an era of lowered expectations and resources such leadership must be of a different kind. There will be a premium on consultation and coalition building and on a diplomacy that encourages cooperation when possible and shields such cooperation from the fallout of inevitable disagreements.

There are positives upon which to build. Anti-Americanism has diminished, and no Great Power rival or set of rivals has emerged to challenge the United States. Yet overall the situation is troubling. Your platform should focus on one clear message: the United States can and must take steps to reduce the chances that an apolar world will become a cauldron of instability.

A key point of attack is that there is little evidence that others are willing to share U.S. global burdens. Washington has pulled back, but others have not come forward to share the burden, they have moved into spaces created by U.S. absence to extract as much advantage as they can for themselves. China's rush to lock down reliable long-term access to natural resources has led Beijing to aggressively buy commodities in Africa, Latin America and other emerging markets. Your challenge that the President was "asleep at the switch" when Russia forcefully re-annexed Georgia was a bright moment of challenge that forced many to reconsider their approach, even though in the end it failed to either stop Russia's actions or to swing the national mood. Europe's failure to step into the breach, however, affirms your argument that even though the U.S. has stepped back others have not stepped forward. The result is a more disorderly and less prosperous world.

In fact, you can make a strong case that the rising powers are simply not ready or willing to stand up for a vast set of principles—the collective defense of democracy, nuclear nonproliferation, trade liberalization, international criminal justice, environmental protection, respect for human rights—that have been enshrined in many international and regional treaties and agreements and that are essential to America's own security, prosperity and democracy. Constructing this web of international norms was the mission of two generations of American leaders, supported by the American people. It was slow and painful work over decades, and now it is unraveling. The "new" powers are still wedded to old principles—sovereignty, self-determination, non-intervention, and autonomous economic development. They are not ready to abandon their traditional stance favoring nonintervention over the collective defense of human rights and democracy.... Trying to gain greater status without a road map, they fall back on their default option: the rhetoric and posturing of bygone days, invoking national sovereignty and nonintervention, calling for limited international jurisdiction, and defending the application of different standards to different nations. Unfortunately, this mood is resonant within America as well. Whereas many Americans and Europeans especially over the last half a century championed cosmopolitan norms of individual rights over collective rights of state sovereignty, actors such as China, Russia and India continue to jealously guard the norms of self-determination, autonomy and sovereignty.

The U.S. did continue one key element of its previous policy framework: it has resisted the further spread of nuclear weapons and unguarded nuclear materials. Given their destructive potential, this effort remains extremely important. But as part of our retrenchment we have shied away from any additional security assurances and defensive systems that could be provided to states which might otherwise feel compelled to develop nuclear programs of their own to counter those of their neighbors. And we have abandoned our ability to work with other key countries to impose robust sanctions—on occasion backed by armed force—to influence the behavior of would-be nuclear states.

In short, you can make a good case that our retrenchment from the world's affairs only hurts us more. Ten years ago, the basic complaint was about the U.S. having too much power; today the even worse— perhaps far worse—challenge is that the U.S. has too little of it.

The way forward is not to propose sweeping adjustments to questions of global governance, but to use U.S. power and its connections to other powers to forge limited coalitions for specific ends. The U.S. should actively form issue-specific major power groupings, most of which will be steered by Washington, that seek to reach informal bargains that can shape broader agreements in more formal mechanisms such as the IMF, NPT or the UN. The Major Economies Forum developed this way, and did the Nuclear Security Group. Such efforts are a relatively effective and efficient mechanism through which to advance U.S. interests and structure relations with other key powers in an apolar world. This is the age of minilateralism.

Reference Notes

p. 32, ... *We would have become Greece* ... Roger C. Altman and Richard N. Haass, "American Profligacy and American Power: The Consequences of Fiscal Irresponsibility," *Foreign Affairs*, November/December 2010; Stephen G. Brooks and William C. Wohlforth, "Reshaping the World Order," *Foreign Affairs*, March/April 2009; John C. Hulsman and A. Rem Korteweg, "Managing Elegant Decline: Transatlantic Relations in the Age of Multipolarity."

p. 34, ... *a new consensus centered on a far more circumspect and reticent America* ... We are indebted to Walter Russell Mead's characterizations of these different domestic traditions in U.S. foreign policy thinking. See Walter Russell Mead, "The Tea Party and American Foreign Policy," *Foreign Affairs*, March/April 2011; Walter Russell Mead, *Special Providence: American Foreign Policy and How it Changed the World* (New York: Routledge, 2002); Michael Lind, "The US foreign-policy future: A progressive-realist union?" (http://www.opendemocracy.net/article/democracy_power/US_world/US_foreign_policy); Altman and Haass, op. cit.

p. 34, ... *focus on problems at home, not engage in adventures abroad* ... For more on these tensions in America's foreign and domestic policy traditions, see Brooks and Wohlforth, op. cit.; Mead, op. cit.; W. McDougall, *Promised Land, Crusader State: The American Encounter with the World Since 1776*, (New York, NY: Mariner Books, 1997); Robert E. Osgood, *Ideals and Self-Interest in America's Foreign Relations: The Great Transformation of the Twentieth Century* (University of Chicago Press, 1953); Robert W. Tucker and David C. Hendrickson,"The Sources of American Legitimacy," *Foreign Affairs*, November/December 2004; Arnold Wolfers, "The Goals of Foreign Policy," chapter 5 in his book *Discord and Collaboration: Essays on International Politics* (Baltimore, MD: The Johns Hopkins Press 1962), pp. 67-80.

p. 35, ... *such global phenomena as outsourcing and offshoring have ... displaced many high-skill service activities* ... For discussion of the impact of outsourcing and offshoring on jobs, see for example Alan S. Blinder, "Offshoring: The Next Industrial Revolution? *Foreign Affairs*, March/April 2006; Kate Bronfenbrenner and Stephanie Luce, "The Changing Nature of Corporate Global Restructuring: The Impact of Production Shifts on Jobs in the U.S., China and Around the Globe," submitted to the U.S.-China Economic and Security Review Commission, October 14, 2004 (http://www.news.cornell.edu/releases/Oct04/jobs.outsourcing.rpt.04.pdf); John Austin, "Defining a Great Lakes Economic Agenda," Brookings Institution,Washington, D.C., 2005; James J. Duderstadt, "The Midwest Region and the Knowledge Economy. A Roadmap to the Future," Midwest Media Project, Chicago Council on Global Affairs, May 15, 2007.

p. 36, ... *transform America's security posture from one premised on forward presence to one based on offshore balancing* ... Christopher Layne is an articulate exponent of the notion of offshore balancing. See for example Christopher Layne, "Who Lost Iraq and Why It Matters: The Case for Offshore Balancing," World Policy Journal Blog, August 19, 2010, http://www.worldpolicy.org/blog/who-lost-iraq-and-why-it-matters-case-offshore-balancing; Christopher Layne, *The Peace of Illusions: American Grand Strategy from 1940 to the Present* (Ithaca, NY: Cornell University Press, 2006);

Christopher Layne and Bradley A. Thayer, *American Empire: A Debate* (London: Routledge, 2006); Benjamin Schwarz and Christopher Layne, "A New Grand Strategy," *The Atlantic*, January 2002; See also Hulsman and Korteweg, op. cit.; Michael Lind, "Beyond American Hegemony," *The National Interest*, May/June 2007.

p. 38, ... the U.S. is no longer able to defend Taiwan from Chinese attack ... See Robert D. Kaplan, "The South China Sea is the Future of Conflict," *Foreign Policy*, September/October 2011; Dilip Hiro, *After Empire: The Birth of a Multipolar World* (New York: Nation Books, 2010); Liselotte Odgaard, *The Balance of Power in Asia-Pacific Security* (New York: Taylor and Francis, 2007).

p. 38, ... greater Asian integration oriented around China is slowly filling the vacuum left by the weakening multilateral order ... Robert D. Kaplan, "A power shift in Asia," *The Washington Post*, September 25, 2011; Hiro, op. cit.; G. John Ikenberry, "The Rise of China and the Future of the West," *Foreign Affairs*, January/February 2008.

p. 39, ... India and China can now project naval power to European shores far more easily than European powers can project power to the Pacific ... Robert D. Kaplan, "The Geography of Chinese Power," *Foreign Affairs*, May/June 2010; Ishaan Thadoor, "China's Navy Grows—And the World Watches Warily," *Time*, May 13, 2009; James Rogers, "Why Europa no longer rules the waves," *Esharp*, May 21, 2009, http://www.esharp.eu/Web-specials/Why-Europa-no-longer-rules-the-waves.

p. 39, Perhaps the greatest impact of a more reticent America, however, has been in the Middle East ... For discussion of the impact of a low-profile U.S. role in the Middle East, see Patrick J. Buchanan, "A Middle East without America? " February 18, 2011, http://www.theamericanconservative.com/blog/2011/02/17/a-middle-east-without-america/; Kenneth Pollack, et. al, *The Arab Awakening: America and the Transformation of the Middle East* (Washington, DC: Brookings Institution Press, 2011). Lee Smith, "A Middle East without American Influence? " Slate.com, March 17, 2010, available at http://www.hudson.org/index.cfm?fuseaction=publication_details&id=6847.

p. 40, ... as other states rise, globalization quickens, and non-state actors play increasingly influential roles ... For discussion and debate about whether the world is heading towards 'multipolarity,' 'non-polarity,' 'apolarity,' or other variants, see, for instance, Richard Haass, "The Age of Nonpolarity," *Foreign Affairs*, May/June 2008; Niall Ferguson, "A World Without Power," *Foreign Policy*, July/August 2004; "A worrying new world order: Europe frets about its place in a different world order, *The Economist*, September 11, 2008; Giovanni Grevi, "The interpolar world: a new scenario," Occasional Paper No. 79, European Institute for Security Studies, June 2009; Elizabeth Dickenson, "New Order: How the multipolar world came to be," *Foreign Policy*, November/December 2009; Fareed Zakaria, *The Post-American World* (New York: W.W. Norton, 2008); Gideon Rachman, *Zero-Sum Future: American Power in an Age of Anxiety* (New York: Simon and Shuster, 2011); Hiro, op. cit.

p. 41, ... The government may be broke, but America is not poor ... Similar debates erupted after the Cold War; see Carnegie Endowment National Commission, *Changing Our Ways: America and the New World* (Washington, DC: Carnegie Endowment for International Peace, 1992).

p. 42, ... how do we "take care of our own"...Changing Our Ways, op. cit.

p. 43, ... We have cut ourselves off from a critical source of American strength—the openness of our country and our people ... See Joseph S. Nye, Jr., "The Future of American Power," *Foreign Affairs*, November/December 2010; Eugene Wittkopf and James M. McCormick, eds., *The Domestic Sources of American Foreign Policy* (New York: Rowman & Littlefield, 2007).

p. 43, ... time to build a consensus on new priorities ... *Changing Our Ways*, op, cit.

p. 43, ... diplomacy that encourages cooperation when possible and shields such cooperation from the fallout of inevitable disagreements ... Hulsman and Korteweg phrase it in this way: "The only question (and it is a seminal one) that remains: Is the United States prepared to pare back its foreign policy ambitions to meet this new financial reality, or will it prove another classic victim of Imperial Overstretch, trying to do everything it once did, while now being forced to live on a budget?" Hulsman & Korteweg, op. cit.

p. 44, ... the rising powers are simply not ready or willing to stand up for a vast set of principles ... Jorge Castañeda, "Not Ready for Prime Time," *Foreign Affairs*, September/October 2010; Jorge Castañeda, "The Trouble with the BRICs," *Foreign Policy*, March 14, 2011, http://www.foreignpolicy.com/articles/2011/03/14/the_trouble_with_the_brics; Stewart Patrick, "Irresponsible Stakeholders? The Difficulty of Integrating Rising Powers," *Foreign Affairs*, November/December 2010; Jonathan Holslag, "Europe's normative disconnect with the emerging powers," *Asia Paper*, Vol. 5, No. 4. Brussels Institute of Contemporary China Studies.

p. 45, ... this effort remains extremely important ... See George Perkovich, "Abolishing Nuclear Weapons: Why the United States Should Lead," *Policy Brief* No. 66, Carnegie Endowment for International Peace, October 2008; George Perkovich, "Principles for Reforming the Nuclear Order," Ifri Security Studies Center Proliferation Paper, Fall 2008; "The growing appeal of zero," *The Economist*, June 16, 2011; William Potter and Gaukhar Mukhatzhanova, eds., *Forecasting Nuclear Proliferation in the 21st Century*, 2 vols. (Stanford: Stanford Security Studies, 2011); Michael E. Brown, et. al, eds., *Going Nuclear: Nuclear Proliferation and International Security in the 21st Century* (Cambridge, MA: Harvard/MIT, 2010).

p. 45, ... our retrenchment from the world's affairs only hurts us more ... See Thomas Friedman and Michael Mandelbaum, *That Used to Be Us: How America Fell Behind in the World It Invented and How We Can Come Back* (New York: Farrar, Strauss and Giroux, 2011); Michael Mandelbaum, *The Frugal Superpower: America's Global Leadership in a Cash-Strapped Era* (New York: Public Affairs, 2010).

p. 45, ... forge limited coalitions for specific ends ... For a discussion of 'minilateralism' vs. 'multilateralism,' see Moises Naim, "Minilateralism: The magic number to get real international action," *Foreign Policy*, July/August 2009, and various responses summarized by Chris Borgen, "Debating "Minilateralism," http://opiniojuris.org/2009/06/28/debating-minilateralism/.

Live and Let Die

June 9, 2020

Memorandum for the Chancellor
Subject: Your Attendance at the Euromark Council

It is somewhat ironic that your meeting with the Euromark Council falls almost exactly 10 years after the European Union first agreed to a bailout package in an effort to stabilize Greece's then-massive debt. At that time, European leaders asserted that Europe has always moved forward through crisis—and this would be true again for the eurozone.

Instead, that decision—or rather, the weakness of it—appears to have been the catalyst which, given underlying trends, set in motion the chain of events that has brought us to the decision before the Euromark Council this weekend: whether to put the Reinfeldt Commission's recommendations for a new European Confederation up to individual member states for ratification. If approved, those states invited to ratify will remain part of a single market and currency zone; the rest will remain outside with loose political coordination among all. The practical effect will simply be to recognize the reality that has set in over the past several years: that the dream of a unified Europe that motivated an earlier generation will never be realized, and instead that the "euromark zone" will be recognized as the new core Europe. And within the euromark zone, Germany will continue to be an even more dominant player than it had been in the old eurozone.

It is worth retracing the steps that brought us to this point. When the eurozone crisis first hit ten years ago, the Lisbon Treaty had just been put into effect. Yet the centrifugal forces pulling Europe apart were already well at work.

Underlying Economic Factors

On the economic side, the most important of these was the interplay between globalization and demographics. In the preceding 50 years, Europe had built a social welfare model based on a large working population, with a globally competitive economic output, supporting a modest elderly population. Each of these foundations, however, had changed by the time of the eurozone crisis.

When women joined the workforce, Europe's working population continued to grow, even as total population growth stabilized and began to reverse. Once women were "in," however, the overall size of the working population itself began to decline, while improvements in health care meant that the size of the retired population continued to grow. This alone would have been enough to put pressure on state budgets as the costs of pensions and health care for the non-working population could not be borne by the size of the residual workforce.

But the rise of lower-cost, less regulated economies around the world meant that while the population was changing, jobs and productivity gradually migrated away from Europe as well, leaving this smaller European workforce without the income-generating possibilities needed to sustain this old economic model.

Immigration has done little to change this dynamic—and indeed Europe's failure to manage its immigration issues has been one of the key components of EU decline. As we have failed to create mechanisms to attract and retain high-skilled labor, Europe has become a magnet for the unskilled, which has only fueled political conflict and given rise to the populist movements that have entered parliaments all across the continent. And even though Europe feared that the revolutions sweeping the Arab world in 2011 and 2012 would generate a massive immigration from North Africa that would bring low-wage workers into a weak economy where there were already not enough jobs for the existing European workforce, in fact the opposite happened. As the "Arab Lion" economies took off, immigration dwindled and even some long-resident populations returned home, further depriving Europe of the influx of human talent it has needed. Although the United States, in its own chaotic way, managed to adapt through population growth, deregulation, and drastic reform of social programs, Europe was literally shrinking.

A further factor was the self-imposed cost of Europe's regulatory choices, most importantly in the energy sector. The year 2010—or perhaps a few years before—marked the beginning of the transformation of global energy markets. Prices of traditional fuels began to rise dramatically as newly developing economies used them to power economic growth. Because they endured almost no costs on the back end by burning them "cleanly," they were able to bid up prices on the front end, raising costs to all consumers.

Those developed nations that invested in market-competitive alternatives—nuclear power in China, Russia, India Brazil and (belatedly) the United States, shale gas in North America, etc.—were able to absorb the impact of the rising cost of traditional fuels. Much of Europe, unfortunately, was not.

The nuclear standards imposed by Europe—as the German price for continued French and central European development—meant that nuclear power was never the cheap alternative it could have been. The European ban on shale gas production after the 2014 Krakow disaster meant that Europe's only access to natural gas was from Russia's monopolistic and diminishing supply, or from LNG—in either case pushing the price of gas in Europe today to nearly 4 times global market levels. And finally, the European mandate on renewables has added as much as a further 35 percent to the cost of electricity production in Europe as compared with global markets.

The high costs of energy have had a significant effect on prices throughout the European economy, and in turn have led to a modest reversal of low external tariffs, as well as diminished European role as an innovation economy. It is simply faster, cheaper, and easier to develop new technologies and processes on the spot in places like India—where they can be brought from drawing board to mass-market in nearly a single and constant motion. European-owned capital, while still significant, invests, profits, and re-invests largely outside of European territory.

The Euro Collapse

It was these underlying factors, setting the conditions for fundamental financial unsustainability, that lay behind the eurozone collapse in 2013, and the continued weakness of the euromark and wider European economy today. Bailouts and austerity measures might have worked, had the underlying factors been favorable. But it became clear to markets, and eventually to European leaders, that no amount of bailout money or painful austerity measures could compensate for these underlying fundamentals.

The European social model had to be reworked—and it had to be applied differently across different member states based on their underlying economic fundamentals. While some could sustain a more generous system, most could not. Once the first debt restructuring was announced in Greece, the floodgates were open. The run on Greece led to the runs on Portugal and Spain. The other eurozone members saw the price of their debt skyrocket to unsustainable levels. What had previously been unthinkable—the dissolution of the eurozone—instead became the only means of self-preservation for the healthy and stressed economies alike. The new "euromark" in the north was all that could be salvaged—and that in turn became the foundation of the two-speed Europe that has since emerged.

As you know more than perhaps any other leader, even this euromark zone remains under long-term economic pressure. The competition from Asia, South Asia, the Middle East, and the Americas remains exceptionally tough, and structural realities within the euromark zone mean that fiscal and monetary policy options remain extremely limited. But at least the well-being of the population in this zone has remained somewhat stable, whereas much of the rest Europe has suffered steep declines in per capita income.

This new, northern Europe also rests more squarely on the shoulders of Germany than the EU as a whole ever did. Indeed, the EU at its origins was created as a way to constrain Germany. Today, German militarism is barely a historical memory, while Germany's fiscal discipline, strong industries, and global trading relationships are more important than ever in sustaining the vitality of the euromark area. And while the euromark zone cannot financially prop up the governments of southern Europe, the underlying strength of the euromark economy has spillover effects that benefit the entire continent.

The southern European states have managed to stabilize currencies and government finances at lower levels of real wages and GDP per capita than had been the case in the old eurozone. While this is a decrease in prosperity on paper, and indeed in reality, it is less significant in practice than expected. The persistence of gray economies, seasonal tourist economies, small-scale agriculture, together with cultural and lifestyle differences with northern Europe have meant that the "decline" in the south has been relatively modest, and the region's economics are now more stable than before.

The euromark zone has also helped stabilize a more constructive relationship with Russia. Russia continues to suffer from its own problems—worse than the rest of Europe, with declining population, a long-term public health crisis, lack of robust economic diversification, internal ethnic and religious strife, and decaying infrastructure. Russia continues to be a major source of energy for the euromark zone, but the euromark zone itself now enjoys a diversity of supplies and a healthy balance sheet, meaning Russia is an economic partner, but has no capacity for mischief affecting Europe.

A Less Perfect Union

It is important to review these economic fundamentals from several years ago, because they led to the political changes that define the Europe we face today.

First among these was the rise of nationalist movements on the right in virtually every EU member state. Initially dismissed as fringe elements, these movements have now become the dominant political forces shaping every European state—much as the Social Democratic movements had done during the period of European construction starting in the 1960s. The difference, however, is that today's movements mark a clear departure from the concept of European "solidarity" that had been championed for so many years. The dream of Europe was seen as an alternative to the dream of strength and prosperity, and publics opted for strength and prosperity at a national level instead.

The politics in each member state is now principally driven by the health of the nation: national well-being, national finances, religious and ethnic affirmation. Whereas the Lisbon Treaty has aimed to build a more integrated Europe through more empowered institutions, the unanticipated effect was that nationalist movements were able to use the new structures to tie central European institutions into knots while they advanced national agendas at home.

This is not to say that the concept of "Europe" has been fully removed from the vocabulary. Rather, it is the meaning of this concept to average Europeans that has changed fundamentally. Instead of a concept that defines oneself, it is instead a concept that defines one's neighborhood. Whereas publics in an earlier era, thinking of themselves as "European," accepted costs, direction, identity, sacrifice—and expected benefits as well—from European Union institutions, publics today accept neither the costs nor the benefits beyond the national level. Europe is back to being a geographic concept, not a political one.

With such changed expectations, the de facto development of a two-speed Europe—the ten euromark countries in the north, and the remainder in the periphery—was only a natural extension. And indeed, seven years on, this looser Europe appears to be stable and even hopeful.

Cheap Security

Perhaps the one bit of good news is that no serious security threats appear to affect Europe. Violence and instability in the Middle East has been replaced with booming economies. Radical Islam has marginalized itself as a political force as Muslim reformers have shown publics a better life on this earth. The terrorism that hit its peak in the 2000's has retreated as a threat to Europe. Though nuclear weapons have spread to 17 nations, the likelihood of their use—and particularly use against any part of Europe—remains extremely low. Russia remains consumed by its internal disintegration. And the regional conflicts in which Europe was engaged a decade ago—Afghanistan, Libya, Syria—have long since ended.

All this means that Europe's maintenance of minimal national defense establishments—no more than a quarter percent of GDP—still carries little risk. While Europe is not able to mount substantial military operations, even for UN peacekeeping missions, the need to do so is also practically non-existent. The United States and South Asia continue to lead on global security matters. Europe is able to contribute to international "policing" operations where appropriate, and usually along its own periphery, but has long since given up the unnecessary ambition to lead truly international operations, or take part in more aggressive interventionist operations. Meetings at NATO's cavernous headquarters in Brussels, though embarrassing and anachronistic, are also largely irrelevant, especially since the United States has stopped attending at ministerial level. The United States looks outside of Europe for dealing with hard security issues, and security issues internal to Europe are outside of NATO's purview.

As with much else, the real issues on security are dealt with at a national level—intelligence, police, cyber, borders. The widespread use of biometric scanners linked to detailed personal data profiles has allowed the euromark zone to maintain a single external border for its core continental members, while their use throughout the rest of Europe states adds to the security of Europe as a whole. All of this has come at far lower cost than the prior investment in high-end conventional military equipment, which was unaffordable in difficult economic times and went largely unused.

A Distant United States

The lack of any real security threats is also important because it means the growing U.S. distance from Europe is of little relevance. While Europe lurched from internal crisis to internal crisis, the United States grappled with its own internal crises. The United States, however, has re-emerged as a strong global political, economic and military player.

After coming to the brink of financial ruin in 2013—when in parallel with the euro's collapse, markets began dumping U.S. Treasury bonds—President Obama and the Republican-controlled Senate and House hammered out a massive restructuring of public finances that slashed social and defense spending and raised revenue through tax reform. At the same time, substantial industry de-regulation was introduced (especially in the energy sector, and at the expense of environmental and labor concerns) in an effort to lure economic activity back to the United States from outsourcing abroad.

Though extraordinarily painful for the first few years—resulting in the weakest showing of the Democratic Party since the Civil War in the 2016 elections—the U.S. economy began rebounding in 2017 and is now experiencing strong growth. The effect of a rebounding U.S. economy has tied it even more tightly to Asia, South Asia and Latin America, which are enjoying strong growth of their own.

In short, the Bush Administration's unilateralism and the Obama Administration's cool *insouciance* toward Europe were not aberrations, but in fact harbingers of what is now a deeply embedded reorientation of the United States to the newly developed world. While the combined US-NATO-EU Summits were relegated to "one-per-Administration" events, APEC, U.S.-ASEAN, OAS, and bilateral U.S.-India, U.S.-China and U.S.-Brazil summits are now all at the top of the U.S. priority list. And as these relationships have matured, the contributions of newly developed countries to global peace and security have largely replaced those made by Europe in the last century.

The New Core Europe

All this brings us back to the subject of this weekend's Euromark Council meeting. The 2015 Luxembourg summit took the first steps in cleaning up the debris of the eurozone collapse: amending the Lisbon Treaty, eliminating layers of accumulated Brussels bureaucracy, establishing coordination mechanisms between euromark and non-euromark European economies, and restoring national sovereignty over nearly all but pure Single-Market issues.

This weekend's gathering will complete that task. It will seek to codify what has stabilized as a less ambitious but more sustainable European order. Gone are the dreams of Europe being a major global actor, of a single Union, an economic powerhouse able to use its strength to leverage soft power in the world. In its place is a diverse Europe with a Single Market, but with significant variance in economic performance, living standards, and external relations.

For the periphery, this has been a mixed bag. Ironically, in Greece, which was the catalyst of the eurozone collapse, day-to-day life has been only marginally affected. While there is little economic growth and wealth creation, and social spending has been slashed since its heyday in the 2000's, the people remain close to agriculture, fishing, and family—and tourism has continued to bring cash into the economy. For Ireland, however, times have been exceptionally hard. In either case, however, it is clear that euromark citizens do not have the capacity to sustain the economies of the periphery.

And yet amid all this, the euromark zone, with its emphasis on economic centralism but political pluralism, has proven itself an effective model for a more modest core Europe. Stripping away the residual baggage of past structures will allow the euromark zone to reform—

tackling more deeply some of the economic fundamentals that caused the collapse of the old eurozone in the first place. If leaders seize this opportunity, it can give an outlook to more robust economic growth in the euromark zone in the future, which can become a driver of growth in the neighboring non-euromark areas.

Reference Notes

p. 50, ... each of these foundations, however, had changed by the time of the eurozone crisis ... Daniel S. Hamilton and Joseph P. Quinlan, *Europe and Globalization: Prospering in the New Whirled Order* (Washington, D.C.: Center for Transatlantic Relations,2008); Jayati Ghosh, Peter Havlik, Marcos P. Ribeiro, Waltraut Urban, "Models of BRICs' Economic Development and Challenges for EU Competitiveness," wiiw Research Report No. 359, December 2009 (Vienna: wiiw, 2009); Luc Soete, "The costs of a non-innovative Europe: the challenges ahead," September 21, 2010, available at http://ec.europa.eu/research/social-sciences/pdf/demeter-costs-non-innovative-europe_en.pdf.

p. 50, ... Europe has become a magnet for the unskilled ... Rainer Münz, "Demographic Change, Labour Force Development and Migration in Europe—Policy Recommendations," http://www.migration-boell.de/web/migration/46_2447.asp; http://www.jonathanlaurence.net/wp-content/uploads/2009/06/transatlantic-academy-final-report-on-immigration.pdf; UN High Commissioner for Refugees, *2008 Global Trends: Refugees, Asylum-seekers, Returnees, Internally Displaced and Stateless Persons* (Geneva, Switzerland: UN High Commissioner for Refugees, 2009), http://www.unhcr.org/4a375c426.html; United Nations High Commissioner for Refugees, *2009 Global Trends*, http://www.unhcr.org; and Ibrahim Awad, *The Global Economic Crisis and Migrant Workers: Impact and Response* (Geneva, Switzerland: International Labor Organization, 2009), http://www.ilo.org/global/About_the_ILO/ Media_and_public_information/Feature_stories/lang-en/WCMS_112537/ index.htm; "The Highly-Skilled as a 'Renewable Resource'," http://www.migration-boell.de/web/migration/46_2456.asp.

p. 50, ... The year 2010—or perhaps a few years before—marked the beginning of the transformation of global energy markets ... Daniel Yergin, *The Quest: Energy, Security, and the Remaking of the Modern World* (New York: Penguin, 2011); Roderick Kefferpütz, "Shale Fever: Replicating the US gas revolution in the EU?" CEPS, 2010, http://www.ceps.eu/book/shale-fever-replicating-us-gas-revolution-eu; Fueling North America's Energy Future, IHS CERA Special Report, IHS Cambridge Energy Research Associates, Cambridge, MA, 2010; Michael Levi, Elizabeth C. Economy, Shannon O'Neil, and Adam Segal, "Globalizing the Energy Revolution: How to Really Win the Clean-Energy Race," *Foreign Affairs*, November/December 2010.

p. 53, ... Russia continues to suffer from its own problems ... See, for example, Marshall Goldman, *Petrostate: Putin, Power and the New Russia* (New York: Oxford University Press, 2010); Andrew Kutchins and Anders Aslund, *The Russia Balance Sheet*

(Washington: Peterson Institute/CSIS, 2009); Andrew Kutchins, Amy Beavin and Anna Bryndza, *Russia's 2020 Strategic Economic Goals and the Role of International Integration*, CSIS Report, July 2008.

p. 53, ... the rise of nationalist movements on the right in virtually every EU member state ... See the chapter by Theo Veenkamp in this volume. Also Ivan Krastev, "The new Europe: respectable populism, clockwork liberalism," Open Democracy, March 21, 2006, http://www.opendemocracy.net/democracy-europe_constitution/new_europe_3376.jsp; Daniele Albertazzi and Duncan McDonnell, eds., *Twenty-First Century Populism: The Spectre of Western European Democracy* (London: Palgrave MacMillan, 2008); Cas Mudde, *Populist Radical Right Parties in Europe* (Cambridge: Cambridge University Press, 2007); Paul Hockenos, "Central Europe's Right Wing Populism," *The Nation*, May 5, 2010.

p. 54, ... Europe ... has long since given up the unnecessary ambition to lead truly international operations ... For discussion of European military capabilities, see the chapter by James Dobbins in this volume; the speech by former U.S. Defense Secretary Robert Gates, "The Future of NATO," Brussels, Belgium, June 10, 2011, http://www.defense.gov/speeches/speech.aspx?speechid=1581; Anders Fogh Rasmussen, NATO Secretary General, "Building security in an age of austerity," February 4, 2011; Daniel Korski, "A Post-Cavalry CSDP," September 26, 2011, http://ecfr.eu/content/entry/commentary_cavalry; Daniel Korski, "Player or Pawn?" *Internationale Politik - Global*, May/June 2010; Lawrence F. Kaplan, "Open Wide—How Libya revealed the huge gap between U.S. and European military might," *The New Republic*, April 26, 2011; Patrick Keller, "Challenges for European Defense Budgets After the Economic Crisis," *AEI Outlook*, July 2011; Tomas Valasek, "What Libya says about the future of the transatlantic alliance," Centre for European Reform, July 29, 2011, http://www.cer.org.uk/publications/archive/essay/2011/what-libya-says-about-future-transatlantic-alliance; Kurt Volker, "Don't Call it a Comeback," *Foreign Policy*, August 23, 2011.

p. 55, ... the Bush Administration's unilateralism and the Obama Administration's cool insouciance toward Europe were not aberrations ... For discussion of U.S. approaches to Europe over different administrations, see Daniel Hamilton and Nikolas Foster, "The Obama Administration and Europe," in Alvaro Vasconcelos and Martin Zaborowski, *The Obama Moment: European and American Perspectives* (Paris, EU Institute for Security Studies, 2009); Esther Brimmer, ed., *Changing Identities and Evolving Values: Is there still a transatlantic community?* (Washington, D.C: Center for Transatlantic Relations, 2006); Esther Brimmer, *Seeing Blue: American Visions of the European Union*, Chaillot Paper, no. 105, (Paris, EU Institute for Security Studies, 2007); Jeremy Shapiro and Nick Witney, *Towards a Post-American Europe: a power audit of EU-US relations* (European Council on Foreign Relations, 2009); John Robert Kelley, "Keep Calm and Carry on: Appraising the Transatlantic Relationship from Iraq to Obama," *European Political Science*, published online January 14, 2011.

With a Little Help from My Friends

June 9, 2020

Memorandum for the President
Subject: Your Participation in the U.S.-EU and G-20 Summits

As you approach the last U.S.-EU and G-20 Summits of the first term of your Presidency, Asia, South Asia, Latin America, and the Middle East are all booming, but the United States and Europe are not. And this confronts the West with some fundamental questions: Is the era of Western global leadership now over? With our emphasis on democratic values, rule of law, private sector economics, and long-ago developed national infrastructure and economies, can we ever successfully compete with the newly developed economies around the world? And is the world now irretrievably moving away from free markets and free trade as the basis of the global economy?

It is too early to know the answers with certainty. One tends to believe that the pendulum always swings back to center. But the possibility that what we are living through is a long-term, structural, one-way shift in global power, resources, and values is worth pondering. And whether or not this is truly the case, the fact that it is an open question is reason enough to consider some radical proposals for reinforcing the U.S.-European partnership that has languished in the past 20 years. If we do nothing, the developing world will continue to eat our lunch; the alternative may be higher external walls, around a single transatlantic marketplace. That, at least, is the European proposal coming into the U.S.-EU Summit, and as hard as it would be to implement, it is certainly worth exploration.

Brave New World

Though we are used to the shape of the global economy today, it is worth recalling just how much it has changed over the past 10 years. China is likely to surpass U.S. GDP next year—far faster than anyone had predicted just 10 years ago, and India is nearing two-thirds of U.S. GDP. Trade between them has grown exponentially—and indeed trade among all countries excluding the U.S. and Europe now accounts for over 80 percent of global trade.

The non-transatlantic nations now account for over two-thirds of all energy production, energy consumption, foreign direct investment destinations, new patents, kilometers of high-speed rail lines, global tourism expenditure and destinations for global tourism, and spending on movies and music. And they account for seven-eighths of the world's population—so there is still room to expand. In short, in just about every conceivable measure of economic performance and cultural output, the traditional transatlantic share of the world has fallen to the status of a distinct minority, and trendlines point to more of the same.

The only area where the transatlantic community still leads the world is debt—which, though reduced as a share of GDP from the crises of 2012 and 2013, still remains extraordinarily high (averaging over two-thirds of GDP across the transatlantic community) given the difficulty in cutting long-assumed social benefits to an aging population, while paying for them with a barely growing workforce.

Moreover, it is not only the quantity of the rest of the world's weight that has changed. It is also the quality. A whopping 40 percent of non-transatlantic GDP—and a majority in strategic industries—is controlled by state-run enterprises. The majority of goods are traded among countries where at least one of them does not have a free-floating currency—so while prices are nominally set by global markets, in reality they are set by state regulators.

While the United States and Europe have tried to emphasize renewable energy and reduced CO_2 emissions, these efforts have been dwarfed by the rest of the world's massive consumption of traditional energy supplies with a view toward fueling rapid growth at the lowest possible cost, meaning that global emissions have continued to rise and are now at double-digit rates of increase.

This has also given rise to significant resource competition among the newly developed countries, pushing up global prices in nearly all areas—from foodstuffs to energy to minerals to water—and affecting the U.S. and European economies significantly, even though we are not driving the change. Thus far, this resource competition has remained in the economic sphere—though it remains possible it could spill over into political or military competition as well.

Although the majority of populations live in countries that we would consider genuine democracies—with China being the main exception—the behavior of most countries in global markets is more one of mercantilist nationalism rather than liberal internationalism. And while committed to democracy at home in most cases, their interest in seeking to advance democratic values abroad is nearly non-existent.

Domestically, in both the United States and Europe, growth has been stagnant for a decade. Jobs lost in the Great Recession have not returned, simply because the cost structures and bureaucratic rigidities on both sides of the Atlantic—as well as their stagnant markets—make it easier to create growth and jobs just about anywhere else in the world. And the ease of global communications and transportation has continued to make the actual location of an industry less and less relevant to its global success.

Shift in Global Security

Alongside the shift in economic weight has been the shift in global security challenges, and in security capacity. While the United States remains the world's largest military power by expenditure, China continues to pour money into new equipment and capabilities, and is able to get far more "bang for the buck." This has prompted growing military spending by others in Asia—including Taiwan, Japan, Korea, Indonesia, India and Singapore—leading to a tense but stable military balance in which the United States has become more of a foot on the scales rather than a singularly dominant military force.

The same can be said for the Broader Middle East region. Pakistan, Iran, Iraq, Saudi Arabia, Israel, Egypt, Syria and Turkey are all beefing up defense establishments as deterrents against each other.

The geographic foci of the world's most intense security competition has shifted to the South China Sea, the Indo-Chinese and Indo-Pakistani borders, Egypt/Saudi Arabia-Iran, the unified Korea and China, and internal borders within southeast Asia. The Israeli-Palestinian conflict—while still unresolved—is by comparison relatively quiet.

Iran's acquisition of nuclear weapons has led to a flurry of other states acquiring nuclear weapons as well, creating a new era of "balance of terror" deterrence, in which Europe and the United States are largely on the sidelines. Fortunately, the simultaneous growth of democratic practices throughout the Broader Middle East and South Asia, including Iran, has given a higher degree of responsible civilian oversight to these multiple nuclear programs.

Russia has proven to be neither a threat nor a partner. Its early ambitions under President Putin for a resource-nationalism-based revival of Russian power and a Russian sphere of influence have come to naught. Russia has enjoyed neither the resource-based income it has sought, nor the good governance needed to put such resources to strategic purpose. Its neighbors, meanwhile, have grown increasingly independent economically, politically, and culturally over the past 25 years, diminishing Russia's influence still farther.

In this new global environment, NATO has become largely irrelevant. The Afghanistan and Libya operations ended long ago, and NATO has retreated to the popular but largely unnecessary task of protecting European territory against military attack. This is due in no small measure to the fact that, on the one hand, Europe has largely stepped out of military affairs, unwilling to fund more than minimalist defense establishments for purely territorial defense, and on the other, the United States has turned its focus clearly to the areas in the Middle East and Asia where today's security problems actually reside. European partners are unable to bring much to the table in these areas, while regional partners have become indispensible for managing regional security competition.

The Decline of Atlanticism

Given all these trends—and the challenges they imply for the United State and Europe—it is therefore surprising to look back in hindsight and see that transatlantic cooperation grew weaker at the same time that the rest of the world was growing stronger.

Rather than joining together because of common values and interests, we allowed the weaknesses of our politics and finances to dictate our relationships. Each side of the Atlantic has actively pursued its own relationships with Asia, with South Asia, the Middle East, and Latin America. This has mostly taken the form of seeking buyers for Western debt securities, and agreeing to structured business deals brokered directly with foreign governments and their state-owned entities. These activities have only served to reinforce the growing state role in the global economic order, rather than international economic liberalism.

Just as these weaknesses in our economies and finances drove us to pursue other relationships with greater vigor, likewise the weakness in our political vision did the same for diplomatic relationships. While the EU-Asia and EU-Africa and EU-Latin America summits—and their American equivalents—have all blossomed, U.S.-EU summits were reduced from twice yearly to annually to once every two years and now to once in four. After NATO in 2016 closed the doors on its Afghanistan operation—its longest, most demanding, and least successful—a NATO summit was held since at the beginning of your term of office, in 2017, and not again since. The next will only be held again in the next term, if then. The G8 has long-since stopped meeting, giving way in full to the G20 instead.

G20—A Troubling Agenda

This brings us full circle to the U.S.-EU and G20 meetings at hand. The Chinese, as G20 hosts, have proposed a new "rules of the road" document aimed at solidifying principles of state-led growth and trade. This includes exempting state-to-state contracts, and state-entity to state-entity contracts from WTO rules. It includes international recognition of privileged "easements" negotiated by states and state-owned entities for unique access to key resources. It explicitly forbids linkage of contractual arrangements between states or state-owned entities to "conditionality" on democracy, human rights, or other issues of governance. The list goes on.

Of course even the Chinese know the G-20 is a fig-leaf organization. It is the bilateral and sub-regional deals that have grown to dominate the newly developed world's economic interactions. Nonetheless, the Chinese aim is to get an international endorsement of the type of bilateral economic deals they have been pursuing successfully for many years. Their behind-the-scenes diplomacy and deal-making has bought them support among a majority of the G20 nations, who are attracted to the predictability implied in the Chinese approach (and the fact that it legitimizes their state-driven trade practices in any event). There will be a heavy push for agreement at the meeting in

Shenzhen—and even in the absence of full agreement due to U.S. and European objections, the substance of the document will be put into practice by the majority of G20 states anyway.

From a transatlantic perspective, however, this new rulebook—whether agreed formally or implemented as a matter of practice—is a direct assault on the liberal economic order that has benefited the global economy, and been sustained through the IMF, WTO and other organizations, for decades. We have lived through the erosion of this order in practice; it is another thing to consign it to history as a matter of decision. Indeed, perhaps the time has come to push back with a new initiative for a liberal marketplace, centered on the transatlantic community.

Reinvesting in the Transatlantic Market

That is what makes this upcoming U.S.-EU summit—two days ahead of the G20 meeting—one of the more important ones we have had in decades. In days gone by, we used to think of the world as "the West and the Rest." Under today's conditions, however, it is "the Rest" that have moved forward, and "the West" that has been reduced in relevance. Given the shifts in economic weight and dynamism, we may be unable in the short term to exert much influence on the economic development going on in the rest of the world. But we do have the opportunity to affect our own "internal" transatlantic economy and political cooperation, and lay the groundwork for potentially greater influence down the road.

To do this, Europe has proposed an ambitious agenda for the U.S.-EU summit. This includes the creation of a single transatlantic marketplace. The establishment of a joint regulatory authority, with mutual recognition and eventual harmonization of existing regulatory regimes. The elimination of restrictions on the movement of people, capital and goods across Europe, Canada and the United States. The adoption of fiscal and monetary policy guidelines, including deficit and debt limits, to help smooth the operation of a single transatlantic market. The raising of external tariffs around this market. The establishment of joint political-consultative bodies to oversee implementation of these proposals over renewable 5-year periods.

Even just two years ago, these proposals would have seemed ridiculously large in scope, dangerously protectionist, and correspondingly impossible to imagine implementing. As the balance of economic power has shifted away from the transatlantic community, however, we are less and less able to assure own individual economic well-being, or to influence the operation of a global marketplace along liberal economic lines.

If trends continue as they now stand, we will see the continued erosion of wealth, jobs, market share, and technological innovation within our own community. It is therefore worth serious consideration whether the creation of a billion-strong Transatlantic Single Market can help to reignite economic dynamism in the transatlantic area, in order to exert a greater influence on the development of the global marketplace.

To be sure, just as we object to the Chinese agenda, there are elements of the European agenda to which we would object as well—and equally, demands we would have, such as on reducing Europe's own labor market rigidities and budget deficits, and relaxing some environmental restrictions. Still, the potential benefits to the United States of "fair" competition within a larger transatlantic market may help offset the increasingly "unfair" competition of a dynamic yet state-led "rest" of the world.

It will not be possible to reach agreement on such a transatlantic agenda in a single meeting. Still—just as the Chinese agenda will not go away even when it is not formally endorsed at the G20 meeting, the idea of a transatlantic marketplace should not go away even though it is fraught with difficulty. It may be the only way to restore our own economic weight and credibility before it is too late.

Reference Notes

p. 59, ... China is likely to surpass U.S. GDP next year ... International Monetary Fund, *World Economic Outlook*, September 2011; Jim O'Neill and Anna Stupnytska, "The Long-Term Outlook for the BRICs and N-11 Post Crisis" (Goldman Sachs Global Economics Paper No: 192, Dec. 4, 2009) (http://www2.goldmansachs. com/ideas/ brics/long-term-outlook-doc.pdf). See also Elizabeth C. Economy and Adam Segal, "The G-2 Mirage, Why the United States and China Are Not Ready to Upgrade Ties," *Foreign Affairs*, May/June 2009; B. Eichengreen and H. Tong,"How China is Reorganizing the World Economy,"*Asian Economic Policy Review* (2006) 1, pp. 73–97.

p. 60, ... in just about every conceivable measure of economic performance and cultural output, the traditional transatlantic share of the world has fallen ... For some current trends, see Daniel S. Hamilton and Joseph P. Quinlan, *The Transatlantic Economy 2011* (Washington, DC: Center for Transatlantic Relations, 2011); Daniel S Hamilton, *Europe 2020: Competitive or Complacent?* (Washington, DC: Center for Transatlantic Relations, 2011); OECD, *Economic Globalisation Indicators 2010*; European Commission, *European Competitiveness Report 2010*.

p. 60, ... the rest of the world's massive consumption of traditional energy supplies ... David Buchan, *Rough Guide to the Energy Crisis* (New York: Penguin, 2010); Daniel Yergin, *The Quest: Energy, Security, and the Remaking of the Modern World* (New York: Penguin, 2011); Sascha Müller-Kraenner, "China's and India's Emerging Energy Foreign Policy," Deutsches Institut für Entwicklungspolitik, 15/2008; Sascha Müller-Kraenner, *Energy Security* (Earthscan 2008).

p. 61, ... The geographic foci of the world's most intense security competition has shifted ... See Robert D. Kaplan, "The South China Sea is the Future of Conflict," *Foreign Policy*, September/October 2011; Abraham Denmark and Nirav Patel, eds, *China's Arrival: A Strategic Framework for a Global Relationship* (Washington, DC: Center for a New American Security, 2009).

p. 62, ... Europe has largely stepped out of military affairs ... Daniel Hamilton, et al., *Alliance Reborn: An Atlantic Compact for the 21st Century* (Washington, DC: The Washington NATO Project, 2009), http://transatlantic.sais-jhu.edu/publications/ books/nato_report_final.pdf; Daniel Korski and Richard Gowan, "Can the EU Rebuild Failing States? A Review of Europe's Civilian Capacities" (London, UK: European Council on Foreign Relations, October 2009); Patrick Keller, "Challenges for European Defense Budgets After the Economic Crisis," *AEI Outlook*, July 2011; Kurt Volker, "Don't Call it a Comeback," *Foreign Policy*, August 23, 2011; Tomas Valasek, "What Libya says about the future of the transatlantic alliance," Centre for European Reform, July 29, 2011, http://www.cer.org.uk/publications/archive/essay/ 2011/what-libya-says-about-future-transatlantic-alliance;

p. 63, ... the weakness in our political vision did the same for diplomatic relationships ... For recommendations regarding ways to improve U.S.-EU, NATO and other transatlantic summits, see Daniel S. Hamilton, ed., *Shoulder to Shoulder: Forging a Strategic U.S.-EU Partnership* (Washington, DC: Center for Transatlantic Relations, 2010); *Alliance Reborn*, op. cit.

p. 63, ... The Chinese ... have proposed ... new "rules of the road" ... See the debate about China's rise: Arvind Subramanian, "The Inevitable Superpower," and Salvatore Babones, "The Middling Kingdom," *Foreign Affairs*, September/October 2011; David M. Lampton, *The Three Faces of Chinese Power: Might, Money and Minds* (Los Angeles/Berkeley: University of California Press, 2008). John Ikenberry, "The Rise of China and the Future of the West," *Foreign Affairs*, January/February 2008; B. Eichengreen and H. Tong,"How China is Reorganizing the World Economy," *Asian Economic Policy Review* (2006) 1, pp. 73–97; Vivek Arora and Athanasios Vamvakidis, "China's Economic Growth: International Spillovers," IMF Working Paper, July 2010, http://www.imf.org/external/pubs/ft/wp/2010/wp10165.pdf.

p. 64, ... "the West and the Rest" ... Fareed Zakaria, *The Post-American World* (New York: W.W. Norton, 2008); Gideon Rachman, *Zero-Sum Future: American Power in an Age of Anxiety* (New York: Simon and Shuster, 2011); Dilip Hiro, *After Empire: The Birth of a Multipolar World* (New York: Nation Books, 2010); G. John Ikenberry, "The Future of the Liberal World Order," *Foreign Affairs*, May/June 2011; Niall Ferguson, *Civilization: The West and the Rest* (London: Allen Lane, 2011).

p. 64, ... the creation of a single transatlantic marketplace ... See Daniel S. Hamilton and Joseph P. Quinlan, *Deep Integration: How Transatlantic Markets are Leading Globalization* (Washington, D.C.: Center for Transatlantic Relations, 2005); *Shoulder to Shoulder*, op. cit. For estimates of the economic impact of a transatlantic marketplace initiative, see also Koen Berden, et. al, *Non-Tariff Measures in EU-US Trade and Investment—An Economic Analysis* (Rotterdam: Ecorys, 2009); Frederik Erixon and Matthias Bauer, *A Transatlantic Zero Agreement: Estimating the Gains from Transatlantic Free Trade in Goods*, ECIPE Occasional Paper No. 4/2010 (Brussels: ECIPE, 2010); Koen Berden, et. al, *The Impact of Free Trade Agreements in the OECD: The Impact of an EU-US FTA, EU-Japan FTA and EU-Australia/New Zealand FTA* (Rotterdam: Ecorys, 2009).

Section I

Rising Powers

Chapter 1

The Rise of New Powers: Implications for the Transatlantic World

Hanns W. Maull

Powers have risen and fallen throughout history, but the particulars of their rise and fall can be understood only in their specific historical context. The most recent rise of "emerging" or "pivotal" powers concerns a group of countries which do not belong to the circle of advanced industrial democracies ("the West"). It takes place in the post-Cold War system of international relations and its specific arrangements of governance. This "system" (the sum of interactions across national boundaries) and its specific arrangements of governance (i.e., the present "international order"), which evolved out of the post-war settlement following World War II, has been characterized a) materially, by a highly dynamic social and economic environment, shaped by rapid and far-reaching scientific and technological advances, and b) politically, by the "post-Cold War settlement," which in the early 1990s replaced the rather rigid security framework of bipolarity under the East-West conflict. In this system, the dynamics of interdependence which during the Cold War had largely been confined to international relations *outside* the communist bloc and its allies, were expanded to engulf those parts of the globe, as well. The post-Cold War international order re-affirmed many of the original principles of the post-World War II order, but soon turned out to be much less durable.[1]

The dynamics of the post-World War II international order offered rising powers avenues for expansion from very early on, and has continued to do so. But this expansion came at a price: successive waves of integrating newcomers led to a serious erosion of the "liberal interna-

---

[1] Daniel Deudney and G. John Ikenberry, "The Unravelling of the Cold War Settlement," *Survival*, 51:6 (Dec. 2009–Jan. 2010), pp. 39-61.

tional order" within which they took place.[2] Over the last two decades, in particular, this order thus has come under increasing strain, largely as a result of diffusion of power within the system, but also of its own successes and its inherent contradictions. Policy mistakes and domestic political dynamics also played a role.

Against this background of an increasingly fragile international order, the most recent wave of rising powers represents a further serious challenge to the *governability* of this *existing* international order—but *not* a fundamental challenge in terms of demands for a "new international order." The new powers want to have a say on policy substance and policy execution, as well as more of a voice, more power and a better status in the extant arrangements of governance *within* the present order, but not any fundamental, revolutionary reconstitution of that order; after all, the existing order enabled them to rise, and they thus are its beneficiaries. This is true only for the international order at the *global* level, however: at the *regional* level, for example in the Persian Gulf and East Asia, some of those emerging powers do challenge existing arrangements of order in ways which are fundamental and could have critical consequences for the system as a whole.

Among the rising powers, China stands out as being in a class of its own, and it will likely remain there for several decades to come. Beyond China, at a lower level, for different reasons and in a different category, Iran also poses a particularly difficult problem from the perspective of international order. China challenges the dominant position of the U.S. in the security architecture of East Asia, and already today, its diplomacy has a global reach; Beijing could thus plausibly develop into a superpower rival to America. Iran certainly does not have that potential, but it does represent a serious challenge to U.S. dominance in the Persian/Arabian Gulf region and the Middle East.

In this new world of international relations, the transatlantic community still would appear best placed to serve as crystallizing focus and catalyst for effectuating international order: the only other plausible alternative that could mobilize sufficient power resources and purpose to do so would be the "G-2"—with America and China acting together as an alternative core for efforts to maintain international

---

[2] G. John Ikenberry, "The Liberal International Order and its Discontents," *Millenium*, 38:3 (2010), pp. 509-521.

order. That alternative may still come about by default, if the transatlantic community fails to rise to the situation, but it still seems far-fetched.[3] In any case, to be viable and sustainable, any future international order will depend on cooperation by others, beyond that core of America and either Europe (and Japan) or China. The rise of new powers therefore confronts governments of the transatlantic community and Japan with the need first to secure the required degree of cooperation among themselves, and then to accommodate others, both in terms of specific policy solutions and institutional arrangements of global governance. To be able to impress its own aspirations and concerns on the international order of, say, 2020, which is likely to be much more complex and contested than that of 2000 or even 2010, the transatlantic community would have to lead by example, by persuasion, and by broad-based international legitimacy for its policy proposals built on perceptions of responsibility and fairness.

The Context: A Liberal Institutional Framework, with U.S. Hegemony at its Core, But Problems Galore

The present international system is characterized materially by processes of rapidly deepening and widening transnational interdependence, propelled outward by technological dynamism and market exchanges (globalization); politically, it is marked by a liberal international order, dominated by the United States as its founder and hegemon. As any order, this order contains its share of inherent tensions and contradictions, such as

- the tension between the expansive exploitation of economic opportunities (e.g., the switch from coal to oil in global energy or the opening of new markets in the South) and the imperatives of political control (such as containment of the Soviet Union or, more recently, the "management" of China's rise);

- the tension between the need to procure common public goods to sustain systemic order and the ability and willingness

---

[3] Elizabeth C. Economy and Adam Segal, "The G-2 Mirage, Why the United States and China Are Not Ready to Upgrade Ties," *Foreign Affairs*, 88:3 (May/ June 2009), pp. 14-23.

of the hegemon to shoulder the costs implicit in providing those goods, and—related to this -

- the difficulties in securing adequate and legitimate arrangements for burden sharing between the hegemon and its allies;

- the dilemma of squaring efficiency with legitimacy in global governance;

- the tension between military and non-military forms of influence and control;

- the problem of persuading domestic audiences, particularly in the U.S., but also among its principal allies, to make available the resources needed to maintain and develop the international order, and finally

- the discrepancy between the norms and values professed and actual policy practice.

The liberal international order particularly suffered from serious blemishes in the behavior of its hegemon, America, and its allies. The United States was not beyond practising double standards by insisting that the rules and norms of international order be followed by others, while exempting itself. Some of its allies represented regimes which were anything but liberal; and at times the U.S. intervened militarily or through covert action in ways that blatantly contradicted central tenets of a liberal international order. In mobilizing domestic political support for its foreign policy posture, America twice (in the late 1940s/early 1950s, and again after September 11, 2001) came dangerously close to doing away with some of the foundations of liberty and democracy at home. Moreover, the demise of the Cold War complicated the conduct of American foreign and security policy by bringing the inherent tensions and contradictions described above to the fore.

Yet despite all these tensions and contradictions the liberal international order has survived and flourished since 1945. Of course, the Cold War greatly facilitated the management of those structural tensions. In the United States, for example, it was mostly the "communist threat" that allowed successive administrations to mobilize societal resources for foreign policy purposes on a massive scale. They were able to do so by a significant re-interpretation of America's traditional foreign policy identity and role concept during and immediately after World War II—the triumph of Wilsonianism which Henry Kissinger so bemoaned in his magisterial study on U.S. diplomacy.[4]

A Progressively Widening Membership

The liberal international order, designed and upheld largely by the United States, offered important opportunities for new powers to rise peacefully. The first powers to do so were those of Western Europe and Japan. While the re-emergence of Europe in the 1950s and 1960s and their integration into the post-war international order overall was in many ways rather easy, it nevertheless did entail the demise of the international monetary and financial order designed at Bretton Woods in 1944, which was replaced by a "non-order"—a system with "dirtily floating" exchange rates, whose fluctuations reflected market forces, but also occasional government (central bank) interventions. A first significant erosion of the post-war international economic order had taken place.

The 1970s also witnessed the demise of the post-war international oil order built around a "public-private partnership,"[5] as David Painter has called it, between the U.S. government, American oil companies and the governments of Saudi Arabia and Iran. It led to the rise of oil power, which was then (as now) heavily concentrated around the Persian Gulf, and thus to a new group of powers from the "Third World". This shift began when domestic oil production in the U.S. peaked in 1970 and then began to decline rapidly, which turned the U.S. into a major oil importer. Oil power also brought financial clout, as became apparent with the at times huge current account surpluses of the Arabian Peninsula oil exporters. Those surpluses have been recycled primarily through Western banks, and have long helped finance U.S. current account deficits.

The third wave of new powers was that of the "mercantilist" or "developmental" East Asian trading states, beginning with Japan and followed by the so-called newly industrializing countries/ economies[6]

---

[4] Henry A. Kissinger, *Diplomacy* (New York: Simon & Schuster 1994).

[5] David Painter, *Oil and the American Century: The Political Economy of US Foreign Oil Policy, 1941–1954* (Baltimore, MD: Johns Hopkins University Press, 1986), p. 2.

Hong Kong, Singapore, South Korea and Taiwan. A third group of manufacturing exporters were ASEAN countries such as Thailand, Malaysia, the Philippines and Indonesia during the 1980s and 1990s, which in turn were followed by Vietnam and, of course, mainland China. The rise of those "developmental states"[7] appeared to challenge the liberal international trading order with the mercantilist strategies pursued by governments, which promoted export-led growth while restricting imports, mostly through non-tariff regulatory barriers. Yet over time, those countries were successfully accommodated within the liberal trading order through a series of mutual adjustments involving voluntary export restraints, market-opening, exchange rate management (such as the Plaza and Louvre agreements on revaluing the yen) and the upgrading of the GATT into the WTO. With regard to China, this process is still incomplete, however, given the scale of China's industrial achievements and ambitions. Finally, the restrictive nuclear non-proliferation order, which the two superpowers had imposed on the rest of the world during the Cold War, also came under strain through "new powers"—first, rather discreetly, Israel and then, more dramatically and persistently, India, Pakistan, North Korea and, probably, soon Iran. Others, however, such as the rising powers Brazil and South Africa, dismantled already initiated nuclear programs and thus reverted to the established non-proliferation order.

All those instances of new powers rising point to the remarkable capacity of the liberal institutional order to accommodate newcomers by reforming the system while leaving its fundamentals untouched, but also to the increasing strains and the growing fragility of this order as a whole. Parts of the problem stemmed from the fact that the newcomers were reluctant to see their success as the result of a level playing field, nor were they necessarily satisfied with the existing principles and institutional arrangements of the liberal international order and the scope of their participation in decision-making. While levels of frustration differed from case to case, nationalist resentment at having to play to the tune of the American hegemon was never far from the surface—even the Europeans bore grudges. Among those grudges

---

[6] Abbreviated as NICs or NIEs. The latter term was used to accommodate mainland Chinese sensitivities about Taiwan not being a "country."

[7] Meredith Woo-Cumings, *The Developmental State* (Ithaca, NY: Cornell University Press, 1999).

were the benefits that America derived from its hegemonic position (thus, it could afford to run ever-growing balance of trade and budget deficits, which it could finance comfortably due to the reserve currency status of the dollar), and also a certain envy at the elevated status and prestige America enjoyed as the hegemon.

Overall, the post-World War II liberal international order, founded in the second half of the 1940s and reconstituted in its essential aspects after the end of the Cold War in the early 1990s, has shown remarkable adaptability. Thus, since the demise of the East-West conflict as the dominant political conflict structure in international relations, the primacy of security politics has been replaced by that of economics and individual rights; today, international relations seemingly are no longer concerned with collective survival but with socio-economic development, prosperity, and human security.

There has been a price for this adaptability, however. As its substance changed, world politics has experienced a loss of coherence; this, in turn, has encouraged a shift in the sources of foreign policy decision-making away from interstate imperatives toward the primacy of domestic concerns. Moreover, the degree and success of adaptation has been uneven. It was most successful in the international trade order, while the non-proliferation regime, the international monetary order and the governance of international oil were more seriously affected. In many areas, a gap seems to have opened up and to be widening between the *needs for political action* to sustain and develop international order in line with the rapid expansion of interdependence, on the one hand, and the *supply of governance* through existing mechanisms of national foreign policy adjustment, cooperation and coordination between states and international regimes and institutions, on the other hand. If those trends are extrapolated in the future, then the prospects for international order seem bleak; international relations appear destined to become yet more turbulent and volatile.

In short, present arrangements and institutions of international order no longer appear adequate; the world needs a more effective system of global governance. This is where the newly rising powers come in. Their rise makes global governance more complicated still. Yet they could also be part of the solution. Will they help or hinder the necessary renovation of the liberal international order?

The Liberal International Order: Reasons for its Resilience

A number of factors may help explain why the integration of new powers until now has caused so remarkably few problems for the liberal international order. First of all, of course, the new powers benefitted from that order's characteristics. It provided them with opportunities, often at quite favorable conditions, since the United States assumed the lion's share of the maintenance costs of that international order.[8] There also often existed domestic political affinity and empathy, as quite a few of the rising powers were fellow democracies (as in the case of European countries and Japan). Others at least shared an understanding about the key principles and norms of that liberal international order, frequently supported by strong transnational ties, particularly through business channels.

Above all else, however, the integration of newcomers into that order was supported by the realities of Cold War bipolarity: the security guarantees extended by the United States to many of the rising powers and the role America played in guaranteeing regional stability in the critical regions of Western Europe, East Asia and the Middle East was probably the single most important cause for emerging states to accept this international order and U.S. hegemony. In fact, not only were many of those emerging states in the past closely aligned to the United States; their rise was often also actively promoted by America out of strategic considerations. Thus, the rapid reconstruction of war-devastated Europe and Japan and the economic build-up of East and South East Asia during the 1950s, 1960s, and 1970s was part and parcel of their integration in U.S.-dominated security arrangements (NATO in Europe, the U.S.-Japan Security Treaty, other bilateral security arrangements with the Republic of Korea, with Taiwan, with Thailand and the Philippines, as well as SEATO).[9]

---

[8] Michael Mandelbaum, *The Case for Goliath, How America Acts as the World's Government in the Twenty-First Century* (New York: Public Affairs, 2006). The notion that Japan's superior economic performance during its take-off phase reflected its low defense expenditure (typically, below one per cent of GNP) and hence its "free-riding" on U.S. security guarantees, held wide sway in the U.S. and even in the literature on U.S.–Japan relations during the 1970s and 1980s.

[9] John Welfield, *An Empire in Eclipse, Japan and the Post-war American Alliance System* (London: Athlone, 1988); Geir Lundestad, *The United States and Western Europe since 1945, from "Empire" by Invitation to Transatlantic Drift* (Oxford: Oxford University Press, 2003).

The economic rise of America's partners was therefore considered desirable for strategic as well as for economic reasons from the standpoint of the U.S. hegemon. The only major exception from this general pattern was the rise of oil exporting countries during the 1970s, which for the first time produced a broader challenge to the existing liberal international order outside the West-West context through demands by developing countries—supported, if somewhat lukewarmly, by the new oil powers—for a "New International Economic Order."[10] But the oil-exporting developing countries organized in OPEC in the end not only showed little effective solidarity with other developing countries, they also failed to maintain the collective discipline and policy coherence among themselves which they would have needed to retain their oil market dominance. When the international oil market turned around in the wake of the Iranian revolution in the early 1980s and prices began to fall, the major new oil powers on the Arabian Peninsula, led by Saudi Arabia, had already been co-opted by the United States into a new version of the old "public-private partnership," in which the United States guaranteed the security of the Arabian gulf states, while those ensured sufficient oil supplies at moderate prices.

The integration of new powers into the liberal international order has thus so far been remarkably smooth, even after the end of the Cold War.[11] Why should this time be different? After all, there still seems to be a fundamental consensus on basic norms and principles concerning this order: none of the presently emerging powers, with the possible exception of Iran, fundamentally challenges the premises of the present international order—and even Iran does not contest

---

[10]The two principal "emerging oil powers" of the 1970s, however, Iran and Saudi Arabia, were also close allies of the United States and thus confirm the pattern noted above. The two new oil powers took divergent positions with regard to international oil prices, with Iran as a "price hawk". This undermined American influence over price developments during the 1970s. Both Iran and Saudi Arabia became the pillars of the U.S.-anchored regional order in the Persian/Arabian Gulf. This order was undermined in 1979 by the Iranian revolution and the fall of the Shah.

[11]Two early, interesting but ultimately inconsequential episodes challenging this order in the Asia-Pacific region were Malaysia's proposal for an East Asia Economic Caucus in 1994 and Japan's proposal for an Asian Monetary Fund in 1997. Both were quickly defeated by the U.S., helped by the onset of the Asian financial crisis in mid-1997. See Yong Wook Lee, "Japan and the Asian Monetary Fund: An Identity-Intention Approach," *International Studies Quarterly* 50 (2006), pp. 339-366.

free markets and private property rights. Most of the new powers even accept the principles of democracy and individual human rights, albeit with significant differences in interpretation and political realities that are often more authoritarian than democratic. Still, even the governments in Russia or China conduct their political discourses in the terminology of Western democracies.[12] There does not seem, therefore, to be anyone seriously challenging the core normative framework of the liberal institutional order, even if there is plenty of unhappiness about the details. What has changed, however, is the salience and the quality of security issues. As a result, the U.S. is often no longer considered critical as a guarantor of national and/or regional security.

Who Are the New Powers?

There is significant disagreement and uncertainty about which states make up this most recent wave of emerging powers. What is clear is that Brazil, China and India belong to it. But even the narrowest definition of this group, the famous concept of the BRIC countries by Goldman Sachs, contains at least one country which hardly qualifies as a "rising power:" Russia. In comparison with the former Soviet Union, to whom it is the successor state, Russia may well seem a declining, rather than a rising power, and its energy wealth is certainly also not new. There are also other good reasons to doubt whether Russia should be seen as a "rising power".[13] Beyond China, India and Brazil, other countries frequently referred to as "rising" or "pivotal powers" are Mexico, Brazil, Algeria, Egypt, South Africa,[14] Turkey, India, Pakistan, and Indonesia,[15] Nigeria, and Iran. At least in the case of South Africa and possibly also Brazil, outstanding charismatic leadership (Nelson Mandela, Lula da Silva) may have contributed to the status as "emerging power."

---

[12]I am grateful for this insight to Volker Stanzel.

[13]Andrew F. Hart and Bruce D. Jones, "How Do Rising Powers Rise?" *Survival* 52:6, Dec.2010–Jan. 2011, pp. 67-88.

[14]Since 2011, South Africa has officially joined the club of the BRIC countries; the acronym therefore was changed to BRICS (for the membership of this grouping consisting of Brazil, India, China and South Africa).

[15]Robert Chase, Emily Hill, Paul Kennedy, "Pivotal States and U.S. Strategy," *Foreign Affairs*, 75:1 (Jan./Feb. 1996), pp. 33-51.

What makes a country an "emerging power"? Andrew Hurrell[16] argues that in order to qualify, a country should, apart from displaying rapid economic growth and considerable economic weight, also dispose, first, of *significant actual or at least potential military and political power*, as well as sufficient *internal cohesion* to plausibly contribute to a revised international order. Second, it should *aspire to a more influential role in global affairs*. Third, the country under consideration should entertain *significant relations with other emerging powers*, and, fourth, it would, unlike established middle powers such as Australia and Canada, *not have been fully integrated in the post-1945 international order until now*—which precludes the European powers and Japan, but also traditional middle powers, such as Australia or Canada.

Following this line of argument, I propose the following criteria for identifying an emerging power:

1. A state which is not part of the inner circle of the existing international order (i.e., no membership in OECD before 1990), but

2. is among the fifteen largest economies in the world today, or will be by 2050,

3. or, alternatively is among the fifteen top countries in terms of investment capital surplus and/or a large energy exporter,

4. is domestically reasonably settled and

5. entertains international ambitions, at a regional or even global level,

6. has shown persistently above-average economic growth for the last decade,

7. is among the world's largest fifteen military spenders, and/or

8. has a nuclear weapons capability or the potential to develop one at short notice, and/or

9. plays a significant (i.e., regional great power) military role in a critical region (Middle East/East Asia/Europe).

---

[16]Andrew Hurrell , "Hegemony, liberalism and global order: what space for would-be great powers?" *International Affairs*, 82:1 (2006), pp. 1-19.

To qualify as a "significant power", a country should meet criteria 1, 2 and/or 3, 4, 5, and 6, as well as at least one of the categories 7–9. Based on this, only a few of the countries mentioned (and listed in the annex) can be considered "significant rising powers", namely China, India, Russia (but not a new power, and of uncertain political resilience), Brazil, Turkey, Iran (?) and Saudi Arabia (?).[17] (In the annex to this chapter, the candidates are listed, with countries meeting the criteria marked in bold).

Two aspects make this wave different from previous ones. First, with China, India and Brazil it includes some of the world's most populous and largest countries with some of its biggest economies; and second, it comes at a time when the dominant position of the United States and its principal allies has already been weakened significantly by previous expansions and mutations of the liberal international order. It also includes one particularly important country—China—which sees itself as an at least partially dissatisfied power and takes a critical attitude towards the United States.

There are also several states which explicitly challenge the dominant position of the U.S. in their respective regions. They include Iran (and, possibly, Turkey) in the Middle East and Brazil in Latin America. Yet those regional challengers fall into two distinct categories: Brazil or Turkey may have very different notions about the organization of their regions from notions entertained in Washington, but such differences should be amenable to mutual adjustment. This will be much more difficult in the cases of Iran or China. China's national unification project (Taiwan) and its reluctance to accept Japan as a co-equal partner in regional co-operation pose a challenge to America's traditional dominance in the Western Pacific, while Iran threatens the U.S. position in the "American Lake" generally known as the Persian/Arabian Gulf.[18] Yet the global supremacy of the United States rests at least in part on its dominant political and security position in those two critical regions. Any challenge to America's regional position in those critical region will therefore also likely have implications at the level of the global international order—if not in terms of its overall

---

[17]The question marks indicate reservations regarding domestic political stability.

[18]Michael T. Klare, *Rising Powers, Shrinking Planet, The New Geopolitics of Energy* (New York: Metropolitan Books, 2008), pp. 177ff.

architecture, then certainly in terms of its ability to function effectively in specific situations.

China: A Special Case

There are good reasons to assume that China will play a special role in the political challenge to international order from this wave of emerging powers. By almost any yardstick, China is by far the biggest new kid on the block, and thus arguably in a category of its own. It is also the only rising power which can plausibly claim to be a global power already now, given its position as a permanent member of the United Nations Security Council and its worldwide economic and political presence. Its economy will probably surpass that of the U.S. economy in terms of purchasing power within the next few years (the IMF predicts the year 2015). Moreover, China is also the only country among the emerging powers that could plausibly challenge the United States politically, as well as economically, as the dominant global power within a generation. China also directly threatens the U.S. position in East Asia, and it is also involved, through its material and political backing for Iran, at least to some degree in the Iranian challenge in the Gulf (but by developing closer ties with Saudi Arabia it is also drawn into Saudi efforts to contain Iran.[19] Its "learning authoritarian system"[20] so far has proved remarkably adept at keeping this huge country together and pushing it forward at almost lightning speed towards industrialization and development.

None of those considerations apply to any of the other emerging powers. Russia, with its huge nuclear weapons arsenal, its influence in the eastern European periphery and shady foreign policy ambitions will certainly continue to present the United States and its allies with difficulties. Iran, with its budding nuclear weapon capability, its radical Islamist foreign policy ideology and its influence in Iraq, as well as its influence with important non-state actors such as Hamas and Hizbullah in Lebanon and Palestine, poses a very serious and difficult challenge to U.S. and Western interests in the Middle East. Still, neither

---

[19]"Saudi Arabia and China: Looking East," *The Economist*, December 11, 2010, pp. 58f.

[20]Sebastian Heilmann, "Maximum Tinkering under Uncertainty: Unorthodox Lessons from China," *Modern China* 35:4 (2009), pp. 450-462.

represents a challenge as large and as complex as that of China. Nor does India: by almost any yardstick other than population, India will continue to play in a lower league than China for decades to come,[21] and its foreign policy is much more cautious, regionally focused and defensive than that of China: it has traditionally focused on regional dominance in South Asia and the Indian Ocean, and on containing Pakistan. Its large border conflict with China also puts India on the defensive.[22] India may thus become a significant constraint on China's foreign policy and an asset to America in its region, but it seems unlikely to develop into a global foreign policy challenge on a par with that of the People's Republic within the next 20 years. This reflects the assumption that India almost certainly will be tending towards closer cooperation with other powers to hedge against, or even to contain China, rather than side with it or be drawn into a Chinese sphere of influence, but also the fact that India's regional environment in South Asia does not have the same critical importance in a global context as does East Asia.

The nature of the challenge which China represents for the present international order and its hegemon, the United States, first and foremost concerns China's search for domestic development, prestige and international status—all of which are considered critical for the maintenance of the rule of the Chinese communist party, the supreme policy objective of Beijing. It may well be the imperatives of socio-economic development in China, rather than strategic conflict, which could cause the greatest frictions with America and the transatlantic community in the future. It is simply not clear when and how the Chinese economy can swing from its present path of industrial modernization based on excessive investment and huge trade surpluses to a trajectory which would be less conflictual in its implications for China's international economic relations. Nor is it clear that this

---

[21]Thus, according to the latest projections by Goldman Sachs, bvy 2050 the Indian economy would still be ´smaller than that of the Unite States and only about half the size of China's. According to those projections, China would overtake the U.S. in 2027 to become the world's largest economy. O'Neill, Jim/Stupnytska, Anna: The Long-Term Outlook for the BRICs and N-11 Post Crisis (Goldman Sachs Global Economics Paper No: 192, Dec. 4, 2009) (http://www2.goldmansachs.com/ideas/brics/long-term-outlook-doc.pdf) [accessed March 10,2011]

[22]Christian Wagner, "India's Gradual Rise," *Politics*, 30: S1 (Dec. 2010), pp. 63-70.

change of direction in the Chinese development model can be achieved without major political discontinuities, which in turn could produce tensions with the West. China's national security strategy, which is focused on its territorial unity and thus directly threatens Taiwan, also implies a direct challenge to America's present strategic position in the Western Pacific. Against this has to be held the massive interdependence which ties the American and Chinese economies together in what correctly has been termed the economic equivalent of "mutual assured destruction" between two former superpowers, the U.S. and the Soviet Union.

China does *not* pose an ideological challenge to America: the alleged difference between economic models ("Washington consensus" versus "Beijing consensus") is less significant than often assumed and concerns more the difference between an advanced industrial country and an industrial latecomer. All established industrial powers, starting with Great Britain and the United States, initially developed their industrial base through a variety of mercantilist strategies, just as China did over the last 30 years.[23] This "developmental state" approach becomes untenable and dysfunctional, however, at a certain level of economic complexity, leading to its reconfiguration within an advanced industrial economy, in which governments and economic actors interact and jointly shape what essentially are mixed economies, rather than economies of particular type.

Will China be a "responsible stakeholder" in the liberal international order, as demanded, famously, by Robert B. Zoellick; an "irresponsible stakeholder";[24] or a "dissatisfied responsible great power"?[25] China's basic foreign policy approach seems to be driven by the search for status recognition,[26] but also by opportunism. It will follow the

---

[23]Barry Naughton, "China's Distinctive System: can it be a model for others? " *Journal of Contemporary China*, 19:65 (2009), pp. 437-460; Ha-Joon Chang, *Bad Samaritans: The Myth of Free Trade and the Secret History of Capitalism* (London: Bloomsbury Press 2008).

[24]Stewart Patrick, "Irresponsible Stakeholders? The Difficulty of Integrating Rising Powers," *Foreign Affairs* 89:6 (Nov./Dec. 2010), pp. 44-53.

[25]Shaun Breslin, "China's Emerging Global Role: Dissatisfied Responsible Great Power," *Politics*, 30:S1 (2019), pp. 52-62.

[26]Yong Deng, *China's Struggle for Status, The Realignment of International Relations* (Cambridge: Cambridge University Press, 2008).

rules and work within the institutions wherever that promises to be beneficial for China. This will include a willingness to make contributions to sustaining the present order (albeit not, of course, without adjustments to accommodate China's weight and influence) where China's material stakes in this order are large, such as in the international trading order or in the present monetary and financial system. Where the Chinese leadership views the rules and institutions as obstacles to China's interests, it will ignore them or bend them wherever that seems possible without serious negative repercussions. And it seems at present very unlikely that China would accept any constraints on its future policy options and its sovereign freedom of action by international rules and institutions. In short, China will insist on being involved in laying down the law and upholding it *vis-à-vis* others, but it will not consider itself bound by that law. This traditional great power attitude is, of course, quite familiar from others, including America itself. But it will also become increasingly problematic in an non-hegemonic, apolar world.

The Rise of the Rest: Implications for the Transatlantic Community

In sum, the most recent wave of emerging states will not challenge the present liberal institutional order in its foundations, but it will make its management vastly more complicated and uncertain. China emergence as the world's largest society and economy will be particularly critical.

Some policy implications of this are fairly obvious: for example, the transatlantic community should concentrate its efforts to sustain and develop further the present international order on the challenges posed by China's rise. This does NOT mean, however, that the West should focus its foreign policies only on China directly. For much of the impact of China's rise, and of this present wave of rising powers in general, is *systemic*, and the responses therefore will also importantly have to focus on the systemic level—but then include China in working on that level.

A constructive approach to China would try to persuade China to modify its present, highly pragmatic and opportunistic foreign policy approach—to induce, in other words, "foreign policy learning."[27] The aim would be to have China reformulate its foreign policy role concept in ways which better reflect its rapidly evolving position in the international order. But such a change in China's foreign policy would—if it were possible to elicit it from abroad at all—would have to be linked to changes in Western policy behavior. Thus, the West could help propagate appropriate standards of behavior for "great powers" by itself setting examples and creating incentives (both material and immaterial, such as standing and status), for new powers. But even assuming that China's foreign policy role concept would shift, nudged by the West, in such a direction, there would still be huge difficulties. For example, "burden-sharing" is an objectively vexing issue: what exactly should being a "responsible stakeholder" involve? The present debate between China and the United States on currency valuations show that the answer to this is neither obvious nor easily achievable without paying a significant domestic price—presumably, on both sides of the divide. Moreover, the rapid changes in the relative weight of China (and others) in international relations will probably require highly flexible, dynamic adjustments in global governance—something which again poses major objective difficulties, even if one assumes that the political will to do so existed.

The picture is further complicated by the challenge to U.S. hegemonic leadership that China does pose, rather directly, in East Asia, and more indirectly also in the Middle East. The complications arise not least out of the complex interdependence between global and regional order in critical regions: transitions to different regional orders in either of the two regions are likely to reverberate at the global level, just as considerations of global order may constrain great power behavior at the regional level. How this would play out is impossible to predict, but the policy implication is clear. In critical regions, it will be important to sustain regional orders not only for their own sake, but also because they represent building blocks of global order. This also works the other way round, at least to some extent: a robust and vibrant international order could help sustain fragile arrangements of regional order. But it would be unwise to rely

[27]Sebastian Harnisch, Cornelia Frank, and Hanns W. Maull, eds., *Role Theory in International Relations* (London: Routledge, 2011).

too much on arrangements and considerations of global order to underpin critical regional orders: their stability and sustainability must be secured independently from each other as much as possible. For example, in the Middle East the present regional order would probably be strengthened by by a meaningful peace process between Israel, the Palestinians and the Arab world (i.e., enhanced regional stability through regional efforts), but also from an inclusive global oil order involving all major producer, consumer and transit countries.[28] The development of more robust multilateral security institutions could serve to strengthen regional order in East Asia through regional efforts, but progress on nuclear non-proliferation at the global level could also contribute to this end, as would a U.S. decision to ratify, and thus join, the UN Law of the Seas Convention.

As China rises, it will change international relations, but it will also be changed itself. One obvious aspect of this is the involvement of ever larger numbers of individual and collective actors (both state and non-state) in China's external relations; another is the growing complexity of this involvement on the ground abroad, as China's presence broadens and deepens. Both developments will tend to undermine the ability of Beijing to carry out coherent and consistent foreign policies. To cite just two recent examples: to what extent were the promotion of a more expansive definition of Chinese interests in the South China Sea or the ramming of a Japanese coast guard ship by a Chinese fishing trawler in the disputed territorial waters off the Senkaku/Diaoyu islands actions undertaken by the Chinese state? the result of bureaucratic politics? or even the consequence of individual ambitions and spontaneous reactions by well-placed individuals? And to what extent are we now confronted with a clearly defined, coherent and consistent Chinese government policies on those issues? The second example concerns Sudan. Originally, Beijing was uncritically and unequivocally backing the regime in Khartoum, but China's increasingly diversified and multi-faceted involvement with thecountry, including the South, has produced significant policy modifications, as China became aware of the possible negative effects of the Darfur conflict and a North-

---

[28]Andreas Wenger, "Towards a More Sustainable Global Energy System: Integrating Demand-Side and Supply-Side Policies," in Andreas Wenger, Robert W. Orttung, and Jerome Perovic, eds., *Energy and the Transformation of International Relations: Towards a Producer-Consumer Framework* (Oxford: Oxford University Press, 2009), pp. 331-362.

South split of the country on Chinese interests. Growing Chinese involvement in world affairs thus complicates Bejing's calculations of interests and its policies.

What does all this imply for the transatlantic community? Clearly, U.S. hegemony is increasingly unsustainable, both internationally and probably also domestically. It will have to be supplemented and, eventually, superseded by more collective forms of management through "effective multilateralism". Yet this is easier said than done. One crucial task in this context will be to mobilize a critical mass of support for international agreements and their effective implementation. While this ultimately will no longer be possible without at least some of the emerging states; the West may have to establish agreement within its own ranks first, so as to overcome the disruptive influence of veto players and free riders. Once there is such a transatlantic basis, it will be easier to find partners among the new powers and beyond. Yet if the West were unable to find agreement within its own ranks, the rising powers are unlikely to come to the support of international order, as they would probably find it even more difficult to agree amongst themselves.[29]

While the rise of China and other powers will at times certainly lead to tensions and conflict within the transatlantic community and the West at large, there is nothing inherent in that rise which would make transatlantic cooperation less feasible, less likely or, indeed, less desirable. The impact of the rise of China and other new powers certainly will often be different in degree, but it will be similar in kind, and therefore should strengthen, rather than weaken transatlantic solidarity. To illustrate: the rise of China will affect the U.S. position in the Western Pacific much more than that of the European Union, which does not have direct security interests in that region. Yet America and Europe share an overall interest in regional stability. It would thus be short-sighted if European countries tried to benefit from tensions between America and China.

---

[29]The most recent illustration of this problem was the decision to appoint Christine Lagarde, formerly the French Minister of Finance, as Managing Director of the IMF to succeed Dominique Strauss-Kahn. Although there was widespread unease about yet another European in this position, with many prominent voices demanding a break with the tradition reserving that position for a European, the BRICS and other rising powers were unable to agree on a candidate of their own, despite a number of well-qualified candidates.

The question then will be not so much whether there is still a *raison d'être* for the transatlantic community, but whether America and Europe will find the political will and the right ways to forge broad winning coalitions for effective global order. To do so, they will increasingly have to rely on forms of power other than their traditional military and economic strengths.[30] This will include 'leadership by example' (both in terms of best practices and normative legitimacy) and 'leadership by down payments' to demonstrate serious commitment. The transatlantic community will have to demonstrate that it will "put its money where its mouth is": double standards and claims to be exempt from international rules and norms, for whatever reasons, are bound to diminish the transatlantic community's legitimacy, and hence also its influence in world politics.

No doubt this kind of foreign policy reorientation would be contested strongly domestically. Governments will have to ask their electorates to mobilize societal resources to help others cope with global challenges at a time when their own societies will likely be grappling with the consequences of low economic growth, demographic aging, overextended public finances, and increasingly stringent external constraints produced by commercial competition, resource scarcities and the growing impact of climate change. The demands on the political skill, leadership and inspiration of transatlantic governments in this context therefore are huge.

Overall, the present dynamics of international relations therefore point towards a world of disorder, painful ruptures and upheavals. To avert this will require levels of regional and global cooperation and even integration with the new powers in general, and with China in particular, that go significantly beyond anything we have seen in recent years. This will test the political mettle of transatlantic leaders, who will need to persuade their societies to make resources available for purposes of foreign policy and international order, rather than—as seems to be the case now—regard foreign policies primarily as a convenient way to advance domestic political interests. As always, but perhaps more than ever before, good foreign policy will therefore have to begin at home.

---

[30]Patrick, op. cit.

Annex I: Emerging Powers Indicators I

Country	Fifteen largest and other economies In 2010, US$ bill., ppp, 2010 prices (rank)[b]	Among fifteen largest economies in 2050, US$ bill., in prices of 2006 (rank)	Stable and focused government	Foreign policy ambitions	Average real economic growth rate, 2000-2008
China	9,872 (2)	70,000 (1)	Yes	Yes	10.0
India	4,046 (4)	39,000 (3)	Yes	Yes	7.2
Russia	2,229 (6)	8,500 (6)	Yes	Yes	7.0
Brazil	2,194 (7)	11,500 (4)	Yes	Yes	3.7
Indonesia	1,033 (15)	7,000 (7)	Yes	(yes)	5.1
Turkey	(879)	4,500 (14)	Yes	Yes	4.7
Iran[a]	(826)	--	Yes	Yes	5.2
Nigeria	(342)	5,000 (11)	(Yes)	(yes)	8.8
Mexico	1,560 (11)	10,500 (5)	Yes	No	2.8
South Africa	(505)	--	Yes	Yes	4.1
Egypt	(469)	--	Yes	Yes	4.9
Saudi Arabia[a]	(591)	--	Yes	Yes	3.9
South Korea	1,467 (12)	4,600 (13)	Yes	Yes	4.8
Venezuela	(344)	--	Yes	Yes	4.4
Pakistan	(451)	--	(Yes)	?	5.5
Vietnam	(278)	4,500 (15)	Yes	?	7.5
Thailand	(580)	--	Yes	?	5.0
Argentina	(596)	--	Yes	?	3.7
Taiwan	(824)	--	Yes	?	3.6
other	USA (1), Japan (3), Germany (5), UK (8), France (9), Italy (10), Spain (13), Canada (14)	USA (2), Japan (8), Germany (9), UK (10), France (12)			

[a]borderline case, but arguably among the most significant emerging powers in the second tier, given its sizeable population, regional military power and political influence, and vast energy resources.
[b]The largest economy according to the CIA World Factbook is the EU, with the U.S. as #2. European economies are also listed separately. The ranking here excludes the EU.

Annex II: Emerging Powers Indicators II

Country	Among largest fifteen military spenders (% of world total) (rank)	Nuclear weapons	Significant regional military power	Among top ten capital investment holders (SWF capital, $ bill., 2010)	Among top ten oil exporters (mbd) (% of world total, 2009)	Among top twenty in terms of population (mio./rank) (2010 est.)
China	100 (6.6) (2)	Yes	Yes	826	-	1,330 (1)
India	36.3 (2.4) (9)	Yes	Yes	--	-	1,173 (2)
Russia	53.3 (3.5) (5)	Yes	Yes	142.5	5.6 (14.6)	139 (9)
Brazil	26.1 (1.7) (11)	--	Yes	--	--	201 (5)
Indonesia	no	--	Yes	--	--	243 (4)
Turkey	no	--	Yes	--	--	78 (17)
Iran[a]	no	program	Yes	--	2.2 (5.7)	77 (18)
Nigeria	no	--	Yes	--	2.1 (5.5)	152 (8)
Mexico	no	--	--	--	--	112 (11)
South Africa	no	abolished	(yes)	--	--	--
Egypt	no	--	Yes	--	--	80 (16)
Saudi Arabia[a]	41.2 (2.7) (8)	--	Yes	415	6.3 (16.4)	--
South Korea	24.1 (1.6) (12)	--	--	--	-	--
Venezuela	no	--	--	--	1,6 (4.1)	--
Pakistan	no	Yes	--	--	-	184 (6)
Vietnam	no	--	--	--	--	90 (13)
Argentina	no	--	--	--	--	--
Thailand	no	--	--	--	--	67 (20)
other	USA (1) France (3) UK (4) Japan (6) Germany (7) Italy (10) Canada (13) Australia (14) Spain (15)	USA France UK Israel DPRK		Singapore (380.5) Kuwait (202.8) Qatar (85) UAE (627)	UAE (2.0) Norway (1.8) Angola (1.8) Iraq (1.9) Canada (1.5)	USA (310) Bangladesh (156) Japan (127) Philipp. (100) Ethiopia (88) Germany (82) Congo (71)

[a]borderline case, but arguably among the most significant emerging powers in the second tier, given sizeable population, energy resource power, regional military power and political influence.

Sources: UN Statistics [www.un.org/esa/policy/link/wesp10_annextables/wesp10_a03.xls]; CIA World Factbook; SIPRI World Military Expenditures; Jim O'Neill/Anna Stuypnytska, The Long-Term Outlook for the BRICs and N-11 Post Crisis (Goldman Sachs Global Economics Paper No: 192, Dec. 4, 2009)

Chapter 2

The U.S. and Europe Face the BRICs: What Kind of Order?

Michael F. Oppenheimer

The liberal world order as we know it—open, non-discriminatory, with strong rule-based institutions of collaboration among democratic, market-driven states led by the U.S.—is in a two-decade long decline. The decline is probably terminal, though the moment of the system's demise will be clear only in retrospect. Failed multilateral trade negotiations, mercantilist trade, currency and foreign investment practices among both established and rising states, weak surveillance of macro-economic policies and exchange rates, growing state to state competition for resources, failure to collectively address emerging issues such as climate change-all demonstrate and contribute to erosion of the liberal system, and all are structural, not consequences (indeed, some are causes) of the recent and continuing global economic crisis.

Arresting the slide is the most to expect over the short term. Though it is easy to invent grand bargains and system-changing institutional projects, this is not a moment for heroic order-building, which presupposes abundant political capital and either hegemonic leverage or consensus among a greater number and diversity of major players. These conditions do not, and for the foreseeable future will not, exist. Making the most of the present requires internal reform within major players to restore growth, employment and competitiveness (among established market economies), rebalance growth (in China), and strengthen institutions of collective decision-making (in the EU). This risks inattention to global challenges, but collective action cannot come from states with disparate interests, stagnant economies and weak institutions.

Over the medium- to long-term, and even under favorable growth assumptions, the challenge posed by the BRICs (and other rising states) to an efficiently functioning, liberal global system will be severe, and the barriers to a common U.S.-European response will be high. This is the case even as the BRICS themselves face growing impediments to growth. Extrapolating recent hyper-economic performance based on continued success of investment/export led growth models can make the BRIC challenge seem more formidable than it is, and can cause us to overlook areas of potential collective action among developed countries and rising states as the problems they encounter begin to converge. At the Center for Global Affairs at NYU, we've been working under a Carnegie Corporation grant to develop alternate future scenarios for pivotal states, and have become convinced of the contingent nature of recent BRIC successes, particularly for China, Russia and Turkey. Growth rates for this set of countries will continue to exceed those for advanced developed countries given their continued, though diminishing, cost advantages, but will not be sustained at recent historic rates, and weak internal institutions, income inequalities, inadequate infrastructure, ageing populations, environmental stresses could cause dramatic declines in economic performance and government legitimacy. As BRIC governments face these inhibitions, some political space could be created for more market-driven development strategies, and a narrowing of differences about how to maintain/extend a liberal global system. The growing disquiet among Western investors concerning their treatment in China, for example, could reinforce outside leverage for liberal reforms.

However, even in a less robust future, the BRICs will continue to challenge the liberal system. Not present at the creation, with often illiberal economic and political institutions, growing power and an uncertain and divided West, we can expect strong assertions of views in conflict with our own, and growing friction between the BRICs and established powers. Global negotiations—on almost anything—will face diminishing returns; regional and bilateral arrangements will proliferate; home-grown systems of economic management and global trade/financial engagement will widen differences and clog negotiating arenas. For at least the medium term future, reform of global institutions to reflect shifts in relative economic power may succeed, but will complicate decision-making without necessarily enhancing legitimacy.

The extent and effects of revisionist challenges to the liberal order will also depend on internal reform and transatlantic collaboration among advanced countries. It is hard to imagine the latter without the former. Without fiscal solvency, economic growth and job creation in the U.S., sustained transatlantic leadership is implausible. Without improved EU institutions and structural reform at national levels, a positive European response to U.S. initiatives is equally implausible. With diffuse leadership and internal preoccupations, disparate and conflicting responses to BRIC challenges (and opportunities) are more likely than not. There is a strong possibility that the West will not meet these tests, that the result could be an illiberal, multipolar and conflict-prone world, delivering far less than optimum growth and with fewer opportunities for the BRICs of the future.

A common U.S.- European agenda that works within this system of diminished relative power and consensus would begin with a rebuilding of economic competitiveness and institutions of common action. For the short term, U.S. fiscal pressures, stubborn unemployment and partisan divides limit bold leadership on behalf of new ideas. Europe's institutional deficit and deepening divisions between north and south limit both its ability to propose new ideas and its capacity to respond to ideas from outside. Yet we should be able to find sufficient political capital to continue present efforts to reform global institutions, improve cross-border financial regulation, bring collective pressure on China for more market-based currency pricing, improve IMF surveillance and seek commitments from major players to limit global trade and financial imbalances. While a restarted Doha is too far a reach, prevention of further protectionist backsliding should be possible. Many of these efforts will not succeed over the short term, but could lay the ground for effective follow-through when internal conditions become more favorable.

It should also be possible to develop a transatlantic dialogue about how to avoid destructive competition for BRIC markets, and enhance our collective leverage with the BRICs on behalf of liberal principles. These guidelines should prioritize action through the WTO and the IMF, but will also entail joint bilateral representations to countries that violate free trade and investment principles. The substance of such actions is well known: IPR, export subsidies, government procurement, currency pricing, FDI-related performance requirements, lack of financial transparency, etc. On some of these issues, the U.S.-Europe coalition would be joined by others. (Brazil on currency issues, for example). As economic conditions improve in the U.S. and Europe, we should also be able to build new momentum into discussions on a U.S.-EU free trade area. We should also try to craft common policies towards pivotal states whose anchoring in the West is feasible and important in solidifying their democratic institutions: Turkey and Ukraine would benefit from such a common approach.

Even as we imagine a restoration of growth and employment, and both structural and institutional reforms in Europe, the enhanced capacity for collective action may not save the liberal system. We will have to decide, at some point in the not-too-distant future, what kind of game we are in with the BRICs, and with China in particular. Is it plausible to imagine a combination of restored Western leverage, reformed global institutions, and the liberalizing pressures of modernization to push the BRICs towards a full embrace of the old rules? If so, the reform agenda is worth significant investment, and the tensions of finding consensus in diversity are tolerable given the ultimate benefits. Patience would be called for as the BRICs work out their own internal adjustments to interdependence, and come to accept responsibility for carrying some of the weight of liberalization, of accepting the constraints on autonomy of full engagement in effective institutions. The contemporary period will come to be seen as transitional, from a deep liberalization limited in geographic scope, to a somewhat more shallow but still functioning liberal order with broader, more diverse membership and manageable frictions. Such a system would deliver higher levels of growth through enhanced market and capital access, common rules for treatment of foreign investors, intellectual property protection, and strong institutions with accepted procedures for dispute resolution.

But all the Western effort we can muster may not be sufficient to get us to this optimistic scenario. The free ride on the open system from which the BRICS have greatly benefited, may be the only condition under which they are prepared to participate. As overdue concessions are demanded for market based currency pricing, liberalization of trade in services and manufactured goods, IPR protection, nondiscriminatory treatment of foreign investors, elimination of trade distorting subsidies, it may become clear that the burden/risk sharing the

West expects from the BRICs is not in the cards. We may already be well into a realist game of power competition and commercial aggrandizement with the BRICs, in which case pursuing a liberal global agenda invites self-deception and a misallocation of political capital.

Improved transatlantic collaboration is essential under either set of circumstances, but the purpose and agenda of such collaboration varies greatly depending on whether the context is liberal or realist. Liberal expectations require recommitment to comprehensive, Doha-like global trade and investment agreements, further institutional reform, internal (to U.S. and EU) negotiating mandates, and patience with illiberal but (assumed) transitory BRIC illiberal practices. Faith in liberal answers to the challenges of growth and stability would be sustained. Protectionist/mercantilist responses to BRIC ingratitude would be resisted. This liberal discipline would have to be reinforced by gains in growth, employment, and deficit reduction in the U.S. and Europe.

A realist context incentivizes a U.S.-Europe collective response to the BRICS aimed at maximizing leverage in competition for markets, resources, capital and technology. We would pay lip service to institutional reform and liberal values, but would invest little in these projects. We would make full use of existing and accepted measures to counteract currency manipulation, export subsidies, import barriers, and protection from import surges, but would operate outside legitimate measures when necessary. We would do so on a coordinated basis whenever possible, in concert with other rising states with similar grievances. We would resist accusations of complicity in the demise of the liberal system, arguing (with Gilpin) that liberal order is possible only under the hegemonic leadership of a liberal state, that these conditions have passed into history, and that it is past time to abandon the self restraint of naïve expectations. The risks here are two: a premature abandonment of these principles that generates self-fulfilling prophecies of protectionism and conflict; and an inability to protect the U.S.-Europe relationship from the same competitive forces that poison the relationship with the BRICs.

By imagining alternate, plausible trajectories for the transatlantic relationship, and for the BRICS, we can construct future scenarios that provide some discipline for our thinking about these issues, and a heads up for policy makers about potential surprises and, hopefully, unrecognized opportunities.

Three fragmentary scenario concepts might include:

Multipolarity/Fragmentation: slow, partial recovery from economic crisis, blocked structural reform in the West, and illiberal competition among the U.S., a fragmenting EU, and the BRICs. No one gains optimum benefits from globalization, but Europe gains the least, the BRICS face new constraints as global growth and market access diminish, and the U.S. is best positioned to succeed on a relative basis given its strong bilateral ties to the BRICs, major European countries, Japan, other rising states, and its hard power advantages, which are more relevant in this scenario. Clearly a worst case, but not necessarily the least likely of the three.

Multipolarity/Effective Balance of Power: successful reform and recovery in the West, and leveraging of collective capacity in a struggle for power and influence with rising states. The West preserves the gains from previous—and continuing—liberal reforms, but is unable to extend these practices to the BRICs. The competition with rising states is expressed in mercantile struggle for economic gains of globalization, and for influence within weakening global institutions and access to natural and other resources.

Liberal Hegemony: successful reform and recovery in the West, and a leveraging of its collective capacity to re-legitimize and extend the liberal system to the BRICs and others. The appeal for the BRICs of fuller participation in, and responsibility for, strengthened institutions is a result of renewed success and credibility of the market-driven growth model, and increasing impediments to sustainable growth in the BRICs. This reassertion of Western power and norms is hegemonic in the sense, not of direct control of the policies and politics of rising states, but of the wide acceptance of Western values in a consent-based system. The best scenario clearly, but not viewed with the same enthusiasm by the BRICs, and therefore not the most likely.

From a policy perspective, the usual 'solution' to the dilemmas posed by such plausible but conflicting realist/liberal scenarios is to seek the upside while preparing for the worst. If only this were a controlled experiment, with transparency among the actors, clarity of purpose, and opportunities to learn from mistakes. Unfortunately, confidence in a common agenda between the BRICs and the West has already eroded, trust is diminishing, transparency is minimal, and incentives to competition—from weak institutions, internal stresses, growing strategic competition—are strong. Preparing for this world, as we must, will cause the upside to recede still further. Focusing on restoring our power and capacity for joint action with Europe is an imperative, but risks drift and decline in the liberal order. One can imagine the BRIC challenge being met by transatlantic collaboration, but aspirations for an order both liberal and global are unlikely to be realized.

Section II:

Prospects for Normative Order

Chapter 3

Normative Future: A U.S. Perspective

Bruce W. Jentleson

Norms are about what is right and just. As such they are more about values than things material. But they do have tangible impact. Work by Joseph Nye and others on "soft power" gets at part of this.[1] So do emphases on how—as bases for judgments about legitimacy—norms create "permissive conditions for action."[2]

In the immediate aftermath of the Cold War, there was a strong sense of global convergence around Western norms: e.g., the end of history, the democratic peace, the Washington consensus. Over time it has become increasingly apparent that normative legitimacy is more contested than consensual. Not as in the post-9/11 "war of ideas" formulation of freedom vs. fundamentalism, but as Steve Weber and I argue, a broader and more complex "global competition of ideas" being driven by debates such as those over globalization, the use of force, the rights and responsibilities of state sovereignty, international justice, optimal balancing of the state and the market, and alternative models for domestic governance.[3] And all this amidst technologies that make for multiple channels of information flow and ever more dynamic forms that flow takes.

With this as general context, I focus on questions about normative challenges in three parts: first, continuity and change in the value placed on the Atlantic Community within the United States; second,

---

[1] Joseph S. Nye, Jr., *The Paradox of American Power: Why the World's Only Superpower Can't Go It Alone* (New York: Oxford University Press, 2002).

[2] Martha Finnemore, "Constructing Norms of Humanitarian Intervention," in Peter J. Katzenstein, ed., *The Culture of National Security* (New York: Columbia University Press, 1996), p. 158.

[3] Steven Weber and Bruce W. Jentleson, *The End of Arrogance: America in the Global Competition of Ideas* (Cambridge, MA: Harvard University Press, 2010).

domestic governance and the Western democracy-capitalism model; third, key normative issues affecting 21st century international order.

American Valuation of the Atlantic Community: Continuity and Change

Shared values are a big reason why the fundamentals of the Atlantic Community are still sound. We have our societal, cultural and political differences in areas such as religiosity, some aspects of the appropriate role of the state, gun control, and the death penalty[4]—although some even question whether these are as stark as often assumed.[5] Either way it is the core commonalities, not differences, that are defining. We are all liberal democracies with a shared philosophical heritage and political values. Our economies are intertwined, with tensions and competition but connected in circumscribing ways. Our societies are interlinked in many ways, both in formal institutions and more informal networks. Our peoples have affinity for one another based on common culture and heritage. This "gestalt" of community is a key reason why even with the end of the Cold War, NATO in particular and the Atlantic Alliance more generally did not conform to the axiom that "alliances are against, or only derivatively for, someone or something."[6] It also provided the undergirding for intense policy conflicts such as over the Iraq war. Indeed, even amidst the animosities of those years, 57% of Europeans and 67% of Americans still saw enough common values to be able to cooperate on international problems.[7]

We do continue to value the same norms. But how much do we value each other?

Two major challenges must be met, one driven by global strategic changes and the other by domestic politics. The global strategic

---

[4] Seymour Martin Lipset, *American Exceptionalism: A Double-Edged Sword* (New York: W.W. Norton, 1996).

[5] Peter Baldwin, *The Narcissism of Minor Differences* (New York: Oxford University Press, 2010).

[6] Bruce W. Jentleson, "The Atlantic Alliance in a Post-American World," *Journal of Transatlantic Studies* (March 2009), pp. 61-72; George Liska, *Nations in Alliance: The Limits of Interdependence* (Baltimore: Johns Hopkins University Press, 1962), p. 12.

[7] *Transatlantic Trends Report: Key Findings 2008.*

change is that the 21ˢᵗ century world is no longer West-centric. The Soviet threat had centrality not just to North American-European relations but in making Europe the central theater of all of world affairs. It's not that Asia is the new central theater, it's that there is no single central theater. I don't subscribe to the zero-sum calculation of a Pacific focus replacing an Atlantic one. It's really more additive, lots of theaters, lots of relationships, lots of issue sets—a global age. Yes, the U.S.-Europe partnership affects and is affected by most if not all of these. But much less determinatively so. Talking and thinking as if this were not true, and especially as if the global strategic context could be made to go back to what it used to be, sets an unrealistic set of expectations.

The other challenge is in the mix of generational and ethnic change within American politics towards cohorts who put less value on relations with Europe. World War II is less part of family lore than part of history books. The FDR-Churchill relationship is still iconic but much more historically distant. Today's American university students still come to Europe in large numbers, but the growth is much more in non-European study abroad. Students in our "Duke Engage" program for research, internship and experiential opportunities take many more summer placements in the developing world than in Europe. Language departments are shrinking or at best holding steady in Romance languages (other than Spanish, but that is about Latin America, not Spain) while growing in Chinese, Arabic, Urdu and the like. Ethnically the country is relatively less Euro-hyphenated, as Carl Haub outlines in his chapter in this book. The point here is less rising antipathy than a degree of apathy, not more conflict but rather less priority.

In sum, while the relationship is not in crisis, it does need tending.[8] Shared values remain important. Shared interests do as well. Shared understandings need to be refreshed. Perspectives need to be adapted. The goal should be to keep the relationship a high priority one but with no illusion of making it as important as it used to be. We cannot

---

[8] For some ideas and proposals, see Daniel S. Hamilton and Frances G. Burwell, *Shoulder to Shoulder: Forging a Strategic U.S.-EU Partnership*, December 2009, http://trans atlantic.sais-jhu.edu/bin/c/s/us-eu_report_final.pdf; Thomas Wright and Richard Weitz, *The Transatlantic Alliance in a Multipolar World*, November 2010, http://www. thechicagocouncil.org/userfiles/file/task%20force%20reports/The%20Transat-lantic%20Alliance%20in%20a%20Multipolar%20World.pdf.

expect the transatlantic relationship to be as valued as highly as in the post-World War II/Cold War period. It needs to be valued for what it can, and needs to, be in the 21st century: the partnership of the world's most stable democracies who have established a security community among themselves and who seek not just to advance their own interests but to promote broad international cooperation and foster a greater sense of global community.

Domestic Governance and the Western Democracy-Capitalism Model

Whether based on Jeffersonian and French Revolution ideals of the rights of man or Churchillian pragmatism of the least bad system, we in the West, and the United States in particular, have held to the normative position of the supremacy of democracy as a domestic system of governance, and of capitalism as an economic system for prosperity. The 20th century provided plenty of supporting evidence. Democracy vs. Nazism, democracy vs. Stalinism, democracy vs. various other dictatorships: pretty clear political verdict. Capitalism vs. Soviet and other socialisms: pretty clear economic bottom line.

But here too the 21st century is bringing new challenges.

How Well Is the Western Model Working?

It was the sense of "rupture" that concerned him. That's how a distinguished Brazilian retired diplomat expressed his concern about what was going on in the United States at a recent conference. That statement has really stuck with me. It digs deeper than just the usual comments about partisanship, or interpretation of particular election results, or who's up and who's down in various policy debates. It gets at the depths to which political differences penetrate into our society, and mix in a dangerous brew with cultural, racial, religious and ethnic differences. One does need to be conscious of too much present-ism and bear in mind that our politics have had prior periods of intense political conflict. Still, when interacting with a number of other forces and with the brew stirred by the unprecedented reach and penchant for sensationalism of the Internet and other new technologies, this does seem to be a particularly worrisome period.

One aspect that bears particularly on the normative appeal internationally of the U.S. model is whether we can live up to our traditional claim of *positive societal heterogeneity*. Electing African-American Barack Obama as President was seen by many around the world as a validation of core U.S. claims of equal opportunity and acceptance of diversity. It was of course more complicated than that, but the impact was still profound. But anti-immigration sentiment—indeed, not just sentiment but policy measures targeted at Hispanics—cut in the other direction. So too does increasing income inequality for African-Americans as well as Hispanic-Americans.

An even greater test is with Muslim-Americans. For a number of years post-9/11 there was much chest-thumping on how more content and less radical Muslim communities in the United States were compared to Britain, France and elsewhere in Europe. But recently there has been a dramatic increase in terrorism linked to Muslim-Americans—the Fort Hood shootings, the Christmas 2009 "underwear bomber" on the aircraft landing in Detroit, the Times Square car bombing, as well as Muslim-Americans heading to Somalia, Pakistan, Yemen and elsewhere for training and active fomenting. All this is ratcheting up pressure, for substantive security reasons as well as politics, for tighter homeland security and counterterrorism measures focusing on Muslim-Americans. How well the security-civil liberties balance is struck will resonate especially widely globally. And this is not just because of al-Jazeera, jihadist bloggers and the like. How well purported norms are upheld at home long has resonated abroad. In 1957 a main reason President Eisenhower sent the National Guard to enforce the integration of the public schools in Little Rock, Arkansas was concern about how segregation at home was playing into the Cold War ideological competition.

Another issue is about *policy capacity*, whether the political system can deliver policies of sufficient coherence to address the crucial problems their societies face. While destructive partisanship has been all too amply demonstrated in recent years, the recent fracas over the debt ceiling took this to new lows, particularly the power exerted by the Tea Party and its political fundamentalism. But the policy capacity problems of the American political system are not just a matter of partisanship. Indeed they go back to James Madison's *Federalist #10*. As part of the *Federalist Papers*, Madison warned about the danger of "factions": a "minority of the whole, who are united and actuated by some common impulse of passion, or of interest, adverse to the rights of other citizens, or to the permanent and aggregate interests of the community." What would Madison think of K Street? If he read *Politico*? The agricultural lobby, the oil lobby, the finance lobby all have plenty of support on both sides of the aisle. It is what political scientists call interest disaggregation, or what we could simply say is the whole of the national interest being greater than the sum of particularized interests. For all the heralding of the cap-and-trade bill that the House of Representatives passed in 2009, even if it had passed the Senate it would have been so broken out into special interest provisions that it would not have amounted to much of a genuinely comprehensive and strategic national energy-environmental policy. The same is the case with health care and financial reform: bills that did pass, and ones that went much further than prior legislation, but still are well short of the policy capacity needed to achieve the posited societal goals.

In sum, the normative appeal of the U.S. model to others depends heavily on how well it works for its own people. There is nothing idealistic about this, it is quite realistic. Nor is it just new age, it is very much age-old. It was no less than the eminent realist scholar Hans Morgenthau who stressed that the Cold War struggle would be determined "by the visible virtues and vices of their [U.S., Soviet] respective political, economic and social systems . . . It is at this point that foreign policy and domestic politics merge . . . The United States ought to again concentrate its effort upon creating a society at home which can again serve as a model for other societies to emulate."[9]

How Universal Its Appeal?

Even if we Americans do get our own house more in order, the question remains whether the Western democracy-capitalism model sets a global norm. The 21st century version of this question is more complex than the 20th century democracy vs. dictatorship and capitalism vs. socialism (and even that was not as straightforward as often posed).

---

[9] Cited in Michael J. Smith, "Ethics and Intervention," *Ethics and International Affairs*, 3 (1989), p. 8.

This is especially true for economic systems. China's economic miracle has not been about conversion to Western-style capitalism so much as its particular blending of the state and the market. Some see this as a new model of state-based capitalism. The other BRICs (Brazil, Russia, India) offer their own variants, each with greater market forces than earlier decades but also with the state playing a significant ownership, planning and strategic investing role. Given whose economies are growing faster, whose financial sector plunged the world into the recent recession, and even in some sectors where the dynamic innovation is (e.g., green technology), it is not hard to understand the appeal of such alternative models.

Underlying the particular policy challenges raised are fundamental normative issues about the state-market balance, which by Bretton Woods standards and according to the prevalent modernization-development model limited the former and maximized the latter. Casting this as about neo-protectionism, or neo-mercantilism, or authoritarian capitalism is much too dichotomous and simplistic to capture current debate and practices. It's more about "purposive state intervention to guide market development and national corporate growth," both internationally (e.g., in currency markets) and as more sophisticated versions of the "developmental state."[10]

The normative challenge here is not a confrontational one, or at least does not have to be. It does, though, point to pluralism more than universality, and the need to accept the legitimacy of a range of economic models beyond Western ones, and to adjust institutional rules and frameworks accordingly. Actually, it should not just be accepting in a concessionary or begrudging way, but being open to ways in which these other models may have strengths that ours do not for international economic stability and prosperity, perhaps even our own national economies, and ourselves doing the learning and adapting.

In terms of political systems, when it comes to civil liberties and individual rights liberal democracy is unrivaled. But effective policy capacity can be a different issue. Even beyond the problems addressed above, this may turn the usual celebration of American exceptionalism on its head. The particularly American version of democracy, struc-

---

[10]Gregory Chin and Ramesh Thakur, "Will China Change the Rules of Global Order?", *Washington Quarterly*, October 2010, pp. 122-125.

tured according to the principle of "that government is best which governs least," reflects the principal motivations of our Founders for achieving self-government and ensuring individual liberty. When juxtaposed against tyranny and repression, these most surely have universality. But for countries with mass poverty, endemic injustice, and other pressing human needs—that is to say, much of the world today—people are looking not just to be protected *from* government, but also to be protected *by* government. That never has and never will justify repressiveness, but it does recognize that in many societies political legitimacy is a function of performance, not just process. To the extent that we advocate democracy, it needs to be democracy that delivers what others want for themselves, not what we want for them. It cannot just be about *freedom from*; it also has to be about the *capacity to*. In this regard one can give due to China's internal problems and systemic negatives, yet still acknowledge the ways in which a system that has pulled hundreds of millions out of poverty in the past twenty years has its attractive elements. The point here is not some great authoritarian wave but also not democracy sweeping the world—another question fundamental to the liberal order that is open and uncertain.

International Norms and 21st Century Global Order

I focus here on six international normative challenges key to 21st century global order.

Multilateralism

The "mixed messages"[11] the U.S. long has sent over the UN and multilateralism generally reflect the core debate over prerogative encroachment vs. policy enhancement. That is, does multilateralism enhance U.S. capacity to achieve policy goals more than the constraints on freedom of action and other impediments encroach U.S. prerogatives? No questions that there are more policy enhancement examples than critics admit. And the policy enhancement gains in today's world are potentially greater than ever. But House Republicans, among oth-

---

[11]Edward Luck, *Mixed Messages: American Politics and International Organizations, 1919-1999* (Brookings, 1999).

ers, remain to be convinced. One of the first initiatives of the incoming chair of the House Foreign Affairs Committee in 2011, Ileana Ross-Lehtinen, was to tie U.S. funding for the UN to whether it "advances American foreign policy goals."[12] In taking on such views, UN proponents inside and outside the administration also need to be serious about addressing the inefficiencies and other "pathologies" that this and many international institutions often have.[13] This is going to take a "tough love" approach, the "love" part being making an even more convincing case that the U.S. is willing to strengthen multilateral institutions even when this means less U.S. control, the "tough" part being serious about institutional capacity and pushing harder for reforms than some ideological multilateralists might like.

On the issue of opening up the leadership of international institutions to greater 21st century representativeness, the United States needs to be more proactive than begrudging. There are potent normative aspects to increasing the roles of non-Western rising and emerging powers. Power and interests are of course part of the equation, but the very formulation of "democratic deficit" speaks to the normative dimension. It is not just rhetoric when Chinese, Indian, Brazilian, Turkish, Indonesian, South African, Qatari and other leaders speak in terms of respect and dignity as why they and their peoples want the affirmation that comes with seats at the various tables, leadership positions and other roles and recognitions.

The G-20 is an important step in this direction. So too are such other recent developments in the formal structure of international institutions such as changes in the IMF quota and voting structure and U.S.-declared support for India as a permanent member of the UN Security Council. These, though, are only partial steps. Key issues remain, including the European hold on the IMF Managing Directorship, the U.S. hold on the World Bank Presidency, and other prospective candidates for UN Security Council expansion.[14]

---

[12]*New York Times*, January 26, 2011, http://www.nytimes.com/2011/01/26/world/26nations.html?_r=1&ref=world.

[13]Michael Barnett and Martha Finnemore, *Rules for the World: International Organizations in Global Politics* (Cornell University Press, 2004)

[14]This includes Germany and Japan although my focus here is more on this as a North-South issue.

There are basic arguments about how larger groups can be less efficient decision-makers. While this is more varying than often portrayed, it is the case that just increasing non-Western roles would not resolve all of the problems international institutions have. There are other factors that affect their effectiveness or lack thereof. Still while not a sufficient condition for effective 21st century international institutions, narrowing the democratic deficit is a necessary condition. The situation is akin to others in life, be it political or personal life, in which one gets more credit for a change that one chooses to make than when one is forced to make it. International institutional expansion and reform is going to happen; it is thus strategic to be a part of making it happen, get some of the credit and have some shaping effect.

Use of Force

The use of force will always be in part discretionary for states. The key question is how much. On the one hand the Bush 2003 Iraq invasion showed the dangers and ramifications of being too unilaterally discretionary. The broader Bush Doctrine context and the "take a number" rhetoric of neo-conservatives (within the administration as well as in the commentariat) made this about not just Iraq but also broader norms regarding the use of force. On the other hand fully subordinating decisions to use force to UN Charter provisions and procedures is unrealistic as a policy matter and is questionable normatively, as demonstrated by the distinction made between the legality (no) but legitimacy (yes) of NATO's 1999 intervention in Kosovo.[15]

The decision process on the March 2011 Libya intervention working through a UN Security Council resolution, with a broad coalition and with support from Arab regional organizations (Arab League, Gulf Cooperation Council, Organization of the Islamic Conference) concretely manifested the Obama administration's commitment to multilateralism in the use of force. Still more generally the administration has been quite explicit that "the United States must reserve the right to act unilaterally if necessary to defend our nation and our interests."[16]

---

[15]Independent International Commission on Kosovo, *The Kosovo Report; Conflict, International Response, Lessons Learned* (Oxford: Oxford University Press , 2000).

[16]Obama Administration, *2010 National Security Strategy*, p. 22, http://www.whitehouse.gov/sites/default/files/rss_viewer/national_security_strategy.pdf

There is a political angle to this: foreswearing the unilateral option other than in clear cases of self-defense would be politically suicidal. But it is not just politics. It also is policy and strategy. Deterrence would be weakened, options would be limited. Indeed, could any state genuinely make such a pledge and keep to it? Still given track records (not just the Bush administration, not just the Cold War, but also going back further in history, as Latin Americans are well aware) the U.S. is under particular scrutiny when it comes to the use of force.

Iran may well be a crucial case. Polls show shared concern on both sides of the Atlantic about Iran acquiring nuclear weapons, but significantly greater American than European support for military action.[17] Some argue that general support for and good feeling towards Barack Obama would modulate European opposition if he did resort to military force against Iran. Others see the potential for even greater disillusionment which even if less violent than anti-Bush demonstrations could cut deeper as happens when people feel let down. Irrespective, global reaction likely would be negative. Even if there were to be some sense of "thank you for cutting off the head of the serpent," that would be muted and tacit—and likely not even expressed in private meetings for fear of more Wikileaks exposure. It also would need to be layered over with more explicit criticism of the United States for acting unilaterally, which would further weaken the claim of normative credibility going forward on this seminal issue.

For its part the UN system has its own challenges. Its general pattern has been to do better on cases of clear interstate aggression (e.g., the 1990 Iraqi invasion of Kuwait and the 1950 North Korean invasion of South Korea) than intrastate (e.g., Bosnia, Rwanda, Kosovo, Darfur, Democratic Republic of Congo). The "Responsibility to Protect" (R2P) has been an important effort with normative as well as procedural and policy components to enhance UN capacity in ways that respect traditional claims of state sovereignty while also being true to the UN Charter as having been, as then-Secretary General Kofi Annan put it, "issued in the name of 'the peoples', not the gov-

---

[17]The German Marshall Fund *Transatlantic Trends 2010* polls found 86% of Americans and 79% of Europeans expressing concern about Iranian nuclear proliferation, but a 65%–43% split on military action; http://www.gmfus.org/trends/doc/2010_English_Key.pdf, pp. 16-17.

ernments, of the United Nations."[18] Striking this balance is inherently difficult. It is further complicated by cover story manipulations both by repressive developing world leaders cloaking their repression in nationalist and anti-colonialist garb, and major powers dressing up interventions largely geared to self-interested objectives in contrived R2P justifications.

Historical Justice

Here too there is some rhetoric in claims of historical injustice at the hands of the West (Europe as colonizer, the U.S. as superpower, the post-World War II "liberal" order). But only some. There also are sincere and solid arguments. Some we may agree with; others we may not agree with but still can see their basis. And, frankly, whether we do or not, the fact remains that many non-Western leaders ground their positions on certain issues on their assessments of historical injustice.

The principle of "common but differentiated responsibility" (CDR) is one of the more interesting efforts to apply this normative debate to particular policy questions. The "common" element gets at shared responsibilities for problems that are global and transnational in scope (e.g., global public goods) and thus require international cooperation. The "differentiated" responsibility takes into account variations in causal impact (who did what and how much to create the problem) and relative capabilities for resolving it. This has been mostly applied to global environmental issues. Success has varied. In the 1989 Montreal Protocol on Ozone Protection and its follow-on agreements, CDR was both important as a principle around which consensus was built and pretty effectively operationalized for policy action. On climate change, while the principle has been affirmed, operationalizing into terms of who does what and who pays for what has been much more problematic.

---

[18]Kofi Annan, "Intervention," Ditchley Foundation Lecture 35, 1998; Gareth Evans, *The Responsibility to Protect: Ending Mass Atrocity Crimes Once and for All* (Washington, D.C.: Brookings Institution Press, 2008); Alex J. Bellamy, *Responsibility to Protect: The Global Effort to End Mass Atrocities* (Cambridge: Polity Press, 2009); Stanley Foundation, *Atrocity Prevention and U.S. National Security: Implementing the Responsibility to Protect*, January 2011, http://www.stanleyfoundation.org/resources.cfm?id=441

Notwithstanding such problems, CDR does capture this normative debate over historical justice in ways that could be applied to other global policy areas (e.g., development, technology transfer, viral ownership). It needs to be refined and adapted. Rhetorical flourishes will not go away, but should not get in the way of policy frameworks and formulas.

Sovereignty Rights and Responsibilities

"What happens in Vegas stays in Vegas," was the tag line of a recent America television commercial. But what happens inside states doesn't stay inside states. Not contagious disease outbreaks, nor carbon emissions, nor terrorist safe havens, nor many other aspects of failed and failing states, nor financial sector policies, nor, as previously discussed, genocide and mass atrocities. The "Vegas dilemma" is how to balance the rights that sovereignty confers on states and the responsibilities that come with it both inward (to their own people) and outward (to the international community).

The liberal order leaves a mixed legacy on this issue. The end of colonialism vastly increased the number of sovereign states. In this historical context the affirmation of the rights of states was largely consistent with the rights of the people within those states to self-determination. But there also was the "organized hypocrisy" by which norms were affirmed in principle but violated in practice by the U.S. as well as the Soviet Union.[19] It thus is harder for those with interventionist pasts to be credible about the mutuality that can be achieved. But while the emphasis of "newly Westphalian" states, whether de jure in terms of newly independent or de facto in terms of having finally achieved global power and stature, on their sovereign rights more than responsibilities is understandable, it further complicates the need for a greater degree of post-Westphalian-ness given the transnational reach of so many threats.

Democracy Promotion and Human Rights Protection

Rhetoric aside, this is a complicated issue for the United States in three respects. First is prioritization in relation to other policy objec-

---

[19]Stephen D. Krasner, *Sovereignty: Organized Hypocrisy* (Princeton: Princeton University Press, 1999).

tives. This long has been evident in policy towards the Arab world in the tension between two old adages, "he may be an SOB but he's our SOB" and "those who make peaceful change impossible make violent revolution inevitable." Traditionally the tilt was largely towards the former. While amidst the "Arab Spring" the overall shift has been in the other direction, there still are tensions across the different cases (e.g., military intervention in Libya but not in Syria, pressure for regime change in Egypt but not in Bahrain) as well as uncertainty about what trade-offs will be made as new regimes take shape. Similar if lower magnitude prioritizations are in play in relations with China, Afghanistan, Pakistan and others.

Second is that in terms of impact, support for democracy and human rights can cut both ways. Too little support can leave democracy movements, dissidents, et al, more vulnerable to repression by regimes calculating that the U.S. and the outside world doesn't much care. Yet that also can put the U.S. so much on the side of the repressive regime that protest movements and successor governments which might not have been anti-U.S. become so. On the other hand U.S. support can be counterproductive if a regime assesses that it can't free a dissident the U.S. champions for fear of losing face, or ties to the U.S. undermine a democracy movement's nationalist credibility, or through other such perverse consequence chains. These tensions also are a part of the China policy mix, as well as with regard to Iran.

Third is consistency. While it may be true that even with its limits the U.S. still has a stronger claim to being pro-democracy and human rights than many other countries, judgments on this issue are less in comparison to others than relative to one's own self-styling and rhetoric. This can create a "relative hypocrisy" gap in which contentions that we do more than others are less salient than that we do less than we claim. A key therefore is to narrow the rhetoric-policy gap, still of course allowing for some speechifying but with more of a pragmatic sense of not preaching more than one is prepared to practice.

The West and Islam

It was striking that the Egyptian revolution was anti-regime but not anti-American. This was despite the close relationship the United States had maintained with Hosni Mubarak for decades; despite Arab public opinion having fallen back from its original enthusiasm for the Obama administration because of the administration's failure to make progress on key issues on the immediate agenda, particularly the Israel-Palestine peace process;[20] and despite the administration's wavering during the 18 days of Tahrir Square. The main reason, in my view, was the very persona of Barack Hussein Obama and the sense that he had empathy and respect for the people of the Arab world. His June 2009 Cairo speech was intended to convey this sense even more than particular policy positions. It persisted despite policy differences and disappointments. As such it demonstrated how normative dimensions can have realpolitik benefits.

There is no guarantee, though, that this sense of affinity will persist. One of the key issues is whether we avoid making the same mistake with political Islam that we did in the Third World in the Cold War when we lumped together most all leaders, parties and movements that in any way smacked of radicalism as part of the Soviet orbit. Some were, like Kim Il Sung in North Korea and Najibullah in Afghanistan. But in so many other cases they had their own local-national identities and agendas which even when having anti-American elements carried possibilities for cooperation or at least coexistence. Political Islam is here to stay. It will be part of the political mix more often than not. It takes varying forms, some extremist-jihadist-violent and others more peaceful and compatible with democracy. Whether the U.S. is able and willing to live with at least some forms of political Islam that while not virulently anti-U.S. also are not pro-U.S. will carry resonant normative messages in the Arab world, also in the broader Islamic world, and more broadly globally.[21]

---

[20]Shibley Telhami, "2010 Arab Public Opinion Poll," http://www.politico.com/static/PPM170_100804_arabpublic.html

[21]Bruce W. Jentleson, "Beware the Duck Test," *The Washington Quarterly* 34 (Summer 2011); Emile Nakhleh, *US-EU Partnership and the Muslim World: How Transatlantic Cooperation Will Enhance Engagement*, Chicago Council on Global Affairs, Transatlantic Paper Series No.2, October 2010, http://www.thechicagocouncil.org/userfiles/file/task%20force%20reports/Trans-Atlantic_Papers_2-Nakhleh.pdf

Conclusion: America and the Leadership Trope

Overarching all these issues is how the United States sees its 21st century global role and how others see it. It remains generally true that most countries believe that we are most likely to resolve or at least effectively manage global problems if the United States plays a constructive role. But that does not mean the U.S. as The Leader. This not only runs counter to others' interests and sense of their capabilities, it also hits at the subjective level of dignity, respect and pride – and as such is normatively objectionable.

Yet in our domestic political discourse America as The Leader is still the bipartisan trope of choice. Instead it needs to be acknowledged that as a group of us wrote during the 2008 campaign, "despite the prevalent presumption that America must always be in charge, effective leadership is not always centered in Washington."[22] It's difficult to conceptualize crisply this "more than this"—"less than that" U.S. role. There's no clear historical precedent in prior international systems, nor an evidently applicable analogy from leadership in business or other sectors, not even an insightful metaphor. But the reality is that whether because of historical relationships, priorities of interests, factor endowments, issue area specializations or other factors, different states have different comparative advantages for taking the lead on different issues. Seeing this reality requires a national self-concept that affirms the crucial role the U.S. does need to play while acknowledging that Washington is not the font of all wisdom or the exemplar of all norms.

---

[22]Phoenix Initiative, *Strategic Leadership: Framework for a 21st Century National Security Strategy*, July 2008, http://www.cnas.org/phoenixinitiative?gclid=CNOB5OK0j6YC FRJY2godhyyNYQ.

Chapter 4

What Norms for a New-Order Transatlantic Relationship?

Giovanni Grevi & Richard Youngs

The waning of Western hegemony challenges Europe and America in different ways and highlights the asymmetry of the transatlantic relationship. It does not necessarily or entirely undermine the liberal international order that they have shaped over decades. The capacity of the EU and of the U.S. to build and sustain viable formats of international cooperation in times of turbulent change will be the litmus test of their leadership, and of their partnership.

Perceptions have been shifting faster than power, compounding narratives of American and above all European decline. Common to the transatlantic partners is that their presumed uniqueness dilutes as power grows more diffused and the market of ideas more competitive. Regardless of their own self-perceptions, ten years down the line the U.S. will likely be regarded as less 'exceptional' and the EU as less of a 'model' for emulation. Different countries and regions will devise their own paths, drawing from different experiences and domestic circumstances.

While the end of deference towards established powers centers and normative engines, such as the U.S. and the EU, need not completely undermine their influence, it will certainly require them to exercise such influence differently. Influence will rest on their socio-economic performance and normative consistency, at home and abroad, more than on claims to past entitlements. It will also depend on their ability to work together to engage others.

The normative identities of the EU and of the U.S. could still be a major asset in fostering their leadership in a less permissive global environment. Retrenching into a fenced community of values defined in opposition to emerging powers would squander such comparative advantage. Such introspection would imperil the liberal order more

119

than it would successfully safeguard the transatlantic community's own core values. This is the key canon that must define the normative orientation of the EU-U.S. relationship in the much-heralded post-Western world order.

The weakening of normative consensus at the international level, from financial matters and development models to democracy promotion and humanitarian intervention, need not determine conflict or trigger the ascendancy of a fundamentally alternative worldview. Instead, it requires the start of a serious debate on the future global order. That will demand often difficult adjustments by all involved, but will unlikely engender the wholesale or definitive demise of liberal internationalism. The latter provides the normative fabric of an international system that most benefit from, or aspire to. It is to this standard that the transatlantic partners must together set their compass.

Europe in a Post-Hegemonic World

In an international system marked by the de-concentration of power and deepening interdependence, establishing the normative and institutional coordinates for cooperation among more, and more heterogeneous, actors is of essence. Milieu-shaping under post-hegemonic conditions, namely when the U.S. is less predominant and its primacy is contested, sets a daunting challenge. For the EU, it is also an existential one. This is not only a matter of interest, since the prosperity of the Union as a major trade power and energy consumer lacking military clout depends on international stability. It is also a matter of identity.

The EU is a community of law built on the rejection of war and bent on the creation of a rule-based international system. While self-perceptions and the surrounding discourse should not be taken at face value, all polities need a narrative and this remains the core European 'story' and principal *raison d'être*. The then-Community has been ritually defined as a civilian power, domesticating international relations through non-coercive means, namely negotiation and compromise.[1]

---

[1] François Dûchene, "The European Community and the Uncertainties of Interdependence," in Max Kohnstamm and Wolfgang Hager, eds., *A Nation Writ Large? Foreign Policy Problems before the European Community* (Basingstoke: Macmillan, 1973).

From its very conception, European integration has been described by Jean Monnet, one of its principal architects, as a step towards a more organized world order.

Crucially, the EU is not a state. As a project, it is endowed with a value-based vision grounded in peace, democracy and sovereignty-sharing, which has proved attractive in Europe and beyond. As a process, it is at the cutting-edge of governance experimentation and innovation, having established over time a mixed system including supranational, inter-governmental and trans-governmental features, unevenly mixed depending on the policy area. As a collective international actor, however, the EU lacks some critical attributes of sovereignty, notably the capacity to speak with one authoritative voice, to mobilize its resources at its discretion, to entertain difficult trade-offs and to guarantee its own security. The latter domain remains largely the preserve of its member states, themselves turning to the U.S. as the protector of last resort. In short, the EU lacks both nimbleness and fist. But it carries economic weight, has shown political endurance and offers solutions that, when achieved, are lasting ones since they are the product of compromise and enshrined in law.[2]

The current transition away from the relatively comfortable post-Cold War world raises the question of the very pertinence of the EU in a post-hegemonic context of growing normative diversity and competition.[3] This question engulfs different dimensions of the EU as a normative actor.

First, it concerns the scope for the EU to invest in multilateral cooperation, thereby fulfilling its vocation to tame sheer power in international relations. It is a matter of both demand, i.e. whether other pivotal actors feel the need to foster rule-based cooperation; and supply, i.e. whether the EU is capable to trigger and sustain governance innovation. Doing so would not least demand surrendering some of the benefits enjoyed by its member states in the traditional

---

[2] Ronald Asmus and Tod Lindberg, with a reaction by Robert Cooper, *Rue de la Loi: The Global Ambition of the European Project*, The Stanley Foundation, Working Paper, September 2008.

[3] Mario Telò, "Introduction: The EU as a model, a global actor and an unprecedented power," in Mario Telò, ed., *The European Union and Global Governance* (London: Routledge, 2009).

multilateral system. It is also a matter of what interpretation of sovereignty will prevail, whether an uncompromising and conservative notion of it as independence from the influence of others, or a progressive one as authority and capacity to engage with others.

Second, the pertinence question addresses the very normative cornerstones of the Union, namely the values of peace, democracy, market economy and rule of law that it embodies and seeks, in principle if not always in practice, to promote. The issue here is whether these values will maintain a universal appeal or will be challenged by truly alternative normative systems, based for example on nationalism, corporatism and state capitalism, which will prove both sustainable and attractive. Deep down, the question is whether modernization necessarily entails approximation to the normative coordinates of political and economic liberalism.[4]

Third, the pertinence of the EU will very much depend on its ability to defend and promote its normative preferences in complex, tough negotiations on issues critical to its prosperity and cohesion. From social to environmental standards, from financial regulation to the application of the precautionary principle to product and food safety, the EU has consistently used institutions as platforms for compromise and norms as channels of influence on the global stage.[5] In so doing, it has acquired a distinctive profile as the driving force for multilateral agenda-setting on issues such as climate change and international justice and it has leveraged its critical economic mass to export its normative preferences, sometimes at odds with American ones. The growing normative assertiveness of rising powers, commensurate with their expanding economic and political clout, and their skills as strategic actors in multilateral negotiations, will test the role of the EU as leading normative entrepreneur. In turn, this challenges the internal legitimacy of the Union as a filter, or shelter, against the hardships of globalization.

---

[4] For different perspectives on this question, see G. John Ikenberry, "The Future of the Liberal World Order," *Foreign Affairs*, May/June 2011, pp. 56-68 and Ian Bremmer, *The End of the Free Market: Who Wins the War Between States and Corporations?* (New York: Portfolio, 2010).

[5] Zaki Laïdi, *La norme sans la force. L'énigme de la puissance européenne* (Paris: Sciences Po, 2005).

In sum, the question is whether the EU's distinctiveness will be an asset or a burden in a polycentric and normatively contested world. In other words, whether the EU is a power 'lost in transition'[6] or whether it is, somewhat counter-intuitively, ahead of the curve, uncomfortably waiting for others to speed up and join it in a post-modern world. As noted by Francis Fukuyama, the end of history is the EU, not the U.S.[7] The problem is that history is in full swing, and is being largely made outside Europe.

Between Multipolarity and Interpolarity

The answer to the crucial 'pertinence' question very much depends on the direction of the transition itself. A range of observers expects the emergence of a multipolar world of balance of power and fierce normative competition, if not clash. In such a context, the end of hegemony would result in a vacuum of leadership and in the disconnect between major power centers bearing different and irreconcilable priorities concerning common challenges.[8] Whether in tackling financial instability, climate change or resource scarcity, international imbalances and transnational risks would go unaddressed and generate ever more frictions. That would further undermine multilateral cooperation and lead to what has been defined a 'zero-sum' world.[9]

This entirely plausible scenario would arguably stretch the Union to a breaking point or anyway result in an even more introverted and defensive Europe, abdicating its role as norm entrepreneur, transformative agent and integration lab. Arguably, a Union deprived of normative aspirations would not be sustainable in the long term, as centrifugal national interests would prevail over the waning commitment to the common good and a better world.

---

[6] Fabrice Pothier, Constanze Stelzenmüller and Tomas Valasek, *Stopping the Drift. Recalibrating the Transatlantic Relationship for a Multipolar Age*, Centre for European Studies, 2011, p. 37.

[7] Quoted in Gideon Rachman, *Zero-Sum World: Politics, Power and Prosperity After the Crash* (London: Atlantic Books, 2010), pp. 207-208.

[8] Ian Bremmer and Nouriel Roubini, "A G-Zero World," *Foreign Affairs*, March/April 2011, pp. 2-7.

[9] Rachman, op. cit.

A zero-sum environment could entail alternative implications for the normative fabric of the transatlantic partnerships. As a key feature of the partnership's profile and projection, the normative edge of Europe and America could take a back seat, overshadowed on either side of the Atlantic by a progressive securitization of the political agenda beyond traditional threats to engulf economic and societal issues. The U.S. would probably still find in many European countries some of its best allies for specific purposes. However, the transatlantic partnership as a community of values would lose traction, not least in the eyes of others. Alternatively, the EU and the U.S. could be drawn closer together as fellows in a turbulent world, promoting their shared values in opposition to those of others and assuming a more or less antagonistic stance in terms of spreading such values. An ideological partnership in a post-hegemonic world would risk building more barriers than creating bridges and could turn differences of interests with other actors into normative alienation.

That said, while plausible, the scenario of a multipolar, zero-sum world is neither the only conceivable one nor, arguably the most probable, as it neglects three basic factors. First is the deepening of global interdependence, encompassing the economy, the environment, resources and security issues in a web of connected, transnational risks. This changes the context of power relations since interdependence entails both shared challenges and mutual vulnerabilities. The second factor is the diffusion of power from states to non-state actors and even individuals, empowered by new technologies. This is perhaps a more consequential trend than power transitions among states over the long term.[10] It does challenge public authorities at the national and international level but it also harbors the potential for eroding normative contrapositions from the bottom up. Transnational advocacy networks and epistemic communities catalyze shared diagnoses and common aspirations, while business can bring solutions where governments fail.[11] The third factor is the potentially game-changing impact of the so-called Arab Spring. The latter could hardly be anticipated and democratic transitions in key Arab countries face many hurdles. However, if sustainable, the shift from authoritarian to demo-

---

[10]Joseph S. Nye, *The Future of Power* (New York: Public Affairs, 2011), pp. 113-122.

[11]Parag Khanna, *How to Run the World* (New York: Random House, 2010).

cratic regimes in North Africa could have a transformative impact in the region and beyond, paving the way for normative convergence in a traditionally volatile theatre.

On balance, the case can be made that deepening interdependence has entered the strategic calculus of all major powers, increasing their stakes in the stability of an open international system and tilting the balance away from confrontation. The conjunction of power shifts and interdependence leads to an interpolar world where leading countries cannot ultimately ensure their prosperity and security by detracting from those of others.[12] Great powers have more to fear from each other's weakness than from each other's strength. Differences between them follow cleavages that vary depending on the issues at hand, thereby making the emergence of opposing blocs unlikely, notably on normative grounds.[13]

In an interpolar world, sufficient political will could be harnessed to devise new formats of cooperation and reform old ones. Under this scenario, the liberal international system would remain the bedrock of global order, although its norms and practices would have to adjust as rising powers bring their agenda to the table.[14] Progress would likely be achieved by trial and error more than by any clear design.

In this context the EU would be, in principle, well equipped to contribute to multilateral agenda-setting and rule-making. The practice of consultation, negotiations and compromise inherent in EU policy-making would be an asset to foster convergence at the international

---

[12]Giovanni Grevi, *The Interpolar World: A New Scenario*, Institute for Security Studies of the European Union, Occasional Paper No. 79, June 2009. See also, among others, Leslie Gelb, "GDP Now Matters More Than Force," *Foreign Affairs*, November/December 2010, pp. 35-43.

[13]For an account of the changing alignments in the context of the G20 negotiations, see Stefan A. Schirm, *The G20, Emerging Powers and Transatlantic Relations*, Transatlantic Academy Paper Series, May 2011.

[14]For the perspectives of emerging powers on challenges including security, the economy and climate change, see Luis Peral, ed., *Global security in a multipolar world*, Institute for Security Studies of the European Union, Chaillot Paper No.118, October 2009; Graeme P. Herd, *Great Powers and Strategic Stability in the 21ˢᵗ Century* (London: Routledge, 2010) and Uri Dadush and William Shaw, *Juggernaut: How Emerging Markets Are Reshaping Globalisation* (Carnegie Endowment for International Peace, 2011).

level and advance new deals. However, the EU would need to become more effective in crafting its positions and in using soft and hard power tools to pursue its normative goals, in ways consistent with the universal values it purports to uphold.[15] America and Europe would remain each other's indispensable partners (but not the only important ones) to shape a new global order, although their initiatives would need to gather the support of a much wider range of actors.

The EU and Global Governance: Full Spectrum Engagement

The EU stakes a lot of its normative identity, and strategic interests, on the sustainability of effective multilateralism. The next decade will challenge the means by which it pursues this central goal. Like a glorious firm producing analog material on the verge of the digital revolution, the EU will have to update its products and business model to shape and fit new modes of international cooperation. Otherwise it risks being pushed to the margins of key governance formats and becoming a venerable brand for vintage collectors, lagging behind the frontier of global governance innovation.

The rise of new powers taking a selective approach to international cooperation and protecting their sovereignty, the proliferation of non-state actors acquiring ever more autonomy as both agents and spoilers of cooperation, and the accumulation of old and new challenges on the international agenda set a tall order for the reform of global governance.[16] The conflation of these trends demands inclusive leadership and operational flexibility from the transatlantic partners. Arguably, the growing governance deficit impacts them in different ways and entails both challenges and opportunities for their partnership.

For America, multilateral engagement is a choice from a wider strategic toolbox. For Europe, it is not just a matter of convenience or, indeed, enlightened self-interest, as it is for the U.S., but one of essence, as it corresponds to the very *raison d'être* of the European project. The U.S., while materially diminished relative to others and

---

[15]Richard Youngs, *Europe's Decline and Fall: The Struggle Against Global Irrelevance* (London: Profile Books, 2010).

[16]National Intelligence Council of the US and Institute for Security Studies of the European Union, *Global Governance 2025: At a Critical Juncture*, 2010.

normatively challenged, is a superpower able to switch through different modes of interaction, from occasional bargains and coalition-building to balance of power and coercion. With the exception of issues where it enjoys exclusive competence, such as aspects of trade policy, the EU struggles to do so, as it is unequipped institutionally and most of its members are reluctant to engage in power politics and trade-offs.

Such differences account for the paradoxical misalignment of American and European approaches to collective action, at a time when the Obama administration announced a new grand strategy centred on enhancing cooperation in a multi-partner world.[17] The U.S. has pushed fast-forward a whatever-works agenda (stitch-up in Copenhagen) while taking unilateral action (quantitative easing) and resorting to traditional power balancing (South China Sea) when other tactics didn't work and U.S. interests were at stake.[18] The EU and its member states have nominally pursued global deals while struggling to define common interests (for example in the G20) and testing alternative channels (bilateral trade agreements) while fighting a rear-guard battle concerning their position in multilateral frameworks (reform of IMF quotas and executive board).

While the U.S. has probably gained more credit as a governance innovator in the last couple of years, for example thanks to the Nuclear Security Summit initiative, neither the pragmatic and selective approach of this American administration nor the principled but stiff and inconsistent approach of the EU have proven particularly effective so far. The relative dissonance between European and American perceptions and tactics is one of the reasons for that. However, the reputation of the EU and of the U.S. as responsible stakeholders is not a given, but relies on the judgment of an ever-growing global public. The deepening debt crisis on both sides of the Atlantic vividly underlines this point. Over the next decade, such a reputation will largely

---

[17]The White House, *National Security Strategy*, May 2010.

[18]For insights on the approach of the Obama administration to multilateral cooperation, see Bruce Jones, "The coming clash? Europe and US multilateralism under Obama," in Alvaro de Vasconcelos, Marcin Zaborowski, *The Obama Moment*, Institute for Security Studies of the European Union, 2009, and Richard Gowan, *The Obama Administration and multilateralism. Europe relegated*, FRIDE, Policy brief No. 39, February 2010.

depend on their ability to do more to underpin and expand cooperative frameworks in addressing three common challenges. First, delinking balanced economic growth from the unbound consumption of energy and other natural resources. Second, delivering global public goods such as preserving the security and openness of the commons for all sorts of (legal) human, material and immaterial flows.[19] Third, supporting and enhancing human development and human security, notably in fragile countries and regions.

For the EU, this will require adopting a policy of full-spectrum engagement, seeking to connect with partners through different channels, as need be. Bilateral partnerships, mini-lateral or pluri-lateral groupings, inter-regional relations and global multilateral institutions should not be seen as alternative vehicles for cooperation but as concurrent platforms for global governance. The EU should devise a strategic approach to pursue its end goals through different formats in a consistent and mutually reinforcing way. This is not about giving up on Europe's multilateral aspirations but pursuing them through a flexible and incremental approach, better fit for a polycentric and diverse world.

The ultimate purpose of the EU's engagement should be to frame fair deals in multilateral treaties and regimes, as the latter enshrine predictable commitments in an uncertain world. But it should do so by seizing, and seeking, opportunities to enhance cooperation beyond traditional institution-building and by working in close partnership with non-state actors to make inroads into new governance territory. On climate change issues, supporting the implementation of the environmental objectives of China's new five year plan, and harnessing public-private partnerships to this end, does not detract from the pursuit of a global post-Kyoto emissions regime. When assisting fragile states and taking preventive action to avert conflict, different levels of governance can and should come into play, and the contribution of non-state actors to mediation or community-building can be harnessed.[20] The codification of best practices to manage natural resources, bilateral partner-

[19]Thomas Wright and Richard Weitz, *The Transatlantic Alliance in a Multipolar World*, The Chicago Council on Global Affairs, Transatlantic Paper Series, November 2010.

[20]The World Bank, *Conflict, Security and Development*, World Development Report 2011.

ships with pivotal regional powers, the joint Africa–EU Strategy and cooperation with the UN are complementary in fostering development and security in Africa. In short, the EU should improve its performance as a venture capitalist to invest in governance innovation with a view to laying the foundations for viable multilateral frameworks.

Political Norms

Another challenge facing the EU and U.S. relates to the type of political norms that will prevail in the emerging international order. The precarious balance between interpolarity and multipolarity, as well as the shifting sands of global governance, leaves some fundamental questions unresolved on this score. One pivotal concern will be the role that democratic norms assume in the reshaped global system. Much has been written on the fate of democracy in a post-Western world order. Some see democracy as increasingly challenged. Others see it has actually gaining appeal as a global norm, as interconnections of all kinds deepen and rising powers hitch themselves fully to the international system. This will be one of the core existential questions that will determine the contours of next-generation international relations: will democracy consolidate itself as the only political norm with truly universal appeal, or will a properly normative perspective be one that allows for greater heterogeneity of political systems in the future? The rise of energy-rich autocracies since the mid-2000s along with China's relatively strong performance in the post-2008 financial crisis have bred democratic pessimism. The Arab Spring has slightly tilted the pendulum back towards a more universalist view of democracy.

Curiously, the EU and U.S. both stress the centrality of democracy to their international policies, but also have a less then fully appreciative view on each others' approach to supporting democratic norms. Rhetorically both the US and EU have long declared support for the international spread of democratic norms to be not merely a standard set of policies like any other dimension of foreign policy, but as constitutive of their whole global 'beingness'. Many comparisons have been made over the years between U.S. and European democracy promotion policies. The complexities, time-sensitivity and country-specificities of these policies have militated against these comparisons reaching clear-cut, parsimonious conclusions. At some moments it has seemed that the EU has been the more committed supporter of democracy, anchoring eastern European transitions while the U.S. tended to the pernicious temptation of unilateral power politics. At other junctures, it seemed that the U.S. was more 'forward-leaning' on democracy, with the EU an insipid *Realpolitik* cynic given to fatuously overblown normative rhetoric.

Curiously then, the ostensibly shared adherence to international democracy has invariably not engendered the transatlantic harmony and unity that one might have expected. Both the U.S. and EU exhibit a tendency to claim that their degree of commitment to democracy makes them unique—by implication, relative to the partner on the other side of the Atlantic. America's 'manifest destiny' competes with the EU proclamation that *its* democracy promotion is an immutable off-shoot of the democracy-embedding multilateralism of its own integration project.

Often the issue of democracy has divided more than it has united the transatlantic partners. The European perspective frequently has the U.S. as fool-hardy missionary zealot, riding rough-shod over domestic sensitivities in the name of a Washingtonian-template democracy constructed solely at the behest of American interests. Such views have a long pedigree but, of course, reached their apogee under the Bush administration. The degree of European animosity to U.S. democracy policies plumbed such depths after 2000 that many European governments began rejecting the whole discourse of democracy promotion and on many issues sided with autocratic regimes against the United States. Such perspectives persisted even when they were objectively a misrepresentation of U.S. policy, which owed far more to traditional realism during the second Bush administration.[21]

Both European and American policymakers have tended to perceive the transatlantic breach on democracy to be wider than it actually is at the level of on-the-ground democracy initiatives and projects. The most comprehensive recent project comparing European and U.S.

---

[21] Tamara Coffman Wittes and Richard Youngs, "Europe, the United States, and Middle Eastern Democracy: Repairing the Breach," Brookings Institute Analysis Paper 18, January 2009.

approaches to democracy concluded that neither European governments nor the US can be accused of having done much to export their
own institutional templates.[22] This is not to suggest that significant
differences do not exist; in general it is true that the U.S.'s 'political'
approach to democracy contrasts with the European 'developmental'
perspective.[23] However, whatever the differences in terms of democ-
racy-promoting strategy, the bigger issue is that the EU and U.S. are
now united in a decline that raises thorny questions over how they can
continue to defend a politically liberal world order. This should be
motive for a new era of deep cooperation on the role of political
norms in foreign policy.

In fact, in recent years some such convergence has been evident—
but, ironically, around a diminished conviction in democracy support.
Naturally, neither European nor American politicians would doubt the
basic legitimacy of democracy as a norm. But the problematic record
of democracy support during the early 2000s produced a striking
degree of caution on both sides of the Atlantic. The transatlantic community came to question its ability positively to influence pro-democracy dynamics more than it evinced any enthusiasm to act as standard
bearer of liberal political change.

The reality of the new international context is that today both the
EU and US share the challenge of keeping some focus on democracy
but in sensitive ways that are attuned to local conditions in different
regions of the world. Neither side of the Atlantic has progressed far in
recalibrating democracy support strategies for a different global order.
The transatlantic community will not be the arbiter of other countries' domestic politics to the same extent as in the fifty years following the end of the World War Two. This need not breed a relativism
of political norms, but it will entail multilateralization of the democracy support agenda. Rising democracies such as India, Turkey, Brazil,
Indonesia and South Africa certainly resist many elements of Western
democracy promotion, but they have also introduced initiatives that

---

[22]T. Risse, 'Conclusions: Towards Transatlantic Democracy Promotion?', in M. A.
McFaul, A. Magen and T. Risse (eds.), *Promoting Democracy and the Rule of Law* (Basingstoke, Palgrave Macmillan, 2009), p. 263.

[23]Tom Carothers, 'Democracy Assistance: Political versus Developmental?', *Journal of
Democracy* 20/1, 2009.

offer positive support to incremental political liberalization in their respective regions.[24] Emerging non-Western donors are also looking seriously at the governance-development nexus, which they prefer to the 'democracy promotion' angle as a route into politically relevant aid programs. There is potential here in respect of which the U.S. and EU need to work together, gently to encourage non-Western democracies to step up their efforts, while according them greater say over the nature of the 'democracy agenda.'

Of course, now the Arab Spring represents an opportunity for democracy support to shift to the front-foot and assume a less defensive air. Both the EU and U.S. have reacted with some admirable new policy commitments in support of Middle Eastern democracy. Both actors have recognized that their rhetoric was not matched by the substance of their reform commitments in the years preceding the Tunisian and Egyptian revolts. Both have recognized that their caution on democracy lagged behind the demands for change, open government and leadership renewal among all sectors of society. Both are beginning to plough money, technical expertise and diplomatic influence into backing Arab reformers. But some cautionary words are still appropriate: it remains to be seen whether the EU and U.S. will be willing fully to welcome the results of free elections across the region; and there are clearly regimes, especially in the Gulf, where a status-quo mentality persists among Western diplomats. Moreover, little in the way of concrete transatlantic coordination on the Arab Spring has yet taken root. If this is a moment of opportunity, the EU and U.S. still need to demonstrate that it is one from which they extract the same conclusions in relation to democracy's broader normative status in the new global order.

Conclusions

The transatlantic relationship needs to move with the times. It cannot remain immune from or disinterested in the broader shifts in global power constellations. Both the EU and U.S. are grappling with

---

[24]T. Carothers and R. Youngs, 'Looking for help: will emerging democracies becomes supporters of international democracy?' Carnegie Endowment for International Peace working paper, July 2011.

the enormously difficult task of refashioning concepts of the 'normative' in a rapidly reshuffling world order. We have shown here that in respect of the two issues of global governance and democracy support, this task remains very much a work in progress. For the transatlantic relationship, the uncertainty of the current juncture is both boon and bane. In recent years, the narrative of a grand normative project has been largely absent from the EU-U.S. relationship. As the partners fight their own respective economic and political crises, and scramble to protect their immediate material interests in the face of relative decline, the notion of a normatively-oriented transatlantic agenda can easily look like an expendable luxury.

Going back to normative basics, however, is the key to unlocking the stalemate at both the domestic and international levels. For one, there is a need to debate the normative compact underpinning increasingly contested social and economic deals at home, to renew the domestic bedrock of international leadership. For another, in a world of relative power, the normative posture of the EU and the U.S. constitutes their comparative advantage at a time when the normative identity of many of their partners is in flux. Precisely when normative perspectives are being debated anew and in some cases redefined, it is of the utmost importance that the U.S. and EU do not embark along different paths. It is equally critical that, with normative differences growing more visible, albeit not necessarily deeper, the EU and the U.S. explore innovative paths for engagement with others and prevent tensions at home from engendering mutual alienation abroad.

Shared normative reassessment is sorely needed across the Atlantic. How far such an endeavor does eventually take shape and succeed will be incomparably important: it will determine whether this is the moment at which the moorings of the transatlantic relationship come definitively adrift or when a normative renaissance becomes possible.

Section III

Demographic Trends

Chapter 5

Europe's Demographic Future:
At the Edge of the Post-Growth Society

Reiner Klingholz

Three major trends are shaping Europe's demographic future: low fertility, aging societies and increasing immigration. Europe's population, already the oldest in the world, is aging faster than those of other continents and will soon start to shrink. Hence Europe—where the so-called population explosion got under way in the 18th century—is again taking on a pioneering role in demographic development. The old continent is setting a demographic trend for stagnant or shrinking populations that sooner or later will reach most corners of the world.

Today, 14 out of 44 European countries already report an excess of deaths over births, a number that will grow over time. The total population of Europe, including Russia, Belarus, Ukraine and Moldova, is 740 million, and is expected to shrink by some 20 to 50 million by 2050. The situation for the EU, Europe's economic heart, which is more attractive for immigrants, is more stable: the population of the 27 EU countries is some 500 million and is still growing. Only one-fifth of population growth in Europe is due to an excess of births over deaths; a much larger part is due to immigration.

The number of EU citizens is expected to peak at 526 million around 2040, followed by a slow decline until 2050. Without immigration the EU would lose 45 million, or 9% of its population by 2050, or roughly the current population of Poland and Greece combined. European stagnation stands in contrast to expectations of 36% growth for the U.S. and Canada, 25% for Latin America and Caribbean, 25% for Asia and 100% for Africa in the same time period. Consequently, the EU's share of the world's population would shrink from 7.3% to 5.5% over the next 40 years.

Nevertheless, some 6% of the world's population is located within a 1,000-kilometer radius of the Czech capital of Prague, a region which can be called Europe's cultural heartland. The only world regions with a higher settlement density are large-scale conurbations in China and India, each of which is home of some 15% of mankind. In effect, Europe is the world's third most important population center. Since the postwar project of European integration, the continent is becoming a powerful and innovative economic unity. Today the EU with its 27 member states, stretching from Portugal to Romania, is a Union that guarantees free movement of goods, persons, services and capital.

Today there are various factors changing the demographic composition of the European continent.

Low Fertility

Europe is the only continent with a fertility rate below the replacement level of 2.1 children per woman. Europe's women give birth to 1.6 children on average. The gap between Europe's "fertility belt"— which stretches from Finland, Norway, Sweden, Ireland and Great Britain to France and where the average is 1.9-2.1 children per woman (comparable to the U.S. level)—and most other European countries (where it is 1.3-1.6) can be attributed mainly to different family and gender policies. EU countries with small gender gaps, with a high proportion of women in the labor force, and relatively equal numbers of men and women working, typically show higher fertility rates.

Aging

In 1958, when the European Union was founded, every one of today's 27 EU members had fertility rates above 2.1 children per woman. The rapid change to today's low levels is the main reason of concern because the large group of the postwar baby boomers is replaced by a next generation that is barely two-thirds as large. The crucial question is how this shrinking post-baby-boomer generation can generate the wealth needed to care for its aging parents and at the same time invest so much into education and innovative industries that it can compete with young and fertile populations on other continents.

Figure 1. Number of individual cohorts, in thousands, by age classes, for the years 2005 and 2050

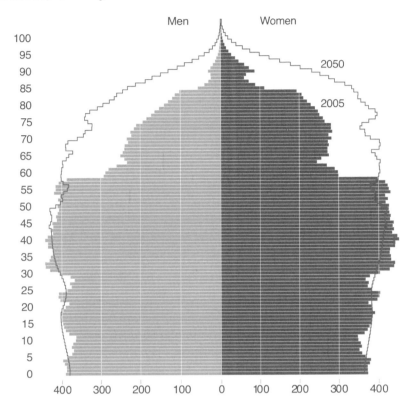

Source: Insee.

In coming years, huge waves of retirement are expected in all industrialized countries around the globe. The working population will then have to support a growing number of pensioners. This will put social security systems under considerable stress. This applies even for countries with replacement fertility like France, Ireland or the U.S. In France, the lower part of the population "pyramid" has evolved into a column, because every child's generation is about as big as their parent generation. France's population is likely to rise by roughly 9 million by 2050, if fertility remains at today's level. But this growth will only lead to an increased number of over-60-year-olds. There will be no growth in the younger cohorts (see Figure 1).

More than 50% of Europeans have already reached the second half of their lives. The average age in Europe is rising by some two days a week. Between today and 2050 the median age of EU citizens will rise from 40 to 49 years, transforming Europe literally into an old continent (see Figure 2). By then, 29% of the people will be 65 and older. Today's EU working age population (336 million) between 15 and 64 years of age will start to shrink even before 2015 and fall to some 299 million in 2050. At today's labor force participation rates, the number of people in the actual workforce will drop from today's 238 million to 212 million in 2050—even to 177 million under the unrealistic assumption of no immigration. Today's pension age cohort of 65 and older will grow from 87 million in 2010 to 150 million in 2050. As a result, the "old age dependency ratio" (number of persons 65+ per 100 working age persons) will double from 26 to 50. In hyper-aging countries like Italy or Germany, one in seven people will be over 80 in 2050. Only in Japan will the population be even older. Given the fact that dementia prevalence is around 20% at 80 and 30% at 90, it is clear that these societies will face challenges unknown in today's countries.

Life expectancy in highly developed western Europe has reached historical levels, whereas some central and eastern European countries have experienced a decline in life expectancy during the transformation period following the fall of the Iron Curtain. Male newborns can expect the longest average lifetime in Iceland, Sweden and Switzerland (80 years) and the lowest in Russia (63). The highest projected life span for females is 85 years in France and 85 in Spain, Italy, and Switzerland. The lowest projected life span for females is 71 in Kosovo and 73 in Moldavia. Compared to the most developed European countries, the U.S. shows a life expectancy of 5 years less, 75 years for males and 80 years for females.

Within Europe divergent demographic trends are observed (see Figure 3). Central and eastern European countries, including East Germany, experienced an enormous decline in birth rates after the fall of the Iron Curtain. Fertility rates in these countries are generally recovering, but they have not reached the level of pre-transformation times and are far below replacement level. As most of these countries have experiences outward migration since 1990, population decline is expected in most regions of the former Eastern bloc over the near future. Romania and Bulgaria are about to shrink by 10% and 15%

Figure 2. Median age

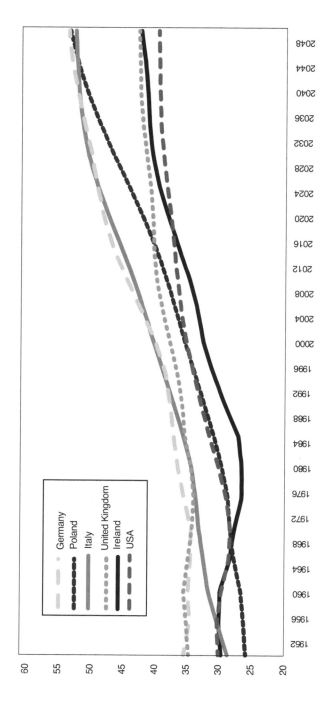

Data sources: 1950-2005: UN Estimate, 2010-2050: UN World Population Prospects, 2008 Revision, Constant Fertility Scenario (for details on assumptions, see http://esa.un.org/unpp/index.asp?panel=4)

Figure 3. Population projection 2004 to 2030, in percent

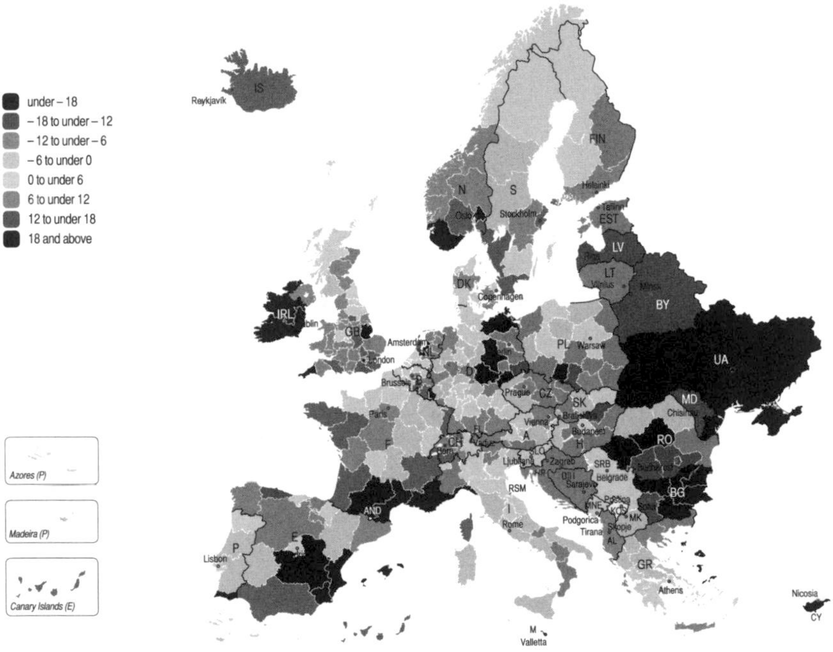

Legend:
- under – 18
- – 18 to under – 12
- – 12 to under – 6
- – 6 to under 0
- 0 to under 6
- 6 to under 12
- 12 to under 18
- 18 and above

Source: Eurostat, United Nations, national statistics offices; data for Belarus, Ukraine, Croatia, and Serbia available only at national level.

respectively by 2030. By the middle of the century, the number of Russia's inhabitants could sink by some 16 million. The working age population will suffer especially heavy losses, shrinking by 15 million, or about 20%, by 2030. Belarus may lose 1 million, or 12 %, by 2030 despite immigration. Ukraine will lose 5 out of today's 45 million in that period. High mortality, mainly related to alcohol abuse especially among men, contributes to these losses in the former Soviet sphere.

In the middle of this crisis Russia has to master an enormous transformation: turning an economy based mainly on exploitation of natural resources—which President Dmitry Medvedev once called "primitive"—into a service and knowledge-based economy supported by a broad, relatively well-educated and healthy middle class. Even security policy questions are increasingly being asked from a demographic perspective. In coming years there won't even be enough recruits to serve in an army of today's size or to protect the 20,000 kilometer- long Russian border.

Migration

Today, Europe's prosperity makes it increasingly attractive for people from other regions of the world. Nearly all EU countries, as well as the 3 associated nations Iceland, Norway and Switzerland, have growing immigrant populations. Some 30 million EU-27+3 residents (6% of the total population) are international migrants. First- and second-generation migrants who have already assumed citizenship in their new home countries are estimated to account for roughly the same share. Together, these people with migration background make up 12% of the entire EU-27+3 population. In countries with a long immigration history during the postwar economic boom, or those with colonial bonds, like Germany, UK and France, around 20% of the population have a migration background.

Even with increasing immigration, however, a number of European countries will not be able to stabilize their populations in the future. Germany, for example, has had a surplus of deaths over newborns every single year since 1972. Immigration was a vital factor for population growth since that time. The natural decrease was compensated by immigration until 2002, but since then migrant inflows have failed to compensate for the decline in population. So far, Germany's population has declined by about one million. A further decline of some 12 million is expected by 2050, despite projections of further immigration of either 100,000 or 200,000 persons per year respectively– the largest decline in the EU (see Figure 4). In East Germany massive outward migration of young people led to a population loss of more than 1.5 million since reunification in 1990. Some remote rural regions in the former GDR are on their way to total desertion. Germany's workforce (between 18 to 64 years) will shrink by 30% in that time period, in East Germany even by 50%. By 2050, the UK and French populations will be larger than Germany's. As the UK and French populations will remain younger than Germany's in 2050 it seems plausible that their economies then could also be more power-

Figure 4. Population projections for Germany.

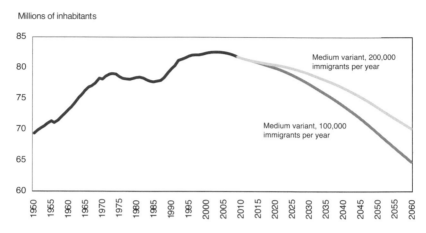

Data source: destatis.

ful than Germany's. The country's influence within the EU will decline proportionally.

Qualified migrants are becoming increasingly important to guarantee the economic prosperity of European nations. The closest sources for Europe's further immigration are the 14 neighboring countries in the Middle East and North Africa, where the number of working age people will double until 2050. Unfortunately, in most European countries there is a rising public and political fear of foreign infiltration. Germany, for example, has made immigration more difficult and as a consequence it has nearly stopped in recent years. One reason for public reluctance against further immigration are the problems all European nations have integrating their migrants adequately into society. Many immigrants have poor qualifications and their children often tend to follow the same trend. This makes it difficult for European governments to justify further immigration of qualified migrants to fill the widening gaps in the labor market.

Policy Options

These population developments, however, do not necessarily mean that Europe is on the road to ruin. Instead, they indicate that European societies face multiple challenges that differ widely from country to country and even more from region to region. Especially remote rural areas in central and eastern Europe will see an accelerated depopulation over coming decades.

As demographic variations follow long term trends, the decline of Europe's native work force and the aging process are inevitable. Therefore, the European populations and governments have no option but to learn to cope with the coming changes. They have to increase their productivity and to fund their social security systems with a smaller number of working age individuals. They have to focus not on human quantities but on human capacities, which are defined by the education and health standards of their populations. The key to mitigate the aging process is education. The continent's most important resources—its minds and talents—will be valued even more highly in the future. Most European countries must develop into knowledge-based societies in which jobs for unskilled workers will become even scarcer in the future. Education and lifelong learning are the preconditions for higher retirement ages, which are needed to make pension systems demographically sound. Education is especially crucial for partly or potentially marginalized groups such as migrants. Unemployment among migrants is at least twice as high as among native-born citizens in most European countries. Income levels of migrants and their share in respected jobs are far below average. At the same time, the EU needs a concerted and appealing migration policy to attract highly skilled workers and their families.

The examples of France or Sweden show that low fertility can be countered by a family policy featuring a mix of financial incentives such as lower income taxes for families and an infrastructure that allows both parents to stay in the workforce after limited parental leave. Reducing the debt burden is another way to prepare for the future as the coming generations will have trouble to pay back what the recent governments have accumulated. Overall, the need to reform might turn into a motor of European innovation.

If these urgent reforms are not approached seriously, however, Europe's competitiveness could fall behind younger and growing countries in other world regions. With regard to demographic challenges, the U.S. is in much better shape, but most of the reforms nec-

**Figure 5. Percentage share of world population for which the EU
and subgroups of EU countries account, 1950 to 2020.**

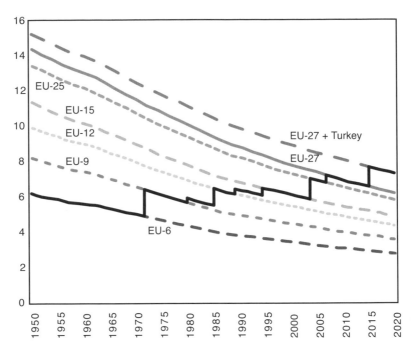

Source: ESPON.

essary for Europe have to be tackled in the U.S. too—especially debt
reduction and social security reform. In these areas the challenges for
the U.S. seem to be higher than in most European countries, whereas
the readiness for reforms appears to be lower.

There is another approach for Europe to remain a vital partner in
the world economy: a strong and growing European Union. Since the
Union was founded in 1950 by its first six member states, their share
of the world population has declined. Their share of world economic
output has been declining since the 1960s. Today the figures are 3 and
11 %, respectively. Only by constantly accepting new member states
has the EU been able to raise its share of world population to roughly
7% and its share of aggregate world economic output to 20%.

European integration was also an attempt by European countries to maintain their international status in a situation marked by rapid demographic and economic development in other world regions. If the EU will be able to accept new countries in the future, it could maintain its global influence, at least as far as the figures are concerned. Turkish accession would boost the EU's share of the world's population to 8%. And while the accession of Norway, Switzerland and Iceland would not change much in demographic terms, it would serve to further increase the EU's share of the world economy. The inclusion of the former Yugoslavian Balkan countries might only be a matter of time, and with the accession of Ukraine, the demographic giant in Eastern Europe, the EU could keep its long-term share of the world population between 6 and 8 % until 2050 (see Figure 5).

How to Survive in the Post-Growth Society

Given that the world population is still growing by 230,000 heads per day and the ecological footprint of the human race is far beyond the limits of sustainability, less European consumers sound like a blessing for the environment (less U.S. citizens would sound even better). Global environmental problems and resource crises will increase as the world's population increases to 9-10 billion by mid-century. The question for Europe is how it can overcome its demographic challenges and the ecological crisis at the same time. The solution might be found in demographic sustainability, a term barely discussed in future studies.

Certainly excessive population growth rates (such as in many African countries) are not sustainable, since they cause a wide array of problems from shortage of schools and jobs to overexploitation of natural resources. But very low fertility rates are unsustainable as well, as they lead to quickly-aging societies, to a disparity between working and pension age groups and to unstable social structures.

Demographic sustainability for Europe would call for a stable or slowly shrinking population, because a constant number of inhabitants can use the existing infrastructure most efficiently. Regarding the actual average fertility rate of some 1.4 children per women in many European countries, there is an urgent need for a better family policy in those countries below this line. But countries with fertility rates above 1.8, like France, UK, Ireland or Sweden do not need a further pro-natal policy. Immigration will fill possible demographic gaps.

Migrants can slow down shortages on the labor market but they cannot prevent societies from aging. Europe's biggest challenge is to survive the peak of its aging process, which will come around 2045. After that point the baby boom generation will leave the population pyramid, and Europe will open a new page in its demographic chronology.

Until then it is important to realize that countries like Germany have already reached the demographic post-growth era, which will most probably lead to an era of no overall and no significant long-term economic growth in the future. These nations are the frontrunners not only in demographic change but also on their way to a sustainable future. They have to invent the models for the well-being of their societies without growth, models that will be highly demanded by more and more countries.

Nearly all countries around the globe have falling fertility rates. One third of all countries already have fertility rates below replacement level. No major highly-developed country has a fertility rate above 2.1 that would guarantee a long-term growing population without immigration. Fertility rates in emerging countries are falling faster than in early industrialized countries. While in Germany the fertility rate fell from 2.5 during the time of the baby boom to 1.4 today, in South Korea it fell from 5 to 1.2 and in China from nearly 6 to 1.5 with only a few years' delay. That means that these countries will face a much more pronounced aging of their societies only a decade after European countries. As most countries have embarked on a path towards development that has meant better education for men and women and therefore falling birth rates, the time of worldwide population growth will come to an end sometime during the second part of this century. Even China, the most populous country of the world, will start to shrink by the end of this decade. The emerging countries' current advantage—their young and productive populations and high economic growth rates—will become relative when their societies enter the massive aging process. China, today a synonym for exploding prosperity, might be the first country in the world to grow old before it has become rich.

All these countries urgently need models for demographic and ecologic sustainability, for prosperity without growth. As the pioneer of demographic shrinking, Europe has no other choice but to build the blueprint for post-growth lifestyle models before others do it. Europe's future will be based more on stability than on growth. The nature of these models remains unknown, because all European governments still follow the paradigm of growth, even though some of them have already entered the demographic post-growth phase. But more and more countries will have to learn to live in prosperity with an aging, stagnant or even shrinking population. These populations will be older, smaller, wiser and more peaceful than today's. Therefore they might be the model societies for a sustainable living on a limited planet.

Chapter 6

Demographic Factors Affecting the Transatlantic Partners

Carl Haub

This chapter examines the ways in which demographic factors are likely to affect future relations between the U.S. and its European partners. In fact, there has already been some effect as European countries begin to grapple with problems brought about by low birth rates and the economic crisis, and the challenges that unprecedented aging is beginning to present to its European (and non-European) allies. The word "crisis" is not used here loosely. That term and others like it are routinely used in Europe to describe the current demographic situation and its portents for the future. The U.S., itself far from immune from future budget challenges due to aging, is likely to find itself with less and less assistance when global issues arise. This chapter suggests that it is time for transatlantic allies to address these issues and, should few solutions be found, to address their consequences. It also suggests that national leaders be more fully informed on the issues, which is almost certainly not the case today.

The European Perspective

The most serious problem facing many European countries today is societal aging, which is proceeding at a pace that could not possibly have been anticipated and, in fact, was not. The severity of the aging process varies but is more evident in several NATO countries of western Europe and in most countries of eastern and southern Europe. The issue in low birth rate countries is often described in terms of the decrease in population size but, except for some countries of the former Soviet Union, decline in projected population *size* by 2050 is quite modest or will not occur until after mid-century. While past decline in birth rates to low or very low levels is the driving issue, many countries now find themselves in an unprecedented condition due to the unusual alteration of their age structures that resulted.

Figures 1 and 2 give the trend in birth rates from 1960 to the present in terms of the total fertility rate (TFR).[1] The TFR is the most useful measure of the birth rate as it captures the rate of childbearing of a given year in terms of the number of children women are currently averaging. When it remains relatively constant for a period of time it gives a very good idea of completed family size and a rather strong suggestion of what may be expected in the future. As can be seen, TFRs have declined to two children or less and, often, to far less than two.

The population "pyramid" of Germany below illustrates the alteration in age structure due to low fertility quite well. Germany is shown as an example, given its importance as a major Western ally, but the situation is roughly the same in most industrialized countries of Europe and in Asia.

The pyramid graphs population by five-year age group and sex, with the youngest group, ages 0-4 (births in the most recent five years), at the bottom moving up to the oldest age group, ages 80+. At the current birth rate, women in Germany would average about 1.36 children each during their lifetimes, far less than the approximately 2.1 needed to "replace" both themselves and their partners. A TFR less than 2.1 will ultimately result in population decrease. The TFR in Germany has been below 2.1 since 1970. Germany is but one of many European countries whose age structures have essentially "pre-programmed" dramatic societal aging that will be difficult and almost impossible to reverse. Pension and health care systems are facing increasing strain while proposals to raise retirement ages are bitterly opposed. As can be seen in the pyramid, the age group of German females 0-4 comprises but two percent of the population whereas that of older groups in the childbearing ages, generally considered to be 15-49, comprise as much as four percent or more. As the age groups below 20 move upward into the childbearing ages, the number of births will decline further even if the TFR increases. In Germany, as in

---

[1] The total fertility rate is the average number of children a woman would bear in her lifetime if the pace of childbearing of a given year were to remain constant.

Figure 1. Total Fertility Rates, Selected Industrialized Countries 1960–2009

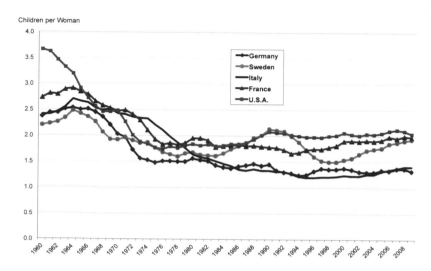

Source: National statistical offices.

Figure 2. Total Fertility Rates, Selected Industrialized Countries 1960–2009

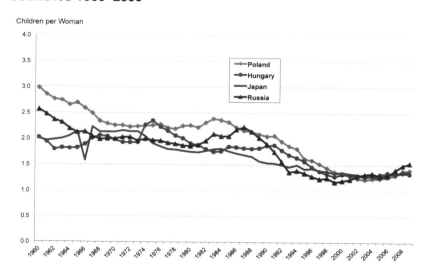

Source: National statistical offices.

Figure 3. Population of Germany by Age and Sex, Dec. 31st, 2008

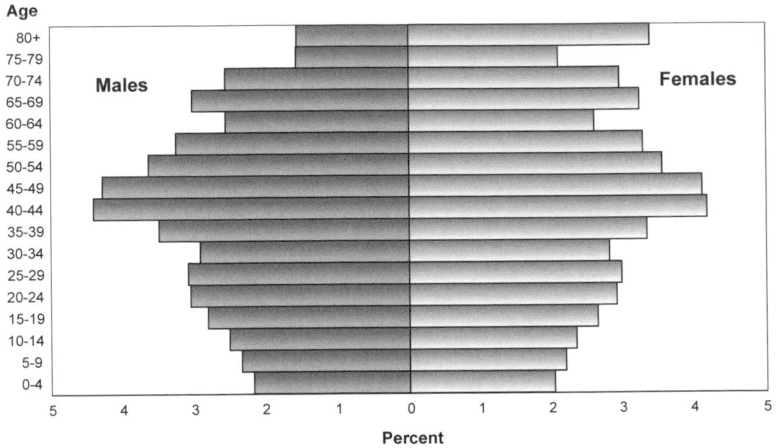

Source: Statistisches Bundesamt, *Statistisches Jahrbuch, 2010.*

much of Europe, childbearing begins late, with the highest birth rates found among those over 30.

At present, the German TFR is not rising despite government efforts to increase financial support to parents and in the face of such direct obstacles as the general unavailability of day-long child care centers, badly needed by two-earner couples. To this can be added a low level of confidence in the economy in general. This will mean a period of twenty years at minimum in which the age structure will frustrate even somewhat successful attempts to increase the number of births. Based upon recent trends and the evidence available, prospects for increases in European birth rates are, at present, very poor.

Countries which find themselves in a situation similar to Germany are all continental countries of the European Union (excepting France) and all of the remaining countries of eastern and southern Europe. Countries of northern Europe, particularly the Scandinavian countries, are in less dire straits, in part due to more liberal accommodations for two-earner families.[2] But, despite some countries having

---

[2] It should be noted that the larger economies of East Asia are in a similar or worse position. In Japan and South Korea, the TFR is 1.4 and 1.2, respectively and not rising, while in Taiwan, the TFR is an incredibly low 0.9 and falling.

Figure 4. Female Population Ages 0-4 As a Percentage of the Largest Female Age Group in the Childbearing Ages, 2008/2010

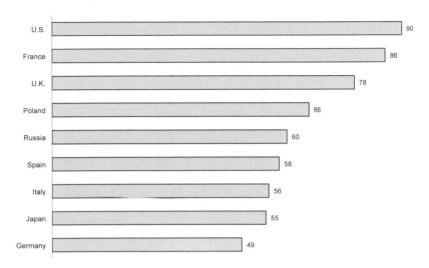

Source: National statistical offices.

better demographic prospects, all industrialized countries face a level of societal aging that will place tremendous pressures on social security systems and health care. Differences are only a matter of degree.

Figure 4 shows the youngest age group, 0-4, as a percentage of the largest age group in the childbearing ages. Different age groups are used for the older ages since the timing of fertility decline has been somewhat different among countries. Clearly, the availability of new parents entering the childbearing ages in the future will often be insufficient to avoid unprecedented aging in many countries. Japan is included as it is an OECD member state. Many of the low fertility countries have moved to address the low birth rate but have waited until the age structure has become a significant obstacle. In some cases where there had been some TFR increase before the current recession, foreign born women have accounted for growing proportion. France (along with the U.S., to be discussed later) has long been supportive of young families with children and the results show.

---

[3] The Population Division produces a comprehensive series of population projections for all countries every other even-numbered year.

Figure 5. Projected Population, Ages 60 and Over, as a Percentage of Total Population, 2050, Two United Nations Variants

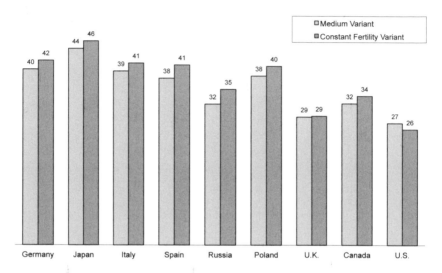

United Nations Population Division, *World Population Prospects, the 2008 Revision.*

The inevitability of aging is evident in Figure 5. The "Medium Variant" of the United Nations Population Division[3] makes the assumption that all low-fertility industrialized countries will see their TFR rise to 1.85 over the next few decades or longer. The projected TFR increase is quite gradual but it must also be emphasized that increase is not happening at present. The "Constant Fertility Variant," as its name implies, assumes in the TFR from the time the UN made its projection (2008). Both of these scenarios result in proportions of the population above age 60 that have never been seen in history even in the case of the U.S., whose current TFR of 2.0 is viewed as a nearly unobtainable goal in many other countries.

Another UN scenario, the "High Variant," is the most optimistic. In it, the TFR exceeds two children per woman by 2050 but the difference in aging is surprisingly little. In the case of Germany, even an increase to 2.1 as early as 2035-2040 results in a percentage 60+ of 35% by 2050, lower but still a major national concern.

The result of these demographic transformations is not difficult to imagine. A population pyramid top-heavy with the aging and retirees will place strains on national budgets that will have to addressed even as the tax-paying younger labor force shrinks. The high social taxes paid during the working lives of many Europeans provide free or low-cost university educations, guaranteed government pensions and government-supplied health care. This is, of course, now well known and the subject of frequent media articles. As the labor force shrinks so, of course, does the population of military age so that many NATO countries will play a decreasing role, placing pressure on the United States to increase its own when needed. The latter is likely to be quite politically unpopular.

Demographic developments are only one cause of the fiscal crises alluded to above. Unemployment was already running high even before current recession. The European Union is now grappling with bailing out the economies of its weaker members and the future of the euro itself is being discussed. It may be argued that the last thing the EU needs is a demographic crisis. In Germany itself, it has been referred with such dramatic expressions as "demographic suicide" and "worse than the 30 Years' War." The United States must fully understand the causes and consequences of "old" Europe perhaps better than it does.

Decreases in labor force sizes have also stirred an immigration debate in Europe that is different from that in the United States. Most other industrialized countries do not have the melting pot tradition of the U.S. and have a much stronger cultural identity which increases resistance to rising proportions of foreigners. In addition, recurrent terrorist attacks and terrorist threats have done little to place immigration in a favorable light, however much it may be needed. Some countries also face significant language assimilation difficulties, such as Germany and Japan, which do not have access to native language speakers from former colonies. In Germany a conservative candidate sought to gain advantage with the electoral slogan *"Kinder statt Inder"* (Children instead of Indians). But, to date, only a decrease in children seems to be likely.

Raising the birth rate takes money, quite a bit of it. In Spain, couples were offered 2,500 euros for each birth in 2007, but the government had to withdraw the offer in 2011 due to budget constraints. In Japan, any expenses for pro-natalist programs will require taking funds from other programs, and huge reconstruction costs resulting from the March 2011 tsunami have strained the budget even further. Russia is one of the few countries whose policies have had some effect. The government began giving the equivalent of $9,000, a huge sum, to couples for each second and subsequent birth in 2007. Vladimir Putin has made raising the birth rate a high national priority and the TFR did rise from 1.3 in 2006 to 1.5 in 2010.

The American Perspective

By any measure, the U.S. is in a very different situation than many European countries. Its population growth rate, a bit below one percent per year, is robust by European standards, its structure comparatively youthful, and its population of 310 million is projected to easily pass 400 million by 2050. It does not have a population "problem" in the same sense as Europe. Nonetheless, the demographic contrasts between many industrialized countries and the U.S. are dramatic but not as dramatic as many Europeans believe.

It should be re-emphasized that the demographic situation of a number of larger NATO allies, particularly France and the United Kingdom, is more similar to that of the U.S. than to their European neighbors. As has been seen in Figures 4 and 5, the U.S. does not face as serious an aging crisis as does Europe in general but, even at that, projections show that funding for Social Security, Medicare, and Medicaid will become a rapidly growing proportion of the U.S. budget.

The U.S. does have a relatively high TFR for an industrialized country, at 2.0 in 2009 (in France it is also 2.0, in the U.K. 1.9, and in northern Europe, 1.9) but it is not "high," as many Europeans believe. The TFR for the group often considered the "majority," i.e., white, non-Hispanic women, was 1.85 in 2009, below a number of European countries. One of the striking contrasts between the U.S. and Europe is the proportion of population growth due to "minorities." The U.S. Hispanic population was estimated by the U.S. Census Bureau to have accounted for 55% of U.S. population growth from July 2008 to July 2009, an estimate that is likely to remain unchanged since the U.S. census count in 2010 was almost exactly as expected. The proportion of births to white, non-Hispanic women was about 51% while that of

Hispanics accounted for 26%. Other groups, such as Blacks, Asians, American Indians, and Pacific Islanders accounted for the remaining 23% of births. The difference in population growth between white non-Hispanics and Hispanics is a result of both the youthfulness of the Hispanic population and its higher TFR of 3.0. The median age of the white-non-Hispanic population is 41.2 years compared to the Hispanic median age of 27.4. As a result of these two factors the ratio of births to deaths among Hispanics is 8.7 births annually to one death, while, among white-non-Hispanics the same ratio is a very low 1.1 birth per one death, the latter much more similar to a European country.

In Figures 6 and 7 the age pyramids of the two largest ethnic groups, which together account for about 80% of the U.S. population, illustrate the vast difference between the age structure of the two groups. It is quite obvious that the majority of the difference is the result of immigration, which has risen to quite high levels since the 1990s. Net immigration (immigrants minus emigrants) reached an estimated one million although there has been a slight reduction since 2008-2009, presumably due to the recession. Thus, it is immigration that keeps the U.S. "young." While there has been increasing opposition to immigration throughout much of Europe, anti-immigrant sentiment in the U.S., where it exists, appears to be primarily targeting undocumented immigrants. Today, in the author's opinion, there is unlikely to be any major constraints placed on legal immigration by Congress in the future. In Germany, recent statements by Chancellor Angela Merkel that immigrants must assimilate German culture is a result of both a desire to maintain traditional cultures as well as a reaction to threatened terrorism. The U.S. has always been a country built by immigrants, who despite early resistance to new groups, has resulted in a relatively homogenous society, a combination of many cultures.

Barring any completely unforeseen changes in future immigration trends, projections of the U.S. Census Bureau show that the current majority population, white-non-Hispanics, will cease to be a majority sometime between 2040 and 2050, and, in any event, there will be virtually no growth in that population in the absence of a "baby boom" type rise in its birth rate and a sudden surge in immigration from Europe and other majority-white population countries. Neither scenario is expected and, at present, would seem quite far-fetched. All

Figure 6. Population of U.S. White non-Hispanics by Age and Sex, 2009

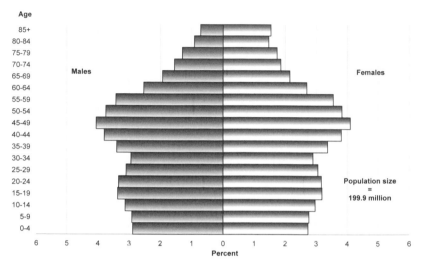

Source: U.S. Census Bureau.

Figure 7. Population of U.S. Hispanics by Age and Sex, 2009

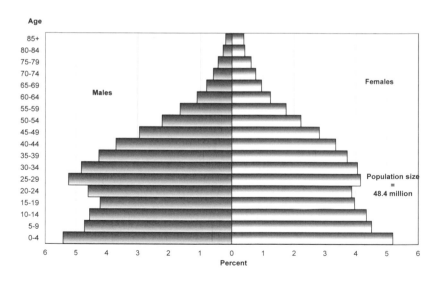

Source: U.S. Census Bureau.

Census Bureau scenarios project a virtual zero-growth white non-Hispanic population out to 2050, barely exceeding the current 200 million.

Summary

From a demographic perspective, industrialized Europe and the United States have entered a period in which their global influence will only continue to wane. The demographic factors are currently being exacerbated by the economic realities of recession, a condition from which the U.S. is likely to exit more easily than its European allies. Some points to highlight are as follows:

- Unprecedented aging in Europe (and in East Asian allies such as Japan, South Korea, and Taiwan) will place great strains on national budgets.

- The U.S. will have a similar experience but perhaps less severe.

- Budget constraints will make it more difficult for low-birth rate countries to fund programs to support younger families and childbearing.

- Both budgets and a reduction in age group pools for the military will likely reduce the ability of low-fertility countries to support global actions where needed.

- One potential impact will be a reduced willingness and ability to provide foreign aid to developing countries in dire need. Such programs are already being called into question in Europe. In order to make foreign aid politically palatable, governments are more and more refusing foreign aid due to corruption in the receiving countries and emphasizing the benefits to the providing country as a result of increasing markets in receiving countries.

- Expanding overseas markets, while helpful to Western countries' bottom lines, often do not bring in social taxes since manufacturing must be transferred overseas to keep products locally affordable.

- Thus, the traditional wealthy nations and former colonial powers are likely to become more isolated and bereft of power. This may not be a bad thing in and of itself, but will emerging developing countries be willing to take military action against rogue states or in cases of genocide as Western powers have done in the past?

- An unknown benefit to former industrialized powers may continue to come in the form of the purchase and resuscitation of corporations in Western countries by successful firms in former colonies. This is already happening to companies in the U.K. by large corporations in India.

- Finally, it is probably time for the transatlantic partners to address mutual demographic realities and seek solutions. Such discussions would certainly be politically sensitive but could lead to such programs as an efficient exchange of labor forces, sharing of knowledge on social issues such as providing a proper climate for the accommodation of families, and keeping national leaders fully aware of the demographic situation in each other's countries.

Section IV

Human Mobility

Chapter 7

Human Mobility in the United States and Europe to 2020

Demetrios G. Papademetriou and Madeleine Sumption

Trends In Immigration And Mobility

A decade into the twenty-first century, international migration is larger and more diverse than at any time in history. More countries than ever before are significant players in the migration game—as countries of origin, transit, or destination, or as a combination of the three. From the old hands to the migration novices, countries across the globe continue to struggle with the fundamental questions the phenomenon brings: how to meet rapidly evolving labor market and economic needs, successfully integrate newcomers and protect their rights and dignity, and ensure that migration serves the interest of their economies and societies. The impacts of migration reach far and wide, touching upon highly sensitive questions of economic prosperity, national identity, social cohesion, and in some cases, national security.

The global economic crisis has cast uncertainty over migration projections for the next ten years. Five years ago, analysts expected the strong growth in international migration to continue uninterrupted. The jobs crisis that the deep and prolonged recession engendered for many large immigrant-receiving countries, however, brought the rise of foreign-born populations in many major host countries to a virtual halt. Some of the migration flows that have previously boomed, such as inflows to Spain, Ireland, Greece, and the United States, dropped dramatically, with large reductions in illegal immigration flows, free movement in the European Union, and, in some countries, corporate transfers, labor migration at various skill levels, and business migration.

How long the impact of the global economic crisis will last, and how quickly immigration flows will "recover," remains unclear. On the one hand, the economic crisis has hardened public opinion toward migration and has strengthened opposition to greater openness across Europe and North America, including in France, Italy, the United Kingdom, and the United States (to mention only a few). If this opposition persists well beyond the economic recovery, the dampening effects of the crisis on migration could be prolonged.

On the other hand, many of the underlying drivers that fuelled migration during the economic boom will continue to be relevant, unless persistent economic troubles bring about a "worst-case scenario" of chronic unemployment and low growth for key immigration countries. The supply or migration "pipeline" is likely to remain robust. The already large pool of significant emigration actors is growing apace, even if only about twenty or so countries provide the vast majority of migrants. Moreover, major sending countries in South East Asia are likely to grow in importance as their citizens become more engaged in the global economy and as their education levels rise (increasing their ability to take advantage of employment opportunities across the world).

Second, "pull factors" such as economic growth, talent and geographical mismatches, persistently below-replacement fertility,[1] and the rising cost of labor will continue to drive immigration flows to traditional immigrant destinations, but also, increasingly, to emerging economies.[2] Alongside these drivers, the globalization of higher education and the continuing growth of global corporations (or firms that recruit globally) are also expected to create movement both to and from emerging economies.

---

[1] Several wealthy countries (particularly in southern and eastern Europe) face extremely low fertility rates, raising the possibility of a mutually beneficial movement of people that could "arbitrage" the demographic differences between regions with very different demographic profiles.

[2] Immigration to developing countries is expected to account for an increasing share of the growth in migrant populations worldwide, according to United Nations projections. United Nations Population Division, "Trends in International Migrant Stock: the 2008 Revision" (United Nations Database, POP/DB/MIG/Stock/Rev.2008).

Figure 1. Immigrants as a Percentage of Host-Country Population

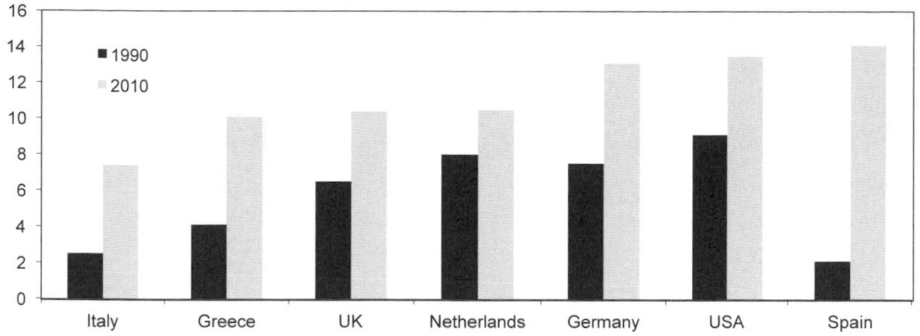

Source: United Nations.
Note: 2010 figures are predicted values made in 2008, before the economic crisis.

In other words, more, rather than less migration is likely in the medium term, unless the effects of the recent recession linger, or a sharp deterioration in public attitudes towards migration creates unexpectedly powerful barriers to movement. Even if, with hindsight, the almost unprecedented growth of immigration in some countries over the past two decades turns out to have been an anomaly, the movement of people is set to remain a central component of the global economic landscape.

It will also be a socially, culturally, and politically complex one. For the biggest immigration actors, migration has already fuelled rapid, profound, and highly visible social and cultural change, with the resulting transformation happening almost literally before people's eyes. This extraordinary pace of change has created deep unease, especially since many new immigrants come from nations with significant social, cultural, religious and racial "distance" from host countries. Further exacerbating these concerns, growing migration during the economic boom came not just in the form of "desirable" immigrants such as skilled workers and degree-level students, but also undesirable ones, namely the unauthorized. This created a popular feeling in some countries that governments had lost control over migration, prompting support for the overhaul of visa systems in some cases, and enormous increases in border and interior enforcement spending in others.

Changing Migration Patterns in the 21st Century

Despite uncertainty about the future flows of international migrants, especially in the next three to five years, some standard observations about the *nature* of migration flows will remain largely reliable. On the one hand, the "traditional" characterization of immigration as the long-term or permanent movement of people from less to more wealthy countries will remain a relevant lens for examining migration during the next decade. However, it will increasingly find rivals in other forms of movement, including more temporary stays by workers from developing countries (both low and middle income ones) and greater mobility among citizens of wealthy nations. These trends foreshadow the emergence of a still relatively small but growing phenomenon whereby *"mobility"* will compete with "migration" as the core concept around which human movements are understood and examined.

This phenomenon manifests itself in various ways. First, states are increasingly significant players as both senders and recipients of immigrants simultaneously. Some of the most developed countries, including the UK, Germany, the U.S. and Canada, already fall into this category and more are likely to join their ranks. These trends are closely linked to the emergence of a more global labor market for workers whose skills in areas such as business, engineering, or scientific research are in high demand worldwide.

On a similar note, corporate mobility is also growing. The movement of people within global corporations has been a feature of modern migration for some time, as firms have located in multiple countries to take advantage of talent, local or regional markets, or simply lower labor costs, taxes, and other incentives. But this share of migration is rising and (sometimes controversially) firms transferring their staff across the globe are now no longer overwhelmingly based in wealthy nations. "Intra-company transfers" make up 60% of employer-sponsored immigration to the United Kingdom, for example, and the use of corporate transfer visas has also increased substantially in the United States, becoming as popular as the more commonly known H-1B visa. (In both countries, India is the major sending country by some distance).[3] The nature of corporate mobility is also changing. Short-

---

[3] Indian nationals received 40% of intra-company transfer visas issued in 2009, and 68% in the United Kingdom. US Department of State, "Visa Statistics" (Washington

term assignments are increasingly supplementing and often replacing the traditional, longer-term expatriate assignment. In some sectors such as IT, these short visits are also strongly associated with the ever rising trade in services.

More generally, the conventional dichotomy between permanent and temporary flows will become less relevant in describing migration decisions. Not only are short-term periods of work abroad now common among the highly educated (especially the most elite professionals and graduates); many migrants also move with open-ended long-term intentions, deferring decisions about permanent residence until their plans have taken shape. On the other end of the skill spectrum, receiving-country policymakers remain interested in encouraging temporary and circular flows among less skilled workers (in part as a means to avoid some of the troubling obligations of immigrant integration when foreign workers stay permanently). These efforts, however, have not been particularly successful, with the exception of a few seasonal work programs involving small numbers of migrants with explicit and tightly regulated contracts.

Another overarching trend is the continuing globalization of higher education, a process through which human mobility and human capital investments have become increasingly interlinked. On the one hand, students are willing and able to travel long distances in order to receive an education that will guarantee the relevance of their skills in the global marketplace. Rising incomes in and beyond the BRIC economies mean that increasingly, students' families can afford the tuition fees and are willing to make investments in their education abroad, in part as insurance against changing personal fortunes or political circumstances. Meanwhile, educational institutions have taken steps to facilitate this movement. An illustration is the global expansion of universities (sometimes with campuses on several continents) and policies in countries such as China and Japan designed to attract foreign students with courses taught in English by an international faculty. On the other hand, employers—especially large firms that make heavy investments in recruiting—are spreading their search

DC: U.S. Department of State), http://travel.state.gov/visa/statistics/statistics_ 1476.html; Migration Advisory Committee, "Limits on Migration" (London: Home Office, November 2010), http://www.ukba.homeoffice.gov.uk/sitecontent/documents/aboutus/workingwithus/mac/mac-limits-t1-t2/report.pdf? view=Binary.

efforts across the globe to identify talented graduates and experienced professionals wherever they are located (including in emerging economies' previously little-known universities and colleges).

Finally, short-term travel for business and tourism have boomed with the falling cost of travel. Despite a decline during the economic crisis, global travel has bounced back to pre-crisis levels,[4] and strong growth is projected over the next ten years.[5] The volume of travel is a product of rising prosperity and brings enormous economic opportunities. However, it has also created anxieties most notably about terrorist threats and serious transnational crime, not to mention more traditional concerns about illegal immigration.

Shared Challenges in the United States and Europe

The size and changing shape of international migration is challenging nations to manage the deep transformations it entails much better. At the heart of this challenge is nothing less daunting than adjusting and even rethinking the accommodations each society has reached, often after decades and centuries of upheavals, on how societal goods and political power are allocated.

Facing skeptical publics, policymakers in both the EU and the U.S. will need to demonstrate that their migration systems are "under control;" that immigration serves the interests of their economies and societies; and that immigrant integration is robust and sustainable. Achieving these goals depends not only on domestic policies (including visa policies as well as education, training, and social policies), but also on cooperation with other nations to tackle problems which are fundamentally transnational in nature.

The Integration of Immigrants and their Descendants

One of the dominant themes in the debate about immigrant integration in the coming decade is likely to be the quest for greater social

---

[4] UN World Tourism Organization, "International Tourist Arrivals Back At Pre-Crisis Peak Level" (Madrid: UNWTO press release, November 9, 2010), http://www.unwto.org/media/news/en/press_det.php?id=6961&idioma=E

[5] UN World Tourism Organization, "Tourism 2020 Vision", http://www.unwto.org/facts/eng/vision.htm.

cohesion. Governments across Europe and North America are struggling to respond to the challenges of immigrant integration, and the results of their efforts are modest at best. In most countries, many immigrant groups and their offspring are well behind natives in educational achievement, economic opportunity, and social and political engagement. These cumulative disadvantages translate into varying degrees of economic, social, and political marginalization. Marginalization, in turn, breeds mutual wariness: many immigrant communities see themselves as aggrieved, while many natives view immigrants and their children with impatience, if not mistrust and suspicion. Moreover, the problem shows no signs of going away, not least because the global economic crisis has fuelled inequalities, hitting already-disadvantaged minorities hardest.[6]

Immigrant-receiving nations of Europe and North America have taken very different approaches to immigrant integration. These range from the nearly half-century German denial of the permanence of immigration and its embedment in the host society's "life,"[7] to the British emphasis on racial equality, the officially "welcoming" but in practice isolating and marginalizing Dutch model, or the United States' *laissez faire* approach that relies on immigrants' rapid incorporation into the labor market. Remarkably, however, alternative policy choices have often had similarly poor outcomes.

Integration challenges vary with a country's circumstances, migration history, and social and economic structures. For example, Germany's immigrants face chronically high unemployment, while the primary challenge to integration in the United States is the large number of unauthorized workers with limited prospects for upward advancement.[8] Each country has its own economically marginalized

---

[6] Demetrios Papademetriou, Madeleine Sumption and Aaron Terrazas, "Migration and Immigrants Two Years After The Financial Collapse: Where Do We Stand?"(Migration Policy Institute and BBC World Service, September 2010), http://www.migrationpolicy.org/pubs/MPI-BBCreport-2010.pdf.

[7] That denial only started to break down with the change in Germany's citizenship laws in the late 1990s, and a more accepting approach became official government policy in the middle of the last decade with the passage and implementation of legislation that focuses explicitly on immigrant integration. See Douglas B. Klusmeyer and Demetrios G. Papademetriou, *Immigration Policy in the Federal Republic of Germany* (Berghahn Books, 2009).

[8] Ibid.

groups (such as unauthorized Hispanic immigrants in the United States, Surinamese and Moroccan youths in the Netherlands, or Pakistanis and Bangladeshis in the United Kingdom, to name just a few). In almost all countries, insufficient social mobility among the children of immigrants from certain key sending countries also drives concerns about integration in the long term.

On both sides of the Atlantic, therefore, ensuring more successful integration that is shared across ethnic groups will be perhaps the single greatest challenge of the coming decade.

Making Immigration More Selective

In all but a few states the majority of overall migration is not "selected" on the basis of its potential economic contribution, but instead comes through channels such as family unification and humanitarian protection. (Australia, New Zealand, Canada, and, in recent years, perhaps the UK, are notable exceptions). Introducing immigration schemes that respond responsibly to economic need and build up a country's human capital infrastructure in economic sectors that fuel growth and prosperity is good policy. It can also be good politics. Where governments can show that immigration serves national economic interests (and where good selection and integration policies succeed in making existing immigrants more economically self-sufficient and socio-culturally incorporated into the communities of which they have become part), public confidence in immigration and its benefits is easier to foster.

A parallel challenge is to select more effectively from the large pool of workers who apply through economic channels. Again, forward-looking countries (and particularly Australia) have already made substantial investments in adapting their systems to admit the workers with the greatest potential to integrate, find employment, and contribute immediately to host societies. But the United States and most European countries still lag behind.

A somewhat wider range of countries have been considering how they can boost their share of the "most talented" immigrants—elite researchers, professionals, and businessmen that almost all observers recognize as valuable assets to the country because of their obvious contributions to capital and skill accumulation, innovation and scientific developments, and (if they return to or invest in their countries of origin) the diffusion of knowledge. This has led to speculation about a nascent "war for talent" between immigrant-receiving countries. While the evidence of direct, zero-sum competition between these countries remains rather limited, greater competition between nations in this field could well grow in the coming decade (even if it does not extend to include competition for the "merely" skilled, for whom supply still significantly exceeds demand).

Controlling Illegal Immigration and Resisting the Irresponsible Growth of Immigration

Being thoughtful about and actively managing migration *across the board* is essential for getting the most out of immigration and regaining control over often negative public perceptions. Yet the active management of legal flows, while critical, is not enough to turn the tables on how immigration is perceived in many countries. To do so also requires success in controlling illegal immigration and maintaining a sense of measure in how to grow a legal immigration flow.

Generally speaking, poorly regulated and illegal migration unsettles receiving communities and the broader public, while undermining immigrant integration and reducing the benefits to receiving communities and economies. Illegal migration may benefit unscrupulous employers, family networks and oblivious consumers; but it takes a social and political toll, in some cases wrapping all migration into a shroud of illegitimacy, such as in the United States. Illegal migration is also deeply entrenched because it enriches the criminal syndicates and smuggling networks that organize it and the "migration facilitating industry" (the network of labor recruiters, travel agents, job brokers, etc.) that makes tens of billions from migration. These networks, organizations and individuals find in human smuggling a highly profitable business whose costs—regardless how they are measured—are worth the risk *in large part because they are borne primarily by the immigrants themselves.*

While illegal immigration is the target of expansive "control and removal" initiatives across the Atlantic, much less thought has been given to the several instances where total immigration was permitted to grow at rates that were unsustainable. Building legislative and institutional frameworks to manage flows and assist with the integration of newcomers requires resources and an ability to evaluate what works and what does not and adapt accordingly. Very rapid immigration growth makes thoughtful policy in these areas difficult. At the same time, the growth in immigration during the economic boom occurred with little regard to the policy consequences of an economic downturn that would reduce the demand for migrant labor. Hence the term "irresponsible" growth of immigration, a term that certainly applies to Spain and Ireland, but also to a lesser degree the UK, the U.S., and Greece. In the years leading up to the recent economic crisis, most of these countries grew their immigration at rates without historical precedent.

In coming years, policymakers will be asked to demonstrate that they know how to grow legal flows "responsibly" while preventing the growth of illegal immigration by chipping away at the drivers that facilitate it (from transnational criminal networks to the employers of unauthorized labor at home). Success in controlling this phenomenon, in turn, creates political space for managing an orderly and flexibly regulated flow of legal immigrants whose contributions to the economy and society are higher in large part *because* the process is successfully regulated.

International Cooperation

Migrant-sending states also have a strong stake in immigration policies. First and foremost, migration provides an essential lifeline to families and economies, in the form of remittances. (According to the World Bank, remittances are expected to have reached $325 billion worldwide in 2010, even excluding substantial informal and other unrecorded transactions).[9] Sending countries also tend to be deeply concerned about two additional issues: the protection of the labor and human rights of their citizens abroad and the risk that both smuggling networks and unscrupulous employers could systematically exploit

---

[9] World Bank, "Migration and Remittances Factbook 2011" (Washington DC: World Bank, 2010), http://econ.worldbank.org/WBSITE/EXTERNAL/EXTDEC/EXTDECPROSPECTS/0,,contentMDK:21122856~pagePK:64165401~piPK:64165026~theSitePK:476883,00.html

them; and the risk that selective immigration policies in receiving countries will drain their most valued human capital (although this theme is not nearly as analytically straightforward as it might appear).

For immigrant-receiving countries, despite the substantial resources and attention devoted to managing migration at the national level, a gnawing concern has emerged among many policymakers that the unilateral approach alone cannot solve some of the persistent problems that many countries face. These problems tend to be fundamentally transnational in nature and thus only partially sensitive to receiving countries' immigration policies. They include: stubbornly high levels of illegal immigration in certain countries; the rise in transnational or criminal networks attempting to smuggle people across borders; the large numbers of individuals seeking humanitarian protection, often for reasons not recognized under current refugee and asylum law; and a host of economic inefficiencies arising from difficulties in evaluating migrant workers' foreign credentials and transferring earned entitlements, such as pensions and other social insurance benefits across national borders.

International cooperation on these issues is not always easy, especially where negotiating partners take only some of the many relevant actors' motivations into account, have conflicting interests and priorities, and have vastly differing capabilities to guarantee that the provisions of any ensuing agreement will be honored fully. However, the potential benefits of greater cooperation at both political and operational levels remain significant, making this an area ripe for further development during the next decade.

Adapting Policy to New Forms of Mobility

The changing nature of migration can put a strain on the existing policies and immigration infrastructure, especially in countries where policies evolve slowly and adaptation is difficult. This is especially a problem for immigration systems if, as we have argued, traditional approaches to both visa policies and immigrant integration strategies may be losing some of their relevance in a world where *mobility* is gaining gradually on (permanent) *immigration* as the dominant paradigm.

First, it is perhaps no surprise that some of the more flexible and strategic immigration nations are embracing temporary-to-permanent or "provisional" immigration pathways.[10] Specifically, instead of assuming that most migration is permanent, this approach allows workers to enter as temporary residents but to transition to permanent residence as their plans and their employers' plans evolve. Indeed, for globally mobile immigrants and their employers, *rapid decisions* on visa approval are likely to be much more important than the immediate access to permanent residence. Similarly, strict visa rules that prevent permanent residents from spending substantial periods of their career abroad without jeopardizing their residence and social protection rights may be burdensome for the most sought-after immigrants (particularly in countries where the process of acquiring permanent residence is cumbersome and time consuming).

A second, related question is how and where to invest in immigrant integration, given the changing nature of human mobility. Integration policies are typically based on investments in human capital (education), workforce skills and experience, and language abilities that pay off over time. Short-term migrants at all skill levels are almost certainly less willing to make these investments, unless they can reap the dividends in the long term (including after they have moved on from the initial destination and/or have returned to their countries of origin). This raises a host of questions about how countries can think more creatively about integration policies, exploring the full range of potential solutions, such as smaller investments that pay off "up front" (including work-focused language skills or skill and language acquisition programs that "cross-walk" between these two typically discrete systems); a stronger role for sending-receiving country cooperation in implementing and financing mutually beneficial training opportunities; and the recognition of qualifications and portability of social rights.

More generally, the changing shape of migration patterns underlines the need for nations to incorporate greater flexibility into their immigration systems. Systematic evaluation of policies on the basis of

---

[10]Demetrios G. Papademetriou, Doris Meissner, Marc R. Rosenblum and Madeleine Sumption, "Aligning Temporary Immigration Visas with US Labor Market Needs: The Case for a New System of Provisional Visas" (Washington DC: Migration Policy Institute, 2009), http://www.migrationpolicy.org/pubs/Provisional_visas.pdf.

clear evidence and extensive data will be essential to any effort to build a flexible and responsive immigration system (whether this analysis is conducted through an independent body such as the Migration Advisory Committee in the United Kingdom, or under a dedicated staff within immigration departments, as in Australia and New Zealand).

Migration, Mobility, and the Transatlantic Relationship

Despite some significant differences in their social models and the degree to which demographics will drive immigration policies, the European Union and United States face similar pressures: publics often skeptical about migration's benefits; strong underlying pressures for migration from neighboring developing countries; the need to manage porous borders effectively; concerns about some immigrant groups' integration; and the imperative to reap the economic benefits of immigration more fully in the face of relatively modest economic growth prospects. In addition, comparable levels of economic development mean that for the most part, it is possible for the two sides to negotiate as equals, without many of the asymmetries that hamper other efforts at cooperation on immigration. Indeed, some policy areas *crucially rely upon* cooperation between the EU and the U.S. in order to allow both to attain their policy objectives. This is clearest in the case of travel and border security, although certain measures to facilitate labor mobility also require international coordination, as we discuss shortly.

The transatlantic relationship is among the most significant relationships between wealthy nations in immigration policy (even if it is, of course, far surpassed by intra-EU or U.S.-Canada cooperation).[11] The sheer size of the North Atlantic economic space and the number of workers and travelers who circulate within it make dialogue on migration both necessary and inevitable.

Facilitating Travel while Maintaining Security

The most concrete area of EU-U.S. cooperation in the field of human mobility, and the one that has absorbed the greatest policy

---

[11]The Five Country Conference of English-speaking immigration nations (Australia, Canada, New Zealand, the United Kingdom, and the United States) is another significant example of international cooperation on immigration.

energy, is without doubt information sharing for the purpose of travel and border security. Over the past decade, states have been developing a new border architecture, the purpose of which is to manage the risks of terrorism, serious organized crime, and illegal immigration, while facilitating mobility for the huge numbers of international travelers who enter and leave the transatlantic space every day.[12] Various innovations characterize this new infrastructure: the collection, sharing, and processing of huge amounts of data about individual travelers; an emphasis on the secure verification of identity (notably through the use of biometrics); and a greater measure of international cooperation on border control and information sharing.[13] The purpose of these policies is to allow countries to anticipate risks by receiving data *before* travelers arrive at their border (and increasingly, before they can board an airplane to travel to any of the participating states); to allow more intensive but also more rapid and cost-effective screening of all travelers; and to reallocate labor-intensive screening resources from the vast majority of less "risky" individuals to the few potential threats.[14]

Cooperation on security measures has taken place both at the political level with the signing of formal international agreements, and at an operational level (for example, in the form of a Working Arrangement signed between Frontex and the U.S. Department of Homeland Security in 2009). A full discussion of the potential for EU-U.S. cooperation on border security and travel is outside the scope of this brief. But it is worth pointing to a few areas of particular importance. The first is a series of agreements between the European Union and the United States (and subsequently with other countries) designed to prevent the misuse of individual travelers' data and protect the rights of those whose data are collected and processed.[15] These agreements are under

---

[12]A much more detailed discussion of this border architecture and the challenges it has raised can be found in Demetrios Papademetriou and Elizabeth Collett, "A New Architecture for Border Management" (Washington DC: Migration Policy Institute, 2011), http://www.migrationpolicy.org/pubs/borderarchitecture.pdf.

[13]Ibid.

[14]To date, the United States has driven the development of new screening practices and technologies, but the European Union, Canada, and others are also increasingly turning to personal traveler information to assist their travel and border control efforts.

[15]Paul De Hert and Rocco Bellanova, "Transatlantic Cooperation on Travelers' Data Sharing: From Sorting Countries to Sorting Individuals" (Washington DC: Migra-

negotiation in early 2011, and will probably form the core of transatlantic cooperation efforts until they are successfully completed.

Second, border security officials often talk about the need to both promote security *and* facilitate mobility. In future, making more progress on the *facilitation* part of the puzzle would be a particularly fruitful priority for the transatlantic partnership. This could include efforts to make registered traveler schemes more accessible to EU and U.S. nationals (building on the existing but so far limited experience of cooperation between the United States and the Netherlands, for example). On a more technical note, it could also include measures to ensure interoperability between the still evolving border management technologies, processes, and systems, so that incompatibility does not stymie future efforts to exchange information so as to accomplish shared objectives.

Facilitating Labor Mobility between Transatlantic Countries

The flows of people across the Atlantic exhibit each one of the characteristics of the emerging global migration system discussed earlier, from foreign student flows and corporate mobility to temporary-to-permanent migration pathways and substantial short-term or circular movement. Transatlantic *labor* migration is predominantly "high-end"—the movement of businesspersons, scholars, researchers, and professionals (indeed, European-born workers in the United States are among the country's highest earners).[16] We briefly discuss two areas in which policies to facilitate these flows—in both directions—deserve much greater attention.

First, licensing and credentialing requirements in individual occupations create a substantial barrier to the movement of professionals. These requirements differ between countries (and sometimes even within countries, between sub-national jurisdictions). Even where concrete differences are minor, practicing in another jurisdiction may still be difficult, requiring complex and time-consuming certification

---

tion Policy Institute, 2011), http://www.migrationpolicy.org/pubs/dataprocessing-2011.pdf.

[16]Madeleine Sumption and Xiaochu Hu, "Immigration and Mobility from The European Union to the United States" (Washington DC: Migration Policy Institute, forthcoming).

and licensing procedures. The mobility chapters of free trade agreements often seek to create processes for mutual recognition of qualifications among professional and licensing bodies.[17] These provisions can be controversial where they have the effect of opening wealthy country labor markets to nationals of lower-wage nations. However, there is much greater scope for EU-U.S. cooperation on this issue, since it could represent an agreement *among equals* for a genuinely two-way movement of highly skilled workers within a gradually expanding circle of professional occupations. In the United States, and agreement of this kind would build upon the experience with "TN" visas created under the North American Free Trade Agreement.

Second, there is clearly a rationale for further action to increase the portability of benefits for workers who divide their careers between countries. Currently, a complex web of bilateral social security and totalization agreements enables labor mobility by avoiding double taxation for social security taxes and making the entitlements that workers earn portable between countries (they cover primarily pensions, but in some cases also health benefits).[18] However, the scope of these agreements is often limited and their provisions vary widely by country.[19] Even private benefits such as tax-deferred private pensions can be difficult to transfer between countries. The creation of a simpler, fully transparent, and more complete framework for transferring earned entitlements, both public and private, across the Atlantic would be a valuable investment of both time and political capital.

---

[17]One current example is the EU-Canada Comprehensive Economic and Trade Agreement (CETA), currently under negotiation. This agreement seeks to smooth access to a wide range of professions throughout Canadian provinces and EU Member States.

[18]The U.S. has bilateral social security and taxation agreements with Australia, Austria, Belgium, Canada, Chile, Czech Republic, Denmark, Finland, France, Germany, Greece, Ireland, Italy, Japan, Luxembourg, Netherlands, Norway, Poland, Portugal, Spain, South Korea, Sweden, Switzerland, and the United Kingdom, spanning a period of three decades. Internal Revenue Service, "Totalization Agreements" (Washington DC: IRS, 2010) http://www.irs.gov/businesses/small/international/article/0,,id=105254,00.html.

[19]Robert Holzmann, Johannes Koettl and Taras Chernetsky, *Portability regimes of pension and health care benefits for international migrants: An analysis of issues and good practices* (Geneva: Global Commission on International Migration, 2005).

Other Forms of Transatlantic Cooperation

Security concerns—in the form of information sharing and data protection—have dominated the EU-U.S. conversation in recent years. However, the EU-U.S. Migration Dialogue agreed to in 2010 aims to bring together policymakers from both sides of the Atlantic (at a range of levels) to discuss broader questions, exchange ideas, and identify areas of potential cooperation. These areas include skills recognition, managing legal migration, policies towards unaccompanied children, and asylum and refugee resettlement. For example, the Migration Dialogue provides a potential venue for training officials in areas requiring technical expertise (such as anti-fraud or asylum processing); for sharing operational-level information about the approach to returning failed asylum seekers to their countries of origin or disrupting human trafficking networks; and for consulting with each other in advance of multilateral meetings on migration issues with other countries (such as the Global Forum on Migration and Development).

If these efforts prove useful and thus continue to receive support, the next decade could see the beginnings of a broader and more productive transatlantic partnership on immigration matters across the board.

Conclusion

Migration links sending, transit, and receiving countries, as well as immigrants, host communities, and employers, in an intricate web of interdependence. Addressing the challenges of the next decade will require the cooperation of all of these actors. It will also require thoughtful policy decisions, consistent implementation, and above all, flexibility and the willingness to continually evaluate and adapt policies in response to changing circumstances. As the nature of migration flows evolves, countries must also be prepared to adapt their policies accordingly. Success in these delicate tasks promises political and economic gains through migration's dynamism and potential for contributing to the host country's growth and prosperity. And as countries grapple with the legacy of the deepest, most profound economic crisis for a generation, finding solutions to the challenges we have outlined becomes all the more difficult *and necessary*.

As we have argued, the scope for international collaboration on migration is substantial. Nations that press ahead with unilateral policies and fortress mentalities without engaging in the possibilities for partnership with other receiving and sending countries, will ultimately lose an opportunity to reap the economic and social dividends that the evolving international migration system has to offer. The United States and the European Union and its member states can learn a lot from each other in all aspects of international migration; and they have even more to teach other nations. Whether they choose to do so is the only remaining question.

Chapter 8

The Rise of Anti-Immigration Populism in Europe and the Future of European Capitalist Democratic Society: An Exploration

Theo Veenkamp

This chapter seeks to tease out deep currents that are relevant to human mobility and imagines the sort of responses that could address these currents.[1]

Migration policy is so very difficult because it is directly connected to many other basic and controversial areas of politics: wealth, work, welfare, security and identity. Throughout history, migration has been driven by very deep currents of hope, often to be met by equally deep currents of fear. It can be a spark for often combustible sentiments that have little to do with migration as such and more to do with slumbering anxieties and broken dreams about changing societal circumstances. For this reason, understanding people flows and the responses they trigger, in particular when it concerns migration, can help us better understand deeper societal developments and concerns.

People Flows to Europe in the Next 10-15 Years: Trends and Patterns

Since a comprehensive analysis of basic trends related to human mobility for the next 10-15 years and how they might affect Europe

---

[1] This chapter builds on but goes beyond a publication by Demos/openDemocracy entitled *People Flow: Managing Migration in a New European Commonwealth* (2003, London), which I wrote together with Tom Bentley and Alessandra Buonfino. The exploration in this chapter is far-ranging. I have embarked upon it as a (retired) reflective practitioner with a political science background and a generalist mind, not shying away from treading adjacent territories like history, sociology and economics. Naturally, my assumptions, tentative conclusions and suggestions therefore deserve to be scrutinized by others who are more qualified than I am.

would far exceed the limits of this chapter, some choices have to be made. We can safely omit "normal" business travel, study abroad, tourism and family visits from the picture. These types of mobility will probably vary with economic indicators, but are not likely to lead us to deeper understanding about what is really going on. So we turn to migration and more in particular to migration *to* and not *from* Europe. Projections of future "reverse brain drain" to countries such as China, India, Turkey, Morocco and others would be interesting, but in the context of this study they would be "mere" illustrations of changing (economic) relations, for which much more dramatic economic and financial indicators are also available.[2]

Narrowing our focus to migration *to* Europe confronts us nevertheless with substantial problems. First of all, migration numbers are notoriously difficult to predict. On the other hand, maybe such numbers are not really what we are looking for. In our search for deep currents we would be better served by knowing something about the overall nature, direction and patterns of future migration trends rather than about their numbers. First, on a global scale the proportion of the population that migrates is and probably remains marginal. Second, as communication and transport costs fall, the growing range of routes and means of migration will probably lead to patterns of movement that will become more complex and diverse, including several forms of circular migration. Third, if the global economy further develops in an overall positive direction, more adventurous migrants will be succeeded by a much larger number of less adventurous career-oriented movers who have become rich and educated enough to further improve their chances elsewhere, i.e. in the U.S. and the EU—until differences in wealth have sufficiently evened out and the migration "hump" flattens to more normal proportions and patterns. At the same time, in the years leading to 2020 pockets of (extreme) misery for economic, political or military reasons will continue to prompt especially younger desperados to migrate, while varied types of refugees will have to be taken care of under the umbrella of the UN and other organizations. If the global economy in the coming 10-15

---

[2] A somewhat related indicator of those changing relations would be a shift in the numbers of especially Asian students, who traditionally have gone to the U.S., Canada, Europe and Australia, and who increasingly would go to top foreign universities in Asia.

years develops unevenly or even stagnates, however, migratory flows will have shapes and intensities that roughly correspond to these developments.

In other words, migration in its varying forms, patterns and numbers is here to stay, and in one form or another the EU will have to take its share. Seen from a long term perspective, one could say that it is "business as usual."

In this respect it is important to note that the EU is employing a variety of policy instruments to achieve more coordinated entry management, including prevention of entry and return of illegal migrants and unaccepted asylum seekers. This very incremental process will continue steadily over the coming decade. It will remain a bumpy road, marked on the one hand by gradually increasing effectiveness and on the other hand by the never-ending cat-and-mouse game among immigraton officials on the one hand and potential migrants and human traffickers on the other, the latter always remaining able to find new entry points through the porous borders of the EU.

As far as integration policies are concerned, the picture will probably remain diverse. Integration policies vary widely among individual EU member states. If there is any overall pattern to be discerned it could be said to exhibit a mix of the following elements:

- ongoing and not very visible "classical" integration of a substantial number of migrants via three generations;
- widely publicized and magnified integration failures and incidents;
- an ongoing public debate fed by entry and integration incidents, with considerable variety in the nature of the debate within and among countries.

Populist Responses to Migration Flows to Europe

Judging from the rise of anti-immigration populist parties in an increasing number of European countries, more and more voters in those countries definitely do not regard immigration as a marginal phenomenon. On the contrary. New populists on nationalistic and anti-migration tickets have won the notable support of voters in recent elections: 11.9% in France (National Front); 8.3% in Italy (Northern League); 15.5% in the Netherlands (Geert Wilders' Dutch Freedom Party); 28.9% in Switzerland (Swiss People's Party); 16.7% in Hungary (Jobbik); 22.9% in Norway (Progress Party); and 29% in Austria (Freedom Party). There are also significant parties of the nationalistic extreme right in Belgium, Latvia, Slovakia, and Slovenia. Finally, the 2010 publication of Thilo Sarrazin's anti-Muslim and nationalistic book "Germany does away with itself" won large support in German opinion polls and revealed a polarization that has long been simmering under the surface.

For a better understanding of the present rise of anti-immigration populism in Europe let us first examine this rise in historical perspective. Leo Lucassen[3] takes the example of the Catholic Irish, who in the beginning of the 19th century were driven by failed harvests and hunger not only to the U.S., but also to England. They landed in the slum areas of Manchester, Liverpool and London, where they were viewed as an indigenous cheap labor threat. But their Catholic background was at least as threatening. Beginning in 1880 William Murphy traveled through the country preaching that through the Irish "Papacy and catholic despotism threatened English liberal freedom," galvanizing mobs to kill Irish and burn their houses. Those riots lasted for decades, and it took a century before the Irish had found their place in society. Even when many second- and third-generation Irish had climbed the social ladder, the dominant image of the Irish was still that of those who were left behind in the slums. Lucassen agrees with U.S. migration expert Aristide Zolberg that the approaches taken toward Catholics in England resemble the views directed against Muslims in present-day Europe.

Anti-immigrant polarization in the 1960s and 1970s in Europe revealed basically similar patterns, though usually less violent. It was also more complex because of additional complications. One compli-

---

[3] The data in this paragraph are mostly extracted from Leo Lucassen, "Het verleden als laboratorium: Immigratie en polarisatie in West-Europa sinds 1850" ("The past as laboratory: Immigration and polarization in Western Europe since 1850"), from 'Polarisatie: bedreigend en verrijkend' ("Polarisation: threatening and enriching"), Raad voor Maatschappelijke Ontwikkeling (Council for Societal Development), 2010.

cation was the independence of all European colonies, which generated new categories and flows of immigrants who often arrived at times of economic recession and higher unemployment, generated in part by the oil crisis. Political entrepreneurs such as Enoch Powell in the UK responded by predicting great chaos and "rivers of blood" in 1968 as a result of ongoing immigration from the West Indies, Pakistan and India—just as four decades later Geert Wilders sketched disasters of apocalyptic proportions in his anti-Islam film *Fitna*.

Today, a large proportion of the grandchildren of these immigrants are doing well. Half of West Indians are married to white English. And despite a lower comparable percentage for the Asian Hindus, many of their grandchildren have reached middle class positions. In the meantime Enoch Powell and the like have done substantial damage, with long-term effects.

The second post-WWII complication resulted from the expansion of the welfare state in most western European countries. As a consequence, temporary laborers from the Mediterranean region did not return home in periods of economic decline. Instead, many stayed because of accumulated rights to certain forms of support, and many also brought their families to join them. Thus, despite the success of many second- and third-generation migrants, this last factor has paradoxically contributed to the growth of persistent pockets of second- and third-generation of unemployment which, as with the Irish, have a disproportionately large effect on the overall image of the group.[4]

Let us now try to look more closely at the latest and still expanding rise of anti-immigration populism in Europe in order to find out whether in this case we are basically dealing with a recurring phenomenon or with something more unique and even more alarming. The necessary distance for evidence-based observations is lacking, and as far as I know no systematic research on the emerging populist wave is yet available. Nevertheless, I will try to identify some specific characteristics of the emerging new wave of anti-immigration populism as it is affecting more and more European countries.

---

[4] See also Hollifield, James F., *Immigrants, Markets and States. The Political Economy of Postwar Europe* (Cambridge Mass.: Harvard University Press, 1992).

Four aspects in particular are striking: the scale, the variety, the link with wider issues and the focus on Islam. I do not believe that Europe has ever experienced such a rise of anti-immigration populism in so many European countries in very different parts of the continent at the same time. On a positive note, one could conclude that this shows that the European Union is, maybe particularly in its crises,[5] becoming more and more a living and interconnected entity. This is all the more intriguing when we realize that the specific contexts and histories of all of these affected countries differ widely.

I will illustrate this point with some sweeping generalizations, just to give an impression of the type and scope of variation. In the northern, more secularized part of Europe, where for instance abortion and homosexuality are less contentious and where social security is most developed, the fear that all of these gains are at risk is coupled with the fear of immigrants and Muslims in particular. In countries such as Belgium, France or Italy, older populist parties with shady roots in postwar fascism now try to ride the new waves as well. In eastern EU member states, poisonous mixtures of post-communist disillusion, trial-and-error democratic development and fragile economic conditions provide fertile soil for new populists. Despite this variation, in almost all cases fragmentation of the political center goes hand in hand with radical and polarizing populism with political programs that connect nationalism and anti-immigrant policy elements with other issues that appeal to many voters.

As far as I can judge, this wider scope is rather unique from a historical perspective. The additional issues that are linked to the anti-immigration/Islam stance seem to address in one way or another deep-felt negative feelings about political elites, the media, the government, the economy and social security, including pensions. Finally, the prominent place of anti-Islam statements clearly resembles the anti-Catholic element in the case of the Irish in England. A new element is that in our age these sentiments can be much more systematically fed into the minds of the electorate with a never-ending supply of new pictures and examples of the "deeply alien and un-Western" nature of the Islam than was ever possible in the 19th century.

---

[5] See also Luuk van Middelaar, *De passage naar Europa:Geschiedenis van een begin* (The passage to Europe: the history of a beginning.) (Groningen, Historische Uitgeverij, 2009).

The Deep Current Underlying Today's Populism: Foreboding of a Systemic Crisis

In trying to identify[6] the mix of emotions that together might constitute the deep current(s) we are looking for, I come to the following enumeration. It is fear of strange outsiders taking over, both based on personal experience and on the imagination that it might come to one's good old neighborhood. It is uneasiness about where their real loyalty lies. It is disbelief about their apparent lack of respect for one's own values. It is anger about what the government has never done for one but is now doing for them. It is powerlessness as one sees the government's lack of control. It is losing respect for the intellectuals who accuse one of racism and in the meantime walk with their smart heads in the clouds and don't see the real dangers on the ground. It is bitterness about traditional parties that have let one down or even betrayed one. It is deep concern about perspectives for one's children and grandchildren as the global economy comes closer and closer. It is disbelief as one sees the unraveling of social cohesion. And it is a growing sense of insecurity triggered by an unholy mix of old crime and new terror dished out daily through the screen in one's living room. It is loss of trust in the sustainability of social security and pensions, Shock about the greed and risky behavior of banks. And finally, it is mixed feelings and groping in the dark about what Europe really is about. A telling aspect of this mix of emotions is that it can quite well go hand in hand with satisfaction about one's personal social and economic situation.

From a long-term perspective one could conclude that, with the swing of the pendulum, these recurring knots of very negative emotions, though always garbed in different clothing, are what politics has been and is and always will be about. As in the past, sooner or later either the political establishment will be able to take over the agenda of the populists, or the populists will join the establishment, while in the meantime the children and grandchildren of the new immigrants will be more and more successful and the economic crisis will be over. From another perspective, however, one can also conclude that this time the phenomenon should be interpreted as a very disturbing sign

---

[6] This section is partly based on my personal analysis of hate mail sent to the Netherlands Agency for the Reception of Asylum-Seekers when I was its general director, and of incidents that took place in that same period.

on the wall, because so many other very crucial concerns are connected with anti-immigration sentiments. But also because the elites themselves seem increasingly shaky about the tectonic vibrations that are disturbing their sense of security, while deep down, many seem just as much groping in the dark about which direction to go.

I believe this second perspective better reflects current realities, and suggest that we label the present rise of populism in Europe as a set of early warning signals for a serious systemic crisis that is emerging in Europe. No less. No less, because populist voters may have better antennae than elites for societal disruptions or even a "big disaster" or "civil war"[7] that hate mail messages tell us may not be far away. They might have better antennae than elites because in one way or another elites are part of the supporting societal infrastructures and populists are not. They may have the sharper eye of the outsider. They would never formulate the danger in the way I just did, but you can 't fool them because they see the signs and turn to leaders who speak their language and share their worries. Recent polls in the Netherlands show that a large proportion of the populist voters knows well that the solutions Geert Wilders propagates are too simplistic. Many also don't agree with his more radical anti-Islam statements—but at least they trust him for shaking up the elite and their systems. If such an insight would be more widespread it would mean that the anti-Islamic aspect of the rise of populism in Europe is not the core of the problem, but the wrapping paper in which it is seen and felt. Since politics is very much also about the way things are seen and felt, the anti-Islamic aspect remains important and must be addressed, also for intrinsic reasons. But from a long-term perspective, the populist voters' unpolished foreboding of a systemic crisis in Europe is in my view the deep current we are looking for.

Searching for Clues to the Crisis and Imagining Levers for Systemic Innovation

In view of the heuristic path we are following it is useful to consider more carefully my point about a systemic crisis: is it really a crisis, and

---

[7] Quotes from hate mail. As one can see, some of them might just as well be called angst mail.

is it really systemic? On the one hand various observers stress that we should not be too alarmed by the ongoing rise of populism because it is basically a necessary corrective reaction to the decades-long neglect by traditional parties of justified worries and fears of a substantial part of the voters, especially with respect to immigrants and their integration. These observers add that, also for several decades, the public discourse has been dominated by self-confident cosmopolitans, so that locally-rooted worried and angry citizens are right to claim their own space in their own way. Those observers also note that until now there is very little anti-democratic populism. On the contrary, democracy is alive and kicking and the arena is still mainly parliament and not the streets. Finally, part of these observers state that populist voters should be taken seriously but deserve better answers than those provided by populist leaders. On the other hand, other observers sense a much deeper change and crisis, which could be well summarized as "systemic." Before trying to choose a position between these different interpretations of what is going on, let us first try to create some sense of the mixed emotions that drive populist voters and that are probably shared by a sizable part of the additional electorate. To really connect with the involved deep current let us not focus on emotions related to immigration directly but to wider and deeper ones. I think that the mixed bag of wider and deeper emotions can be paraphrased into the following cluster of populist statements, formulated on a more abstract level:

— "our government is losing its grip";

— "the economy is running wild";

— "our society is falling apart".

In even more abstract terms these statements indicate very fundamental worries about democracy, capitalism and society as evidenced by the day-to-day experiences of populist voters. An appropriate label for the composite cluster of the systems that is at stake here could be "capitalist democratic society."

Let us now return to the interpretation of what is going on. Since one of the leading departure points in this chapter is to take populist voters seriously and listen carefully to what they try to say, I choose the more dramatic interpretation and stick to my original choice to see the populist mood as a foreboding of a systemic crisis, because if we take the three statements at face value that is basically what they are concerned about.

In order to further specify this interpretation the next question must be whether the voters' intuition that a systemic crisis is approaching should be seen as an early warning for a systemic collapse or as an early warning for the need of a fundamental system improvement. If we look at the hate mail, the voters just don't know and at times fear the worst. That is where the elite, including the political leadership, must come in and help with reading the signs on the basis of additional overview and knowledge.

My own conviction is that Europe still has a lot of potential in a world that is changing fast in unprecedented ways—but only if it begins today to prepare its defining systems for the future. Systems that are based on a number of crucial paradigms that were invented in Europe 3-4 centuries ago. In other words: Europe must prepare for capitalist democratic society 2.0,[8] starting today. The rest of this chapter will explore this point with a view towards finding out what this may mean for Europe and the United States in the year 2020.

An uncomfortable question now presents itself: how on earth can we ever hope to advance policies that can tackle the three identified major worries with respect to a cluster of systems of such awe-inspiring size and complexity? Our chances of answering this question increase if, from the outset, we realize two things.

First, the three statements are exaggerations, but exaggerations are the stuff of populist politicians. Still, they must contain at least several clues that guide us to real problems, otherwise they could not be so potent. Let us therefore try to identify for each of the three involved systems at least one of those clues and see whether we can thus find entry points for the sort of policies that we are seeking. Second, the government, the economy and the society are not realities that can be improved or redesigned at one stroke or with one massive effort. They are huge, complex and dynamic systems. The best we can ever hope to achieve is to design or find key levers, both for stimulating construc-

---

[8] I use the label '2.0' as a metaphoric indicator for a next and more sophisticated generation of a major innovation.

tive and discouraging destructive dynamics in a more sophisticated direction.

Democracy: "The Government is Losing its Grip"

It would of course be impossible to identify in this paragraph *the* central clue that could help us both to explain why the government is losing its grip and to find the lever for moving in the direction of democracy 2.0.[9] There are probably several such clues. I want to identify at least one plausible clue and explore how it could lead us to at least one lever for triggering 2.0-oriented changes in the democratic system.

A Clue: Decreasing Public Manageability of Increasing Man-made Complexity

Governments have probably never been able to meet fully the expectations and demands of their subjects or citizens. Simply, because there were always unforeseen side-effects of their decisions and unexpected events to which they had to react. Also, I presume that, before modernization started, subjects and citizens as a rule had more or less static expectations of what their government could do for them. However, in Europe the Renaissance unleashed an ongoing interaction between governments and citizens, continuing until today, in which governments became more and more ambitious and citizens more and more demanding. The cumulative results of this process have led to a splendid civilization with unholy dark sides and staggering man-made complexity that is itself driven by man-made acceleration.

The process I just described in a few sweeping statements is usually called modernization and is the original trademark of the West. An intrinsic part of this modernization process in Europe[10] was an ongoing process of introducing such elements as separation of powers, popular elections, sophisticated bureaucracies and respect for human rights. The post-WWII period in several ways has been a continuation of this process, including through the introduction of social secu-

---

[9] Actually, we should speak of democracy 3.0 since modern democracy was partially developed on the basis of rediscovering ancient Greek democracy.

[10] There were and are marked differences in this respect between the various regions of Europe, but I assume that the underlying dynamics basically form one interconnected historical process.

rity systems and the emergence of the European Union. In order to search in an open manner for a clue that could possibly explain governments' "loss of grip," I suggest to replace—at least for the rest of this chapter—the term "government" by "public affairs infrastructure." In this way we can examine not only the government bureaucracy and cabinet but also parliament, the judiciary and the galaxy of (semi-)public institutions that are circling around modern governments, and which together make up the present democratic system in Europe.

There are clear signs that at the start of the new millennium the many complexities that have in one way or another to be dealt with via the public affairs infrastructure are increasingly too much and too difficult to handle. Let us focus on the key aspect of decision-making on policies. Modern parliamentary democracy was one of the innovations resulting from the modernization process. This innovation has basically three functions: the prevention of civil war by ensuring peaceful change of political power; involving citizens in public affairs and creating a reasonably fair mechanism for meaningful decision making on public affairs. Parliamentary democracy can therefore be regarded as a never-ending battle for political power, disguised as a never-ending search for good policies in a way that ensures sufficient grass-roots support. This triple function increasingly becomes a handicap and weak point as complexity increases. From a strictly "technical" point of view, modern parliamentary democracy as we know it is not the best set of institutions, rules and practices for generating sound and implementable policies on increasingly complex public issues. As man-made complexities continue to increase this becomes more evident. The ever-ongoing acceleration further aggravates this development.[11] When public issues become more complex, it takes more time to take a decision on them, even more so when that has to be done on EU level. At the same time the acceleration of especially economic and financial changes gives less and less time for decision making. All this can lead to a creeping but potentially very dangerous decrease of public authority: the famous gap. The far-reaching implications of this evolving systemic shortcoming of modern parliamentary democracy in

---

[11]See also Hartmut Rosa and William E. Scheuerman (eds), *High Speed Society: Social Acceleration, Power and Modernity* (University Park: Pennsylvania University Press, 2009).

Europe become immediately clear when we realize that this is the public decision-making system that has to deal with the dilemmas underlying the various themes that are the subject of the Transatlantic 2020 project.

It is important for a proper understanding to be as precise as possible on the question whether this "law" of diminishing public manageability of increasing man-made complexity is typical of parliamentary democracy, or whether it pertains to modernization in any political system. I assume that the latter is the case. Any public affairs infrastructure is ultimately fueled by political decision-making that is inevitably the result of extremely complicated processes in which a variety of actors with a variety of interests and positions participate. This phenomenon has as such little to do with the question whether a particular public affairs infrastructure is part of a parliamentary democracy, an authoritarian system or the court of Louis XIV. It is inherent in the exercise of political power. And likewise, any public affairs infrastructure is in principle capable of realizing an ongoing modernization of its society that is at least comparable to the ones at both sides of the Atlantic. To be sure, the type of resulting man-made complexity might show some differences varying with the type of political system. Also, the modernization of the public affairs infrastructure itself will show some differences in outcome, varying with the type of political system.[12] But what they share is that they are all under the spell of ongoing modernization[13], gradually leading to a fundamental shift in the capacity of invidual humans to grasp public issues and manage the public realm.

Societies prior to the Renaissance were undeniably complex, but nevertheless in those days it seemed in principle possible for one gifted person—a ruler or a scholar—to master the complexity of his society in accordance with his needs. A ruler with his advisers or a

---

[12]For an empirical assessment of some of those differences between developing countries, see Goran Hyden, Julius Court and Kenneth Mease, *Making Sense of Governance: Empirical Evidence from Sixteen Developing Countries* (Boulder: Lynne Rienner Publishers, 2004).

[13]I regard modernization as an ongoing process for a long time to come and don't go into the issue whether in some respects we have reached a post-modern phase. It might nevertheless be useful to distinguish some phases of modernization.

council of administrators could decide on major issues on the basis of mutual consultation within a common frame of reference. Each could in principle grasp the whole and the dialogue or debate seemed mainly necessary for inventarizing all arguments, considerations and interests. Likewise, in those days it was in principle still possible to become a universal scholar mastering in an integrated manner all branches of science as they existed at the time. The main reason that this was so was of course not that at those times human and physical nature were basically less complex than nowadays. Rather, in those days the desire to master this complexity to such an extent that man could fundamentally reshape his environment and fate had not surfaced yet.

The paradox of modernization therefore seems to be that in the name of shaping ourselves a better world, we have produced a world of such complexity that no single person—however gifted he or she may be—could even dream of encompassing it. The impressive civilization which we have built during the last few centuries rests on a human foundation which has grown weaker over time—a foundation of individual people among whom no single person can even strive to grasp the totality of what we have wrought.[14]

This incremental process of increasing vulnerability does not become quicly evident because on an *individual* level modernization seems to lead—admittedly with its ups and downs—to more control over one's life for more people during longer periods. On *a collective* level, however, public decision-making inevitably suffers increasingly from a lack of common grasp of complex public issues, thus enlarging the chances for uproductive polarization instead of tough but constructive debates.

It seems to be the price we all have to pay unwillingly for ongoing modernization. The most relevant difference for our quest is that

---

[14]See also Theo Veenkamp, *Into the third millennium:the need for societal innovations?*. Paper prepared for the Symposium 'Europe into the third millennium', organised by the University of Exeter from 9-12 April 1992 under the auspices of UNESCO, the Council of Europe and the Vienna Academy for the Study of the Future. This paper was a modified version of Theo Veenkamp, *Europe on the Threshold of a New Era: Time Bomb or Catalyst?*, Provost's Lecture 1992, Ball State University, 10 February 1992.

Western societies are farthest ahead on this inclined plane, simply because they are farthest with modernization.

A Lever: Paradigm Laboratories

Moving in the direction of 2.0 requires that we introduce a crucial innovation into the political decision-making machinery that will enable the system to deal with the increased man-made complexity in a more sophisticated manner and in less time. The multi-actor, complex and sometimes very polarized political decision-making machinery that is increasingly unable to produce on-time policies and regulations that match the complexity of public issues must in my view be accepted as a fact of life that can from time to time be changed cosmetically, but not intrinsically. The exercise of political power is not imaginable without an at-times-bloody political arena. It is part of the human condition. Therefore, the only possible innovation for dealing faster and in a more sophisticated manner with increasing man-made complexity that I can think of at the moment must come from outside the existing political decision making machinery. Really innovative changes from within in the end are all doomed to failure.

At present it seems that more and more good ideas and analyses are more or less torn apart in the decision-making arena, while the shreds are used for constructing a politically acceptable but hardly implementable compromise. I am not naive: compromise is the heart of politics, but complex societies demand sophisticated compromises. What I therefore have in mind is truly external, very sophisticated input into the political decision-making machinery that is so plausible and attractive[15] in several ways that the different parts of the machinery can hardly resist using it as a solid and common departure point for the decision-making process. As a quasi-replacement for the missing shared frame of reference from the pre-Renaissance period. I am heartened in this opinion by Richard Sennett,[16] who in a Spinoza Lecture in The Hague drew an intriguing lesson from the start of the Renaissance. Sennett described how the Renaissance began with individuals who, influenced by humanist thinkers, opened up their minds and

---

[15]Among others by, when appropriate, containing a strong narrative as crucial part of the input.

[16]Richard Sennet, in his Spinoza Lecture, The Hague, 24 November 2010.

repositioned themselves as observers of the evolution of their lives. Man as work-in-progress instead of man as God's creature. This change in attitude became visible first and foremost in a practical and material way. During the 15th and 16th centuries the strictly organized and supervised medieval guild workshop changed gradually into a wider institution: a laboratory that was open to experiments with materials, tools and new technologies. The dominant rule in the early-modern workshop was that informal, open cooperation is the best way to experience differences in expertise, views, ideas, etc. Each component of this rule is important. *Informal* means that contacts between people with different expertise and (field of) interests are rich when they are messy and weak when they are strictly regulated, as in dull meetings following strict formal rules. *Open* means that you want to know on what somebody else is working without needing to know to what it shall lead. In other words, from the very start you want to avoid the iron law of usefulness that determines a product or a policy goal. *Cooperation* is the simplest and most important term, implying that you go for the gains that result from the exchange between different parties, instead of going for the battle between parties in order for one of them to win. Sennett concluded that the high-tech laboratories of today still operate on the basis of this informal open cooperation, while the same rule seems totally absent in trying to deal with the complexities of modern society. This absence leads in his view to all sorts of inhumane consequences. So, laboratories that generate highly sophisticated and innovative input on complex public and societal issues and that operate in the same way as high-tech laboratories on the basis of the rule of informal open cooperation are what we are seeking.

In view of the deeply-rooted arena character of the political decision-making machine, such laboratories can only be created totally outside the public affairs infrastructure. During my long career in the public realm I have tried several times to create safe informal creative spaces within this infrastructure, but in the end I always felt a little bit like Don Quixote. The parallel with high-tech laboratories is important, because such laboratories are clever in developing very seductive high-tech products, which in the end are hard to resist. That should also be the ambition of complex societal issue-oriented laboratories, with the major difference that they are not technology-driven but paradigm-driven. Precisely because so many complex societal issues have the shape of a real (often ideological) dilemma, the trick that liberates the necessary creative energy usually is a paradigm shift, leading to one or more sometimes totally new ways of looking at the dilemma. In other words, the creation of paradigm laboratories might produce the lever that we are seeking.

Fortunately enough, I have an example of such an attempt at hand: the Netherlands National Think Tank Foundation.[17] The Foundation was launched in 2005 as an initiative of a number of young scholars, supported by the University of Amsterdam, McKinsey & Company and the Dutch Innovation Platform. The Foundation selects each year a multidisciplinary team of approximately 20 promising master students, recent graduates and Ph.D candidates. The team functions as the yearly National Think Tank. During a three-month period the team must develop an innovative and creative solution for a complex societal problem. The team can make use of input from many experts from the domains of science, economy and government. In addition to that there is full-time support from a renowned consultancy firm. The innovative proposals must be concrete and implementable. The final outcome is presented in a public report each year. This pressure-cooker approach has until now led to influential reports on the care of chronically ill (2006), education (2007), stimulating young people to choose a healthy life style (2008), energy transition (2009) and trust in a changing society (2010). "Alumni" of the yearly think tank remain connected through a virtual community.

The use of paradigm labs is no magic wand or quick fix. But if such labs are used more and more systematically, in the long run they may lead to a fundamental change of the dominant political/administrative culture in the direction of less ideological polarization and more cooperative idealist pragmatism. In the end this has the potential to influence the nature of political parties, the profile of politicians and the roles of civil servants.

Capitalism: "The Economy is Running Wild"

Just as in the section on democracy I will try to identify at least one plausible clue that can help us in understanding what really is going on and in finding a lever for moving in the 2.0 direction.

---

[17]www.nationale-denktank.nl. There is no English language website yet.

A Clue: Growing Vulnerability to the Inevitable Destruction of Jobs

The twins of capitalism and modernization was born in Europe. One can regard capitalism as a growth-oriented way of generating wealth, financed by investors motivated by maximum return, that makes innovative use of modern technology—with the important side-effect of ongoing creation and destruction of jobs (the famous "creative destruction" of Schumpeter). The results, in Europe, on the whole are impressive.[18] But capitalism has always had one major weak spot: employment can ultimately never be more than a side effect. Capitalism is wealth-driven, not employment-driven. The inevitable periodic and unpredictable creation and destruction of jobs has been going on in Europe for quite a few centuries. But it seems that in Europe the periodic destruction of jobs is becoming more and more a problem that has destabilizing effects with unacceptable ramifications.

In western Europe the postwar welfare state was developed with the purpose of reducing these ramifications, but it now turns out that the costs of maintaining it at the existing level are too high—and not immigrant-proof. In central and eastern Europe, (artificial) communist job security has been replaced by a rough sort of capitalism. The transition is difficult. For demographic reasons—the aging of the population—unemployment is unlikely to become a large problem for several decades, but at the same time persistent pockets of unemployment—notably of (descendants of) immigrants—could have disproportionately destabilizing effects on the whole society, in any case much more so than before WWII. Lucassen argues that for a variety of reasons today's (descendents of) Mediterranean immigrants have less chances in the labor market than their 19th century Polish and Italian predecessors.[19] Also, more general unemployment can quickly rise to high levels, as we see today in for instance some Southern European countries.

An additional complication is that the financing factor is becoming more and more an additional cause of unpredictable dynamics, rather than only a facilitating factor, adding to employment volatility. But there is a more fundamental factor at play: the problem of never-end-

---

[18]I leave aside the environmental sustainability aspect.

[19]Lucassen, op. cit.

ing acceleration. Mostly because of ongoing globalization it becomes increasingly important to be quick and creative in generating new types of employment. But in a sizable number of EU countries there is a mixed bag of structural and cultural restraints that prevents reacting in such a manner. Finally, in the wider circle of countries bordering Europe there are huge numbers of educated youth with no job perspective, creating a potentially destabilizing force both in their own country and vis-a-vis Europe.

The trend that is sketched in the previous paragraph in a rather impressionistic way produces a steady stream of negative news bits, which for populist voters results in the growing conviction that the economy is running wild and that there are hard times ahead for one's children and grandchildren. Those voters are not like their cosmopolitan colleagues, who are (still) confident that they and their children will be able to ride the waves. They, however, increasingly grope in the dark about how their offspring can best prepare for such an unpredictable future. This emergent anxiety is extremely important because it is all about jobs. Let us hear what Ben Verwaayen, CEO of Alcatel-Lucent, has to say about jobs:

> What, especially today, is the core of a society? It is jobs. Jobs create prosperity; jobs create well-being; jobs create cohesion. Jobs give people identity; independence, further development and self-confidence. But we live in a changing world. In which centres of power are shifting and in which the criteria for participating in the economy are broadened. In that world the existing balance of jobs cannot be taken for granted anymore, in the West, in Europe.[20]

What is basically going on here? My hypothesis is that the globalizing capitalist wealth-creating machinery—driven by the ongoing interaction between investors, entrepreneurs and consumers—increasingly runs the risk of losing its various national political and societal foundations because it is less and less able to create meaningful jobs on time for those whose jobs are destroyed by ongoing economic developments. My guess is that one of the reasons for this process is that, precisely because of geographically expanding global-

---

[20]In a *Volkskrant* interview of April 6, 2010.

ization, the chances of national mismatch of and time lag between supply and demand of jobs increase steadily. Moreover, the pain that is caused by the loss of jobs becomes larger as modernization becomes more succesful, simply because there is more to lose, which fact at the same time makes it more difficult to move to where the work is. I assume that these unnerving constrains are felt and feared most by populist voters. Seen from a historical perspective a large proportion of them probably belong to the last that have moved upward thanks to modernization only to be the first to fall back again thanks to concomitant globalization. Socially and politically, this is a potentially explosive situation. Especially as such an existential threat can easily be seen and construed as primarily coming from the others, from outside. I think that the dynamics that erode incrementally globalizing capitalism in the way that I am describing here are at play in one way or another in all existing modernizing societies. But if ongoing modernization means that more and more people reach a position in which there is more and more to lose, then the social and political risks in the West are the greatest, again, because modernization has most progressed there. In the US and Europe in different manifestations, because of different social and political cultures and infrastructures, but probably basically sharing, the same degree of risk.

A Lever: An Additional Instrument for Creating Employment

It must not come as a surprise that in my view a crucial lever for moving out of this dangerous situation and in the direction of Capitalism 2.0 could be the creation of an additional instrument for creating employment. Since employment basically is only a side effect of the capitalist way of wealth creation, it is not realistic to expect that such an additional instrument can be positioned in the heart of the existing capitalist machinery. The dominant role of maximal-return-oriented investors in fueling the machinery will prevent that, especially in Europe, with its relatively high wages. Also, government-financed employment is reaching its limits, again, particularly in Europe. We are therefore forced to be truly innovative.

I think that what we are looking for is an additional and new way of creating employment that

- operates in a real but strictly local market;

- is financed by strictly local investors who operate via banks and not via the stock market;

- operates on the basis of employment-oriented interaction between investors, entrepreneurs and consumers who are each driven by more complex motives than presumed in the existing capitalist philosophy:

  —multiple return-oriented investors;

  —multiple profit-oriented entrepreneurs;

  —multiple satisfaction-oriented consumers;

  —multiple reward-oriented employees.

At first glance it seems revolutionary, but actually it is already in the air, thanks to a new generation of economists who have reconstructed homo economicus as a much more complex ideal type than the original one. Each element of the additional way of creating employment that I have just suggested needs clarification.

- *A local market* as a relatively stable countervailing economic reality against the dynamics of globalization;

- *Employment-oriented* as an indication of an economic activity whereby available human resources are taken as the starting point and ideas, technology and funds consequently are added;[21]

- *Local multiple return-oriented investors (not via the stock market)* as an indication of investors who want a reasonable return plus a non-financial bonus in the form of certain privileges, connections or otherwise; because they are local; and not investing via the stock market, because being part of the enterprise in one way or another is rewarding to them;

- *Local multiple profit-oriented entrepreneurs* as an indication of entrepreneurs who want a reasonable profit plus a non-finan-

---

[21]I saw a first example of such an approach when I visited a number of beautiful palaces in Jaipur, India. When I asked my guide, a history teacher, why these palaces were lying so close to one another, he answered that building them was primarily meant by the involved maharadjas as a way to create employment for their subjects.

cial bonus in the form of satisfaction derived from the adventure and from the contribution he or she is giving to society and from the status that or she receives; or otherwise;

- *Multiple satisfaction-oriented consumers* as an indication of consumers who are willing to pay a reasonable price plus a non-financial bonus in the form of certain privileges, a sense of belonging to the larger enterprise, or otherwise;

- *Multiple reward-oriented employees* as an indication of employees who want a reasonable salary but who are also willing to be paid additionally by on-the-job training as far as necessary for doing the work.

In a macroeconomic sense this new type of multiple profit-oriented enterprise would mean the enriching of the economies of all modernizing societies with an additional driver, taking untapped and possibly "unrefined" human resources as a departure point for new economic activities culminating in irresistible products and services of competitive quality to be bought by multiple satisfaction-oriented consumers.

Bringing this new type of enterprise to the market implies having to solve a lot of thorny problems which will differ per national context. I see no *initiating* role for governments here, except some (crucial) facilitating activities. Many banks owe us quite a bit these days, and it would be creative thinking in a very strategic way if they would try to pay us back by returning to their core business of facilitating innovative economic activities, but this time of the kind I am describing here, and if necessary with the help of paradigm laboratories. Banks 2.0 functioning as one of the key levers for moving in the direction of Capitalism 2.0. There is a new generation of young bankers waiting to do it all very differently.

Society: "Our Society is Falling Apart"

In this section we will try again to a) find at least one clue that can help us both with understanding the justified fear of populist voters that their society is falling apart and b) find at least one lever that can help reverse this trend into the direction of Society 2.0.

A Clue: The Emerging Culture War

Ongoing modernization usually triggers two sorts of basic reactions: on balance a sense of enrichment by the open-minded (living in an adventurous mode) and on balance a sense of loss by the closed-minded (living in a safe mode). Analysis of election results shows that the closed-minded are strongly represented in the populist voters. In line with my approach to focus on what the populist voter is trying to say, this aspect needs further scrutiny. In most European countries people with closed minds have a problem: their habitat and other certainties are disappearing. Their rural towns and villages are becoming empty and dead. Higher education students with all their new ideas are "in" and good old professionals like carpenters and plumbers are "out." And when your children have graduated from university, they are still out, because they don't know the codes. Strange people you don't understand, who have strange habits and whom you cannot really trust, have come to live on your street. What happened to the time when you could stay with one boss during your whole career? To make things worse, liberal and cultural elites make fun of your favorite TV programs, look down on your simplicity and almost force you, in a condescending way, to become more open and tolerant, as they call it. But that goes against your grain, mentally and physically. They are fitter, stronger and better equipped than you in riding the waves of modernization, and you feel humiliated. You start to resent them and hate them. When someone finally comes along who says it all out loud and who wants to lead the attack, he or she is your person.[22]

These days we have a word for this: "culture wars"—emerging clashes within civilizations rather than between civilizations, whether "Muslim" or "Western," much more fluid and enigmatic than good old class struggle, but paradoxically enough no less real, especially in its virtual manifestations. In any society there are always many divisions, but culture wars seem to become the main new driver of divisiveness, of polarization. As far as I can judge this process is on its way in most European countries but in different degrees and different disguises. In many but not all cases anti-immigration and anti-Muslim feelings function as catalysts, but they are not the driver. The driver is ongoing modernization and the dramatic changes that it brings about.

---

[22]Partially quoted from Geert Jan Kuip, *NRC Handelsblad*, November 18, 2010.

I assume that the emerging culture wars are the visible manifestation of the disintegration of the old underlying (mostly immaterial) infrastructures that kept communities separate and together in ways that were manageable. They are an unforeseen side effect of ongoing modernization. Because of this disintegration, it seems as if nobody knows his or her place in society any more, regardless of whether an individual is part of the common people or part of the elites.

A Lever: Promote Upgrading of Societal Infrastructure

When trying to imagine a lever than can move us out of the dangerous culture war situation into a process in the direction of society 2.0., it occurs to me that we are dealing here with a very different type of human invention than democracy and capitalism. It is not too difficult to decide roughly when and how modern democracy and capitalism were invented—even though they each required substantial time to mature. Society, as a construct, is probably one of the most important human inventions ever, but we are used to see our present and previous societies as the result of many shaping forces and not as a conscious human construct. I guess and hope that there are historians and anthropologists who can show us that the ongoing development of specific societies can be better understood by digging up their underlying paradigms and how they shifted in an implicit way from time to time into new paradigms. It seems as if, for the first time in history, we are in need of a more explicit paradigm to help us deal in a more conscious manner with the destructive effects of ongoing modernization on our societies. Such a paradigm should contain the key elements of a more sophisticated *societal infrastructure* that can serve as a beacon for upgrading the present disintegrating societal infratstructure. With this in mind I have constructed a first draft of such a paradigm, which on the one hand connects with what should remain and on the other hand can serve as a reference point for 2.0-oriented change.[23] I have labeled this paradigm, as if it were a new chemical product, JMCC: "Just Multiple Connected Coexistence."[24]

---

[23]Society X+1.0 would be a more appropriate label since we simply don't know how many generations of society there have been before our type of society.

[24]See also Theo Veenkamp, 'After Tolerance,' *openDemocracy*, November 24, 2004.

Multiple indicates the acceptance that different people have different strategies for survival and growth, according to choice or necessity. Therefore all people will have the best chance of becoming successful when being able to access a strategy that suits them best: for instance living in an ethnic community (the safe mode) or a mixed community (the adventurous mode); sending children to an ethnic school (the safe mode) or a mixed school (the adventurous mode). *Multiple* implies that there is no intrinsic preference for any of these strategies, but at the same time there is a an acceptance of equal minimum standards of living, quality and security for people, regardless of the path that they follow. If this requires governments and institutions to operate differently in different circumstances, so be it.

Connected implies an acknowledgement that modern, increasingly multicultural[25] society is becoming so all-pervasive and multi-faceted that physical and psychological withdrawal into one's own perceived micro-world becomes a natural and understandable reaction. But such a reaction, if unchecked, could undermine the minimum of cohesion and shared emotions, memories and values, necessary for any society to sustain itself. Thus an essential component of JMCC is active promotion of all sorts of connections between micro-worlds.

Just refers to the leading, uncompromising and overarching principle that characterizes a resilient open society, despite the freedom to choose any strategy to respond to its multicultural character: namely, the rule of law. The rule of law also means *not* rule by religion, race, the market, violence, media, or money. It includes the choice of parliamentary democracy as a way of creating law and the separation of powers to implement and apply law. It includes adherence to those human rights that are enshrined in constitutions and international treaties. It is an indispensable but not sufficient element for holding society together.

Coexistence in itself may not appear to dreamers of a better world to be a very ambitious concept. But in combination with the other three elements it can create the basis for peaceful coexistence, for coexistence that can facilitate the emergence of all sorts of constructive and

---

[25]'Multicultural' is used here purely as a description of the type of society in which most Europeans now live, and not as a normative concept.

creative surpluses. For coexistence that is sustainable in an ever-changing world.

Infrastructure indicates the interrelated set of conditions that facilitate just multiple connected coexistence. It can refer to material conditions such as the design of neighborhoods and roads and immaterial conditions, like new narratives or competitions between schools—ethnic or mixed—in determining which one delivers student populations with the highest degree of connectedness.

The JMSS paradigm can help us as a conceptual lever for promoting an innovative upgrading of existing societal infrastructures in such a way that they become sophisticated enough, for facilitating people and communities to respond in constructive ways to the eroding effects of ongoing modernization. Such a promotional effort is by far the most difficult challenge that I have suggested in this chapter. It basically is about changing our societal patterns in such ways that our open society remains sustainable within the context of ongoing modernization.

Trying to move in the direction of Society 2.0 is difficult for several reasons. In the first place, the social sciences are lagging behind the physical sciences when it comes to their orientation to developing innovation. In order to prove their legitimacy as a science the main emphasis in the social sciences until now has been on empirical research—with impressive results—and not on research and development. It is time for a next phase, with a proliferation of R&D paradigm labs. The second difficulty is that moving in the direction of a more sophisticated society basically must be a help-yourself job. In Europe we have had our share of disastrous utopian dreams trying to mold society from above. Revitalizing society and making it more resilient and creative can only lead to anything substantial when the initiatives come from society itself. In a metaphoric sense the process should be seen as a rite of passage for the coming of age of societies in Europe after too much dependence on government and too much magical belief in the market.

Moving in the Direction of Capitalist Democratic Societies 2.0. in Europe

The purpose of this section was to explore connecting deep currents underlying the growth of anti-immigration parties in Europe with specific policy responses focused on dealing in a constructive way with those currents. The unexpected outcome of my trial-and-error exploration is that the identified deep currents should not primarily be addressed by government policy responses but by creative responses from non-governmental sources: young scholars, helped by universities and consultancy firms, for dealing in a more sophisticated manner with man-made complexities; banks and entrepreneurs for developing an additional and more sophisticated manner for creating employment; private initiatives for promoting a more cohesive, sophisticated and sustainable open society. To the extent that these non-governmental actors are committed, government can move in by intelligent facilitation—not the other way around. Also, though I did not dwell on it, it is clear that such efforts can have greater impact the more they are coordinated, simply because they are (sometimes deeply) related.[26] It therefore becomes at least imaginable that launching a lever oriented European Capitalist Democratic Society 2.0.Program in one form or another might by a rather sensible thing to strive for.

The Wider Context

In this short section I will touch on a few aspects of the wider context of my explorations: the regional context, the transatlantic context, the Islamic dimension and the "West and the Rest."

The Regional Context

The European Union is connected at its eastern and southern flanks with a ring of societies that are unstable to varying degrees and that are each in their own way in an ongoing process of modernization. The 'Arab Spring' being the most recent example. It is official policy of the EU to gradually turn this into a zone of positive interdependence. If an inspiring nongovernmental EU group would launch a Capitalist Democratic Society 2.0 EU Program, such a step would simultaneously create many chances for shared initiatives focused on strengthening ongoing modernization processes in non-EU countries. Promoting multiple profit employment-oriented enterprises could

---

[26]Indicative for this interdependence is that one could have an endless debate about whether it should be Capitalist Democratic Societies or Democratic Capitalist Societies.

have a particularly strong and positive multiplier effect.[27] Of course, all of this, if necessary, would be facilitated by the EU government.

The Transatlantic Context

I have the impression that the deep currents that are identified in this chapter basically are also at work in the U.S., but perhaps less connected with anti-migration sentiments and more directly connected to ongoing political polarization. I think that in a general sense a good case could be made for initiating in one way or another also in the U.S. a capitalist democratic society program 2.0. At the same time, the argumentation, flavor and tone for initiating such a program in the U.S. would probably have to be quite different, among other reasons because of the very different societal and political belief system, type of capitalism, global position and importance attached to military power. Still, or rather, precisely because of that, an interconnected approach between the EU and the U.S. would probably have great mutual additional value.

The Muslim Dimension

It is time to return to the comparison with the anti-Catholic dimension of the anti-immigration sentiments directed against the Irish in the UK. That took several decades to wither away. My assumption is that the same will happen with respect to the anti-Islam dimension of the emerging anti-immigrant populism in Europe—although perhaps lasting longer because of the very visible connection with some international incidents and dilemmas. In my view the basic strategy should be in all cases to deconstruct the[28] problem of Islam into its underlying contexts, i.e. into specific socio-economic, cultural, and (geo)political problems, and to address those. In most of these cases the Islamic dimension may cause some very specific additional complications, but as a rule those complications will not be the main

---

[27]Hamed Abdel-Samad, an Egyptian born German, predicts in his book *Der Untergang der islamischen Welt. Eine Prognose* (Munich: Droemer Knauer, 2010) a total collapse of the Middle Eastern region as a consequence of inability to respond to ongoing modernization, resulting in mass migration to Europe.

[28]The more we talk about *the* Islam as a fundamental problem the more we dance to the tune of Al Qaeda and the like.

cause of the problem to be addressed. For the rest, leave the ongoing debate about the modernization of Islam to the national and international Muslim communities themselves. Such a strategy would probably have as a result that in the coming decades there would be marked differences between individual EU countries with respect to the persistence of the problematic nature of the Islamic dimension. Such differences would then mainly be caused by differences in content and timing of integration policies in the involved countries. Likewise, EU policy with respect to the Middle East would differ from country to country and would also take into account on a country-by-country basis the specific nature of the Islamic dimension.[29]

The West and the Rest

The West and the Rest are intimately connected with each other by ongoing modernization processes. This growing interconnectedness has developed itself since the European Renaissance. The road that led to this interconnectedness was bumpy, at times even rather bloody, and fed deeply-rooted cultures of superiority in the West and humiliation in the Rest.[30] I think we have now arrived at a period in time in which, *as far as ongoing modernization is concerned*, the overall global picture is becoming more and more diffuse, while historically-rooted cultures of superiority and humiliation are lagging behind in this process and remain more distinct. It is even more complex because cultures of hope and optimism are now emerging in the Rest and cultures of uncertainty and pessimism are becoming more dominant in the West. The point that I want to make is that when interests clash in the international arena the old superiority can still very quickly rankle the old humiliation, making it much more difficult to find a solution for the clashing of interests. The concept of "liberal world order" implies that the world is made up of countries that have a modern parliamentary democracy, rely on a capitalist mode of wealth creation and have an open society. If preaching the blessings of these three building blocks of a liberal world order by the West could be replaced by swapping uncertainties about how to deal

---

[29]See also Jan Michiel Otto (ed), *Sharia Incorporated: A Comparative Overview of the Legal Systems of Twelve Muslim Countries in Past and Present* (Leiden: Leiden University Press, 2010).

[30]Dominique Moisi, *The Geopolitics of Emotion* (New York: Anchor Books/Random House, 2010).

with complicated side effects of ongoing modernization, that would give an enormous boost to the emergence of a new more constructive and balanced type of interconnectedness.

A joint EU-U.S. capitalist democratic society 2.0 program could act as a powerful catalyst of such a switch, especially when such a program would be open to participants from the Rest. In the process such an initiative could also contribute to new optimism in the West. I used the term "catalyst" because change is in the air already in many ways. A dramatic example is that the West and the Rest are equally hijacked by Islamist terrorists of various backgrounds, being rather effective in triggering a culture of fear in their rearguard action against ongoing modernization, which therefore also triggers real cooperation between the West and the Rest. Old labels never die; they just fade away. Let us therefore not cling to these labels in actions and words any longer than is strictly necessary.

Conclusion

Writing this chapter turned out to be an inspiring journey for me personally. It remains to be seen whether the outcome of this journey can also contribute to the Transatlantic 2020 project. That could be best further explored by discussing at least the following questions:

— Did I hit upon some plausible deep currents related to immigration to Europe?

— Did I imagine some potentially meaningful and implementable responses to these deep currents?

— Are these outcomes relevant in a transatlantic context?

— On a more abstract level: could striving towards something like "capitalist democratic society 2.0" be a suitable lever for triggering constructive and inspiring processes of change in and of the liberal world order and between the "West and the Rest?"

Section V

Questions of Energy Sustainability

Chapter 9

Alternating Currents:
How Global and Domestic Energy Trends will
Affect the European Union, the United States,
and the Transatlantic Partnership in 2020

Alexander Ochs and Shakuntala Makhijani

Over the next decade, energy choices will play a central role in relations between countries, with resource constraints and climate change providing challenges as well as opportunities for international collaboration. As global economic leaders and major energy consumers, the European Union and the United States will be key actors in determining the direction of world energy trends.[1] In this article we examine continuities and changes in the past and present of EU and U.S. energy policies in order to discuss how they might look like a decade from now and to explore how these policies will shape transatlantic relations. In other words, we assess the transatlantic energy policy situation around the year 2020 based on an analysis of the current landscape, past trends, and an understanding of policy-making processes on both sides of the Atlantic. Insofar, it follows the hope that we can see the future, as "it is much like the present, only longer."[2]

Several factors, including physical, situational, ideological and institutional ones, interact to shape a country or region's energy policy. Naturally, available energy resources and technologies are first and

---

[1] It is likely that China and India will become the two largest energy markets in this century. Other key countries determining the future international energy system are the fossil-fuel rich nations, at least for a few more decades, and increasingly the countries that have committed themselves to develop sustainable energy systems based on renewable energy production and a highly efficient consumption.

[2] "I've seen the future and it's much like the present, only longer." Dan Quisenberry, pitcher for the Kansas City Royals. http://www.baseball-almanac.com/quotes/quoquis.shtml

fundamental determinants of energy strategies as they limit any actor's choices of what sources can be accessed. But strategic options are also influenced by socioeconomic, political and normative considerations, with some countries reluctant to prioritize renewable and efficient energy options despite their environmental, health, and long-term economic benefits until immediate technology installation costs become smaller and payback periods shorter. Other technical considerations like grid capacity and proximity of consumption centers to available energy resources and production sites can further limit the attractiveness for capitalizing on domestic, alternative energy sources.

The importance granted to energy security concerns also shapes policy decisions. Energy security considerations can lead countries to prioritize domestic resources to minimize foreign imports, especially due to risks from dependence on fossil fuels from politically unstable regions. Decision-makers also prioritize sustainability concerns differently. These include the environmental and public health impacts of various energy resources and, increasingly, climate-related goals that help determine limits on greenhouse gas emissions from energy use. Some governments still consider fossil fuels indispensable, while others emphasize longer-term national benefits from harnessing renewable resources.

The influence of these various factors on energy policy outcomes is not predetermined. Rather, it is defined by the political players in each country. Their actions, in turn, are influenced by the perceived political realities surrounding them, including the configuration of their "own" domestic political system. Forecasting the nature of EU and U.S. energy policies in 2020 thus requires predicting public decisions in the next ten years regarding, among others, energy resource deployment, energy security, climate, environmental and development policy goals as well as international geopolitical developments. Insofar, predicting future energy policy might be "very difficult" indeed.[3]

---

[3] "Prediction is very difficult, especially about the future." Neils Bohr, Nobel Prize winning physicist. http://en.wikiquote.org/wiki/Niels_Bohr

Power Differences: Current EU and U.S. Energy Portfolios

Understanding the current state of energy production and consumption in the EU and U.S. is essential for predicting future trends and policies. Resource constraints and sustainability pressures increasingly require a shift away from fossil fuel dependence. The 21st century energy system in many countries will feature energy efficiency, renewables, and smart grids as central components. Others will remain on a carbon-intense fossil-fueled path for some time. Transition versus stagnancy of the energy system is thus a key trend to analyze if we want to understand whether the transatlantic community is drifting apart or growing together in this issue area. This section provides an overview of domestic primary energy consumption in the EU and the U.S., with a particular look at renewable energy development over the past two decades.

Similar Mixes, Divergent Trends:
Electricity Generation and Energy Consumption

In 2009, U.S. electricity generation totaled 4.2 million gigawatt-hours (GWh), with fossil fuels accounting for 70 percent of this generation. Coal alone contributed 46 percent of U.S. electricity production. Nuclear power accounted for an additional 19 percent of generation, with the remaining 11 percent provided by renewable energy sources, mostly hydropower.

EU-27 electricity generation in 2009 was significantly lower than in the U.S., at 3.2 GWh. Fossil fuels provided just over half of this generation, with coal playing a much smaller role than in the U.S., contributing 27 percent of total production. Nuclear and renewable generation played a larger role in Europe, at 28 and 19 percent respectively, with hydropower accounting for over half of renewable generation. Figure 1 displays the U.S. and EU electricity generation mixes for comparison.

Growing versus Developing Rapidly:
Renewable Electricity Generation

Electricity generation from renewable sources grew much more rapidly in the EU than in the U.S. in the period from 1990 through

Figure 1. Shares of U.S. and EU Electricity Generation by Source, 2009

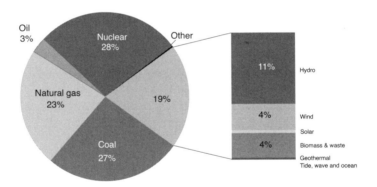

2009 U.S. Electricity Generation by Source

Oil 1%

Natural gas 23%

Nuclear 19%

Other

11%

Coal 46%

7%   Hydro

2%   Wind
     Solar
2%   Biomass & waste
     Geothermal

2009 EU Electricity Generation by Source

Oil 3%

Nuclear 28%

Other

Natural gas 23%

19%

Coal 27%

11%   Hydro

4%   Wind
     Solar
4%   Biomass & waste
     Geothermal
     Tide, wave and ocean

Worldwatch Institute, data source: World Energy Statistics (2011 Edition), Data Services. International Energy Agency, http://data.iea.org/ieastore/statslisting.asp

2009. In the EU-27 over this period, overall electricity generation grew by 24 percent, while renewable generation grew by 93 percent. In contrast, the 18 percent growth in renewable electricity generation in the U.S. for this period lagged behind the overall electricity generation increase of 30 percent.

The relative growth in solar and wind electricity generation in the U.S. and EU illustrate the much more rapid European expansion.

Figure 2. U.S. and EU Renewable Electricity Generation by Source, 1990–2009

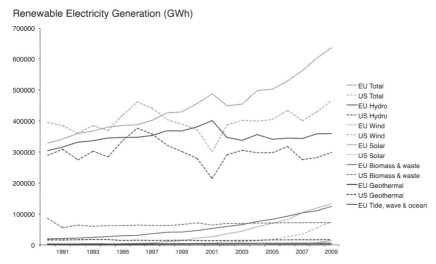

Renewable Electricity Generation (GWh)

Worldwatch Institute, data source: World Energy Statistics (2011 Edition), Data Services. International Energy Agency, http://data.iea.org/ieastore/statslisting.asp

Solar generation in the EU-27 increased over 1,000-fold from 1990 to 2009, while solar power in the U.S. increased less than 3-fold. Similarly, EU-27 wind generation increased by nearly 170 times over the same period, while the U.S. saw a significant but still far smaller 23-fold increase in wind generation from 1990 through 2009.

Figure 2 displays renewable electricity generation by source over the 1990 to 2009 period. Hydropower continues to dominate in both the U.S. and Europe, but wind generation growth is increasingly determining the path of overall renewable electricity growth. The quicker growth of renewables in Europe are not due to better potentials but the result of concrete targets and specific support mechanisms, as discussed below.

Energy Intensity, Energy Efficiency

The EU leads the U.S. in energy efficiency measures. In 2008, the energy intensity of the EU-27 was nearly one-third lower than the U.S. 7,603 Btu of primary energy consumption per 2005 USD, at

Figure 3. U.S. and EU Energy Intensity, 1990–2009

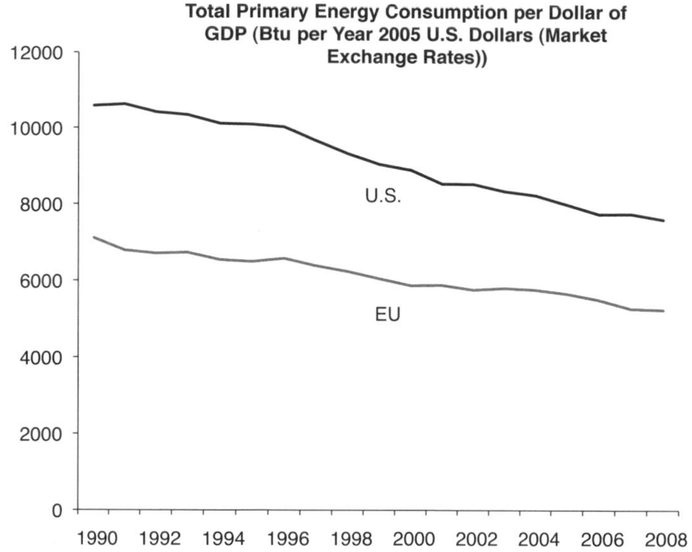

Total Primary Energy Consumption per Dollar of GDP (Btu per Year 2005 U.S. Dollars (Market Exchange Rates))

Worldwatch Institute, data source: World Energy Statistics (2011 Edition), Data Services. International Energy Agency, http://data.iea.org/ieastore/statslisting.asp

5,238 Btu.[4] Figure 3 tracks the decline in energy intensity in both regions, with the U.S. consistently higher than the EU-27. The lower energy intensity of the EU-27 is especially notable as it includes not only western European countries, but also outdated energy systems in new member states of central and eastern Europe. The EU-15 countries that are more comparable to the U.S. in terms of industrial development and other socioeconomic factors are about twice as efficient as the U.S. in terms of value of production per unit of energy consumed.

The U.S. also trails the EU in combined heat and power (CHP) generation, a process through which waste heat from electricity generation is recaptured for local heating uses. Efficiency rates for CHP systems range from 65 to 80 percent, compared with the average efficiency of 33 percent for conventional U.S. fossil fuel plants.[5] Electric

---

[4] International Energy Statistics, United States Energy Information Administration, site accessed 20 September 2011. http://www.eia.gov/cfapps/ipdbproject/IEDIndex3.cfm?tid=5&pid=53&aid=1

[5] "Efficiency Benefits," Combined Heat and Power Partnership, United States Envi-

power generation from CHP plants in the U.S. totaled 81.5 TWh in 2009,[6] compared to 366 TWh (11 percent of total electricity generation) in the EU in 2006. CHP generation accounts for 2 percent of the overall 20 percent energy efficiency improvement target set by the EU for 2020.[7]

Average energy consumption per person in the U.S. is more than twice that in Europe, at 330 million Btu per capita in the U.S. compared to 155 million Btu in the EU-27. Per capita consumption remained relatively stable for both the U.S. and Europe from 1990 through 2008.[8]

Grid Capacity and Energy Storage: Norwegian Water Storing German and Danish Wind

In terms of grid integration and storage considerations to accommodate new renewable capacity, Europe in general is farther along in creating incentives for advanced metering infrastructure, interconnections between different regional grids, and more integrated electricity markets—all of which contribute to grid flexibility and enable a higher share of renewable energies. As a result, regional grid capacity, though differing immensely within Europe, is in large parts of the continent well ahead of the outdated U.S. systems.

Renewable energies can be used off-grid (e.g., at the household level) and in micro-grids. For their large-scale, on-grid employment, however, due to their intermittencies, they need either very robust, smart, wide-ranging transmission lines bringing many different producers on-line, or "natural allies" of renewables like natural gas that can be fed into the grid to cover renewable production lows or con-

---

ronmental Protection Agency, site accessed 14 July 2011. http://www.epa.gov/chp/basic/efficiency.html

[6] "Useful Thermal Output by Energy Source by Combined Heat and Power Producers," Electricity, United States Energy Information Administration, site accessed 14 July 2011. http://www.eia.gov/cneaf/electricity/epa/epat2p2.html

[7] "Combined Heat and Power generation," Europa Press Release, 13 November 2008, http://europa.eu/rapid/pressReleasesAction.do?reference=MEMO/08/695&format=HTML

[8] International Energy Statistics, United States Energy Information Administration, site accessed 20 September 2011. http://www.eia.gov/cfapps/ipdbproject/IEDIndex3.cfm?tid=5&pid=53&aid=1

Figure 4. US and EU Energy-Related Carbon Dioxide Emissions

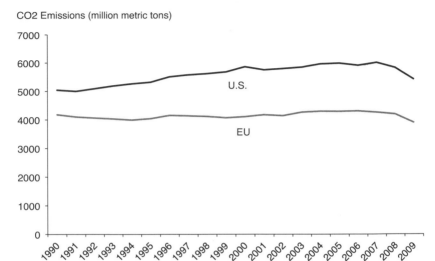

CO2 Emissions (million metric tons)

Worldwatch Institute, data source: International Energy Statistics, United States Energy Information Administration, site accessed 20 September 2011. http://www.eia.gov/cfapps/ipdbproject/IEDIndex3.cfm?tid=5&pid=53&aid=1

sumption peaks, or storage—and in the best case all of the above. So far, Scandinavian hydroelectric pumped storage capacity has been sufficient to buffer a lot of the recent growth in wind generation in Germany and Denmark, but this potential may be exhausted soon. As in the U.S., other grid-scale storage options have not yet become widespread, and excess wind power is frequently curtailed when the grid cannot accommodate it.

Carbon Emissions: Introducing One of the Greatest Polluters of All

U.S. energy-related carbon dioxide (CO_2) emissions increased nearly 16 percent between 1990 and 2008, from 5,020 to 5,810 million metric tons. In contrast, EU emissions fell more than 6 percent, on the path to compliance with Kyoto Protocol commitments. The United States is the world's second biggest greenhouse gas producer in the world, and has just recently been passed by China as the planet's number 1 polluter.

The carbon intensity of U.S. society becomes even more obvious if we look at energy-related per capita emissions. Whereas EU 27 citizens emit about 7.9 tons of CO_2 per capita per year, still well above world average, the average U.S. American releases 19.2 tons into the atmosphere. Only Canadians deplete more.[9]

What's Left, What's Renewable?
Fossil Resources and Alternative Energy Potentials in Europe and the United States

Availability of domestic fossil fuel resources can discourage countries from investing in renewable resources. This section examines fossil fuel reserves in the EU and the U.S. as well as the current exploitation and potential of renewable energies to describe what energy path both regions have taken in the past, and what their future options are.

Fossil Fuel Resources: Abundance and Scarcity

While both regions face diminishing oil reserves, the U.S. still enjoys relatively abundant coal and gas resources. In contrast, EU-27 domestic fossil fuel resources appear to be reaching a state of shortage. In the ten years leading up to 2007, annual decline in extraction averaged 4.9 percent for coal and lignite and 2.8 percent for crude petroleum and natural gas.[10] Net fossil fuel imports as a share of primary energy consumption increased from 47.8 percent in 2000 to 54.5 percent in 2007. The largest share of EU imports for all three fossil fuels now comes from Russia, with Norway providing significant additional oil and gas resources.[11]

Coal

Coal is still a dominant power source in both Europe and the U.S., but past trends and future projections of coal availability and consumption differ between the two.

---

[9] Climate Analysis Indicators Tool (CAIT) Version 8.0. (Washington, DC: World Resources Institute, 2011), http://cait.wri.org/

[10] "Energy extraction statistics," European Commission, Eurostat, site accessed 14 July 2011. http://epp.eurostat.ec.europa.eu/statistics_explained/index.php/Energy_extraction_statistics

[11] "ENER12 Net Energy Import Dependency." European Environment Agency, September 2010.

Figure 5. U.S. Coal Resources

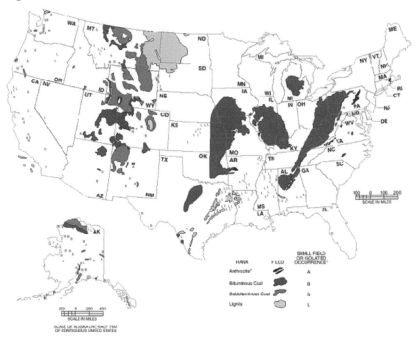

U.S. Coal Reserves: 1997 Update, U.S. Energy Information Administration.

Total U.S. recoverable coal reserves were estimated at 260 billion short tons in 2009, nearly 30 percent of the estimated world total.[12] At current rates of consumption, U.S. recoverable coal reserves would last 249 years. However, if EIA-projected coal consumption increases continue into the future, these reserves would be exhausted in 119 years.[13]

Figure 5 displays U.S. coal resources, which are mostly concentrated in Illinois, Kentucky and West Virginia (bituminous coal), and in Montana and Wyoming (subbituminous coal).

---

[12]International Energy Statistics, United States Energy Information Administration, accessed 20 September 2011. http://www.eia.gov/cfapps/ipdbproject/IEDIndex3.cfm?tid=5&pid=53&aid=1

[13]"Coal Explained: How Much Coal is Left," U.S. Energy Information Administration, site accessed 14 July 2011, http://www.eia.gov/energyexplained/index.cfm?page=coal_reserves

Figure 6. U.S. and EU Total Coal Consumption, 1990–2009

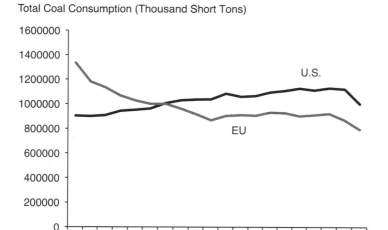

Total Coal Consumption (Thousand Short Tons)

Worldwatch Institute, data source: International Energy Statistics, United States Energy Information Administration, accessed 20 September 2011. http://www.eia.gov/cfapps/ipdbproject/IEDIndex3.cfm?tid= 5&pid=53&aid=1

Total recoverable coal reserves in the EU-27 were estimated at 62.9 billion short tons in 2009. At current rates of consumption, these reserves will last for 78 years. However, EU coal consumption has been steadily declining for the past two decades, which means that domestic reserves will likely last longer.[14]

Figure 6 displays coal consumption trends in the U.S. and EU-27 from 1990 to 2009. The significant divergence in these trends led the U.S. to surpass the EU-27 in coal consumption in 1996. Over the 20-year period, U.S. coal consumption increased by more than 10 percent, in contrast to the dramatic 40 percent decline in EU-27 coal consumption.

EU-27 coal imports grew from 15 percent of consumption in 1990 to nearly 30 percent in 2009. Meanwhile, the EU-27 exported less than 5 percent of its coal consumption. In contrast, the U.S. imported

---

[14]International Energy Statistics, United States Energy Information Administration, accessed 20 September 2011. http://www.eia.gov/cfapps/ipdbproject/IEDIndex3. cfm?tid=5&pid=53&aid=1

only 2 percent of its coal consumption in 2009, and exported 6 percent. However, U.S. coal imports increased more than five-and-a-half times from 1990 to 2009, while exports dropped by almost half.[15]

In the U.S. especially, coal is hailed as a low-cost, domestic source of energy. However, this cheap abundance already shows signs of decline. Furthermore, there are significant health and environmental costs from coal mining, production and combustion that are not reflected in the production cost paid by electricity producers (or the electricity price paid by consumers) but need to be covered by the society as a whole. A recent study published by the New York Academy of Sciences compiled data on the range of coal energy costs to determine its unaccounted-for external costs, summarized below.[16]

As coal is often used as a substitute energy source when oil and natural gas become too expensive, its prices respond to fluctuations in those markets. This sensitivity combined with increasing electricity demand worldwide caused global coal prices to more than double from $41 to $85 per ton from March 2007 to March 2008 and remain above $70 in 2010. Furthermore, estimates of coal reserves typically do not take profitability into account or fully consider geologic, economic, legal and transportation constraints for expanding coal mining, which means that the economically competitive coal reserves might not last more than two or three decades.

Coal electricity production from mining to combustion causes significant environmental damage, despite regulations on some impacts. Coal is the most carbon-intensive major source of energy, emitting 1.5 times as much carbon dioxide as oil and twice as much as natural gas for the same amount of energy produced. Although coal generated 50 percent of U.S. electricity in 2005, it accounted for 81 percent of electricity-related carbon emissions. With greenhouse gas emissions now a central energy-related environmental concern, high carbon intensity is a major drawback for expansion of coal generation.

---

[15] Ibid.

[16] Paul R. Epstein, Jonathan J. Buonocore, Kevin Eckerle, Michael Hendryx, Benjamin M. Stout III, Richard Heinberg, Richard W. Clapp, Beverly May, Nancy L. Reinhart, Melissa M. Ahern, Samir K. Doshi, and Leslie Glustrom. 2011. Full cost accounting for the life cycle of coal in "Ecological Economics Reviews." Robert Costanza, Karin Limburg & Ida Kubiszewski, Eds. Ann. N.Y. Acad. Sci. 1219: 73–98.

Coal releases tons of numerous additional toxic and carcinogenic substances into the environment through mining, processing and combustion, including mercury, lead, cadmium, arsenic, manganese, beryllium, chromium, nitrous oxides, sulfur dioxide and particulate matter. These have significant public health and ecological impacts through contamination of air and water resources. All in all, the study's best estimate for U.S. coal externality costs in 2008 was $345.3 billion, or 17.84 cents per kWh. This dramatic figure suggests that if the full environmental and health costs of energy sources were taken into account, coal would be much more costly and a range of renewable energy sources would become cost competitive.[17]

Oil

Petroleum consumption in the U.S. and Europe is mostly linked to transportation. In 2009, transportation accounted for 72 percent of U.S. oil consumption. Domestic reserves of oil in both regions are in decline and imports are increasing. While the EU is dealing with its constrained oil supply by limiting consumption, the U.S. is turning to increasingly aggressive and environmentally harmful methods of expanding U.S. oil production.

Figure 7 shows the trends of oil consumption in the U.S. and EU since 1990. EU oil consumption has been in steady decline since 2005, while U.S. oil consumption began to increase again in 2010 after a few years of decline. Since 1990, U.S. oil consumption has increased by 13 percent, while EU-27 consumption increased by only 4 percent.

EU-27 oil production has also seen a downward trend for over a decade, unlike U.S. production, which has increased.[18]

U.S. proved crude oil reserves were estimated at 20.7 billion barrels in 2009, down more than 20 percent since 1990.[19] Most of these reserves are concentrated in Texas, Alaska and California, as well as offshore in the Gulf of Mexico.[20] U.S. oil consumption in 2010 was 7

---

[17]Ibid.

[18]Ibid.

[19]Ibid.

[20]"U.S. Crude Oil, Natural Gas, and Natural Gas Liquids Proved Reserves, 2009," Natural Gas, United States Energy Information Administration, 30 November 2010,

Figure 7. U.S. and EU-27 Petroleum Consumption, 1990–2010

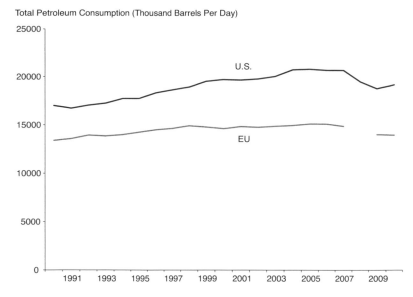

Worldwatch Institute, data source: International Energy Statistics, United States Energy Information Administration, accessed 20 September 2011. http://www.eia.gov/cfapps/ipdbproject/IEDIndex3.cfm?tid= 5&pid=53&aid=1

billion barrels, of which only half was met with domestic production despite fairly steady increases in annual production over the past two decades.[21]

EU-27 proved oil reserves are much lower and in faster decline than in the U.S. Proved oil reserves in the EU-27 in 2011 are estimated at 5.8 billion barrels, down 37 percent from 9.2 billion barrels in 2000. The United Kingdom holds nearly half of these remaining reserves, with most of the rest located in Denmark, Romania, Italy and the Netherlands.[22] European oil consumption in 2010 was 5.1 billion

http://www.eia.gov/oil_gas/natural_gas/data_publications/crude_oil_natural_gas_res erves/cr.html

[21]International Energy Statistics, United States Energy Information Administration, accessed 20 September 2011. http://www.eia.gov/cfapps/ipdbproject/IEDIndex3. cfm?tid=5&pid=53&aid=1

[22]Ibid.

Figure 8. U.S. and EU-27 Oil Imports, 1990–2007

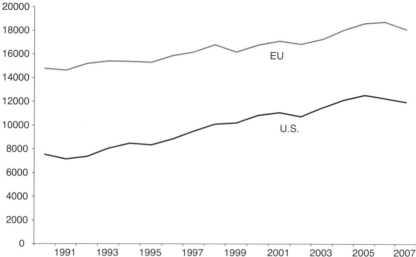

Total Oil Imports - Crude Oil & Refined Petroleum Products (Thousand Barrels Per Day)

Worldwatch Institute, data source: International Energy Statistics, United States Energy Information Administration, accessed 20 September 2011. http://www.eia.gov/cfapps/ipdbproject/IEDIndex3.cfm?tid=5&pid=53&aid=1

barrels (nearly equivalent to reserve levels) while production was only 1 billion barrels, leaving Europe highly dependent on imports.

Figure 8 displays average daily oil import trends in the U.S. and the EU. Despite the EU-27 countries' lower level of oil consumption, the region still imports more oil than the U.S. due to fewer domestic resources. Imports are rising in both the U.S. and Europe as domestic supplies decline.

Canada is the largest single-country source of U.S. oil imports, accounting for 21 percent of imports in 2010. Nevertheless, the U.S. still relies heavily on OPEC for its oil supply, which made up 49 percent of 2010 U.S. oil imports.[23]

---

[23]"U.S. Imports by Country of Origin," Petroleum & Other Liquids, United States Energy Information Administration, site accessed 20 September 2011, http://www.eia.gov/dnav/pet/pet_move_impcus_a2_nus_epc0_im0_mbblpd_a.htm

The EU-27 receives the largest share of its oil imports from the former Soviet Union, with Russia alone providing 30 percent of EU oil imports in 2010. African imports provided the next largest share at 22 percent, half of which came from Libya. The Middle East and other European countries combined accounted for most of the remaining one-third of EU-27 oil imports.[24]

In an attempt to expand domestic oil production despite declining reserves, the U.S. is turning to increasingly controversial resources. The Obama Administration is moving forward with granting permits for offshore drilling,[25] despite the April 2010 BP oil rig explosion which killed 11 workers and resulted in widespread economic and environmental damage.[26,27]

The Pacific Outer Continental Shelf (OCS) is another U.S. off-shore resource, currently producing about 61,100 barrels per day.[28] The total endowment including undiscovered resources is currently

---

[24] "Market observatory: EU Crude oil imports," 2010 (EU27) from non EU countries, European Commission, site accessed 20 September 2011. http://ec.europa.eu/energy/observatory/oil/import_export_en.htm

[25] "Remarks by the President on America's Energy Security," The White House, Office of the Press Secretary, 20 March 2011, http://www.whitehouse.gov/the-press-office/2011/03/30/remarks-president-americas-energy-security

[26] The spill was capped nearly two months after it began and only after releasing 4.9 million barrels of oil into the Gulf of Mexico. Since the oil spill, BP has reimbursed the Administration for over $700 million in clean-up costs including for compensation benefits, dissemination of public information, clean-up personnel, monitoring and assessment, and clean up equipment and materials. The BP oil spill caused serious economic disruptions to tourism and fisheries in addition to its ecological impacts to sea turtle and marine mammal populations.

[27] "BP/Transocean Deepwater Horizon Oil Rig Blowout," United States Chemical Safety Board, 20 April 2010, http://www.csb.gov/investigations/detail.aspx?SID=96; Joel Achenbach and David A. Fahrenthold, "Oil spill dumped 4.9 million barrels into Gulf of Mexico, latest measure shows, *The Washington Post*, 3 August 2010, http://www.washingtonpost.com/wp-dyn/content/article/2010/08/02/AR2010080204695.html; "Oil Spill Cost and Reimbursement Fact Sheet," RestoreTheGulf.gov, 12 July 2011, http://www.restorethegulf.gov/release/2011/07/12/oil-spill-cost-and-reimbursement-fact-sheet

[28] "Offshore Production, Development & Resources," United States Bureau of Ocean Energy Management, Regulation and Enforcement, site accessed 14 July 2011, http://www.boemre.gov/omm/pacific/production-development-resources/prod-dev-resource-eval.htm

13.05 billion barrels of oil, only 1.46 of which are economically recoverable reserves.[29] The risks and expense of offshore drilling draw into question the value of exploiting the relatively minor Pacific OCS reserve.

The Arctic National Wildlife Refuge (ANWR) in Alaska is another hotly contested domestic oil resource. While drilling advocates have argued for exploiting ANWR for oil despite its protected status as valuable wildlife habitat, the added resource would make little impact in national supply. According to 2008 U.S. Energy Information Administration (EIA) projections that assumed the start of ANWR oil production in 2018, annual production from the region would be expected to peak at around 780,000 barrels per day in 2027, compared to the projected national production peak at 6.3 million barrels per day in 2018. Cumulative ANWR oil production from 2018 through 2030 is projected at 2.6 billion barrels, less than half of what the U.S. currently consumes in one year. The market impacts of opening ANWR to oil drilling would likewise be miniscule, lowering global oil prices by only $0.75 per barrel in 2025, a small enough shift for OPEC countries to counteract by reducing their oil exports.[30]

The U.S. also relies on neighbor and friend Canada for 20 percent of its crude oil imports. Currently 40 percent of Canada's oil production comes from tar sands, a proportion that is rapidly expanding. Unlike liquid crude which is extracted through drilling, tar sands are accessed through open pit mining and refined to crude oil through an energy-intensive process. Producing one barrel of oil requires two tons of tar sands.[31] Most of Canada's tar sands are located in Alberta which had 170 billion barrels of oil recoverable at 2006 prices, making the country's oil reserves second only to Saudi Arabia. Canadian tar

---

[29]"Assessment of Undiscovered Technically Recoverable Oil and Gas Resources of the Nation's Outer Continental Shelf, 2006," United States Department of the Interior, Mineral Management Service, February 2006, http://www.boemre.gov/revaldiv/PDFs/2006NationalAssessmentBrochure.pdf

[30]"Analysis of Crude Oil Production in the Arctic National Wildlife Refuge," United States Energy Information Administration, May 2008, http://www.eia.gov/oiaf/servicerpt/anwr/results.html

[31]"About Tar Sands," Oil Shale & Tar Sands Programme EIS, Argonne National Laboratory, site accessed 14 July 2011, http://ostseis.anl.gov/guide/tarsands/index.cfm

sand production is rapidly increasing, growing from 760,000 to 1.3 million barrels per day from 2005 to 2006, and expected to reach at least 3.3 million barrels per day by 2020. Oil production from tar sands has serious environmental consequences, including water contamination and low rates of land reclamation following mining processes. It also emits higher levels of greenhouse gases than conventional oil, a step in the wrong direction given the urgency of addressing climate change.[32]

Improved fuel economy, advanced biofuels, improved public transportation systems, and commercialization of electric vehicles are all viable alternatives to the U.S. track of exploiting expensive and environmentally damaging offshore and unconventional oil resources. The EU has been much more proactive in implementing these alternative measures and steadily reducing oil consumption.

Natural Gas

The U.S. is one of the world's largest natural gas producers, and gas production has grown rapidly in recent years due to exploitation of shale gas reserves. In contrast, the European Union has far more limited gas reserves, both conventional and unconventional, and has been more conservative in tapping into shale gas resources.

Figure 9 displays U.S. and EU natural gas consumption since 1990, which shows overall higher levels in the U.S. and a recent decline in the EU.

The United States has long been one of the world's largest natural gas producers, and while rising production from other regions including the former Soviet Union and the Middle East have drawn market share from the U.S., it remains the source of almost one-fifth of global natural gas production today.[33] At the end of 2009, the U.S. had 272.5 trillion cubic feet (7.7 trillion cubic meters) of proved natural gas

---

[32]Schindler, David, "Tar sands need solid science," *Nature*, 25 November 2010, Vol. 468, Issue 7323, pp. 499-501, http://www.nature.com/nature/journal/v468/n7323/full/468499a.html

[33]BP, *Statistical Review of World Energy 2011*, site accessed 14 July 2011, http://www.bp.com/sectionbodycopy.do?categoryId=7500&contentId=7068481

Figure 9. U.S. and EU-27 Natural Gas Consumption, 1990–2009

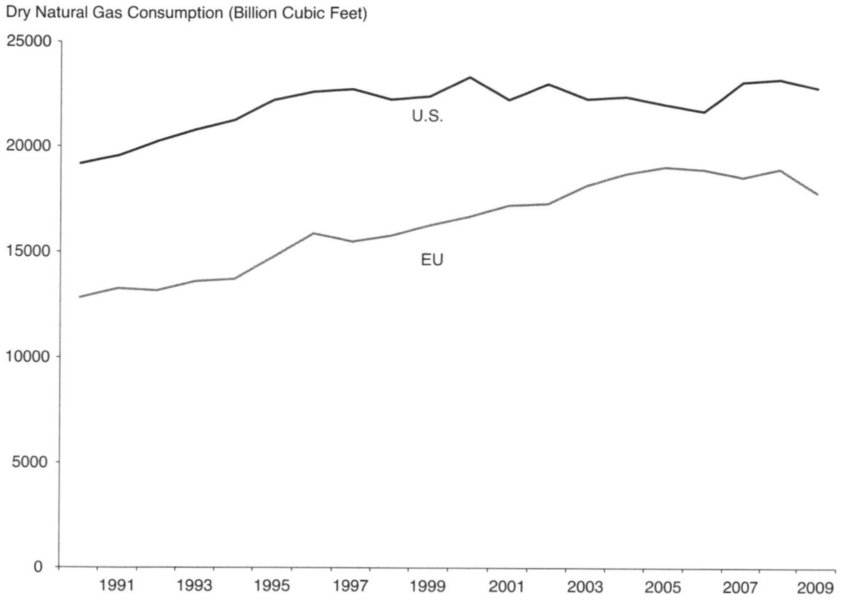

Dry Natural Gas Consumption (Billion Cubic Feet)

Worldwatch Institute, data source: International Energy Statistics, United States Energy Information Administration, accessed 20 September 2011. http://www.eia.gov/cfapps/ipdbproject/IEDIndex3.cfm?tid= 5&pid=53&aid=1

reserves, while the EU and Norway had a combined 158.3 trillion cubic feet (4.5 trillion cubic meters).[34]

Natural gas is the cleanest burning fossil fuel, emitting only half the amount of carbon dioxide as coal and two-thirds that of oil for the same amount of energy produced.[35] In the near- to midterm, natural gas can serve as a substitute for coal baseload power, and as a bridge technology to renewable energy sources. Because natural gas electricity can be quickly turned on and off, it can serve as an ally to renewable sources while new grid and storage solutions are still being developed to manage variability issues.

---

[34]Ibid.

[35]"Air Emissions," Clean Energy, United States Environmental Protection Agency, http://www.epa.gov/cleanenergy/energy-and-you/affect/air-emissions.html

In recent years, the U.S. has seen a boom in natural gas production, largely due to rapid growth (average annual rate of 48 percent between 2006 and 2010) in production from shale formations.[36] In 2009, shale gas made up about 16 percent of U.S. natural gas production, and the U.S. Energy Information Agency (EIA) projects that share could grow to 47 percent by 2035.[37] The EIA estimates technically recoverable shale gas resources in the U.S. to be 862 trillion cubic feet, equivalent to about 38 years of U.S. natural gas consumption at 2010 levels.[38]

The European Union, by contrast, accounted for only about one-twentieth of global natural gas production in 2010. Norway (not an EU member state) is by far the largest European producer of natural gas, with 3.3 percent of global natural gas production in 2010.[39]

European conventional natural gas production is expected to decline, potentially by 30 percent or more, by 2035, while natural gas demand continues to rise.[40] In the absence of a significant increase in domestic natural gas production, the EU will face growing import dependence. In an effort to diversify its natural gas supply mix (the current Russian dominance of which has proven dangerous to European energy security), the EU has pursued multiple policies, including the construction of pipelines to transport natural gas from the Caspian region to Southeastern Europe without transiting Russia and the construction of new import terminals for liquefied natural gas (LNG). Whereas the U.S. imported about 11 percent of the natural gas it consumed in 2010, many European countries imported more than 70 percent of their natural gas.[41]

---

[36]*Annual Energy Outlook 2011*, United States Energy Information Administration, site accessed 14 July 2011 http://www.eia.gov/forecasts/aeo

[37]Ibid.

[38]*World Shale Gas Resources: An Initial Assessment of 14 Regions Outside the United States* United States Energy Information Administration, April 2011, http://www.eia.gov/analysis/studies/worldshalegas/pdf/fullreport.pdf

[39]Ibid.

[40]*Impacts of shale gas and shale oil extraction on the environment and on human health*, European Parliament, Directorate-General for International Policies, Economic and Scientific Policy Department, 2011.

[41]*BP Statistical Review of World Energy 2011*, site accessed 14 July 2011 http://www.bp.com/sectionbodycopy.do?categoryId=7500&contentId=7068481

Figure 10. U.S. and EU-27 Natural Gas Imports, 1990–2009

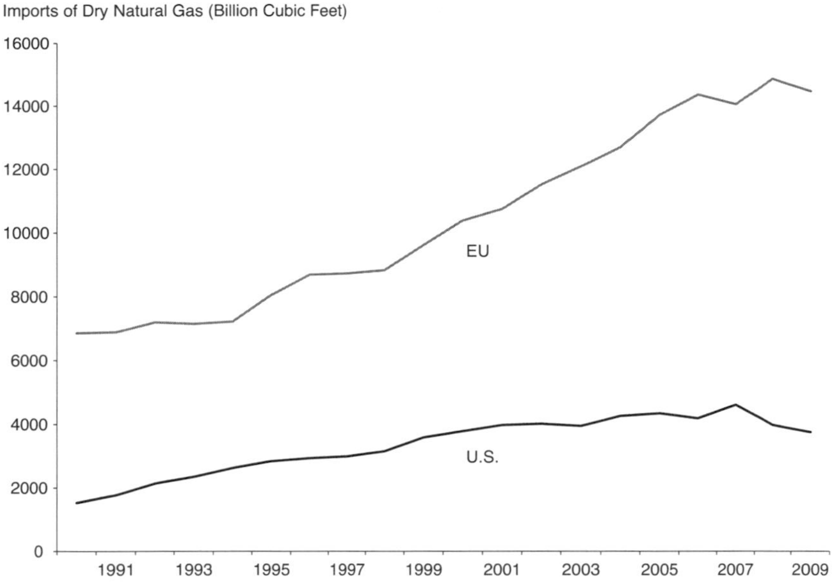

Imports of Dry Natural Gas (Billion Cubic Feet)

Worldwatch Institute, data source: International Energy Statistics, United States Energy Information Administration, accessed 20 September 2011. http://www.eia.gov/cfapps/ipdbproject/IEDIndex3.cfm?tid= 5&pid=53&aid=1

Figure 10 illustrates the rapid increase in EU-27 import dependence for natural gas supplies since 1990, while U.S. imports have been lower and increased more slowly. The recent shale gas boom has allowed for a decline in U.S. natural gas imports since 2007.[42]

Shale gas has been greeted by some within Europe as a potential solution to the energy security concerns caused by Europe's import dependence on Russia. The U.S. State Department, through the U.S. Shale Gas Initiative, has also sought to promote responsible shale gas develop in certain European countries with at least one stated purpose being the strengthening of regional energy security.[43] Some have also proposed that given its lower carbon content and the higher efficiency

---

[42]International Energy Statistics, United States Energy Information Administration, accessed 20 September 2011. http://www.eia.gov/cfapps/ipdbproject/IEDIndex3. cfm?tid=5&pid=53&aid=1

[43]"Global Shale Gas Initiative," United States Department of State, site accessed 14 July 2011, http://www.state.gov/s/ciea/gsgi/index.htm

of the power plants in which it is used, that new supplies of natural gas from shale could enable some European countries (i.e. countries such as Poland with high coal dependence) to mitigate greenhouse gas emissions associated with their power sectors.

However, the extent to which estimated shale reserves could provide enough production to significantly change the energy mix or energy security is a matter of debate. Perceptions vary significantly from country to country, and officials in countries such as France and Germany have justifiably argued that any incremental natural gas supplies could displace renewable or nuclear power, rather than coal. The EIA estimates technically recoverable natural gas from shale basins in 14 European countries to be about 639 trillion cubic feet, or about 44 years of those countries' natural gas consumption in 2009.[44] Some 70 percent of these reserves are located in Poland, France, and Norway.[45]

The environmental and public health impacts of producing shale gas in Europe have been the subject of much debate. Critics have argued that Europeans would not tolerate the number of instances in the U.S. of water and land contamination with methane, leaked or spilled fracturing fluids and high-saline produced water, air pollution, well blowouts, and community impacts such as noise and light pollution. Many suggest that in Europe, higher population density and lower water availability will make widespread shale gas production much more difficult than in the United States. In addition, unlike in many parts of the United States where individual land-owners hold the rights to minerals below their property and therefore have strong financial incentives to allow drilling on their land, in most European countries the government retains the rights to all minerals, and land-owners have a far lower incentive to allow drilling, especially if it is perceived to be environmentally risky.

At the very least, most Europeans who believe that shale gas development could benefit Europe argue that member countries must avoid repeating the mistakes of the U.S. shale gas boom by waiting for

---

[44]*World Shale Gas Resources: An Initial Assessment of 14 Regions Outside the United States*, United States Energy Information Administration, April 2011, http://www.eia.gov/analysis/studies/worldshalegas/pdf/fullreport.pdf

[45]Ibid.

the results of extensive environmental impact studies before permitting drilling and by creating much stricter regulations governing drilling and hydraulic fracturing. In combination with a much lower availability of drilling rigs in Europe than existed in the U.S. at the onset of the shale gas boom, that political reality will almost certainly result in a much slower pace of shale gas development than has been seen in the U.S.

The Nuclear Option: A Fallout Everywhere

Even before the nuclear tragedy in Fukushima in the summer of 2011, nuclear power globally was the only energy source with negative growth in recent years. Nuclear power generation declined for the fourth year in a row in 2009, falling by 2 percent. The European Union still accounts for about half of nuclear generation worldwide, with France accounting for about half of that. The U.S. follows Europe, contributing almost one-third of world nuclear generation.

The U.S. is currently operating 104 commercial nuclear reactors, more than any other country, and with a combined capacity of 101 GW in 2009.[46] However, no successful orders for new plants have been placed since 1973, and 138 reactor projects have been cancelled. The last U.S. reactor was completed in 1996.

Of 28 recent license applications, four nuclear power plant projects had been granted early site permits as of February 2011, which some have taken as indication of a nuclear renaissance. However, none of the reactor designs for these projects have been approved, and those plants in competitive markets will require loan guarantees which could involve prohibitively high fees. The remaining 24 applications have been cancelled, suspended or delayed. Despite the permitting difficulties for nuclear power projects, the long hiatus and slow restart to new investments are not due lack of permits but rather the unwillingness of utilities to cover the financial risks of nuclear power without state guarantees.

---

[46]"U.S. Nuclear Generation and Generating Capacity," United States Energy Information Adminsitration, 18 August 2011, site accessed 20 September 2011, http://www.eia.gov/cneaf/nuclear/page/nuc_generation/gensum.html

EU-27 installed nuclear capacity was 133 GW in 2004, just under half of which was located in France, which is the greatest exception to Europe's overall nuclear phase-out.[47] Nuclear power in Europe is following the global downward trend with 143 operational plants as of April 1, 2011, compared to the maximum of 177 plants in 1989, as aging reactors are being retired much more quickly than new ones are being considered for construction. The vast majority of these plants are in the original EU-15 member states, where currently only two new plants are under construction. Two additional plants are under construction in the new member states, with four more in planning stages, and expansion approved for two existing plants.

Phase-out plans in many EU countries are contributing to the transition away from nuclear power. In the wake of the Fukushima disaster, the German government accelerated its phase-out schedule, committing in May 2011 to shut down all of the country's nuclear reactors by 2022. In 2009, Lithuania ended its nuclear power program by shutting down its only plant, a Chernobyl-style reactor that accounted for 76 percent of the country's electricity generation. Other European countries have taken initial steps. Belgium is currently considering a phase out program, Spain has a policy of no new nuclear construction, and Sweden only allows new reactor construction if an existing plant is shut down.

Nuclear power countries around the world are rethinking nuclear safety issues in light of the ongoing Fukushima crisis. The accident bankrupted the world's fourth largest power company, demonstrating the tremendous financial risks of nuclear power. Lifetime extensions for operating plants will also be reconsidered, as older reactors present a greater safety concern.

The U.S. response to Fukushima was mixed. Interestingly, major nuclear energy companies such as Exelon and NRG were the most forthcoming about the economic unviability of future nuclear construction. Republican lawmakers and Energy Department officials on the other hand continue to emphasize nuclear power as an important

---

[47]"EU electricity market: Wind powered electricity generating capacity increased over 150% in the EU25 since 2000," Europa Press Release, 22 May 2006, http://europa.eu/rapid/pressReleasesAction.do?reference=STAT/06/66&format=HTML&aged=0

part of future U.S. energy development, despite the need to prioritize safety above all other concerns.

Reactions in the EU were generally more cautious. Just days after the Fukushima disaster began, EU Energy Commissioner Günther Oettinger put forth the idea of a nuclear energy-free Europe in the foreseeable future. Shortly thereafter, the European Council called for safety reviews and assessments in all EU nuclear plants and a review of current safety regulations.[48]

Nuclear power will play a diminishing role in the future in both the U.S. and the EU as old plants are decommissioned, and despite some remaining U.S. enthusiasm for new nuclear projects, new capacity cannot keep pace with the retirement of existing nuclear plants. Security issues, waste and safety concerns are major contributors to the decline, but the excessive costs and siting issues with nuclear plants and waste facilities will continue to pose the greatest barrier to new nuclear investment.

Renewable Energy: Great Unused Potential

The EU has demonstrated greater urgency in transitioning to renewable energy due to its more limited availability of domestic fossil fuel resources compared to the U.S. Climate change concerns related to greenhouse gas emissions from fossil fuel combustion should be a major in both the U.S. and Europe. This section examines the existing capacity, generation and resource potential of various renewable energy sources in the U.S. and EU to determine where the major areas of past development have occurred, and what renewable resources provide the greatest opportunities for future expansion.

Hydropower

The U.S. and Europe have similar hydropower profiles, both in terms of existing capacity, share of electricity generation, and potential for future hydro development. Between 1998 and 2009, conventional

---

[48]Mycle Schneider, Antony Froggatt and Steve Thomas, "The World Nuclear Industry Status Report 2010-2011: Nuclear Power in a Post-Fukushima World," Worldwatch Institute, April 2011, http://www.worldwatch.org/system/files/pdf/WorldNuclearIndustryStatusReport2011_%20FINAL.pdf

hydropower generated between six and nine percent of U.S. electricity, with the variation due to water availability fluctuations.[49] Hydropower accounted for over 60 percent of U.S. renewable electricity generation in 2009.[50] Large hydro accounts for 80 percent of hydro generation, with small-scale plants making up the remaining 20 percent.[51] In 2008, hydropower provided 10 percent of EU-27 electricity production, and accounted for 63 percent of renewable electricity generation.[52] EU-27 total installed hydro capacity is about 102 GW, 90 percent of which is provided by large hydropower plants.

As for additional hydro potential, according the Department of Energy, the U.S. currently has about 80 gigawatts (GW) of installed hydroelectric capacity, with an additional 30 GW of undeveloped capacity at 5,677 sites.[53] A 2004 joint study by Idaho National Laboratory and the U.S. Geological Survey identified 18 GW of small hydro potential at 5,400 sites.[54] Over half of favorable sites for hydro development in the EU-27 have already been exploited, and environmental and technical concerns make expansion to additional large-scale sites unlikely. Expansion of hydro generation will most likely come from

[49]"Hydropower has a long history in the United States," United States Energy Information Administration, 8 July 2011, site accessed 14 July 2011, http://www.eia.gov/todayinenergy/detail.cfm?id=2130

[50]http://www.eia.gov/energyexplained/index.cfm?page=electricity_in_the_united_states

[51]Douglas G. Hall, et al. "Feasibility Assessment of the Water Energy Resources of the United States for New Low Power and Small Hydro Classes of Hydroelectric Plants," United States Department of Energy, Office of Energy Efficiency and Renewable Energy, January 2006, http://www1.eere.energy.gov/windandhydro/pdfs/doewater-11263.pdf

[52]"Hydropower" European Commision Strategic energy technologies information system, site accessed 14 July 2011, http://setis.ec.europa.eu/technologies/Hydropower/print_version

[53]"Hydropower Resource Potential," United States Department of Energy Office of Energy Efficiency and Renewable Energy, Wind & Water Power Program, site accessed 14 July 2011, http://www1.eere.energy.gov/windandhydro/hydro_potential.html

[54]Douglas G. Hall, et al. "Feasibility Assessment of the Water Energy Resources of the United States for New Low Power and Small Hydro Classes of Hydroelectric Plants," United States Department of Energy, Office of Energy Efficiency and Renewable Energy, January 2006, http://www1.eere.energy.gov/windandhydro/pdfs/doewater-11263.pdf

new low head plants and improvements to existing plants. If significant investments occur in these areas, large and small hydro capacity could increase to 112 and 19 GW by 2030, respectively.[55]

Wind

U.S. wind generation grew by 33.5 percent in 2009 to reach 73.9 TWh, or 1.9 percent of total electricity generation. Installed wind capacity 2009 was 34.3 GW.[56] In 2010 it accounted for 11 percent of primary renewable energy consumption, up from just 4 percent in 2006.[57] Despite the still relatively low share of total generation, new wind power has grown at a faster rate than any other electricity source for several years.[58] A 2010 study estimated U.S. wind energy potential capacity at nearly 11,000 GW and over 38,000 terawatt hours (TWh) of potential generation,[59] ten times the 3,741 TWh of all electricity consumed in the United States in 2009.[60]

Wind power is experiencing even more rapid growth in Europe, where it has accounted for one-third of new electricity generating capacity since 2000.[61] In 2008, 65 GW of installed wind capacity gen-

---

[55]"Hydropower Generation," European Commision Strategic energy technologies information system, site accessed 14 July 2011, http://setis.ec.europa.eu/newsroom-items-folder/hydropower-generation

[56]"Wind," United States Energy Information Adminsitration, January 2011, site accessed 14 Juyl 2011, http://www.eia.gov/cneaf/solar.renewables/page/wind/wind.html

[57]"Renewable Energy Consumption and Electricity Preliminary Statistics 2010," United States Energy Information Administration, 28 June 2011, site accessed 14 July 2011, http://www.eia.gov/renewable/annual/preliminary/

[58]"Wind," United States Energy Information Adminsitration, January 2011, site accessed 14 Juyl 2011, http://www.eia.gov/cneaf/solar.renewables/page/wind/wind.html

[59]"New Wind Resource Maps and Wind Potential Estimate for the United States," United States Department of Energy Office of Energy Efficiency and Renewable Energy, 19 February 2010, site accessed 14 July 2011, http://www.windpoweringamerica.gov/filter_detail.asp?itemid=2542

[60]International Energy Statistics, United States Energy Information Administration, accessed 20 September 2011. http://www.eia.gov/cfapps/ipdbproject/IEDIndex3.cfm?tid=5&pid=53&aid=1

[61]"Wind Energy," European Commission Research & Innovation, site accessed 14 July 2011, http://ec.europa.eu/research/energy/eu/research/wind/index_en.htm

erated 4.2 percent of total EU electricity.[62] Wind energy production is unevenly distributed the EU, with over two-thirds of the total installed capacity located in Germany, Spain and Denmark.[63] Based on environmental, technical and economic considerations, the European Environment Agency estimates wind electricity generation potential in 2020 at 9,600 terawatt hours (TWh) onshore and 2,600 TWh offshore, more than triple the projected demand for that year.[64]

Solar

Solar power production is increasing in both the U.S. and Europe, but the solar expansion is much more rapid in the EU due to effective policy measures of several European countries to promote solar development. Both regions have vast untapped solar potential, but the main drivers of solar power development are policies and incentives, not resource availability.

U.S. thermal and photovoltaic solar energy consumption is growing rapidly, at average annual rate of 12 percent between 2006 and 2010.[65] Nevertheless, it still accounted for only 0.2 percent of renewable electricity generation.[66] Installed solar photovoltaic (PV) and thermal capacity reached 603 MW by 2009.[67] Solar PV energy accounted for 2.2 percent of total EU electricity capacity in 2009, but only 0.4 per-

[62]"Europe's onshore and offshore wind energy potential," European Environment Agency, 2009.

[63]"Wind Energy Technical Background," European Commission Research & Innovation, site accessed 14 July 2011, http://ec.europa.eu/research/energy/eu/research/wind/background/index_en.htm

[64]"Europe's onshore and offshore wind energy potential," European Environment Agency, 2009.

[65]"Renewable Energy Consumption and Electricity Preliminary Statistics 2010," United States Energy Information Administration, 28 June 2011, site accessed 14 July 2011, http://www.eia.gov/renewable/annual/preliminary/

[66]"Renewable Energy Consumption for Electricity Generation by Energy Use Sector and Energy Source, 2004-2008," United States Energy Information Administration, August 2010, http://www.eia.gov/cneaf/solar.renewables/page/rea_data/table1_3.pdf

[67]"U.S. Electric Net Summer Capacity," United States Energy Information Administration, August 2010, site accessed 14 July 2011, http://www.eia.gov/cneaf/alternate/page/renew_energy_consump/table4.html

cent of generation due to variability.[68] PV installations increased by 5.8 GW (21 percent of total new capacity) to reach 16 GW at the end of 2009.[69] PV additions accelerated in 2010 with an estimated 10 GW of new capacity that year.[70] Planned CSP installation in the EU is mostly centered in southern Europe, especially Spain, where the solar resource is strongest. Projects currently underway in the region will bring total CSP capacity to 4 GW in 2012.[71]

A 2009 article in *Energy Policy* described the vast potential for solar PV and concentrated solar power (CSP) to meet U.S. energy needs. The study examined technical, geographical and economic considerations and found that solar generation for the grid could be cost-competitive by 2020, and meet 69 percent of U.S. electricity (35 percent of total energy) needs by 2050.[72] Best estimates for solar PV potential in the EU-27 are greater than 1,500 TWh per year, boosted to more than 2,000 TWh with the inclusion of Turkey and Croatia.[73] Best CSP potential in Europe is concentrated in the Mediterranean countries. Potential for capacity and generation in this region is estimated at 30 GW and 85 TWh per year in 2020, and 60 GW and 170 TWh per year in 2030. This significant expansion will capitalize on further cost reductions, as the European Commission states that CSP energy could be cost competitive as soon as 2015.[74]

---

[68]"EU leading the way in newly installed solar cells," European Commission Joint Research Centre, 6 September 2010, site accessed 14 July 2011, http://ec.europa.eu/dgs/jrc/index.cfm?id=1410&obj_id=11380&dt_code=NWS&lang=en

[69]Ibid.

[70]"Solar Photovoltaic," European Commission Strategic energy technologies information system, site accessed 14 July 2011, http://setis.ec.europa.eu/technologies/Solar-photovoltaic/info

[71]"Concentrated Solar Power Technical Background," European Commission Research & Innovation, site accessed 14 July 2011, http://ec.europa.eu/research/energy/eu/research/csp/background/index_en.htm

[72]Vasilis Fthenakis, James E. Mason and Ken Zweibel, "The technical, geographical, and economic feasibility for solar energy to supply the energy needs of the US," *Energy Policy*, February 2009, Vol. 37, Issue 2, pp. 387-399, http://www.sciencedirect.com/science/article/pii/S0301421508004072

[73]Thomas Winkel et al. "Potential of Solar Energy: A literature study on European potential assessments," EcoFys, June 2009, http://eea.eionet.europa.eu/Public/irc/eionet-circle/energy/library?l=/environment_10-1105/potential_finalpdf/_EN_1.0_&a=d

[74]"Concentrated Solar Power Technical Background," European Commission

Figure 11. Top 10 Countries with Greatest Installed Solar Capacity, 2010

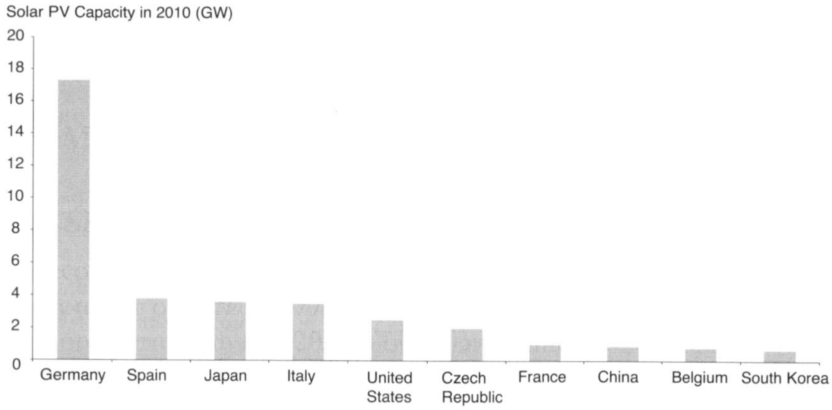

Solar PV Capacity in 2010 (GW)

Worldwatch Institute, data source: "Renewables 2011: Global Status Report," REN21 Renewable Energy Policy Network for the 21st Century, 2011, REN21 Secretariat.

A Matter of Political Will

The importance of policies and incentives to promote solar development can be seen in the case of Germany, which is by far the world leader in total installed solar PV capacity. Figure 11 shows Germany leading the top ten countries with the greatest installed PV capacity of 17.3 GW in 2010, nearly seven times greater than the U.S. PV capacity of 2.5 GW that year.

As the maps in Figure 12 illustrate, this impressive capacity is not due to a favorable solar resource, which in fact is fairly weak in Germany compared to the U.S., but because of political will to incentivize solar development.

Figure 13 tracks the rapid increase in Germany's renewable electricity generation in response to several effective policies.

Research & Innovation, site accessed 14 July 2011, http://ec.europa.eu/research/energy/eu/research/csp/background/index_en.htm

Figure 12. Photovoltaic Solar Resource: United States and Germany

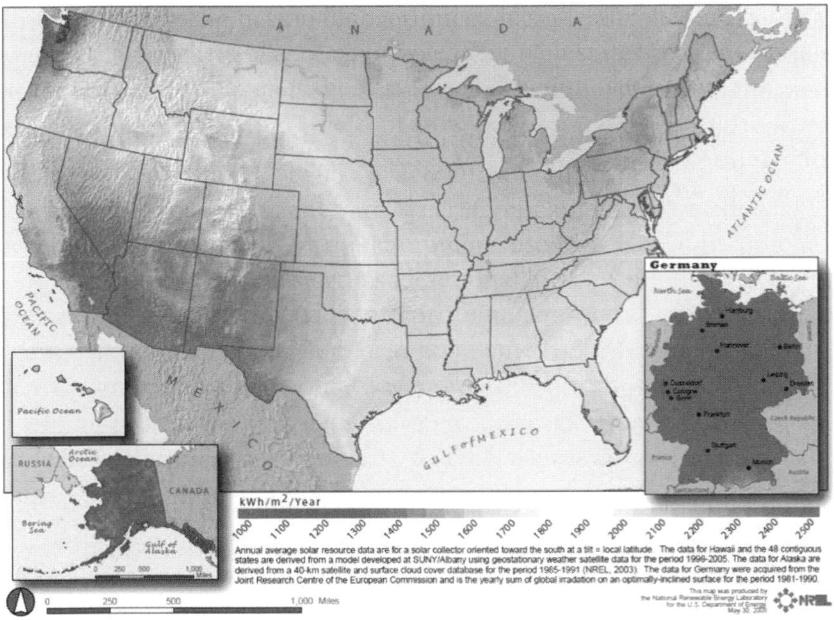

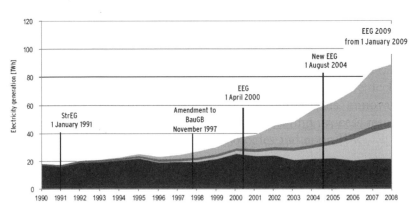

United States National Renewable Energy Laboratory.

Figure 13. Renewable Electricity Generation Growth and Policies in Germany, 1990–2008

German Ministry of the Environment, 2009.

Biomass

Biomass accounted for over half of U.S. primary renewable energy consumption in 2010.[75] Biomass consumption grew by over 30 percent between 2006 and 2010, with the change mostly driven by a more than doubling of biofuel (ethanol and biodiesel) consumption for transportation which now accounts for nearly half of overall biomass consumption.[76] Installed biomass electricity generating capacity reached 11.4 GW in 2009 and generated 55.4 terwatt-hours (TWh).[77] The U.S. produced 10.6 billion gallons of ethanol and 12 million gallons of biodiesel in 2009.[78]

The European Union required that biofuels displace diesel and petroleum consumption by accounting for 5.75 percent of transportation fuel consumption by 2010. An estimated 4 to 13 percent of total EU agricultural land was required to produce this amount of biofuels. The EU Biofuels Research Advisory Council estimated that the EU could sustainably meet one-quarter of its transportation fuel needs with biofuels by 2030.[79]

Biomass provided 802 TWh of EU energy generation in 2003, accounting for 4 percent of energy use. The European Union set targets to reach 722 TWh of biomass heat and 162 TWh of biomass electricity by 2010, and increase the share of biofuels in oil consumption to 10 percent by 2020.[80] An analysis by the European Environ-

---

[75]"Renewable Energy Consumption and Electricity Preliminary Statistics 2010," United States Energy Information Administration, 28 June 2011, site accessed 14 July 2011, http://www.eia.gov/renewable/annual/preliminary/

[76]"U.S. Energy Consumption by Source, 2006-2010," United States Energy Information Administration, sitea accessed 14 July 2011, http://www.eia.gov/renewable/annual/preliminary/pdf/table1.pdf

[77]"U.S. Electric Net Summer Capacity," United States Energy Information Administration, August 2010, site accessed 14 July 2011, http://www.eia.gov/cneaf/alternate/page/renew_energy_consump/table4.html

[78]Biomass Energy Data Book, United States Department of Energy Office of Energy Efficiency and Renewable Energy, 2010, site accessed 14 July 2011, http://cta.ornl.gov/bedb/biofuels.shtml

[79]"Biofuels in the European Union: A vision for 2030 and Beyond," Biofuels Research Advisory Council, 14 March 2006, http://ec.europa.eu/research/energy/pdf/draft_vision_report_en.pdf

[80]"Bioenergy," European Commission Research & Innovation, site accessed 14 July 2011, http://ec.europa.eu/research/energy/eu/research/bioenergy/index_en.htm

ment Agency (EEA) estimates that environmentally-compatible biomass energy generation could increase to nearly 3,500 TWh by 2030.[81]

There are limits to growth in the ability of biomass to meet future energy needs. Biomass and biofuel potential worldwide depends on the availability of land and resources to generate energy crops. A 2008 study found that only 5 percent of total global energy demand could be sustainably met with biomass energy, mostly through use of abandoned agricultural land, without negatively impacting climate or food security. Because biomass energy is mostly used for transportation fuels, alternative energy technologies such as plug-in hybrids and fuel cells are needed to substitute petroleum, in addition to the limited contribution from biofuels.

Geothermal

Currently, shallow geothermal resources provide most of the geothermal electric capacity in the U.S., with 2.8 GW installed in 2006. As technologies advance, developable resources are expected to expand further to co-produced and geopressured and deep geothermal resources providing more than an estimated 260 GW capacity of developable resources by 2050. Geothermal heat pumps provide the greatest current and projected thermal capacity, with 7.4 MW of developed thermal power in 2006, and more than 1,000 GW of developable resources estimated for 2050.[82]

The EU currently has 0.95 GW of operational geothermal electricity capacity which generates about 7,000 GWh each year. Direct and indirect thermal capacity is close to 9 GW and produces 23.6 TWh of heat annually.[83]

---

[81]"Biomass Potential in Europe," European Commission DG Environment News Alert Issue 5, January 2006, http://ec.europa.eu/environment/integration/research/newsalert/pdf/5na2.pdf

[82]Bruce D. Green and R. Gerald Nix, "Geothermal—The Energy under Our Feet: Geothermal Resource Estimates for the United States," United States National Renewable Energy Laboratory, November 2006, http://www1.eere.energy.gov/geothermal/pdfs/40665.pdf

[83]"Geothermal Energy Technical Background," European Commission Research & Innovation, site accessed 14 July 2011, http://ec.europa.eu/research/energy/eu/research/geothermal/background/index_en.htm

The European Commission estimates that the maximum capacity for geothermal electricity will reach 6 GW by 2020 and 8 GW by 2030, 1 and 1.3 percent of projected electricity demand in those years. Maximum geothermal capacity for heating is projected to reach 40 GW by 2020 and 70 GW by 2030.[84]

Summary

As the above overview reveals, the United States has significantly greater coal and natural gas resources than the European Union, and consumes those fossil energy sources at a greater rate. Both sides of the Atlantic face serious oil resource constraints, but continue to consume significant quantities by relying on imports. Nuclear generation and hydropower are stagnating or declining in both regions as a result of burdensome environmental, safety and financial concerns.

Due in part to its more limited fossil fuel resource base, the EU is expanding its renewable energy use much more rapidly than the U.S., despite comparable or even inferior physical resources. The EU leads in wind and biomass development, and its solar capacity and generation is several times that of the U.S.

Climate and Energy Policies and Politics in Europe and the United States

Examining past policy decisions in the U.S. and EU including climate and energy targets set by both can shed some light on what we might expect to see in the next decade.

Federal Goals: About Leaders and Laggards

The United States to date has failed to pass mandatory federal renewable energy or greenhouse gas emission standards. The passage of a comprehensive economy-wide cap-and-trade bill in the U.S. House of Representatives in 2009 provided some hope for progress, but the Senate's failure to even vote on a comparable bill in 2010 has left little chance for such a policy to be enacted at the federal level in the next couple of years or more.

---

[84]Ibid.

In contrast, the EU has passed renewable energy and greenhouse gas emission targets into law that are internationally recognized as ambitious and have established Europe's position as a global leader in promoting clean energy. Europe has demonstrated climate leadership by both pushing for binding and ambitious targets in the UN climate change negotiation process as well as leading by example through implementing strong support mechanisms at home. The central goals for 2020 are to reduce EU-27 greenhouse gas (GHG) emissions by 20 percent below 1990 levels, meet 20 percent of energy consumption with renewable energy, and increase energy efficiency by 20 percent above 2005 levels. The EU is on track to meet the 20 percent GHG target and even exceed its renewable energy goals, but is so far falling far short of energy efficiency targets.[85]

The EU adopted GHG reduction goals for 2020 in an extension of their Kyoto commitments to reduce emissions by 8 percent below 1990 levels from 2008 to 2012. The EU-15 (the original Member States that adopted this goal) had collectively reduced emissions by 6.9 percent below 1990 levels in 2008, putting the Kyoto target well in reach. Some countries within the EU have fallen short of emission reduction goals, but the overall EU progress is made possible by dramatic reductions elsewhere. France, Germany, Sweden and the UK, among others, have already exceeded their individual targets.[86]

Meanwhile, the EU-27 is moving forward with further goals. In addition to the unilateral 20 percent emission reduction by 2020 policy, the EU has also pledged to increase that ambition to a 30 percent reduction if other countries take comparable action. These reductions will be spread across the EU, with some countries like Germany taking on much stricter limits, while many new Member States in Central and Eastern Europe that are heavily coal-reliant and face substantial economic challenges will be granted more lenient targets and in some cases will even be allowed to increase emissions. While the 27 socioeconomically and politically diverse nations of the EU can agree

---

[85]"Energy Policy," European Environmental Bureau, site accessed 14 July 2011, http://www.eeb.org/index.cfm/activities/climate-energy/energy-policy/

[86]"EU greenhouse gas emissions: more than halfway to the '20% target by 2020'," European Environment Agency, 2 June 2010, http://www.eea.europa.eu/pressroom/newsreleases/eu-greenhouse-gas-emissions-more.

on such a "bubble," committing internationally to a joint reduction goal that is shouldered with common but differentiated responsibility, the United States has been unable to forge such agreement even at a national level.

The Importance of Policies at the State (U.S.) and Country (EU) Levels

Individual U.S. states have stepped up to try to fill the climate and energy policy vacuum left by the federal government. Twenty-three states have enacted greenhouse gas emission targets, albeit at varying levels of stringency and enforceability. California has established itself as a leader in climate policy, enacting the country's first state-level economy-wide GHG cap-and-trade program with enforceable penalties in 2006.[87]

Multi-state regional initiatives across the U.S. including the Midwest Greenhouse Gas Reduction Accord, Western Climate Initiative, and Regional Greenhouse Gas Initiative (RGGI) have also been implemented in the absence of a nationwide program. RGGI was established in 2005 as the first mandatory carbon dioxide cap-and-trade program in the U.S. to limit emissions from power plants. Currently, the ten northeastern and mid-Atlantic states participating in RGGI have committed to reduce power sector CO_2 emissions by 10 percent below 2009 levels by 2018.[88]

Overall, state-level and regional goals fall far short of EU-wide and most individual EU countries' goals. Starting in 2013 under the EU Emissions Trading System (ETS), all countries within the EU will be subject to the same rules for emission allowance allocations under a single EU-wide cap, meaning that individual country plans for GHG reductions within ETS sectors will not be necessary.[89] However, for sec-

[87]"Greenhouse Gas Emission Targets," Pew Center on Global Climate Change, site accessed 14 July 2011, http://www.pewclimate.org/sites/default/modules/usmap/pdf.php?file=5902

[88]"Fact Sheet: The Regional Greenhouse Gas Initiative (RGGI)," Regional Greenhouse Gas Initiative, site accessed 14 July 2011, http://www.rggi.org/docs/RGGI_Fact_Sheet.pdf

[89]"Emissions Trading System (EU ETS)," European Commission Climate Action, site accessed 14 July 2011 http://ec.europa.eu/clima/faq/ets/index_en.htm

tors not subject to the cap including housing, transportation and agriculture, an effort-sharing program has been established to set different emission targets for Member States. Countries with low GDP per capita will be allowed to increase emissions, while countries with high GDP per capita will be required to implement more stringent reductions.

Nearly half of U.S. states have also adopted renewable portfolio standards (RPS). Nineteen states and Washington, DC have set mandatory targets, while another seven states have set goals without financial penalties for enforcement. RPS goals range from 10 to 40 percent, with target dates from 2010 to 2030.[90] Decentralized energy and climate policies take on a different significance in the EU, where overarching mandates from above dictate region-wide targets. Unlike the U.S., where state policies are seen as a way to make progress on energy goals while a federal policy is still lacking, country-level policies in Europe are used mostly as a way to effectively implement EU statutes. Likewise, renewable energy targets vary at the national level and were set to ensure compatibility with the EU-wide goal of 20 percent by 2020. Targets range from 11 percent in Luxembourg to 49 percent in Sweden.

Policy Changes on the Horizon?

When the environmental movement first started gaining momentum four decades ago, the U.S. assumed a leadership role by establishing standards and protections and innovating new forms of environmental policies. More recently however, especially in the context of climate change, the U.S. has shown itself to be far more hesitant to take bold action, and the EU has emerged as the global leader in implementing ambitious energy and climate goals. This section will examine the political and institutional factors contributing to this evolution and divergence.

Gridlock in U.S. energy politics

The U.S. political system was designed to promote stability and prevent abuses of power. The separation of powers between the executive, legislative and judicial branches enable checks that ensure that no

---

[90]"Renewable Portfolio Standards (RPS) and Goals," United States Federal Energy Regulatory Commission, 3 May 2011, http://www.ferc.gov/market-oversight/othr-mkts/renew/othr-rnw-rps.pdf

one branch becomes too authoritative.[91] The distinct powers of Congress and the executive administration in particular can place the two entities at odds, especially when the partisan interests of each do not align.

One important consequence of this institutional structure is that the stable political system is slow to change in response to new pressures and evidence, including those in the areas of energy and the environment. The limited ability of the President to influence the legislative process and the President's veto power over legislation passed in Congress makes it difficult to make headway on far-reaching goals such as a comprehensive climate and energy policy that would impact nearly every sector of the U.S. economy. The promise of a veto on any climate legislation that reached the President's desk during the Bush presidency, and the anti-climate bias and preoccupation with other political priorities in the current Congress have halted progress. The possibility of gridlock was shown to be even more dramatic in the summer of 2010, when the threat of filibuster alone prevented the Senate from even voting on a climate bill despite House-passed legislation, a Democratic majority, and support from the Obama Administration. Furthermore, the two-party system puts pressure on lawmakers to moderate proposals toward a middle ground, which has tended to erode, undermine, and deter consideration of viable climate bills.

Another characteristic of the U.S. political system that has played a role in slow progress on clean energy and climate policy is its susceptibility to influence from vested private interests. Due to their extensive financial resources, coal and oil companies with an interest in maintaining the status quo as relates to fossil fuel reliance have exerted influence on policy-makers through campaign contributions and corporate lobbying. Superior resources and established relationships with lawmakers generally enable these corporations to have greater access to the halls of power than environmental organizations and clean energy interest groups. Aside from the willful mischaracterization of climate science that has dominated much of the debates, climate legis-

---

[91]For an early, detailed explanatory attempt of U.S. gridlock vs. EU leadership in climate policies, see Joshua Busby and Alexander Ochs, "From Mars and Venus Down to Earth," in David Michel, ed., *Climate Policy for the 21st Century* (Washington, DC: Center for Transatlantic Relations, 2005), pp. 35-76.

lation is also consistently portrayed by certain business and political interests in the U.S. as a battle of environmental versus economic trade-offs.

Policy change and inclusiveness in the EU parliamentary system

The parliamentary systems in many of the EU's member states tend to enable more rapid and substantial policy changes. The partisan alignment of prime ministers with their respective parliaments makes it easier for the dominant party to push through policy agendas, including on climate change. Many EU countries also have multi-party political systems as opposed to the two-party system in the United States. Multi-party systems allow a greater range of issues and positions to enter serious consideration in the policy-making process. With particular regard to climate policy, Green Party positions in EU countries are generally taken seriously and help shape the policy debate, as opposed to the U.S. Green Party, which is highly marginalized. In particular contrast to the framing of energy policy issues in the U.S., renewable energy, energy efficiency and climate policies are seen as measures that can have wide-ranging economic benefits by providing green jobs and allowing Europe to get an early start in capturing a rapidly expanding global clean energy market.

The dominant influence of more economically powerful EU member states with strong climate policy agendas such as Germany, in addition to the institutional characteristics described above, have led to the passage of robust EU-wide energy and climate policies.

Value and political orientation changes in the last 30 years

The United States was a leader and innovator in environmental regulation starting in 1969 with the passage of the National Environmental Policy Act. European countries often followed the U.S. lead through their own initiative or due to U.S.-led international pressure, sometimes even adopting policies wholesale as with the mandate requiring catalytic converters in 1974.

The United States began to slip from its leadership role with the start of the Reagan Administration in 1981 which ushered in an era of deregulation that affected environmental policy among other issue areas. As climate change emerged onto the environmental policy agenda with increasing dominance over the past two decades, the EU filled the environmental leadership gap left by the U.S.[92]

In the absence of pressing energy security concerns, a major problem for addressing environmental and climate challenges is the increased partisanship of U.S. policy.[93] Republican Senators, including former climate "champions" like John McCain, in 2010 closed ranks and opposed climate legislation as a block. It remains Senator McCain's own secret why, in 2003, he introduced cap-and-trade legislation much like the bills he later opposed. Like its decision-makers, the country as a whole is increasingly paralyzed by a monumental societal divide. On the one side of a society that has drifted further to the right since the early Reagan years, are moderates and very few progressives who want to find political answers to the most pressing questions the nation faces; on the other side is the Tea Party, Fox News, and the "no" faction—no government, no taxes, no change, no climate and energy legislation.

Reading Tea Leaves: EU and U.S. Energy Policy in 2020

Relative fossil fuel abundance, stagnating political trends with regard to environmental issues, a system thus far unable to produce the change mandated by national environmental and health as well as international climate challenges have stalled significant U.S. energy policy advancements. Meanwhile, the EU has pulled ahead to establish its position as a global leader in renewable energy generation and climate protection. This disparity in sustainable development ambitions has begun to strain transatlantic relations. In April 2011, European

---

[92]Alexander Ochs and Detlef Sprinz, "Europa Riding the Hegemon? Transatlantic Climate Policy Relations," in: Davis B. Bobrow and William Keller, *Hegemony Constrained: Evasion, Modification, and Resistance to American Foreign Policy* (Pittsburgh: University of Pittsburgh Press, 2008), pp. 144-166; Alexander Ochs, "America's Opposite Hand: Germany's Parties Agree on the Necessity of Environmental Protection and a Green New Deal" (Washington, DC: AICGS, June 2009).

[93]This paragraph and fragments of the following section follow, in part verbatim, Alexander Ochs, "From Flop'enhagen to Can'tcun? US climate policy before the mid-term elections and the UN summit," in: *Bridges*, vol. 27, October 2010; Alexander Ochs, "Obama und der Klimaschutz: Was vom Ehrgeiz übrig blieb," in: *Süddeutsche Zeitung*, November 2, 2010.

Commission Director General for Climate Jos Debelke criticized the U.S. for its lack of leadership and commitment in international climate negotiations. Debelke highlighted resource scarcity as an impetus for engagement in climate talks, citing the discovery of abundant shale gas reserves as a key factor in U.S. reluctance to shift its energy consumption away from fossil fuels.[94]

U.S. state and local initiatives on climate and renewable energy policy can provide some momentum and best practice experience, even when national leadership is lacking. But we predict that the political environment will long remain unfavorable to comprehensive federal climate change and energy legislation and a transition of the national energy system. Disparities in clean energy and climate ambitions between EU member countries to some extent mirror the varying state commitments in the U.S., but overall, the EU appears much more determined to continue the transition of its energy system away from fossil fuels to one that is based on energy efficiency, renewable energies, and smart grids.

In theory, were the U.S. able to break its partisan gridlock and begin to implement ambitious energy and climate goals in the next few years, energy policy could provide common ground and a basis for increased transatlantic cooperation. By setting a strong collective example and demonstrating the benefits of the transition to a green economy, the U.S. and EU together could then play a critical role in leading the transition to a low-carbon energy world.[95] In reality, however, this is highly unlikely. Due to the resource, technology, ideological and institutional reasons explored above, in the United States, comprehensive climate and energy legislation including binding emission targets and renewable energy standards seems to be off the table for the foreseeable future. There is a remaining flicker of hope that the EPA will make use of its court-backed authority to regulate industry greenhouse gas emissions as pollutants under the Clean Air Act.

---

[94]Ewa Krukowska, "EU Praises Chinese Action on Climate, Blames U.S. for Blocking Global Deal," *Bloomberg*, 15 April 2011, http://www.bloomberg.com/news/2011-04-15/eu-praises-chinese-action-on-climate-blames-u-s-for-blocking-global-deal.html

[95]Alexander Ochs and Markus Schaper, "Konflikt oder Kooperation? Transatlantische Umweltbeziehungen," in Thomas Jäger, Alexander Höse, and Kai Oppermann, *Transatlantic Beziehungen* (Wiesbaden: 2005), pp. 235-52.

This would be an important step forward, but it cannot substitute for the relatively bold, visionary, comprehensive, and long-term policies the EU and some of its member states have enacted.

This all means no good news for the international climate negotiation process and the development of a sustainable global energy system. In addition to the damage they are doing at home, U.S. legislators hold the international climate negotiation process hostage. Europe has to find a strategy for how to deal with a transatlantic partner tied up in internal divergences. To be sure, collaboration with the United States on climate and energy should remain a priority for European policymakers; but it seems to be most promising in contexts other than the UNFCCC such as the G20, the Major Economies Forum/Clean Energy Ministerial, and multiple technology-oriented partnerships. As for the UN process, Europe needs to concentrate on the areas where progress with the U.S. seems possible—financial assistance for developing countries being the most prominent—and build new alliances with those who are willing and able to move forward on the issues that are unlikely to be accepted by the U.S.[96] China, India, Mexico, South Korea, among others are, or soon will be, as reliant on fossil energy imports and as motivated to build a low-carbon economy as the EU.

The more it becomes clear that sustainability means economic boom, not doom[97]—compare the current economic performance of many environmental leaders to those who took a free ticket—we might see U.S. industry and decision-makers rethink their position. But this will in all likelihood take many years to create the significant changes in the U.S. climate and energy position that Europe and much of the world would like to see. It is much more probable that the EU and U.S. will continue to drift apart in their energy, climate and environmental performances, and that this divergence will create significant tension between the long-time partners with impacts well exceeding these individual issue areas.

---

[96]Alexander Ochs, "The Good, the Bad, and the Ugly? Europe, the United States, and China at the World Climate Conference," FACET Commentary No. 6, February 2008.

[97]Alexander Ochs, "Mapping the future: Why bidding farewell to fossil fuels is in our interests—and how it can be done," in: *Climate Action 2010*. London & Nairobi: UNEP & Sustainable Development International (launched at COP 16, Cancun), November 2010, p. 60 ff.

Chapter 10

Buying Time: Energy and the Art of Sustainable Advancement in Transatlantic Relations

Christof van Agt

This chapter investigates major developments in the energy security and sustainability policies of the European Union (EU) in relation to the United States (U.S.). Will energy and sustainability challenges bring these key transatlantic partners together or drive them apart between now and 2020? The impact of sentiment and perception on fundamental socioeconomic developments is growing, fueled by access to instant information and hypercommunication through global media reach and portable screens. Policy optics and/or postures are therefore more likely to affect international relations and global markets in future than the rule of law, economic disciplines and universal norms alone. Both the EU and U.S. should therefore handle their positioning and messaging to partners prudently.

Global economic, energy and climate trends are unsustainable.[1] Business-as-usual scenarios point to unprecedented crisis in energy networks and in supply and demand patterns of critical resources to satisfy demand. Major disasters expose systemic vulnerabilities, ranging from Hurricane Katrina and the Macondo oil well spill in the Gulf of Mexico to the impact of earthquakes and tsunamis in the Pacific on the use of nuclear power. Rising resource nationalism, transit disputes and the reinforcement of authoritarian trends in energy producing states reveal that energy governance advancement of market economic integration and value- based social economic growth appears to have

---

[1] See for instance the *IEA World Energy Outlook* of 2009 and 2010, which describe the contemporary challenges to global energy security and sustainability in the context of major financial economic crisis and fragile recovery: "The present world faces unprecedented uncertainty," which government policy must address.

stalled. Fear of potential and actual resource scarcities[2] sharpen geopolitical rather than market dependencies, signaling a policy race to the bottom.

A bidding war for access to both resources and markets in a zero-sum-game among adversaries appears to be taking over the post-Cold-War globalization game of the 1990s. The latter's long-term rule-based market vision of unlocking value from mutual co-dependencies among producers and consumers only faintly projects itself amidst rising insecurities, economic crises and unsustainable futures. The turbulence created by a world re-polarizing around resources worsens problems in developing countries and negatively affects stability and growth in other less-well-integrated and or potentially bypassed regions. Now that both the EU and U.S. are fiscally constrained, as well as geopolitically challenged by emerging economies, the bottom line is that new, essentially protectionist policy trends may emerge that alter the governance disciplines for energy and sustainability. This in turn risks a departure from the value- and rule-based market economic governance system that largely defines the transatlantic relationship and global market integration itself. As Europe risks edging towards a fortress Europe policy stance and the U.S. risks retreating into itself on the back of its shale gas revolution and national energy policy, the transatlantic relationship could fall apart, at the expense of global energy market security and overall socioeconomic sustainability. Weathering the storm and ensuring the enduring viability of transatlantic partnership requires, counter intuitively, a steady-handed policy stance by governments focused on doing less rather than more, while enabling well-functioning markets, the self-regulating effect of fundamental co-dependencies, enhanced interconnectivity and last but not least the general applicability of universal norms.

Since the turn of the millennium the U.S. and EU member states have been assessing options and rolling out policies to move together towards more viable pathways that could lead to a more secure and

---

[2] Predictions of disruption are not uncommon, and range from the Club of Rome's *Limits to Growth* and gloomy global predictions of the late 1970s to alarmist peak oilers and the advent of catastrophic climate change today. See for instance Walter J. Levy, "Oil and the Decline of the West," *Foreign Affairs*, Vol. 58 No. 5 (Summer 1980), pp. 999-1015.

prosperous future. Dialogue has intensified at the highest EU-U.S. policy levels[3] to deal with common energy and sustainability challenges. Ultimately, Europeans and Americans will make their own choices, due to different market structures, import needs and other macroeconomic dependencies. From an oil and gas market perspective this may look like a transatlantic flight into a new yet far-from-certain 'green' economy that can be bridged by unconventional gas resources in the U.S. and through gas import diversity in the EU. This however may also pressure producer-consumer relations and risks adverse policy reflexes.

On the other hand, the civil uprisings in the Middle East and North Africa (MENA) expose weaknesses in the institutional arrangements governing transatlantic relations as well as varying perspectives regarding the very nature of long-term challenges. Most revealing today is the risk to energy security and sustainability when normative foreign policy is subsumed to transatlantic preoccupations, or when security of supply and sustainability concerns are based only on considerations regarding investment, trade and technology. Comprehensive transatlantic energy diplomacy across the full ambit of foreign policy will be essential if these relationship risks are to be managed credibly.

A complex yet complementary system of governance and institutional structures defines transatlantic relations. This relationship must evolve and be strengthened to deal with energy sustainability challenges for both sides of the Atlantic as well as globally beyond 2020. The alternative option is that its texture, which already appears strained by the "rise of the rest," as well as its own institutional rigidities and poor policy reflexes, cause the transatlantic partnership to unravel in ad-hoc approaches and brinkmanship. The erosion of EU-U.S. global engagement has strengthened geopolitical undercurrents in a subtle but steady de-globalization process.

---

[3] 'New EU-US Energy Council to boost transatlantic energy cooperation' EUROPA – Press Releases IP/09/1674, Brussels, 4 November 2009 at http://europa.eu/rapid/pressReleasesAction.do?reference=IP/09/1674; 'EU-US Energy Council Press Statement' Council of the European Union, Lisbon, 19 November 2010 16724/10 Presse 314 at http://www.consilium.europa.eu/uedocs/cms_data/docs/pressdata/EN/foraff/117862.pdf.

Thus the key question is how energy security and sustainability trends and challenges affect the advancement of the fundamental norms and values shared by the EU and U.S. The transatlantic rule-set encompasses the market model, as applied to investment, trade, transport, transit and innovation, with the energy sector as an engine for growth to service these universal humanist values and norms. In the lengthening shadows of growing global imbalances, this model appears to be facing its biggest test.

Shared Legacies, Economic Recovery, Energy Sector Cooperation and Events

Over the postwar period the transatlantic economies moved from reconstruction under the Marshall Plan for the rebuilding of Europe to state industry and subsequent progressive trade liberalization, market opening and deepening economic integration. This required decreasing state ownership of undertakings and increasing degrees of policy coordination in the Organization for European Economic Cooperation established in 1948, which become the Organization for Economic Cooperation and Development (OECD) in 1961 and which is undergoing further reform today.

The benefits Robert Schuman and Jean Monnet saw in energy sector and industrial cooperation for Western European economic recovery led to the formation of the European Coal and Steel Community in 1951 and the European Community for Atomic Energy, or "Euratom," in 1958; both instruments used energy, industrial policy cooperation and embrace of new technologies to boost economic growth and implement the vision of the EU's founding fathers of socio-economic integration in postwar Europe.[4] This mirrored post-

---

[4] Former European Commission President Jacques Delors and European Parliament President and former Polish Prime Minister Jerzy Buzek followed somewhat haphazardly into the footsteps of these men in May 2010 by declaring energy to be the center of EU integration and economic recovery. They argued that rules granting equitable access to common resources no longer existed and that, beyond market liberalization and interconnection, new bolder approaches were required. Their new "European Energy Community" proposes a variety of initiatives, including the creation of combined purchasing concepts, possibly involving a degree of regionalization of the internal market through enhanced cooperation among its member states.

war developments in the U.S., where new nuclear technology was deployed for civil economic advancement through the 1954 Atomic Energy Act.

Together with EU enlargement and neighborhood policies this model functions. Some argue for an even broader vision of U.S.-EU-Russia energy cooperation, the feasibility of which remains hard to estimate though its logic is self-evident. This is because of the variation in energy market models and application of norms. After efforts towards market integration with OECD policies in the 1990s under the Energy Charter and Multilateral Agreement on Investments, Russia has returned to manage its energy resources with a strong geopolitical edge. Though market disciplines and norms are shared at the policy level with the EU and U.S., their implementation remains "fluid." While in general Russian exports have been reliable, there have been exceptions, prompting Western concern, for instance regarding gas market upsets in countries providing transit[5] and disputes with foreign investors. Moreover, the lack of independent outlets for Central Asian resources to Western markets enables Russia to act as a monopoly marketer of Caspian gas to the EU.

OPEC's 1973 embargo of U.S. and European oil markets, which included oil export cutoffs to the Netherlands and Portugal, served as retaliation for Western support of Israel in the Yom Kippur War. The International Energy Agency (IEA), which U.S. Secretary of State Henry Kissinger proposed in 1973 and was established in 1974 as an autonomous institution within the OECD, strengthened transatlantic energy security and policy coordination to overcome the OECD's fragile emergency response capability. The OECD's mechanisms had proved ineffective because member states failed to act collectively and decisively, even though individual or fragmented efforts increase the risks and cost to all. Globally the IEA has successfully evolved as the transatlantic platform[6] for intergovernmental cooperation on energy

---

Recent Commission efforts to forge a common EU energy policy have moved forward roughly along these lines.

[5] Sijbran de Jong, Jan Wouters & Steven Sterkx, "The Russian-Ukrainian Gas Dispute: Lessons for European Energy Crisis Management after Lisbon," *European Foreign Affairs Review* 15: 511-538 (Kluwer law International B.V., 2010).

[6] This is reflected in the widening of its Eurocentric membership and the relative weight of membership voting rights.

security, policy dialogue and technology transfer. In this capacity the IEA remains the singular stage for transatlantic oil market security and energy policy dialogue regarding global energy market dynamics. To maintain its effectiveness and extend the success of its policies into the 21st century, outreach has increased steadily since the 1990s. This has involved oil and gas producers such as Russia and the Middle East; cooperation with OPEC; and efforts to engage with China, India and Brazil, the major energy consumers of the emerging economies group.[7] Outreach is at the core of the IEA's mission today. Indeed, how the IEA engages in global energy dialogue to accommodate current challenges to energy security and sustainability and facilitate congruent energy policy and security measures by key non-member countries will in large part define the enduring nature of transatlantic energy relations.

The June 2011 IEA stock release in response to the outage of Libyan supplies of light sweet crude and conservative OPEC production policies was allegedly driven by fears among some IEA member states of an oil product supply crunch and the challenge high oil prices pose to economic recovery[8]. While the action is a *'first of its kind'*[9] by the IEA's own admission and was acclaimed as a success in terms of market response, it has also prompted criticism and raised questions about the IEA's role in upholding market discipline. Previous IEA stock releases were associated with mitigating the effect of oil market disruptions occurring as a consequence of major geopolitical upheavals or extreme weather related outages, for instance at the onset of operation Desert Storm during the 1991 Gulf War or the impact of Hurricane Katrina on the Gulf of Mexico oil industry in 2005. The subsequent Iraq War did not necessitate a stock release, even though the IEA had readied itself for such an eventuality. In the June 2011

---

[7] See for instance Henry Kissinger's views on the 'The Future Role of the IEA' in his speech for the 35th anniversary of the International Energy Agency, Paris, October 14, 2009 at http://www.henryakissinger.com/speeches/101409.html; and Jeff Colgan, "The International Energy Agency, Challenges for the 21st Century," GPPi Policy Papers Series No.(6) 2009, at www.gppi.net.

[8] IEA 30-Day Review of Libya Collective Action, at http://www.iea.org/press/pressdetail.asp?PRESS_REL_ID=421.

[9] IEA Farewell to IEA Executive Director Tanaka *IEA News* July 2011, at http://www.iea.org/IEAnews/news5511.htm).

IEA collective action, its Executive Director Nubuo Tanaka acted pre-emptively, thus enabling IEA member states to utilize the Agency as 'central commodity banker.' This *'first of its kind'* action outraged OPEC's Iranian Secretary-General Abdallah El-Badri and prompted pundits to question whether this is an appropriate role for the IEA to take.[10] No doubt this newly established practice of acting preemptively ahead of market forces shall affect the IEA's credibility.

Other intergovernmental platforms and organizations, such as the International Energy Forum IEF,[11] embed transatlantic energy relations in a wider system of energy market governance that also involves emerging economies outside the OECD/IEA. Because views differ as to how and when norms and values apply to the specific socioeconomic circumstances of the countries involved, this wider governance system involves flexible and varying degrees of commitment, and is therefore inherently fragile. Though informal forms of cooperation enable the formulation of coherent policy responses to energy and sustainability challenges with greater flexibility and larger political effect, when put to the test their implementation often seems rhetorical. Here the focus is on confidence-building and process, not on the application of multilateral market disciplines on energy markets, which would enable the application of more fundamental norms and values. Given current energy security and sustainability challenges, there is therefore a danger that transatlantic values and service to broader "human interests" could be sacrificed to expedient government policies and a false sense of urgency advanced by market actors intent on capitalizing on economic opportunities.

In this regard it is useful to ask whether the challenges we see are still the challenges we need to address, and whether the venues we choose are really still the best.

Among the informal platforms that embed the transatlantic relationship in the wider world is the G8 and its subsequent and expanded incarnation, the G20. The G-8 evolved from a 1975 summit meeting

---

[10]OPEC Outrage at IEA's release of Oil reserves, *Economy Watch* 29th June 2011, at http://www.economywatch.com/in-the-news/opec-outrage-at-iea-release-of-oil-reserves.29-06.htm.

[11]Bassam Fattouh and Coby van der Linde, *The International Energy Forum: 20 Years of Producer – Consumer Dialogue in a Changing World* (IEF Riyadh, Saudi Arabia 2011).

among six key industrialized economies at Rambouillet.[12] The objective was to address the impact of oil market dynamics on macroeconomic development while escaping the rigidity of existing institutions and avoiding protectionist reflexes. Today the G20 offers the world's most prominent policy stage, yet it is still an 'informal' meeting of the major economies to deal with energy security from a macroeconomic, fiscal and monetary policy perspective. The prospect of global economic recovery from the current financial economic crisis remains uncertain, also because of rising energy security and sustainability concerns. The perceptions of impending resource scarcity, catastrophic climate change or geopolitical maneuverings between Russia and the U.S. and EU in wider Europe have become a cause of concern to the U.S., also in respect of the EU's gas market diversification to Caspian and Central Asian gas resources. Political events unfolding in the MENA, spiked by nuclear disaster in Japan, will impact energy security and sustainability. Even with proper diversification, Russia's oil and gas market dominance in the EU's future energy mix will last. Alleviating normative governance hurdles, regardless of inconsistencies among market models alone, is therefore critical for energy security and sustainability and must therefore become a priority in dialogue between the transatlantic partners and the rising 'Rest.' Indeed the tragic events in the MENA underscore the unprecedented uncertainty to which global energy markets are exposed if they are not sufficiently anchored in shared values and socioeconomic policy goals.

The International Energy Forum (IEF), which resulted from the 1991 producer-consumer dialogue among IEA members and MENA provides a key platform for dialogue between major energy producer and consuming countries. Taken together, the countries involved represent 90% of the world's oil and gas supply-demand balance. The IEF, which has been served by a permanent secretariat in Riyadh since 2002, gathers energy ministers to foster informal dialogue on oil and gas market fundamentals and underlying investment and trade patterns, while contributing to market stability through enhancing market data transparency in the Joint Oil Data Initiative (JODI) and Joint Gas Data Initiative.

---

[12]The 'Group of Six' comprised the United States, the United Kingdom, France, Germany, Italy and Japan.

The G20 economies' ever-tighter codependency requires strengthened multilateral cooperation and formulation of shared visions in support of global macroeconomic stability and sustainable economic growth. Yet energy sector volatility and climate threats affect North Atlantic and emerging economies differently. These differences exacerbate major trade and monetary imbalances and lead to conflicting priorities. The February 2011 communiqué issued by the G20 finance ministers and central bank governors meeting welcomed the collaborative work undertaken by IEA IEF, OPEC on JODI to at least improve data transparency and mutual understanding of market fundamentals. The G20 Paris communiqué called on these organizations to recommend how it could extend its work on oil price volatility to gas and coal by October 2011—thus embracing organizations as varied as the International Monetary Fund (IMF) and the Gas Exporting Countries Forum—a gas producer organization said to be modeled after OPEC (GECF).[13]

At the extraordinary IEF ministerial meeting on February 22, 2011 in Riyadh, ministers signed the IEF charter, which enshrines the work and organization of the forum as a neutral facilitator for intergovernmental dialogue among producing, consuming and transit states in a legally non-binding document. The communiqué announces that signature of the Charter:

> marks a new era of international energy cooperation built on greater mutual understanding and trust, with significant reinforced political commitment to an informal, open, informed and continuing dialogue in the framework of the IEF... With all the major energy producers and consumers united in this dialogue framework, this fact sends a powerful positive signal to the energy world and energy markets that difficult issues can and will be tackled in a *global context*, whenever necessary.[14]

---

[13]See item 5 of the 'Communique Meeting of Finance Ministers and Central Bank Governors', G20 France Paris, 18-19 February 2011 at http://www.g20.org/Documents2011/02/COMMUNIQUE-G20_MGM%20_18-19_February_2011.pdf.

[14]Extraordinary IEF Ministerial Meeting Concluding Statement by the Kingdom of Saudi Arabia and the Secretariats of IEA, IEF and OPEC, 22 February 2011, Riyadh at http://www.ief.org/whatsnew/Pages/ExtraordinaryIEFMinisterialMeeting,22February2011,Riyadh.aspx.

In addition to the welcome diplomatic engagement of the IEF globally, basic norms and values codified in predictable and transparent rule of law, including fiscal and regulatory stability, will continue to be essential to let societies prosper and boost the necessary investor confidence to address the world's energy and sustainability challenges. The transatlantic relationship may be in some disrepair due to geopolitical and economic dynamics in the post-9/11 world, but its long-standing and well-established fundamental disciplines and humanist bearings did not turn post-modern with the turn of the century; indeed, the Arab Spring shows how they in great part represent a self-propelling and universal human force. Alternative rule sets and terms of international engagement are difficult to envisage if they largely serve industry interests. Because of the universality of these values, which govern basic transatlantic market, trade and investment disciplines, the EU and U.S. are duty bound to help carry them forward until there are sufficient other safe harbors out there.

During the 1990s there was a broad trend of multilateral energy market integration; this has given way in large part to greater government-orchestrated efforts to attain energy security and sustainability goals. This interventionist trend mirrors the resource nationalism of producers whose integrated companies seek to capture the premium values that are best attained, despite their indebtedness, on open liberalized EU and U.S. markets. This now prompts energy-consuming governments to declare the need to "protect the integrity of internal markets"[15] and hedge against real and perceived risks of scarcity and the intangibilities of geopolitical concerns. With the wisdom of hindsight and well-established market principles tested in practice, such initiatives are not very convincing, diminish EU and U.S. security by questioning their commitment to established norms and policies, and in practice will most likely prove to be self-defeating. Most importantly, however, is that their rather self-serving tit-for tat character creates poor policy optics in wider contexts. It reveals a lack of confidence in the adequacy of the existing governance system and rule-set

---

[15]"*The EU should continue to develop stronger common actions and accompanying measures on external energy matters to increase its influence on regional and global energy markets and to protect the integrity of the internal market and the security of energy supplies for all its members.*" Cited from: Stock taking document Towards a new Energy Strategy for Europe 2011-2022 para 2, p. 14.

in terms of overcomming or accommodating energy security and sustainability challenges that could spawn bigger catastrophes globally before 2020.

Sluggish multilateral progress regarding the Energy Charter Treaty[16] and the Climate Summits in Copenhagen and Cancun of the United Nations Framework Convention on Climate Change[17]

---

[16]The Energy Charter was signed in the Hague in 1991 by the member states of the OECD and the newly independent states of the Former Soviet Union to promote energy sector trade & investment and spur economic integration and recovery. The Energy Charter Treaty signed in Lisbon in 1994 sets out non-discriminatory market rules for energy trade, transit and investment and dispute settlement procedures thus creating a level playing field between producer consumers and transit states. The United States and Canada though signatories to the 1991 Energy Charter and negotiating parties did ultimately not sign the 1994 Energy Charter Treaty due to the federal governance system of their energy sectors and the obstacle provided in the Jackson-Vanik Amendment. Ratification of the 1994 Energy Charter Treaty is still pending for Norway, Iceland and Belarus. Russia withdrew its signature from the 1994 Energy Charter Treaty to end its provisional application and because it believes the Treaty to be out of date with the substantially changed circumstances in global energy markets. Negotiations on a Energy Charter Protocol on Transit were launched in 1998 but have not been concluded to date. The Energy Charter Conference remains the intergovernmental body for negotiation of multilateral energy market rules. Also in light of Russia's concerns and the proposal of President Medvedev of Russia for a new conceptual approach for a legal basis in international cooperation in energy in April 2009, the Energy Charter is considering modernization in a strategy group and a new Russian draft convention on energy security circulated in November 2010. For a discussion see Christof van Agt, 'Tabula Russia, Escape from the Energy Charter Treaty' Clingendael International Energy Paper, October 2009 at http://www.clingendael.nl/publications/2009/20091001_ciep_paper_cvanagt_russia.pdf. The original new concept can be retrieved at *Konceptual'nyj podchod k novoj pravovoj baze mezhdunarodnovo sotrudnichestva v sfere energetiki (celi i principy)*" President of Russia, Official Web Portal, 21 April 2009, retrieved at http://www.kremlin.ru/text/docs/2009/04/215303.shtml

[17]The Conference of the Parties COP 15 Copenhagen summit of December 2009 was meant to agree on a legally binding treaty to replace the 1997 Kyoto Protocol that expires in 2012 and sets binding targets for reducing greenhouse gas emissions on mature industrialized economies through the principle of common but differentiated responsibilities relative to emissions in 1990.The rising expectations to make progress ultimately became an obstacle to move forward. The Kyoto Protocol a separate legally binding agreement under the 1992 UNFCCC is not ratified by the United States though under the current administration there is much more engagement for reaching a an effective arrangement for the second commitment period

(UNFCCC) are often cited as proof that the transatlantic relationship has become inadequate or insufficient with regard to the globalization of energy security and viable governance arrangements regarding sustainability. Due to the rising need to cater to public perceptions, EU and U.S. governments have surrendered to a fundamentally flawed assumption that lies behind these allegations, namely that governance has to be fast and furious when confronting crisis and glamorous for the voting public to perceive it as operating effectively. The truth is that international governance's main characteristic is that it is a painstakingly slow process in which process and product serve equally important goals. Its torturous tendency towards patience is only broken in case of clear and present breaches of national and human integrity and, as the Libyan intervention demonstrated, only in the face of great disunity.

A more broadly shared vision for socio-economic integration and growth derived from transparent and nondiscriminatory energy market rules and robust engagement on climate change could possibly be achieved in the context of the WTO. There is no need for new institutions or yet another informal intergovernmental initiative. In fact, there is even an argument to be made to leave the now rather bizarre and rising complexities of multilateral negotiations on energy and climate in the context of the Energy Charter or UNFCCC for what they have achieved, and first make progress in other more homogeneous regional contexts. Ultimately, such efforts at 'buying time' will require multilateral validation to obtain the required critical mass. This means that progress between the U.S. and EU as key stakeholders in the transatlantic relationship through the WTO will be a key test of their

---

after 2012. Despite strong efforts by the European Union to become a lead actor in making progress, President Obama's grabbed the headlines as the broker of a non binding agreement to salvage the gridlock and keep the process moving. The COP 16 Cancun summit in Mexico in December 2010 was characterized by a much more operational approach and made progress on some important elements of what might ultimately become a comprehensive agreement but pushed the agreement on a legally binding commitment for mature economies only or all further over the horizon. As a consequence the EU is now like the US moving ahead more unilaterally on its climate policy goals. See Richard Wolf, 'Obama claims partial victory in Copenhagen,' *USA Today*, December 18, 2009, at http://content.usatoday.com/communities/theoval/post/2009/12/obama-claims-partial-victory-in-copenhagen/1.

ability to further develop their relationship while welcoming the 'Rise of the Rest' within multilateral frameworks.

In July 2011 the WTO ruled against export restrictions imposed by China on its raw materials on environmental grounds since 2009. This provided some comfort to importing parties and enhances confidence in the ability of multilateral frameworks to deal with rising tensions effectively. "This is a clear verdict for open trade and fair access to raw materials. It sends a strong signal to refrain from imposing unfair restrictions to trade and takes us one step closer to a level playing field for raw materials," noted EU Trade Commissioner Karel De Gucht.[18]

It is of interest that in relation to Russia's impending accession to WTO and the "reset" of relations between Russia and the U.S. that Vice President Joe Biden encouraged the strengthening of political freedoms and rule of law in Russia even as Prime Minister Putin made the lifting of visa restrictions a condition for moving forward towards a "new moral atmosphere":[19] *"The reset is working, working for all of us, working for Russia and I would presumptuously say working for the world."*[20]

Transatlantic energy and sustainability concerns institutionalized in the OECD/IEA and embedded in the wider world through the informal context of the G20 and other platforms and institutions such as the, IEF, Energy Charter and UNFCCC can thus still be strengthened and extended, notably through the WTO, by virtue of its general cross-sector approach. "A stronger rule book could benefit the energy sector"[21] and help to maintain a predictable and transparent basis for rational energy market development and sustainability goals. This will avoid fragmentation of effort and zero-sum games between various stakeholders and country groups, much like the IEA did for the coun-

---

[18]Karel de Gucht, cited in 'EU hails WTO ruling on Chinese raw materials export restrictions' *Platts*, 6 July 2011, at http://www.platts.com/RSSFeedDetailed News/RSSFeed/Metals/8083493.

[19]Speech of Vice President Joseph Biden at Moscow State University cited in 'US Warns Russia for investor risk" *Financial Times*, March 11, 2011, p. 2.

[20]Speech of Vice President Joseph Biden at Moscow State University cited in 'US Warns Russia for investor risk" *Financial Times*, March 11, 2011, p. 2.

[21]Remarks by Pascal Lamy Director General World Trade Organizations during the 21st World Energy Congress cited in 'Lamy: *"A stronger WTO rule book could benefit the energy sector,"'* WTO, 16 September 2010.

tries of the OECD and WTO disciplines for opening markets and strengthening of universal norms.

For these reasons energy security and rule-based economic integration, as well as sustainable growth are back at the center of the U.S.-EU agenda:

> Energy is an important component of the EU-U.S. dialogue in the 21st century, because it has effects across our foreign, economic and development policies. By working together on energy, the EU and the U.S. are increasing our mutual security and prosperity; underpinning stable, reliable and transparent global energy markets; and coordinating our regulatory regimes and research programmes to speed the development of tomorrow´s clean and efficient energy technologies.[22]

Changes in the geopolitical landscape of the modern world show that, although historic, the transatlantic relationship is no longer the "one and only" nor can or should it claim exclusive authority over the now much more widely acknowledged norms and values at its core. The transatlantic relationship could in fact become a victim of its own success due to

- the fact that economic growth and rising energy demand of Asian-Pacific and other rising non-OECD economies may crowd out the impact of transatlantic policies on global energy and foreign economic relations;

- the growing macro-economic gravity of other interdependencies, such as U.S.-China monetary relations or the economic co-dependency between Russia and the EU in energy issues;

- the EU's ambition to become a more effective and cohesive actor on the international stage to confront risks from globalization, demographic trends, energy and sustainability and its mistaken ambitions (when considering EU capabilities), floated occasionally, to 'go it alone' or seek new non-transatlantic or U.S. alliances.

---

[22] See 'EU-US Energy Council, Press Statement' Council of the European Union, Lisbon, 19 November 2010 16724/10 Presse 314 first paragraph at http://www.consilium.europa.eu/uedocs/cms_data/docs/pressdata/EN/foraff/117862.pdf.

Europe's 'California Dreaming'

The entry into force of the Lisbon Treaty on December 1, 2009 reformed the workings of EU institutions to enable EU member states to "act as one" in confronting 21st century challenges, which means "rethinking some of the ground rules for working together."[23] While these public relations intonations may sound catchy, they reveal that Europe might be edging into panic mode to harness political unity and protect the integrity of its internal market rather then extending these rules externally. New measures to ring-fence open market disciplines and norms, as if these are the EU's exclusive domain and not also governed by international treaties, with measures to leverage market power against monopolist energy suppliers such as Russia's Gazprom, in favor of possible new market entrants such as gas supplies from a normatively underperforming Turkmenistan, represent the opening move in a dangerous and not-so-great game. Here real and perceived security of supply concerns cut through much broader foreign policy goals of the EU and the fundamental norms and values that the transatlantic relationship must carry at its core. The ambivalence shared by the EU and U.S. towards Russia and their preoccupation with project-specific policies in the Caspian region reflect divisions in a cumbersome and failing energy dialogue. They call into mind statements made by U.S. Secretary of State Henry Kissinger in 1973 at the Pilgrims society, where he launched the concept of the International Energy Agency. Indeed these words could be voiced today from a Russian perspective as well:

> Europe's unity must not come at the expense of the Atlantic community, or both sides of the Atlantic will suffer, it is not that we are impatient with the cumbersome machinery of Europe, it is rather the tendency to highlight division rather than unity with us which concerns us.[24]

---

[23]From the EU website notice marking the entry into force of the Lisbon Treaty on the 1st of December 2009 'Taking Europe into the 21st Century' Europa, gateway to the European Union at http://europa.eu/lisbon_treaty/take/index_en.htm.

[24]Henry Kissinger, Text of address in London to the Pilgrims society on energy and European problems, *New York Times*, December 13, 1973.

Of course the world, the EU and U.S. have changed since the Arab oil embargo in 1973 and with the end of the Cold War in 1991. The EU has enlarged its membership and seeks a more active engagement with its neighborhood policies, although this does not involve key Central Asian energy producers such as Kazakhstan, Uzbekistan or Turkmenistan, even though they are the focal point of EU and U.S. efforts to diversify gas markets via establishment of a Southern corridor around Russia.

Emerging economies such as China and India have increased the living standards of millions, but as a consequence they have also become more dependent on energy imports. China has made rapid progress in securing oil and gas supplies across the world and notably in Central Asia, with speedy and straightforward government-financed deals. Here the issue the transatlantic partners face is not so much new competition over resources but the fact that particular Asian-Pacific players fail to buy into the application of economic and other values and norms. On the transatlantic side, business-like cooperation with key MENA energy producers has improved in the producer-consumer dialogue and become more effective, as demonstrated by the willingness of OPEC producers to boost oil production and calm world energy markets in the wake of the Libya crisis, even though ultimately this was considered not enough.[25]

The geopolitical turmoil unleashed by the 9/11 terrorist attacks has tested the mettle of transatlantic partnership and considerably damaged the global market economic vision the twin towers stood for and was widely shared in the post-Cold-War world of the 1990s. Russia's policy turns in utilizing its energy wealth as a geopolitical lever in response to military intervention in Iraq and Afghanistan or the U.S. Congress denial of CNOOC's bid to take over UNOCAL are at least illustrative of the loss of confidence in level playing fields globally. Yet as the dust settles a decade on now we do see increasing system convergence around an enduring social and economic value-set reemerging.

Evidence hereof lies in the success of emerging economies in the Asia-Pacific and in Latin America, which today drive much of the world´s economic growth; and in the growing populations in MENA's

---

[25]'Members of Opec join Saudis in oil boost,' *Financial Times Europe*, March 8, 2011, p. 1.

opening societies, who no longer wish to be excluded from the freedoms and benefits that transatlantic societies stand for. In addition, countries in the EU's Eastern and Mediterranean partnership seek to become more closely associated with the EU. This should encourage the transatlantic relationship not to respond defensively to the rise of the rest, but rather take to a more daring posture claiming co-ownership and therefore being entitled to press for implementation of market disciplines and socio-economic values and norms. This provides the impetus to regain the confidence of the 1990s and to equip transatlantic partners with a clear basis from which to more confidently project their foreign economic policy.

Looking forward into the 21st century, what is certain is that the world and its macroeconomic and fundamental energy market dynamics will change in ways that are difficult to foresee. Finally, the shale gas revolution in the U.S. and the wide application of biofuels in Brazil are both examples of how the deployment of technology can affect market dynamics and sentiment.[26] But crises in the Gulf of Mexico and Japan also show that vigilance with respect to the management of industrial risk is also needed.

Meet You in Geneva

In times of unprecedented uncertainty, innovative approaches that sidestep norms or economic discipline in anticipation of future challenges will not strengthen stability and investor confidence. Dilution of market discipline will diminish options for further engagement between the EU and the U.S., and will weaken the ability of the transatlantic partners to engage constructively with emerging economies. In the absence of more even-handed and effective multilateral approaches (think of Russia's escape from the Energy Charter in relation to its impending WTO accession), the standing and credibility of the transatlantic rule-set will be lost. In this scenario, transatlantic states expose themselves in the eyes of the people of the "rising rest" to claims of neglect for taking responsibility for the protection

---

[26]John Deutch, 'The Good News About Gas, The Natural Gas Revolution and its Consequences,' *Foreign Affairs*, January-February 2011.

and advancement of values and norms that also determine their well-being and prosperity.

Shared Visions, from Stable to Dynamically Evolving

The IEA/OECD ensures the cohesion and consistency of energy market policy and regulation among its members precisely because there are important differences in energy governance, market structures and external dependencies between the EU as a whole, its member states, the U.S. and other transatlantic partners.

Despite the Lisbon Treaty's[27] chapter on energy,[28] the EU mixes community competencies with intergovernmental forms of cooperation among EU member states. These retain sovereignty over their resources, the composition of their energy mixes and investment policies. Though parallels can be drawn between the federal governance system in the U.S. and the governance structure of the EU these are often misleading. First, the U.S. represents a stable federal governance system with a single department for energy and federal regulatory authority that ensures coherence in energy policy and regulation. The EU is, with the Lisbon Treaty in place, still a political process of governance formation in which the institutional set-up and division of competencies among EU bodies and member states is in dynamic evolution. Second, the use and ownership of subsoil energy resources in the EU are governed by EU member states, but are often privately held in the U.S., with the notable exemption of offshore resources. Although the predictability of the rule of law, policy objectives and market economic, fiscal and commercial disciplines are now equally shared as implementation of the EU's "third energy package" is underway,[29] the U.S. does not have a requirement for full-scale energy market liberal-

---

[27]Consolidated versions of the Treaty on European Union (TEU) and the Treaty on the Functioning of the European Union (TFEU), *Official Journal of the European Union* (OJ) C115 Volume 5 Notice 2008-C115-01 (Brussels 9th of May 2008).

[28]TFEU Title XXI Article 194 Energy C115 Volume 5 Notice 2008-C115-01 (Brussels 9th of May 2008).

[29]See the 'Third Energy Package': (OJ L 211, 14 August 2009) Legislative acts that formally entered into force on the 3rd of March 2011. Due to the delay's by some EU member states the Commission would only consider next steps and or infringement procedures in 4Q 2011 at best. See also 'Brussels weighs legal action on internal

ization. Unlike the EU's state traditions in economic governance, private enterprise is at the core of U.S. policymaking. This means that significant differences still exist between EU member states and U.S. states. Finally, governance in common law and civil law cultures mean that policy and regulatory approaches cannot automatically be transposed and that their utility and effect are not necessarily the same.

The division of responsibilities among senior representatives of the EU and member state institutions means that EU energy policy emerges from a complex process of negotiations and compromise between stakeholders with divergent perspectives, in particular with regard to its external relations. The EU, a post-modern entity in which the actors and elements together make up the EU's single voice on foreign policy, focuses through a kaleidoscope of interests that can both blur and sharpen views. In the search for an external energy policy therefore, not only cohesion and consistency, but above all caution, remain key:

> There is a need for better coordination of EU and Member States' activities with a view to ensuring consistency and coherence in the EU's *external relations* with key producer, transit, and consumer countries. The Commission is invited to submit by June 2011 a communication on security of supply and international cooperation aimed at further improving the consistency and coherence of the EU's external action in the field of energy. The Member States are invited to inform from 1 January 2012 the Commission on all their new and existing bilateral energy agreements with third countries; the Commission will make this information available to all other Member states in an appropriate form, having regard to the need for protection of commercially sensitive information. The High Representative is invited to take fully account of the energy security dimension in her work. Energy security should also be fully reflected in the EU's neighborhood policy.[30]

---

energy market' EurActiv, 01.03.11, and The internal energy market—Time to switch into higher gear.'

[30]Conclusions on Energy European Council EUCO 2/11 CO EUR 2 CONCL 1(Brussels 4 February 2011) item 11 pp 4 at http://www.consilium.europa.eu/uedocs/cms_data/docs/pressdata/en/ec/119141.pdf.

By establishing an Agency for Cooperation of Energy Regulators (ACER)[31] the EU has moved one step further in the direction of an independent European regulator that may contribute to a more optimal regulatory environment, as the U.S. ensures through the Federal Energy Regulatory Commission (FERC). Indeed, here the EU appears to have followed the U.S. lead.[32] Another important policy trend is that since the 1990s, when the policy consensus was for energy to be governed by general non-discriminatory economic rules and commercial principles checked by competition and antitrust law, the policy and regulatory domain today seems more characteristic of the 1950s in terms of financing and industrial needs for dealing with real and perceived challenges and achieving a "green economy."[33] The weaknesses observed in the application of multilateral frameworks for open energy market integration gives rise to complaints over the absence of a European energy policy to cover also more clearly the external energy dimension of Europe's internal energy market and to protect its integrity over the dominance of external monopoly power. The opportunities this creates for new "innovative" approaches are reflected in the concept of a Caspian Development Corporation[34] and other initiatives that in their most radical interpretation will amount to ring-fencing the EU's internal energy market.[35] It is unclear how

---

[31] See Regulation (EC) No 713/2009 of the European Parliament and of the Council of 13 July 2009 establishing an Agency for the Cooperation of Energy Regulators.

[32] *'Issues for consideration for the longer-term: Strengthening the role of ACER & ENTSO (European Network of Transmission System Operators ed) to develop a more integrated regional and **European energy market**'* (emphasis added) cited from Stock taking document Towards a new Energy Strategy for Europe 2011-2022 para 2, p. 12.

[33] See Sami Andoura, Leigh Hancher and Marc van der Woude *'Policy Proposal by Jacques Delors Towards a European Energy Community: a Policy Proposal'* (Notre Europe March 2010) that proposes to put energy itself at the centre of EU policy in marked contrast to its own multilateral open market model and universal appeal of humanist rules.

[34] To enhance, in its totality the competition on the EU's own internal gas market, the European Commission jointly with the European Investment Bank, World Bank and the Public Private Infrastructure Advisory Facility investigates the option on bundling European gas demand in a single corporate vehicle to purchase gas and facilitate infrastructure investment with Turkmenistan and other Caspian and Middle Eastern producers. See also CERA HIS Caspian Development Corporation Final Implementation Report December 2010 presented to WB, EC, EIB *Confidential Report.*

[35] Full text of the Buzek and Delors Declaration on the creation of a European Energy Community, The President of the European Parliament, Press Releases (Brussels – Wednesday, May 5th, 2010) pargraph 7.

such approaches will pass the test of the EU's own general market rules[36] or add cohesion and consistency to the EU's own multilateral policy posture[37] within the transatlantic relationship on the international scene, but as is already mentioned above these policy optics look rather poor.

Looking at the energy and sustainability challenges themselves, these center on managing rising import dependencies notably for gas in the EU and oil in the U.S. as well as the need to manage climate change and sustainable economic growth by reducing carbon emissions and decreasing the energy intensity in GDP. Energy efficiency, innovation and transition to alternative non-fossil sources of energy such as biofuels, wind and solar and other renewable energies are key. This is part of the Europe 2020 strategy for smart, sustainable and inclusive growth,[38] which among its five goals lays down where the EU should be on climate and energy in 2020:

- 20% reduction of greenhouse emissions (binding and on track)[39]

- 20% increase in the share of renewable in the EU's energy mix (binding and on track)

- 20% improvement of energy efficiency targets (non-binding and not on track)[40]

---

[36]General market rules as provided for in the EU Third energy legislative package and EU competition rules.

[37]See in addition to multilateral energy market rules under in international frameworks such as the Energy Charter Treaty and WTO TEU Title V Chapter 1 General Provisions on the Union's External Action Art. 21(2) paragraphs (a),(d),(e),(f),(g),(h). *Official Journal of the European Union* C115 (Brussel 9th of May 2008).

[38]Europe 2020 strategy for smart, sustainable and inclusive growth last updated on 6 August 2010 at http://ec.europa.eu/economy_finance/structural_reforms/europe_2020/index_en.htm.

[39]Without prejudice to an offer in international negotiations to raise this to a 30% target.

[40]But if this could be met through full implementation of the revised Energy Efficiency Plan this would enable a 25% reduction in greenhouse gas emissions by 2020 instead of the 20% reduction target today. See Communication from the Commission to the European Parliament, the Council, the European Economic and Social Committee and the Committee on the Regions A roadmap for moving to a low carbon economy in 2050, (Brussels COM 2011 xxx) p 12.

Next to climate change, this also serves security of supply and strategic economic interests in a resource-efficient economy to create jobs and boost competitiveness by stimulating investment in innovation and deployment of new more efficient "green" technologies.[41]

Unlike the U.S. and other transatlantic partners, the EU must manage these challenges while completing its internal market and moving forward with its own political and institutional integration in accordance with the Lisbon Treaty. This means that it can rely less on merely creating fiscal and regulatory conditions, as for instance is provided for by FERC in the U.S., or fostering public private partnerships to enable that ultimately market mechanisms ensure these challenges are met in an optimal and economically viable manner. The EU must focus permanently on policy coordination and consistency of effort among its member states. Thus the EU is becoming much more reliant than the U.S.—if not entrapped—on strategic inward planning and cooperation,[42] which relies on a complex procedural universe internally that has become a science in its own right. For this reason next to the already observed sluggish multilateral negotiations internationally the EU will continue to need the U.S. to voice international policy clear and effectively. The fundamental belief in the U.S. in markets, combined with a federal system that works effectively,[43] means

---

[41]Communication from the Commission to the European Parliament, the Council, the European Economic and Social Committee and the Committee on the Regions A Resource efficient Europe Flagship initiative under the 2020 strategy at Europe http://ec.europa.eu/resource-efficient-europe/.

[42]*'The third internal energy market package laid the basis for European network planning and investment by creating the requirement for Transmission System Operators (TSOs) to cooperate and elaborate regional and European 10-year network development plans (TYNDP) for electricity and gas in the framework of the European Network of TSOs (ENTSO and by establishing rules of cooperation for national regulators on cross-border investments in the framework of the Agency for the Cooperation of Energy Regulators (ACER)'* Communication from the Commission to the European Parliament, the Council, the European Economic and Social Committee and the Committee on the Regions Energy infrastructure priorities for 2020 and beyond—A Blueprint for an integrated European energy network, (Brussels 17 November 2010) COM (210) 677 final p 8. at http://eur-lex.europa.eu/LexUriServ/LexUriServ.do?uri=SPLIT_COM:2010:0677 (01):FIN:EN:PDF.

[43]Compare the role of FERC in facilitating the expansion of interstate gas infrastructure—a major obstacle to integrate the gas market in the EU and diversify gas supplies—in the period 1998-2008 the interstate grid was expanded by some 30.000 km

that the U.S. can project foreign policy much more swiftly and straightforwardly than the EU, with or without an effective External European Action service and despite the EU's ambition, laid down in the Lisbon Treaty's new article on energy, that individual EU member state energy security and sustainability policies are to be governed in 'a spirit of solidarity.' This appears to go against the principle of subsidiarity, by which EU member states retain authority on how best to implement EU policy.[44]

In parallel to the adoption of the Lisbon Treaty and implementation of the third energy package, the EU is launching (among a wide range of new policy initiatives) major strategic approaches to tackle the challenges it sees on energy and sustainability. Among these are:

1. **The Energy 2020 Strategy (2020 Strategy)**[45]: Sets out the EU's key priorities in a step change to meet the energy challenge ('the life blood of our society ... one of the greatest tests which Europe has to face')[46] in five goals:

   i)   Achieving an energy efficient Europe;

   ii) Building a truly pan-European integrated energy market;

   iii) Empowering consumers and achieving the highest level of safety and security;

   iv) Extending Europe's leadership in energy technology and innovation;

---

see Aad Corrélje, Dick de Jong, Jacques de Jong 'Crossing Borders in European Gas Networks, the missing links' Clingendael International Energy Programme (CIEP) Energy Paper 2009 at http://www.clingendael.nl/publications/2009/20090900_ciep_paper_gas_networks.pdf.

[44]TFEU Title XXI Article 194 Energy C115 Volume 5 Notice 2008-C115-01 (Brussels 9th of May 2008).

[45]Communication from the Commission to the European Parliament, the Council, the European Economic and Social Committee and the Committee on the Regions Energy 2020 A strategy for competitive, sustainable and secure energy, (Brussels 10 November) 2010 COM (2010) 639 final at http://www.energy.eu/directives/com-2010-0639.pdf.

[46]Ibid., A strategy for competitive, sustainable and secure energy, (Brussels 10 November) 2010 COM (2010) 639 final p.1 at http://www.energy.eu/directives/com-2010-0639.pdf.

v) Strengthening the external dimension of the EU energy market.[47]

2. **The European Energy Infrastructure Package (EIP)**[48]: Sets out the EU's vision of what is needed to mobilize the EU's infrastructure investment needs, estimated at one trillion euro, making oil gas and electricity networks efficient and resilient to meet energy and sustainability needs by 2020:

i) Efficient and transparent project authorization and permitting procedures;

ii) Financing incentives that the current regulatory framework does not provide;

iii) Cross-border cooperation on European value-added as opposed to member state policy.

It maps out the necessary infrastructure, qualifies those of 'European interest' and offers a tool box for their timely implementation that includes a public co-financing Connecting Europe Facility.[49]

3. **The Roadmap for moving to a low carbon economy and energy policy beyond 2020 towards 2050 (Roadmap 2050)**[50]: Sets out the EU's roadmap for action to fulfill its objective to reduce GHG emissions by 80-95% compared to 1990 that enable a 50% reduction in emissions globally by 2050[51] outlining milestones achieving 40-60% reduction lev-

---

[47]Ibid, p. 5-6.

[48]Communication from the Commission to the European Parliament, the Council, the European Economic and Social Committee and the Committee on the Regions Energy infrastructure priorities for 2020 and beyond – A Blueprint for an integrated European energy network, (Brussels 17 November 2010) COM (210) 677 final at http://eur-lex.europa.eu/LexUriServ/LexUriServ.do?uri=SPLIT_COM:2010:0677 (01):FIN:EN:PDF.

[49]Ibid., A Blueprint for an integrated European energy network, (Brussels 17 November 2010) COM (210) 677 final at http://eur-lex.europa.eu/LexUriServ/LexUriServ.do?uri≠SPLIT_COM:2010:0677(01):FIN:EN:PDF pp. 5-6.

[50]Communication from the Commission to the European Parliament, the Council, the European Economic and Social Committee and the Committee on the Regions A roadmap for moving to a low carbon economy in 2050, (Brussels COM 2011 xxx).

[51]In accordance with necessary reductions by IPCC taken on by developed countries as a group and multilateral agreements on climate change struck at Copenhagen and

els by 2030 and 2040 respectively, energy policy challenges, investments and opportunities. It identifies electricity as the key enabler to eliminate CO_2 emissions in 2050.

This is in addition to a communication on security of supply and international cooperation aimed at further improving the consistency and coherence of the EU's external action in the field of energy. While the EU affirms open energy market integration and the application of competition policy as its foreign economic 'leitmotif,' it will look at foreign energy relations more on a case-by-case basis, rolling out the 'principle of differentiation' that remains to be tested notably in EU support for negotiations for an intergovernmental agreement on a Trans-Caspian gas pipeline between Azerbaijan and Turkmenistan.[52]

Summary: A False Sense of Urgency?

After a period of high geopolitical and energy market volatility, a striking feature is the sense of alarm about the energy security and sustainability challenges and the apparent frustration with the EU's own functioning that resonates throughout these documents though the above referred to communication on external energy relations radiates more policy calm, The EU's ambition to shepper Caspian intergovernmental gas relations may provide comfort to some, while for others this is a cause for alarm. The sense of urgency is also apparent in the swift succession of initiatives to foster new rules and the leadership role the EU contemplates to take on globally to tackle the challenges it sees. This can also be derived from a general report on the EU's activities that discusses energy, climate and environment prominently in chapter III.[53] Options for more Europe (EU), govern-

---

Cancun to limit climate change to 2ºC.

[52]Conclusions on Energy European Council EUCO 2/11 CO EUR 2 CONCL 1(Brussels 4 February 2011) item 11 pp 4 at http://www.consilium.europa.eu/uedocs/cms_data/docs/pressdata/en/ec/119141.pdf. See also Communication from the Commission to the European Parliament, the Council, the European Economic and Social Committee and the Committee of the Regions On security of energy supply and international cooperation—"The EU Energy Policy: Engaging with Partners beyond Our Borders" Brussels, 7.9.2011 COM(2011) 539 final.

[53]The *General Report on the Activities of the European Union — 2010* was adopted by the European Commission on 16 February 2011 under reference number SEC(2011) 189 See at http://europa.eu/generalreport/pdf/rg2010_en.pdf.

ment intervention, public funding and coordination to deal more innovatively with the EU's increasing energy market exposure to largely imported sources of fossil energy are recurrent themes. Policies and technologies are increasingly mandated aside of actual EU governance and market realities due to the preponderance of a strategizing bureaucracy based on yet to be tested extrapolation of existing trends. This creates both process and perception risks for EU governance in relations with the U.S. and with external partners,[54] apart from reactions by the EU's own member states, which despite the Lisbon Treaty's appeal for solidarity retain important competencies over energy security and sustainability.

Make Haste with Slow Policy

More consolidated approaches based on agreed policy such as through implementation of the third energy package in the EU and working through multilateral frameworks and dialogue by Transatlantic partners on the international scene should add rationality and predictability. This will allow energy markets, themselves characterized by long-term approaches and an "ecosystem" of complex codependent international relations, to develop and capitalize on new opportunities while adapting to enduring challenges of climate change and energy security based on market needs. Time and transparency are of the essence to foster the necessary trust and confidence in effective multilateral frameworks through cooperative approaches by governments and competition by the energy industry. This enables deployment of the most economically viable options offered by new technology or allow markets to retain sufficient flexibility to capitalize on other unforeseen market developments effectively.[55]

The February 2011 EU Council meeting conclusions on energy and innovation contributed to instill some calm and discipline in EU

---

[54]Interview with Alexander Medvedev: "There is no need to build the Great Wall of China on the gas market" *Gazprom* (14 october 2010) retrieved at: http://www.gazprom.com/press/reportages/interview-medvedev/.

[55]See the speech by the former executive director of the international energy agency Mr. Claude Mandil on energy security to the Clingendael International Energy Programme Advisory Board meeting on the 14th of December 2010 in The Hague at http://www.clingendael.nl//ciep/events/20101214/CIEP%20Lecture%20by%20Mr %20Mandil%2014%20December%202010.pdf.

policymaking on energy security and international cooperation, especially with respect to its foreign policy implications. The EU gears up to navigate the still rather uncharted limits of all that the Lisbon Treaty provides for, and certainly transatlantic partners have been eager to have a more robust partner on their side. This assessment however finds that in principle a transatlantic energy and climate policy is best served by buying time to recalibrate much more cautiously approaches based on market austerity and a reengagement on normative policy. A spirit of solidarity should accommodate diversity of situations among its partners rather than superimpose a centrally administered protectionist EU energy policy. U.S.-EU cooperation should be geared to 2020 by avoiding strident approaches and focusing on well-measured steps in a highly fluid energy market context to minimize rather than exacerbate geopolitical turbulence.

Conclusions

Today's events, notably in relations between the transatlantic partners and the Middle East and North Africa, but less so with former cold war foes China and Russia, underscore the unprecedented uncertainty to which global energy security and sustainability is exposed when normative foreign policy is made secondary to transatlantic preoccupations with security of supply and sustainability concerns. These show that new U.S. and EU energy policy choices, whatever they might be, should be embedded much more convincingly into the values and norms that the transatlantic partners share in their foreign affairs and security policies. This is not only in the interest of economic development, primarily driven by emerging economies, but required to embed more firmly energy security and sustainability concerns in socioeconomic stability. Universal application of fundamental values and norms, which the transatlantic partners provide safe harbor to but do not hold on their own exclusively, must come to the fore in the articulation of a new and more appealing narrative on long-term energy market stability and sustainable economic growth.

Outreach is at the core of the OECD and IEA's mission today. How these institutions engage in global dialogue to facilitate compatible governance, energy policy and security measures by non-member countries shall define the endurance and nature of transatlantic energy relations. Transatlantic energy and sustainability policies institutionalized in the OECD/IEA are also embedded in the wider world through the informal context of the G20 and other platforms and institutions such as the IEF, Energy Charter and UNFCCC. Though policy dialogue can still be strengthened and extended here, the WTO stands out as a more appropriate venue to move towards further inclusion and implementation notably by virtue of its general cross-sector approach and genuine global appeal.

More consolidated approaches based on agreed policy and through multilateral frameworks and dialogue on the international scene is a sluggish undertaking. Informal venues may provide political impetus and some relief, but cannot provide a viable alternative. Time is an essential component in advancing multilateral market disciplines. With the exception of elementary norms and values, the transatlantic partners should not expect to receive instant gratification on these where we disagree. However, increased U.S. engagement in the multilateral scene is urgently required to add weight and augment appeal through modernization and re-engagement. Emphasis could be shifted from debating market models with Russia, MENA and the Asia Pacific towards more fertile ground, such as their own modernization, governance and development needs.

While buying time by avoiding the launch of new organizations, initiatives and rules on energy, a new policy narrative on energy security and sustainability needs to be created. This should enable the formulation of a credible and comprehensive energy diplomacy for the 21st century that the transatlantic partnership urgently needs. Such a narrative should go beyond market fundamentals, investment and trade terms that carry themselves quite well, but dare to speak to the norms and values that characterize the transatlantic relationship at its core and need to be carried more convincingly, as they ultimately provide for its global appeal.

Section VI

The Future of the Knowledge Economy

Chapter 11

The Changing Global Knowledge Landscape: The Need for a Transatlantic Vision and a New Pragmatism

Bengt-Åke Lundvall

"No matter if it is a white cat or a black cat; as long as it can catch mice, it is a good cat."—*Deng Xiaoping 1962, actually a Sichuan proverb*

In the first part of this chapter I present data on the global distribution of knowledge production and innovation capabilities. They show a remarkable growth of investment in academic knowledge in China and stagnation in the U.S. and Europe. But they also show that innovation capacity is still limited in China. This is the background for the priority given to 'indigenous' innovation in China's medium to long term plan presented in Appendix 1. How should Europe and the U.S. tackle this situation? Is the right response increased techno-nationalism?

In the second part of the chapter I present results from new research that indicates the need for a broader approach to innovation and innovation policy that brings to the forefront 'the social dimension of the learning economy.' I discuss implications for innovation policy in Europe and the United States. I propose that the U.S. and Europe need a new vision based upon a learning economy perspective as well as a more pragmatic perspective upon the respective roles of market and state.

Table 1. Global Distribution of R&D 1990, 2000 and 2007

Share of total global R&D in percent and R&D as a share of GNP in percent[a]

	1990		2000		2007	
	Share	R&D-Int.	Share	R&D-Int.	Share	R&D-Int.
USA	38.2	2.3	37.2	2.3	34.7	2.3
Japan	16.3	3.1	13.0	2.9	13.0	3.4
China	3.0	0.8	6.7	1.0	9.2	1.5
India	0.6	0.8	2.6	0.7	2.2	0.8

[a] E. Arond and M. Bell, "Trends in the Global Distribution of R&D since the 1970s: Data, Their Interpretation and Limitations," STEPS-Working Paper, SPRU and IDS, Sussex University, 2010.

The Changing Global Knowledge Landscape

Arond and Bell give a unique global coverage of R&D efforts for the period 1970-2010.[1] In table 1 I have summarized some of the most important trends.

Europe does not appear in the table. Actually, the distribution of research efforts within Europe went through a radical transformation in connection with the dissolution of the Soviet Union. The share of global R&D expenditure of the former Soviet republics was for instance drastically reduced from 33% to 3% between 1973 and 2000. But it is well known that the 3% target for R&D as share of GNP that was set by the European Council in Barcelona 2002 to be reached 2010 for the EU15 has not been met. Actually the EU-area's R&D-intensity stagnated at around 1.8% between 2000 and 2008 and in 2010 was still about 2.0%.

The growth of China's share and R&D-intensity 2000-2007 reflects an annual growth rate of R&D expenditure of 20% per annum. China's 15-year plan aims at raising its R&D-intensity to 2.5%, which presupposes a similar rate of growth per annum between 2006 and 2020.

---

[1] E. Arond and M. Bell, "Trends in the Global Distribution of R&D since the 1970s: Data, Their Interpretation and Limitations," *STEPS-Working Paper*, SPRU and IDS, Sussex University, 2010.

Table 2. Global Distribution of Scientific Publications 1990, 2000 and 2005

Share of total global number of scientific publications in per cent and annual rate of growth in %.

	1995	2000	2005	Annual growth rate 95-05
USA	34	31	29	0.5%
European Union	35	35	33	1%
Japan	8	9	8	2%
China	1.6	2.9	5.9	16.5%
India	1.7	1.6	2.1	4.5%

Reinhilde Veugelers contributes to the picture of the changes in the knowledge landscape based upon data on the global distribution of scientific publications.[2] I have presented some of her data in Table 2.

For the whole world the annual rate of R&D expenditure growth is around 2%. Japan has a corresponding rate of growth while the growth in the U.S. and in the European Union is below the average. The rate of growth in India and China is above the average.

Veugelers also presents data on doctoral degrees in different parts of the world. She does not give aggregate data on the EU so instead we include Germany as a representative of Europe.

Table 3 offers a picture very similar to that derived from the growth of R&D and the mapping of scientific publications. Both input and output in the academic system are growing much more rapidly in China than in the rest of the world. The investment in science and the output from science have either stagnated or grown moderately in the U.S. and in the EU. Japan seems to be more committed to investment in knowledge than the U.S. and EU. India has registered even stronger growth rates in scientific output than Japan.

Another process that contributes to the on-going changes in the global knowledge landscape is the mobility of students and scientists between countries and continents. In 2005 there were 2.7 million students studying abroad. As can be seen from Table 4, the biggest share

---

[2] Reinhilde Veugelers, "Towards a Multipolar Science World," *Scientometrics*, Vol. 82, No. 2, 2010, pp. 439-456.

Table 3. Doctoral Degrees Awarded in Selected Countries 1995-2003 and Growth Rates 1995-2005[a]

	1995	2003	Annual growth rate 95-05
USA	41.747	40.740	0.4%
Germany	22.387	23.043	1,5%
Japan	12.645	16.314	2.9%
China	4.364	18.806	18.7%
India	9.070	13.733	4.2%

[a]E. Arond and M. Bell, "Trends in the Global Distribution of R&D since the 1970s: Data, Their Interpretation and Limitations," STEPS-Working Paper, SPRU and IDS, Sussex University, 2010.

Table 4. The International Flow of Students 2005

Share of the total origin country outflow that goes to a specific country of destination in percent[a]

	Country of destination			
	US	UK	Germany	France
Country of origin share				
China 16%	23%	13%	7%	4.0%
India 5.5%	60%	12%	3%	0.4%
Brazil 0.7%	38%	6%	9%	9%
Russia 1.6%	12%	5%	28%	6%
Host country share	27%	17%	14%	6%

[a]E. Arond and M. Bell, "Trends in the Global Distribution of R&D since the 1970s: Data, Their Interpretation and Limitations," STEPS-Working Paper, SPRU and IDS, Sussex University, 2010.

came from China, followed by India. The country receiving most foreign students was the U.S., followed by the UK.

The proportion of students who stay on in their host country once their studies are completed is quite high, especially for students coming from China and India (around 90%). This is reflected, not least, in the high presence of university scholars coming from abroad in the U.S. (in 2005 almost 100,000, constituting 30-40% of the total number of university researchers). The number of Chinese scholars in the U.S. is estimated to be around 20,000 (between 5% and 10% of all university researchers in the U.S.). They constitute even bigger proportions of doctoral students in natural science and mathematics.

Not surprisingly, co-publication data tend to reflect the patterns of mobility of students and scholars. Co-publication data demonstrate that the U.S. remains an important node in global academic networking. 40% of China's co-published papers were co-published with U.S. authors in 2005, while the share of papers co-published with European authors was significantly lower. The U.S. share was stable while the EU share fell between 2000 and 2006.[3]

Global Patenting Shows China's Weakness in Technical Innovation

The data presented above indicate a dramatic increase in China's relative contribution to the production of scientific knowledge. The results can be used to argue that the U.S. and Europe are falling seriously behind. The true picture, however, is somewhat less dramatic. First, in a system in which the leading authorities set up ambitious goals for investment in knowledge there will be a tendency to overstate numbers when reporting results both at the lower level of the system and at the level of central statistics. A closer analysis also indicates that the 'quality' of input and output is systematically lower than what we find in the U.S. and Europe. Yet even with such caveats taken into account, the scale and growth of the effort is impressive.

Second, and this is more important, the increase in the production of scientific knowledge and in the training of scientists is not yet reflected in a corresponding increase in technical innovation. Currently, Chinese firms contribute very little directly to innovation at the global level. Boeing and Sandner present data on patenting that indicate that China's capacity to transform academic knowledge into radical innovation remains weak.[4] They divide patents into three classes—high, medium and low. They assume that very valuable patents will be filed in all major markets, and therefore they define high-value patents as those filed in the Triad (U.S., Japan and Europe). Intermediate-value patents are defined as patents taken out both in

---

[3] Ibid.

[4] S. P. Boeing and P. Sandner, "The Innovative Performance of China's National Innovation System," Working Paper presented at the DRUID Academy, January 2011, Frankfurt School of Finance & Management.

the home country and in one of the Triad-countries. Low-value patents are those only applied for in the home country.

In the following citation the two authors compare China's performance with that of the U.S. and Germany:

> The comparatively low total volumes of high value patent family applications represent the strong filter function of the triadic patent family. China starts with 5 patent applications in 1990 and reaches 25 patent applications in 2005. In comparison, we can observe 2,139 patent applications in 1990 and 606 in 2005 for Germany. The corresponding volumes for the United States are 5,784 in 1990 and 1,722 in 2005. Considering the growth rate, applications in China increase by 400 percent in 2005 in comparison to the base year 1990. In the intermediate value class ... 1990, we observe 51 patent applications in China, compared to 10,101 in Germany and 40,232 in the United States. Thus, China starts with 0.5 percent of the German and around 0.1 percent of the United State's volume. In 2005 we observe 2,528 patent applications in China, an increase of roughly 5,000 percent in yearly application compared to the base year 1990. Despite the impressive growth rate, China reaches only 14 percent of German applications and 5 percent of the patent applications of the United States in 2005. China's total patent applications in the entire period sum up to 6,500. This figure presents a fraction of around 3 percent of the German and around 0.75 percent of the United States' volume. Considering the low value class, volumes in Germany and the United States rises moderately but volatile over the period, whereas China reaches a strong growth rate in the late 1990s and increases continuously until 2005. For China, we observe 27,343 patent applications in 1990 and 187,067 patents applications in 2005—an increase in yearly applications by approximately 500 percent. In total, China accumulated around 1.2 million patent applications in the entire period.[5]

---

[5] Ibid.

While the annual growth rate for patents is impressive in all classes (for 1995–2005 it is 33% for the low class patents) the starting point is low and in comparison to Japan, the U.S. and Germany the very modest contribution to TRIAD-patents indicates a weakness in terms of radical high value innovation. This is accentuated by an analysis that takes into account the international origin of firms operating in China and applying for TRIAD-patents. Of the 25 Chinese patent applications in this class in 2005 no less than 21 came from foreign firms operating in China. There were only three Chinese firms engaged in triad patenting—Huawei and ZTV, each of which operates in the telecommunications industry; and BYD, which operates in the automotive and high-tech battery industry.

Various indicators suggest that so far the massive investment in research has been translated only to a limited extent into corresponding innovation performance in Chinese enterprises. Above we have focused upon an indicator that allows for comparisons across countries: the frequency of different types of patent applications. This indicator is far from unproblematic since institutional and historical conditions will affect the propensity to legally protect new technologies. As regards China, we must bear in mind that a regular legal framework for the protection of intellectual property was introduced only a few decades ago. Therefore, we must assume that also for this reason, Chinese enterprises may lag behind Western firms when it comes to patenting. Nevertheless, we find that the gap between China and the West is surprisingly large in this respect.

A Synthetic Indicator of Innovation Performance

Archibugi, et. al present a global innovation scoreboard aiming at comparing innovation performance across countries and regions.[6] The indicator combines information about firms, human resources and infrastructure. Table 5 compares the EU, Japan, the U.S., India and China, focusing on 1995 and 2005. The overall picture is that the gap between the Triad and the emerging economies remains big but that

---

[6] D. Archibugi, M. Denni and A. Filipetti, "The global innovation scoreboard 2008: The dynamics of the innovative performances of countries," *Innometrics* (Brussels: European Commission, 2009).

Table 5. Ranking in the Global Innovation Scoreboard 2005 for USA, EU, Japan, China and India (with the 1995-2005 change in ranking in parenthesis), based upon a total of 48 countries.

	Overall	Firm activities	Human resources	Infrastructure and absorptive capacity
USA	6 (-3)	8 (-2)	6 (-1)	7 (-6)
European Union	20 (-3)	16 (-1)	19 (-4)	21 (-2)
Japan	5 (-1)	1 (+2)	13 (-3)	9 (-4)
China	34 (+8)	25 (+7)	48 (-3)	31 (+9)
India	46 (+1)	35 (+11)	42 (0)	38 (+7)

there is a process of catching up. It should be noted that four EU countries (Sweden, Finland, Denmark and Germany) are ranked among the top ten—the relatively weak position of the EU reflects its heterogeneous character.

It is worth noting that the catching-up is especially strong in the field of infrastructure and absorptive capacity. This indicator gives equal weight to ICT expenditures per capita, broadband penetration and public R&D as share of GDP. It seems as if the weakening position of the U.S. and Europe is related to stagnating public efforts to build infrastructure.[7]

Can China Change its Comparative Advantage?

So far China's economic growth has been based upon a rapid expansion of manufacturing for exports. A major driver has been the

---

[7] The global innovation scoreboard represents a systematic effort to compare innovation capacity. But it is dependent first on what is easy to measure, and second it is strongly biased in favor of formal academic codified knowledge. The quality of linkages in the innovation system, the quality of the overall labor force, corporate governance, managerial competences, social capital, social cohesion and the organization of work are all crucial factors for innovation performance but are not included in the scoreboard. Here a wider set of data such as those presented in Castellaci and Natera might be helpful. But even those omit important systemic features related to how organizational learning at the workplace takes place. See F. Castellaci and J.M. Natera, "A new panel data set for cross-country analyses of national systems, growth and development," *NUPI working paper*. Oslo, NUPI (2011).

extremely high rate of capital accumulation combined with imitation strategy. The annual savings ratio and investment ratio has been between 40-50% and the annual growth rate around 10%. The pattern corresponds well with the kind of strategy that the classical development economists (Hirschman, Sen and Rosenstein Rodan) saw as the most realistic way toward economic development for poor countries. But the current growth pattern is not sustainable. There are environmental, social and international barriers that makes it impossible to move much further ahead along the current trajectory.[8]

Attempts to compensate and bring innovation into the domestic economy through attracting foreign direct investments on a large scale have not been as successful as expected. China attracts more foreign direct investments than any other country in the world with the exception of the U.S. and the UK. During the past five years, hundreds of new R&D centers have been established by foreign companies in China. In several recent surveys, executives from multinational companies rated China as the most attractive country for future R&D investments. China has become a large exporter of high technology products, which accounted for one-fourth of China's total exports in 2005.

Nonetheless, as seen from its limited contribution to high value patenting, China's strategy of attracting foreign technology and knowledge has only partially been successful. A large share of China's high-tech exports consists of imports of high-tech components which are assembled in China and then exported abroad. Moreover, no less than 80% of China's high technology exports emanates from firms that are wholly or partially owned by foreign capitalists. This is the background for the emphasis on 'independent innovation' in the new plan.

The openness to foreign capital and the massive entrance of Chinese diaspora capitalists from other parts of Asia brought with it management and marketing skills. But the spill over from FDI in terms of increased capacity to innovate to the population of domestic firms has been quite limited. This may reflect weak corporate governance in state owned enterprises—top managers pass through as part of a

---

[8] See S. Gu and B.-Å. Lundvall, "China's innovation system and the move toward harmonious growth and endogenous innovation," *Innovation: Management, Policy & Practice*, Vol. 8, No. 1-2 (2006), pp. 1-26.

mainly political career reinforcing short-termism.[9] It may also reflect a corporate culture that does not make use of the creativity of employees. The education system does not promote creativity but it seems as if foreign firms have been more successful than the domestic ones to overcome this barrier to innovation within China.

For China as a whole this indicates a comparative advantage in the production of standard commodities that are intensive in the use of physical capital and labor. But, as mentioned, there are limits to how far this trajectory can followed and it is obvious that the vision of China's current leaders is to change China's comparative advantage to make it more 'innovation-intensive.' They refer to 'indigenous innovation' as indicating a new model of economic growth where Chinese owned firms begin to contribute much more to new, high-value innovations.

One significant step in this direction was taken by the 2006 15-year medium-long term plan for science and technology, where almost 100 specific initiatives were defined with tasks allocated to specific authorities and individuals (See Appendix 1). When the first version of the plan was sent forward to Prime Minister Wen Jiabao (former professor in Geology) from the Ministry of Science and Technology, he refused to accept it because it was too vague. He forced all parties to specify their contributions.[10]

The strong and direct engagement of China's top leaders in science and technology policy reflects their academic background and is characteristic for China. Eight of the nine members of the standing committee of the Politburo of the Communist Party have an academic background in engineering or natural science—the ninth combines a degree in law with a Ph.D. in economics. Four of them are graduates from the prestigious Tsinghua University.

---

[9] J. Liu, and A. Tylecote, "Corporate Governance and Technological Capability Development: Three Case Studies in the Chinese Auto Industry," *Industry & Innovation*, Vol. 16, Issue 4-5 (2009), pp. 525-544.

[10] S. Gu, B.-Å. Lundvall, F. Malerba, J. Liu and S. Schwaag Serger, "China's System and Vision of Innovation: An Analysis in Relation to the Strategic Adjustment and the Medium- to Long-Term S&T Development Plan (2006-20)," *Industry and Innovation*, Vol. 16, Issue 4-5 (2009), pp. 369-388.

Actually, many Chinese economists are quite critical of the technology enthusiasm and the emphasis given to innovation by the current top leaders. The current debate is not so different from the one in Japan in the 1950s between MITI engineers and Bank of Japan economists over the right industrialization track to follow. As the Japanese case illustrates, a change in comparative advantage may be a way to accelerate economic development.

How Should Europe and the U.S. Respond?

Does the acceleration of knowledge investments in China signal the decline of the West, and should it be countered by aggressive technonationalism in Europe and the U.S. in the form of intellectual protectionism? A broader and deeper understanding of the innovation process leads to a more nuanced picture and to a different kind of response.

As we have seen, China's capacity to innovate is still quite limited as compared to that of Europe and especially to the capacity of the U.S. The U.S. competitive advantage is an innovation mode that combines strong technological capacity with entrepreneurial initiative, managerial competence and advanced markets for services. Parts of Europe, not least the egalitarian welfare states in Scandinavia, have a unique potential when it comes to mobilize employees in processes of change and to engage consumers as advanced users.

Retain and further developing these competitive advantages may be the best way to respond to China's growing contribution to the global knowledge base. That would make it possible to transform new scientific ideas developed abroad, including those developed in China, into attractive and useful new products and services. But in order to do so a certain 'absorptive capacity' is of course needed, and this absorptive capacity requires domestic/regional production of scientific knowledge. It is therefore necessary (but not sufficient) to host high-quality academic research, technological institutes engaged in applied science and firms with strong R&D departments in order to be able to transform new knowledge into innovation.

Rather than viewing the growth of China's effort as a threat, the U.S. and Europe should welcome its contribution to the knowledge commons. It is true that the current emphasis in China upon 'indigenous innovation' and the tendency among Chinese firms to 'borrow and steal' technologies both from domestic competitors and from Western companies seems to contradict such a perspective. But it is nonetheless the case that both the U.S.-system of innovation and firms from EU and the U.S. already reaped significant benefits from China's investment in higher education and science. The Chinese intellectuals in the U.S. and the research laboratories located in China owned by firms from the U.S. and from Europe have in different ways contributed to innovation in the U.S. and in Europe.

A major challenge will be to cope with China's strategic shift toward 'indigenous innovation'. One rational response might be to give China a stronger position in the international rule-setting system, including the WTO, and to use this system as well as informal mechanisms to develop fair and transparent global rules for how to share and protect knowledge at the global level—rules that establish positive sum games and maximize common benefits world-wide, not forgetting about the region that stands as the major loser in the new context—Africa. On this basis a broadening and deepening of technological collaboration between the U.S. and Europe with China could take place.

The Learning Economy and the Need for a Broader Understanding of the Innovation System

The concept of 'the learning economy' refers to a specific phase of capitalist development where a combination of factors such as globalization, deregulation of finance and the widespread use of information and communication technologies *speeds up the rate of change* in different dimensions (on the demand side user needs change rapidly, and on the supply side there is acceleration in the creation, diffusion and use of new technology).[11]

The learning economy is characterized by cumulative circular causation. The selection by employers of more learning-prone employees and the market selection in favor of change-oriented firms accelerate further innovation and change. In this context the key to economic success for a national or regional economy is its capacity to renew

---

[11]B.-Å. Lundvall and B. Johnson, 'The learning economy,' *Journal of Industry Studies*, Vol. 1, No. 2, December 1994, pp. 23-42.

competences in order to be able to move into activities that are less exposed to global competition.

The mapping of knowledge pursued above has not captured the characteristics that determine success in the learning economy. The data sets cover mainly academic knowledge and do not capture learning processes taking place in the production system.

The same narrow perspective dominates the innovation policy strategies developed in China as well as in Europe and the U.S. Too much emphasis is on the role of codified scientific knowledge and too little attention is given to organizational learning. The innovation system is understood as encompassing mainly research, education and high technology industry, and innovation policy is correspondingly narrowly defined. The important role of employees in the innovation process is neglected.

Over the last 20 years I have been engaged in research that shows that the innovation process can be successful only if it combines science-based learning with experience-based learning, and that we therefore need a broad definition both of the innovation system and innovation policy.[12] In this section I will build upon some recent outcomes of research showing:

— that innovation requires a combination of science-based and experience based knowledge;[13]

— that innovation thrives in countries where a big proportion of the employees are engaged in work activities involving problem solving and learning;[14]

---

[12]See for instance the Post-Script in B.-Å. Lundvall, ed., *National systems of innovation: Towards a theory of innovation and interactive learning* (London: Anthem Press. 1992/2010).

[13]M.B. Jensen, B. Johnson, E. Lorenz and B.-Å. Lundvall, "Forms of knowledge and modes of innovation," *Research Policy*, Vol. 36, No. 5, June 2007.

[14]A. Arundel, E. Lorenz, B.-Å. Lundvall and A. Valeyre, "How Europe's economies learn: a comparison of work organization and innovation mode for the EU-15," *Industrial and Corporate Change*, Vol. 16, No. 6 (2007).

— that the dramatic differences within Europe in how people learn at the workplace reflect differences in national institutional settings in relation to education and labor markets;[15]

— that workers engage more widely in processes of change in innovation systems with strong welfare states and egalitarian income distribution.[16]

Below I present some of the evidence. For detail and insight in the underlying methodology I refer to the referenced publications.

How Europe's Economies Learn

Figure 1 indicates that countries with wide participation in discretionary learning have a bigger share of firms that develop their own innovations and innovations new to the market.

In Holm et. al[17] we show that the frequency of discretionary learning is correlated with certain institutional characteristics that can be affected by public policy. The results suggest first that continuing vocational training goes hand in hand with high shares of discretionary learning. They also point to a north/south divide within Europe. The Nordic countries are characterized by relatively high levels of vocational training and by relatively high-level use of discretionary learning forms.

Another important field of public policy that sets the framework for how work is organized is labor market policy. EU member states display large differences in systems of employment and unemployment protection. The analysis indicates that systems combining high levels of unemployment protection with relatively low levels of employment protection may have an advantage in terms of the adoption of the forms of work organisation that promote learning and 'new to the market'-innovation.[18]

---

[15]J.R. Holm, E. Lorenz, B.-A. Lundvall and A. Valeyre, "Organisational Learning and Systems of Labour Market Regulation in Europe," *Industrial and Corporate Change*, Volume 19, Issue 4 (2010), pp. 1141-1173.

[16]B.-Å. Lundvall, 'Innovation systems and economic development,' *Innovation and Development*, Vol. 1, No. 1, pp.

[17]Ibid.

[18]Holm, op. cit.

Figure 1. Lead Innovators by Discretionary Learning

% Lead innovators by % discretionary learning

% discretionary learning

R-squared = .39

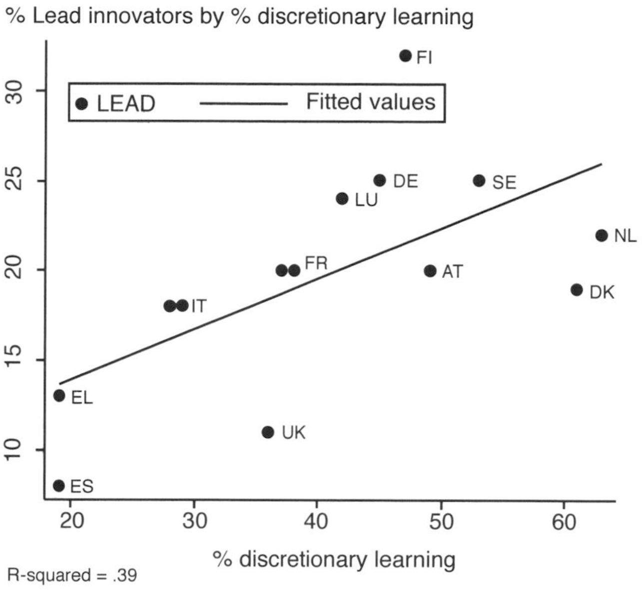

On the Competitive Advantage of Egalitarian Innovation Systems

The data referenced above on organizational models of learning in different European countries make it possible also to develop a more dynamic and adequate indicator of inequality than the ones based upon income distribution.[19]

In Table 7 we compare degree of inequality in access to learning with corresponding international differences in income inequality for the EU-15. The data on income inequality emanate from a paper by Brandolini and Smeeding (2007)[20] on inequality patterns and refer to the Gini coefficient with respect to disposable income. Both data sets cover the year 2000.

---

[19]B.-Å, Lundvall, P. Rasmussen, P. and E. Lorenz, 'Education in the Learning Economy: a European perspective,' *Policy Futures in Education*, Volume 6 Number 2, 2008, pp. 681-700.

[20]A. Brandolini and C. Smeeding, 'Inequality Patterns in Western-Type Democracies: Cross-Country Differences and Time Changes', Working Paper, *Syracuse University*, 2007.

Table 6. National Differences in Organizational Models

Percent of employees by organizational class

	Discretionary learning	Share of managers in discretionary learning	Share of workers in discretionary learning	Learning inequality index*
North				
Netherlands	64.0	81.6	51.1	37.3
Denmark	60.0	85.0	56.2	35.9
Sweden	52.6	76.4	38.2	50.3
Finland	47.8	62.0	38.5	37.9
Austria	47.5	74.1	44.6	39.9
Center				
Germany	44.3	65.4	36.8	43.8
Luxembourg	42.8	70.3	33.1	52.9
Belgium	38.9	65.7	30.8	53.1
France	38.0	66.5	25.4	61.9
West				
UK	34.8	58.9	20.1	65.9
Ireland	24.0	46.7	16.4	64.9
South				
Italy	30.0	63.7	20.8	67.3
Portugal	26.1	59.0	18.2	69.2
Spain	20.1	52.4	19.1	63.5
Greece	18.7	40.4	17.0	57.9

*The index is constructed by dividing the share of 'workers' engaged in discretionary learning by the share of 'managers' engaged in discretionary learning and subtracting the resulting percentage from 100. If the share of workers and managers were the same, the index would equal 0, and if the share of workers was 0 the index would equal 100.

The most striking result is that the countries with the highest degree of income inequality (UK and Portugal) are amongst those most unequal in terms of access to discretionary learning, and that those countries with the most equal income distribution (Denmark and Netherlands) also offer the most egalitarian access to jobs with discretionary learning.

This pattern indicates that workers are given and take on more responsibility at the workplace in countries in countries where income distribution is more egalitarian. There seems to be a major 'system effect' from income distribution upon the degree of participation in processes of work. In an era with growing income inequality in the

Table 7. Comparing Income Inequality with Organizational Learning Inequality

	Income inequality Gini Coefficient	Ranking income inequality	Inequality in organizational learning	Ranking inequality in organizational learning
Austria	0.257	11	39.9	12
Belgium	0.279	7	53.1	8
Denmark	0.225	15	35.9	15
Finland	0.246	12	37.9	13
France	0.278	8	61.9	6
Germany	0.275	9	43.8	11
Greece	0.334	4-5	57.9	7
Italy	0.334	4-5	67.3	2
Ireland	0.313	6	64.9	4
Luxembourg	0.260	10	52.9	9
Netherlands	0.231	14	37.3	14
Portugal	0.363	1	69.2	1
Spain	0.336	3	63.5	5
Sweden	0.252	12	50.3	10
United Kingdom	0.343	2	65.9	3

Sources: Brandolini and Schmeeding 2007 p. 31 and the last column of Table 3.

U.S., in China and in most European countries this raises important questions about how increased inequality affects participatory learning. One fundamental cause of the weakening of the competitiveness of countries may be 'below the radar' and reflect that growing income inequality reduces the willingness of workers to take an active part in processes of organisational learning.

The learning-economy perspective may help explain the fact that the Nordic welfare states come out strong in all rankings related to innovation. Most interesting forms of learning take place in interaction between people. When it comes to implement innovation a close interaction between workers and managers is crucial for success.

Implications for Europe, the United States and China

A more complete and relevant mapping of the global knowledge landscape should include the learning that takes place among employees, but the data are missing. The outcome of global technological competition will reflect not only the investment in higher education and in research. It will depend upon a broader institutional setting and a wider set of public policies including labour market policy, education policy and not least programs supporting adult vocational training.

The current problems of the European monetary union reflect structural weaknesses, and the low frequency of discretionary learning in the so-called peripheral countries may be seen as a relevant indicator for this weakness. They also reflect the failure of the EU's Lisbon strategy to realize its goals of 'more social cohesion' and knowledge-based economic growth. Specifically, it did not succeed in transforming education and labor market institutions in the peripheral countries so that the institutional setting could support organizational learning. European leaders did not understand the requirements of the learning economy and therefore they made the mistake of regarding that 'social cohesion' as a burden and not as an asset.

Currently, Europe's weakest point is its high degree of inequality. Galbraith has shown that Europe is much more unequal in terms of regional income distribution than the U.S.: "When this comparison is undertaken, the results are quite striking. A European cross-regions Gini coefficient comes in at about .235, or more than twice the value of .101 computed across the 51 [sic] American states."[21]

Galbraith argues quite convincingly that increasing regional equality would be an efficient way to increase employment, since employment rates are higher in more egalitarian countries and regions. Here we would add that a more egalitarian Europe would be better prepared to cope with the globalizing learning economy and contribute more to innovation. One of Galbraith's interesting proposals is to let Europe fund and build *European* universities, throughout the European periphery, on a scale and of a quality to rival higher education in the United States.

The U.S. and Europe are pushing China to become more like themselves, not only when it comes to human rights and democracy,

---

[21]J.K. Galbraith, 'Maastricht 2042 and the Fate of Europe: Toward Convergence and Full Employment,' University of Texas Inequality Project, *UTIP Working Paper*, no. 39, September, 2006.

but also when it comes to finance, intellectual property rights and competition. And it is correct that 'systemic differences' do give rise to increasing friction as national systems get closer to each other through an increase in their economic interaction.[22] But it might be a mistake to expect all the adaptation to take place in China. Chinese leaders have excelled in pragmatism when it comes to promoting economic reform (installing private ownership and market mechanisms whenever it serves their purpose) while the political and ideological leaders of the West suffer from the heritage of a neo-liberal vision where markets are always for the good and governments and planning are often seen as threats to freedom.

There is both in the U.S. and in Europe a need for a paradigmatic shift where the exaggerated belief in markets is changed into a pragmatic perspective where governments take on the tasks necessary to promote sustainable economic growth. This includes establishing a strict regulation of financial markets. But most importantly it involves a rethinking and redesign of policies and institutions so that they take seriously that we are in a new phase where knowledge is the most important resource and learning the most important process. This includes building institutions that make it possible to engage more people as active contributors to the process of innovation.

The EU's new Europe 2020 strategy sets ambitious goals for the EU, including 'smart growth' as materialised in an Innovation Union. But the experience from the Lisbon strategy is that the goals will not be reached within the current mode of governance. To achieve such goals, the integration process must accelerate and the current monetary union must be transformed into an economic and social union. Movement toward a fiscal union is needed to bolster the building of a European welfare state and a European knowledge infrastructure. The basis for such movement could be a European vision that takes seriously the original idea behind the Lisbon Strategy—the combination of social cohesion and competitiveness.

---

[22]S. Ostry and R. R. Nelson, *Techno-Nationalism and Techno-Globalism: Conflict and Cooperation* (Washington: Brookings Institution Press, 1995).

Appendix: China's 2006-2020 Science Technology Development Plan[23]

On February 9, 2006, the State Council presented its strategy for strengthening China's scientific and technological progress in the coming 15 years (State Council 2006a). The plan reflects ambitions to make China one of the world's most innovative countries. In addition, it contains an explicit target to reduce China's dependence on foreign research and development using public procurement as a way of strengthening its domestic capabilities. The aim of this Appendix is to provide a critical assessment of the plan. First, we identify key components of the plan and examine the actors, processes and driving forces explaining its development. Second, we analyze the plan in the context of China's larger socio-economic challenges. Finally, we assess how the 15-year plan relates to some of the principal weaknesses in China's innovation policy and its innovation system.

The General Targets of the Plan

The plan sets eight major objectives to be reached over the 15-year plan horizon:

1. Industries important for the country's national competitiveness, should develop and master core technologies at world-class level.

2. The scientific and technological base of agricultural production should become one of the most advanced in the world.

3. Breakthroughs should take place in energy exploration, energy-saving technology and clean energy technology.

4. Scientific and technological efforts should support building of a resource-efficient and environment-friendly society.

---

[23]This section draws upon S. Gu, B.-Å. Lundvall, F. Malerba, J. Liu and S. Schwaag Serger, "China's System and Vision of Innovation: An Analysis in Relation to the Strategic Adjustment and the Medium- to Long-Term S&T Development Plan (2006-20)," *Industry and Innovation*, Vol. 16, Issue 4-5 (2009), pp. 369-388.

5. Major progress should be achieved in fighting major diseases and in epidemics prevention.

6. The development of S&T for national defense should support R&D of modern weapons and equipment, for information technology for the army, and for safeguarding national security.

7. Scientists and research teams should reach world-class levels, and breakthroughs in science should be achieved specifically in information, biology, materials and space technologies.

8. World-class research institutions as well as internationally competitive business R&D institutes should be developed.

The aim is a complete national innovation system with Chinese characteristics.

The plan lists sixteen key projects. The common criteria for these projects are that they address significant socioeconomic problems, and that they will develop technologies where China already possesses sufficient competence. Examples of key projects are to put a Chinese on the moon and to develop the next generation of jumbo jets. Others focus on the development of fast processors, high-performance chips, oil and gas exploitation, nuclear power technology, water purification, new drugs, fighting AIDS and hepatitis, and developing the next generation of broad band technology.

The plan addresses strategic technologies. Among these are biotechnology, IT, advanced materials, production technology, advanced energy technology, oceanography, laser and space technology. These priorities are not radically different from what has been behind earlier generations of science and technology programs. But the urgency in relation to finding solutions on environmental and energy problems is stronger and the ambition to build 'independent innovation capacity' is more explicit. There are also some major differences in the tools proposed for implementing the plan. Public procurement and tax subsidies are given stronger emphasis and in general there seems to be a new kind of mobilization around the strategy.

One novel method suggested in the plan is tax incentives for small and medium-sized enterprises which are intended to encourage companies to invest in R&D and even to establish R&D activities abroad. The latter is particularly interesting and it might be unique for China. It signals that 'independent innovation' does not aim at decoupling Chinese firms from global sources of knowledge and innovation.

The Main Features of the Plan

An NSI-perspective

According to the documents presenting the plan, for the first time the concept of *national innovation system* is used to structure a mid-and-long-term plan (Lu 2007). The plan defines the national innovation system as a social system where government is in a guiding position, market plays a fundamental role to deploy resources, and various sources of S&T innovation link tightly and interact effectively. It is referred to 'a national innovation system with Chinese characteristics.'

Governance

To promote and improve the building of a national innovation system, institutional reform will take place in the country's S&T system. According to the plan, "the national S&T decision making system and macro coordination mechanism for S&T policy will be improved. General planning and administration of the development of S&T by the government will be strengthened. S&T policies will act as the country's fundamental public policy. The system for examining and appraising S&T quality, and as the system for assessing and rewarding S&T achievements are to be reformed. Justice, fairness, openness, and innovation-friendliness will be embodied into the system."

The Purpose of the Plan and the Brave Target Numbers

The plan explicitly sets some rather ambitious quantitative targets to be reached over the 15 year period. First, the proportion of R&D expenditures of GDP will be raised from 1.3% to 2.5% of GDP. Second, more than half of economic growth should emanate from 'technical progress'—i.e. not from the extended use of labor and capital. Third, reliance on foreign technology should be reduced from 60% to 30%.

Enterprises as Main Force for Innovation

As indicated by the basic definition of the 'system of innovation,' it is assumed that the national government has a lead role, but it is also argued that markets play a major role. The plan states that enterprises should be seen as being at the very core of the innovation system.

According to the plan, an innovation-friendly tax policy will be adopted. For instance, 150% of R&D expenditure can be deducted from taxable income of the same year. Companies will be allowed to accelerate depreciation of the equipment used for R&D. Income tax will be remitted for new startups in national high-tech industrial zones for two years once they become profit-making and after these two years the income tax rate for these companies is 15% which is 10 percentage points lower than that for ordinary companies.

Public Procurement

Government procurement is to be used as an important tool to encourage indigenous innovation. The system of procurement of innovative products will be enhanced. The government is to purchase the first vintage of innovation products created by domestic enterprises or research institutions when the innovative products have significant market potential. A control and evaluation system giving guidelines for procuring domestic and foreign products will be set up. Normally, in the purchasing process, domestic products have priority over foreign products. When government procures products from foreign companies, those companies that are willing to transfer technology to local companies will be given priority over other candidates.

Indigenous Innovation

One of most characteristic features of the new plan is the declared intention to strengthen 'independent' or 'indigenous' innovation. Indigenous innovation is defined as a value-creating process resulting in new products based upon core technologies and upon IPR.

Several different policies aim at using IPR to reach the aim. Government will strongly support the IPRs of core technologies and key products. According to the plan, China will actively participate in international standard setting and will promote domestic market-centred technological standards. The plan calls for the government to support research on standards of core technologies, it will guide joint research by industries, universities, and research institutes on technological standards, and it will promote the integration of R&D, design, and manufacturing.

International Cooperation for S&T Development is Highlighted

While there is a strong emphasis on strengthening the domestic capacity to innovate there is no intention to reduce international cooperation on knowledge production. There is a strong emphasis on the potential for drawing upon global sources of knowledge through international cooperation and through attracting expertise from the rest of the world.

The plan envisages that various forms of international and regional cooperation and exchange on S&T will be expanded. Research institutes and universities are encouraged to set up joint laboratories or R&D centers with overseas R&D institutes. International cooperation projects under bilateral or multilateral frameworks of cooperation agreements for S&T will be supported. Companies are encouraged to "go global." Companies that set up overseas R&D institutes and industrialization bases will be encouraged and supported. Multinational companies will be encouraged to set up R&D institutes in China.

Scientists and S&T institutes will be encouraged to join major international scientific projects and international academic organisations. They will also be supported to participate in or lead major international or regional scientific projects.

Dual Use of Scientific Research in Defense and Civilian Sectors

One of the areas where national priorities as well as secrecy are important is scientific and technological research for military purposes. The plan aims to form a dual-use technological and industrial base that serves both military and civilian needs. So far government investment in science and technology development has been divided into two parts, one for military use, and the other for civil use. According to the plan document, over half of all the military R&D projects overlap with civilian ones and it is argued that this has resulted in a lack of investment and a waste of human resources in both areas.

To make full use of economic and social resources the two systems will be integrated. Military research institutes will be encouraged to shoulder tasks of scientific research for civilian use. At the same time, civilian research institutes and enterprises are allowed to take part in national defence research projects. The purchase of military articles will also be expanded to more areas of civilian research organizations and enterprises.

References

Gu, Shulin, *China's Industrial Technology, Market Reform and Organizational Change*, Routledge in association with the UNU Press, London and New York, 1999.

Gu, S., Lundvall, B.-Å., Malerba, F., Liu, J. and Schwaag, Serger, 'China's System and Vision of Innovation: An Analysis in Relation to the Strategic Adjustment and the Medium- to Long-Term S&T Development Plan (2006-20)', *Industry and Innovation*, vol. 16, issue 4-5, (2009), pp. 369-388.

Hong, "Decline of the center: the decentralizing process of knowledge transfer of Chinese universities from 1985 to 2004", *Research Policy*, Vol. 37, (2008), pp. 580-95.

Lin, Zhongping, "The Influence of MNCs upon China's Independent Innovation Capacity", *China S&T Investment*, May 2006, pp.40-43.

Lu, W., "To Improve the National Innovation System and Strengthen Innovation Ability", paper presented at 2007 China Development Forum, Development Research Center of the State Council, Beijing, 2007.

MOST, Preparation of China.s National Medium & Long-Term S & T Development Plan and Its Progress., White Paper by *Ministry of Science and Technology*, 2004.

Mu, R. and Qu, W., 'The development of science and technology in China: A comparison with India and the United States, *Technology in Society*, Vol 3, (2008), pp. 319-29.

State Council of the People's Republic of China (SCPRC) (2006a), Outline of the Long-Term National Plan for the Development of Science and Technology (2006-2020);

State Council Decision Notice of the Implementation of the Long-Term Plan for the Development of Science and Technology and the Increase of Independent Innovation, China Legal Publishing House, Beijing. State Council of the People's Republic of China (SCPRC) (2006b).

Section VII

New and Traditional
Dimensions of Security

Chapter 12

A More Secure World?

Andrew Mack

Since the end of World War II the global security environment has undergone a series of profound changes whose causes remain curiously little examined—even by security analysts.

As Figure 1 reveals, the total number of conflicts—international and civil wars—being waged around the world increased threefold during the Cold War years, then sharply declined, with this latter change going largely unheralded, even at the United Nations.

The forces that have been driving this decline are likely to be sustained, or to increase, in the years ahead, providing grounds for cautious—though qualified—optimism about future security trends.

Patterns of Warfare in the Post-Cold War World

Almost all of the increase in conflict numbers from the end of World War II until the end of the Cold War was accounted for by the proliferation of intrastate conflicts—civil wars. But, as Figure I indicates, following the end of the Cold War, the number of conflicts—almost all intrastate—dropped sharply. By 2008, there were a third fewer conflicts than in 1992.[1]

---

[1] Figure 1 only counts conflicts in which a government is one of the warring parties and is either fighting another government (international conflict) or a non-state armed group (intrastate conflict). Conflicts in which a government in *not* one of the warring parties—intercommunal conflicts, or those between rival rebel groups or warlords, are not counted. There are however relatively few of these conflicts and they are *far* less deadly on average than conflicts in which a state is one of the warring parties. Conflicts are defined here as violent contestations that result in least 25 battle deaths a year. Battle deaths include so-called "collateral damage"—i.e., civilians caught in the crossfire.

Figure 1. Trends in Armed Conflicts by Type, 1946–2008

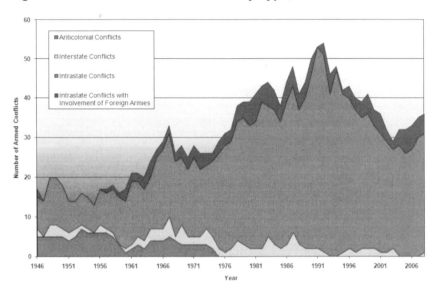

Data source: Uppsala Conflict Data Program/Peace Research Institute Oslo 2009.

From 2003 to 2008 overall conflict numbers increased by some 25 percent. This was due primarily due to an increase in minor conflicts that killed relatively few people. But the number of high-intensity wars (those with an annual battle death toll of 1,000 or more) have continued to decline. By 2008 there were 78 percent fewer of these conflicts being fought around the world than at the end of the 1980s.

Remarkably, not a single full-length study has been devoted to explaining why this extraordinary reduction in conflict numbers— almost all of which were civil wars—has taken place.

How Wars Have Become Less Deadly

The average war in the 1950s killed about 10,000 people a year; in the new millennium the average was a little less than one thousand.

The remarkable, but extremely uneven, reduction in death tolls revealed in Figure 2 has been caused, in part, by the long-term decline in international conflicts (which kill far more people on average than

Figure 2. Trends in Reported Battle Deaths from Armed Conflicts by Region, 1946–2008.

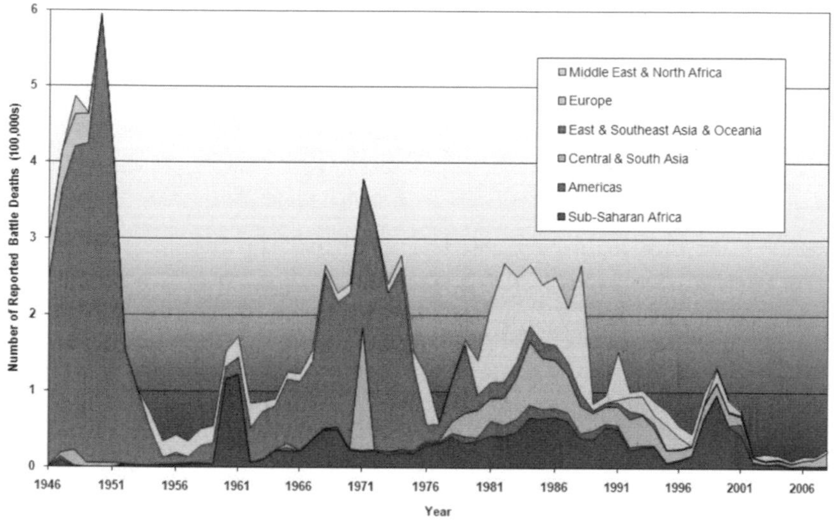

Source: Uppsala Conflict Data Program/Human Security Report Project Dataset 2009.

civil wars), and by the sharp decline in the direct and indirect military interventions by the superpowers in other countries wars that were characteristic of the major conflicts of the Cold War years. These conflicts—from the Chinese Civil War and the Korean and Vietnam Wars to the Soviet invasion and occupation of Afghanistan—typically involved prolonged engagements between huge armies, at least one of which was equipped with heavy conventional weapons such as strike aircraft, tanks, or long-range artillery. Death tolls often exceeded a million.

In the post-Cold War world, wars are mostly fought within, not between, states and by small armies mostly equipped with small arms and light weapons. While often characterized by extreme brutality towards civilians, they have killed relatively few people compared to the major wars of the Cold War period.

And it is not just battle deaths that have declined. Deaths from conflict-exacerbated disease and malnutrition have also been reduced by long-term improvements in public health, notably immunization, that have caused child and adult mortality rates to decline sharply across the developing world over the past 30 years. These improvements, have not only steadily reduced mortality rates in peacetime, but also saved countless lives in wartime.

In addition there have been major increases in the level, scope, and effectiveness of humanitarian assistance to war-affected populations in countries in conflict. These interventions have reduced wartime death tolls still further.

Can We Be Confident About the Trends?

These findings present a picture that is very much at odds with popular—mostly media-derived—depictions of a progressively more violent world. And they raise an obvious question: how reliable are the data? The short answer is that we can be quite confident about the *number* of conflicts, but battle death data are far less reliable. Exaggerated, politically-driven claims about death tolls are common in some conflicts, while undercounting is a problem in most—particularly in wars in very poor countries. But there is no doubt that the 50-plus year trend in battle-related deaths is downwards—no serious scholar would deny that today's wars are, on average, *far* less deadly than those of the Cold War years.

Predicting future security trends is an exercise fraught with peril, as the near-universal failure of the security studies community to predict the end of the Cold War reminds us. But while current statistical models do very poorly at predicting exactly when and where wars will start, considerable progress has been made in establishing the conditions, dynamics and policies that increase—and decrease—the *risks* that countries will succumb to war.

Ironically given the huge, and sometimes disproportionate attention, paid to the risks of war and terrorism, to say nothing of some 1.5-plus trillion dollars a year being devoted to military expenditure around the world, there has been far less attention paid to what prevents or stops wars than what causes them. As Australian historian Geoffrey Blainey succinctly put it. "For every thousand pages on the causes of war, there is less than one page directly on the causes of peace."[2]

---

[2] Geoffrey Blainey, *The Causes of War*, Third Edition (New York, Free Press, 1988), p. 3.

Figure 3. Average Number of International Conflicts per Year, 1950–2008.

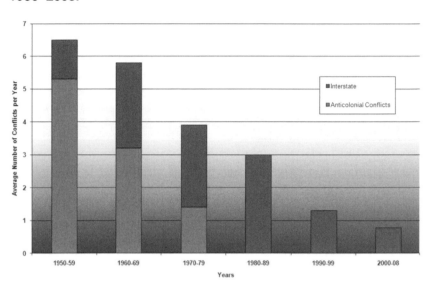

Source: Uppsala Conflict Data Program/Peace Research Institute Oslo 2009.

Understanding the drivers of peace in the post-World War II world at minimum requires explaining the decline international conflicts since the 1950s, and decline in civil wars since the end of the Cold War. The next two sections attempt this, while the final section reflects on the implications these analyses for global security over the next decade.

Explaining the 60-Year Decline in the Incidence of International Conflict

In the 1950s, there were, on average, just over six international conflicts being fought around the world each year—anti-colonial conflicts are included in this category. In the new millennium there has been fewer than one international conflict each year on average, as Figure 3 makes clear.

Moreover, there has not been a single war *between* the major powers for an unprecedented 60-plus years. This does not mean that the major powers are war-averse—far from it. In fact France, the UK, the U.S., and Russia (USSR) top the list of countries that have fought the most wars since 1946—though their wars were almost all fought in poor countries, never against other major powers.

International conflicts are not only fewer in number, they have also become far less deadly. In the 1950s, the average international conflict killed some 20,000 people a year on the battlefield. In the post-Cold War 1990s, the average annual battle-death toll was less than 6,000; in the new millennium the figure was around 3,000.

International relations scholars have offered a number of—contested—explanations for the causes of war and peace in the nuclear age. However, notwithstanding heated debates among their proponents, most of the contested theories are complementary.

A Nuclear Peace?

For "realist" scholars, the absence of war between the major powers during the Cold War years is best explained by the existence of a stable balance of power between East and West—in particular by the deterrence created by the mutual possession of nuclear arsenals with "second strike" capacities.

Kenneth Waltz, the leading proponent of the pacifying impact of nuclear weapons, has argued that, "Peace has become the privilege of states having nuclear weapons, while wars are fought by those who lack them."[3]

But while nuclear arsenals undoubtedly induced a measure of caution in the behavior of the superpowers and their allies towards each other, Waltz' assertion is wrong for two reasons.

First, nuclear weapons states are not embroiled in fewer wars. Quite the contrary. Each of the four countries that have fought most international wars since the end of World War II—France, the UK, the U.S., and Russia (USSR)—is a nuclear weapons state.

---

[3] Kenneth Waltz, "Peace, Stability, and Nuclear Weapons," Institute on Global Conflict and Cooperation, Policy Paper No. 15, University of California, Berkeley, August 1995, p. 9.

Second, since the end of World War II, non-nuclear states have repeatedly attacked nuclear weapons states. U.S. nuclear weapons did not deter China from attacking U.S. forces in the Korean War, nor North Vietnam from attacking South Vietnam and U.S. forces in the 1960s. Israeli nuclear weapons did not dissuade Egypt from attacking Israel in 1973. British nuclear weapons did not deter Argentina from invading the Falkland Islands in 1982, and the Soviet nuclear arsenal did not deter the mujahedeen from waging war against the Soviet army in Afghanistan in the 1980s—nor did it prevent a Soviet defeat.

Somewhat ironically, nuclear weapons are of greatest utility to the very governments that are of greatest proliferation concern to the international community. For small states—like North Korea—that perceive themselves to be under military threat from far more powerful adversaries and that lack powerful allies, nuclear weapons are a relatively low-cost "strategic equalizer." Whether or not the threat they perceive is real is immaterial—it is the perception that counts. This is why the prospect of the paranoid North Koreans giving up their nuclear arsenal any time soon is remote.

The best the international community can hope for here is a "capping" regime that keeps the North Korean nuclear arsenal down to a handful of weapons, plus a verifiable agreement to prevent the cash-strapped regime from selling nuclear technology and materiel to other would-be nuclear powers.

Dissuading Iran from continuing to pursue its nuclear weapons program will be difficult, if not impossible, for essentially the same reason.

While the prospect of further nuclear proliferation is a major security concern, it is important to remember that almost all states that seek a nuclear capability do so for essentially defensive reasons—nuclear weapons have little value as weapons of aggression. And of course they have zero utility in the civil wars that now make up more than 90 percent of all conflicts.

Peace Through Democratization and Interdependence

"Liberal" scholars, who have a much less pessimistic view of human nature and institutions than "realists," believe that the risk of war between states has been reduced since the end of World War II by the steady growth in the number of democracies in the international system and by growing international economic interdependence.

The best-known liberal theory is the "democratic peace," whose central—and uncontested—finding is that fully democratic states never, or to be more precise, *almost* never, go to war against each other.

Proponents of democratic peace theory do not argue that democracies are *generally* peaceful; democracies frequently fight non-democracies. What they argue, simply, is that democratic states do not fight *each other.* If the democratic peace theory is correct, the dramatic increase in the number of democracies around the world over the last three decades will have reduced the number of countries in the world likely to fight each other.

Other liberal scholars place much less stress on the conflict-reducing effect of democracy and a lot more on the security impact of the ever-growing interdependencies that are associated with today's globalized economy. Interdependence increases the costs of going to war, while reducing its benefits. One study by the libertarian Cato Institute argued that when measures of both democratization and economic liberalization are included in statistical analyses, "economic freedom is about 50 times more effective than democracy in diminishing violent conflict."[4]

The debate among quantitative scholars over the *relative* impact of democracy versus economic interdependence on the risk of war is both unresolved and highly technical, but there is little dissent from the proposition that increasing levels of international trade and foreign direct investment (FDI) are associated with a reduced risk of war.

But, increased interdependence is not the only economic driver of reduced war risks. In the modern era there are far fewer economic incentives for embarking on war than there were in the era of colonial expansion. Today it is almost always cheaper—politically as well as economically—to buy raw materials from other countries than to mount invasions in order to seize them.

---

[4] Executive Summary, *Economic Freedom of the World, 2005* (Washington D.C., Cato Institute, 2005), http://www.cato.org/pubs/efw/efw2005/efw2005es.pdf. p. 3.

Peace through Ideas: The Change in Attitudes to War

In the 21st century the traditional economic benefits of conquest have not only largely disappeared, but the resort to war as an instrument of statecraft has become legally and normatively proscribed except in self-defense, or with the authorization of the UN Security Council.

This shift in global norms is evident in the universal recognition of the illegitimacy of colonial conquest and the absence among national governments the world over of the sort of aggressive hyper-nationalism associated with German and Japanese Fascism prior to World War II. What the French call *bellicisme*—the glorification of warfare—has almost completely disappeared from the developed world and very rare elsewhere—though it is characteristic of some radical Islamist organizations like al-Qaeda.

The importance of the anti-war norm is not negated by the fact that it is sometimes violated. All norms are violated to some degree, this does not mean that they are ineffectual.

Explaining the Decline in Civil Wars

The most robust finding to have emerged from two decades of statistical research on the causes of war is that there is a strong association between rising levels of economic development and the risk of war onsets. As national incomes increase, the risk of war declines. Economic development, in other words, appears to be a powerful long-term form of conflict prevention.

Several reasons have been advanced to explain *why* higher incomes should be associated with reduced risks of civil war. The most compelling and best supported, is that income is a "proxy" indicator for state capacity. As national incomes rise, tax revenues increase and state capacity grows. This in turn provides governments with the political, economic, and military resources to prevent rebellions—and to crush militarily those that cannot be stopped via negotiation, or by buying off grievances, or political co-optation.

Rebel groups, often living in the rural periphery, are generally excluded from the benefits of rising levels of development, so the balance of resources relevant to preventing wars, and winning those that cannot be prevented, will—other things being equal—tilt progressively in favour of governments as incomes rise.

Given that economic growth generally increases the capacities of governments relative to those of insurgent organizations, we might expect to see fewer insurgent victories as poor-country incomes rise.

This is in fact the case. In East and Southeast Asia, for example, there has not been a single insurgent military victory since the end of the 1970s, while among the "strong" states of the Middle East and North Africa, there has been just one (Yemen) in the same period. The greatest number of insurgent victories over the past 30 years has been in sub-Saharan Africa—the region with the weakest states.

If, as seems likely, poor-country incomes continue to rise, the prospect for insurgent victories will continue to decline. Confronting diminishing returns from political violence, some would-be rebels may in future be deterred from starting wars.

The Impact of the End of the Cold War

The extraordinary post-Cold War decline in the number of high-intensity conflicts went largely unnoticed in the policy community, the media, and by many in the research community. In the 1990s this was perhaps not surprising. Most people believed that conflict numbers were *increasing*—and they were partly correct. In fact, *twice* as many conflicts *started* in the 1990s, as in the 1980s. But an even greater number of conflicts *ended* in the latter decade. It was this little-recognized, development, that led to the *net* decline in conflict numbers.

The end of the Cold War directly caused, or indirectly catalyzed, a series of changes that had a major impact on the global security landscape.

First, the deep ideological division that had driven conflicts both between and within states in the international system for more than 40 years simply disappeared.

Second, the flow of resources from the US and the Soviet Union and their allies to the warring parties in various "proxy" wars in the developing world simply shrivelled up. One consequence was the ending of "... nearly all the large scale communist insurgencies in the world."[5]

Third, the UN, freed from the political stasis imposed by more than four decades of East-West rivalry, spearheaded an extraordinary upsurge of security initiatives by the international community.

Most notable were "peacemaking" (UN-speak for negotiations to end wars) and post-conflict "peacebuilding," whose central security task, as its name suggests, is to prevent wars that have ended from starting again.

Preventive diplomacy was talked about a great deal but little practiced. This was in part because the UN Security Council is so consumed by the demands of constant crisis management that it has little time to pursue prevention initiatives, and in part because many states in the developing world worried that inviting the UN in to play a dispute resolution role would give unwanted international legitimacy to insurgent groups.

The UN was not alone in its security activism, of course. The World Bank, other international agencies, regional security organizations, donor governments, and huge numbers of international NGOs (nongovernmental organizations) were also actively involved, as were the national governments and national NGOs of the war-affected countries.

The increase in the level of international security activism has been extraordinary. It has included:

- A threefold increase in UN and non-UN peace operations from 1988 to 2008—there are currently more than 30 such operations underway around the world, with a comparable number of non-UN missions in the field.

- An increase in UN Security Council "Chapter VII" resolutions from zero in 1989 to 40 in 2008. Chapter VII resolutions authorize the Security Council to respond to threats to the peace with military force, sanctions, or other means.

---

[5] Ann Hironaka, *Neverending Wars: the International Community, Weak States, and the Perpetuation of Civil War* (Cambridge: Harvard University Press, 2005), p. 124.

- A fivefold increase between 1989 and 2008 in the number of Special Representatives of the Secretary-General of the UN, most of whom have a security-related mandate.

- A tenfold increase between 1991 and 2001 in the number of "Friends of the Secretary-General," "contact groups," and other political arrangements that support peacemaking and post-conflict peacebuilding initiatives.

- A thirteen-fold increase in the number of multilateral-sanctions regimes in place each year between 1991 and 2008.

- A nine-fold increase in the number of ongoing disarmament, demobilization, and reintegration operations from 1989 to 2008.

In some important areas—notably mediation initiatives to end civil wars—we still lack reliable global data. But, there is little doubt that the trends are similar.

Conclusion

The security history of the post-World War II era, despite some major failures, provides grounds for some cautious optimism about the future.

Two system-wide drivers of armed conflict—the imposition of colonial rule on much of the developing world and the Cold War—ceased to exist in this period. Neither will return. No obvious new system-wide source of conflict appears likely to replace them.

Some might argue that the threat of Islamist radicalism exemplified by al-Qaeda is already a major threat to international security. But support for extremist Islamist ideology has declined substantially throughout the Muslim world. Absent popular support, Islamist radicals cannot wage a successful "peoples' war," and without conventional armies, which none have, they cannot overthrow governments. It appears extremely unlikely that radical Islamists can ever energise a effective global campaign comparable to the anti-colonial and Marxist political movements of the Cold War period.

There are other reasons for cautious optimism. First, absent a global economic crisis that is far greater than the current one, economic interdependence will continue to grow. This will likely further increase the costs and decrease the benefits of interstate war—and hence the risk of it occurring.

Second, incomes will almost certainly continue to grow in the developing world. This will continue to enhance state capacity, which almost all the statistical studies agree, reduces the risks of armed conflict.

Third, there are no signs that the international community's commitment to peacemaking and peacebuilding is waning—indeed the contrary is true.

Fourth, in the two decades since the Cold War ended, a dynamic, inchoate, rarely efficient, but nonetheless quite effective, system of global security governance has emerged. Its central focus is civil war in the developing world, and it comprises a loose network of international organizations—most importantly the UN and the World Bank—national governments and NGOs, plus informal clusters of like-minded states such as the various "Friends of the Secretary-General" groups—that share core values and objectives and are created to support peace negotiations and peacebuilding missions.

This is not a mode of governance that eschews the use of the military—indeed peacekeeping is central its peacebuilding policy. But its major security objectives—conflict prevention, peacemaking and post-conflict peacebuilding—are pursued primarily by non-military means.

The evolution of this mode of security governance has been, and remains, messy, disputatious, and—as Rwanda and Darfur remind us—prone to tragic failures. But the security initiatives that have been pursued have been a major driver of the dramatic post-Cold War decline in armed conflict. This is no mean achievement.

Chapter 13

International Security in 2020

James Dobbins

Much of today's geopolitical punditry rests on two assumptions; that American power has passed its zenith and will continue to decline, and that this will occur in a world of increasing disorder and rising conflict. Both these predictions represent straight line projections of what are perceived as current trends: the rise of China, America's diminishing clout, the decline of the West, the growth of terrorism and the importance of non state actors, the shift from a uni- to multi-polar world and the consequent rise in turbulence. As predictions, these two prognoses may or may not be true. As descriptions of the recent past, they are both largely false.

The End of American Hegemony

The early 1990s is generally seen as the apogee of American power. With its Soviet adversary vanquished and no other competitor in sight, the United States emerged as the world only superpower. Yet by any objective measure, the real peak of American power was between 1945 and 1950, when the United States produced and consumed half the world's wealth and had a monopoly on nuclear weapons. By 1970, the American share of global GDP had fallen from half to one-quarter of the world total, and there were four other nuclear powers, two of them hostile.

The relative decline in American power that occurred between 1945 and 1970 was in some measure the product of American policy, specifically its efforts to turn both former allies into prosperous competitors and former enemies into well-armed allies. Since the 1970s, American economic power has remained steady, at about a quarter of global GDP, while American military dominance has grown, not diminished, to the point where today the U.S. defense budget is almost as large as that of every other nation in the world combined. Recent American setbacks in Iraq and Afghanistan have demonstrated the limits on that power, but the United States had an even harder time forty years ago and enjoyed less success in pacifying a significantly smaller and less populous, country, South Vietnam. A comparison of the Vietnam, Afghan and Iraqi campaigns does not suggest any degradation in American military capacity, nor indeed of its political weight, since the United States has been able to secure more international support for both of the latter two ventures than it did for its Vietnam intervention.

Whereas the United States economy has grown at about the global average since the 1970s, Europe, Japan and Russia have grown more slowly than the norm, even as China, Taiwan, South Korea, Indian and Brazil have expanded more quickly. As a result, the rise of China (and these others) has come at the expense not of the United States, but of Europe, Japan and Russia, all of which have seen their share of global GDP, and their resultant influence shrink over the past several decades. Their comparative decline has been even more precipitate in the military sphere for both Europe and Russia.

The United States has also grown demographically at a faster rate than the rest of the world, to include even China. Thus the American population has grown 10 percent since 2000, while its economy expanded by 21 percent, and its defense budget by 55 percent. The United States also has a higher proportion of working age people to dependents than do Russia, Japan, China and most European nations—another source of economic strength.[1]

The Rise of China

While America's global predominance has not significantly diminished since the 1970s, and has indeed grown since the disappearance of the Soviet Union twenty years ago, China and to a lesser extent India are emerging, or reemerging, as major powers. Nevertheless, China still has a way to go before it enters the superpower bracket.

---

[1] Charles Wolf, "Facts About American Decline," *Wall Street Journal*, April 13, 2011.

The Chinese economy is presently 40 to 60 percent the size of the American, depending on whether one uses market exchange rates or purchasing power parity as methods of comparison. The Indian economy is either 26 percent or 42 percent the size of the Chinese, again depending on which method is used. China has been growing faster than India for decades, but the gap in growth rates is narrowing. A RAND analysis of 27 different expert forecasts finds that the projected average annual GDP growth for the two economies through 2025 is approximately the same, 5.7 percent for China, 5.6 percent for India. Assuming that the American economy grows at about half this rate over the same period, China's GDP will be about half that of America's in 2025 at market exchange rates, while India's will remain less than half of China's.[2]

China has a much healthier and better educated population than India and it spends a good deal more on research and development. China has the world's third highest expenditure on R&D, after the United States and Japan. China commits one percent of its GDP to R&D, versus 0.8 percent for India and 2.6 percent for the United States. Given the different size of the three economies, this means China spends three to five times more on R&D as India, whereas the United States spends four to eight times more than China.

China has sustained its high growth rate longer than did the earlier Asian tigers, but it is about to encounter some severe demographic headwinds. Historically, societies have become rich before they became old, as rising prosperity led to declining birth rates and increased longevity. China's one child policy has greatly accelerated this process, and is about to produce the first aged society that is still relatively poor. By 2025, India's population will equal China's after which China's overall population will begin to fall while India's will continue to grow. More significantly, China's working age population will begin to fall much earlier than that, while India's will continue to

---

[2] Data for 2008 from the World Bank, "Country Data," www.worldbank.org. Detailed analyses of Chinese and Indian economic prospects and projections of their future defense spending can be found *in Indian Defense & Defense Procurement Spending to 2025*, Eric Larson and Meilind Huang, RAND, 2010, and *Chinese Defense & Defense Procurement Spending to 2025*, Keith Crane et al, RAND, 2005. A forthcoming RAND study will provide a comparative assessment of the two countries' development over the next fifteen years.

grow for another twenty years and then decline much more slowly. As China's working age population declines, its elderly population will grow. Dependency ratios will rise, savings rates will decline, and the government will face heightened pressures to increase spending on health care and pensions. These demographic factors are among the chief reasons that Chinese and Indian economic growth rates are likely to converge.

Although much has been written about increases in Chinese defense spending, China has in this regard actually been falling further behind the United States. In 2000 the American defense budget was seven times that of China, in 2010 it was ten times bigger. Of course, China is not fighting any wars, which accounts for much of the American increase.[3]

China and India both spend about 2.5 percent of their GDP on defense, more or less equal to the shares of the United Kingdom or Russia, but about half the current American proportion. RAND economists estimate that China defense spending will be a little more than half that of the United States by 2025, while India's will be a half to a quarter that of China's. China will thus begin to narrow the military gap with the United States over the next fifteen years, while India will remain pretty much its current distance behind China.

As these figures suggest, for another generation, at least, the United States will remain the world's predominant power, albeit less dominant than heretofore. China and India will become more influential actors. China is already the world's second largest economy and will soon be its second largest military power. India will maintain but probably not gain measurably on its current position vis-à-vis China. Europe, Japan and Russia may see their relative positions wane further.

The End of History and the Decline of the West

China and Russia may not themselves be models of democracy, but neither state is seeking to export any alternative ideology. Indeed both China and Russia regularly vote for and fund UN efforts to hold free elections in fragile states around the globe. Only strict Islamists cur-

---

[3] Wolf, op. cit.

rently offer any systematic alternative to representative democracy, and this ideology has shown only limited appeal in Muslim societies and none whatsoever beyond them. Iran, the sole exemplar, has not had the slightest success exporting its system. Frank Fukuyama may have been somewhat premature in declaring that the collapse of communism represented the end of history, in the sense of competing ideologies, but it is certainly true that history has been moving in this direction for several decades. Only the Arab Middle East has escaped until very recently the democratizing trend that has swept through Europe, Latin America, Asia and even Africa. Thus, since the 1980s the global number of democratic nations has doubled, from under thirty to almost sixty.[4] In the spring of 2011 several Arab societies sought to jump on the democratic bandwagon.

If one defines the West geographically as the United States and Europe, or in Cold War geopolitical terms as the United States, Europe and Japan, then there has already been some relative decline vis-à-vis China, a decline which will likely be accentuated further over the next decade. If, by contrast, the West is conceived ideologically to include all established democracies that are marked by representative governments, the regular alternance in power, civil liberties and free market economies, then nearly all of the world's fastest growing states, with the exception of China, but including India, South Korea, Taiwan, and Brazil, must be counted on the Western side of the global equation. So defined, the "West", far from declining, has seen an extraordinary expansion over the past several decades, its values now almost universally espoused and increasingly widely practiced.

New World Disorder

Americans and Europeans tend to recall the Cold War era as tense and occasionally scary era, but basically stable and peaceful. They contrast this oddly nostalgic image with the much more fluid and uncertain international environment they have experienced, or at least observed over the past twenty years. The immediacy and global reach of modern communications heighten their perception of turbulence and rising violence and intensifies the anxieties that go with it.

---

[4] Polity IV Project, University of Maryland.

Contrary to this picture of a peaceful cold war and an increasingly violent aftermath, actual trends have been just the opposite, with rising conflict throughout the duration of the Cold War, and a falling incidence of warfare thereafter. From the 1950s to the early 1990s the number of wars, mostly civil, rose year after year. In the early 1990s, even as the Soviet Union was disappearing into history, the number of conflicts simultaneously underway around the world had risen to over fifty. The social impact of these wars, as measured in casualties, refugees and physical destruction, also rose commensurately throughout this forty year period.[5] The Cold War was certainly peaceful compared to the historically unparalleled half century of bloodletting that preceded it, but it was much more violent than anything that has followed.

As Andrew Mack makes clear in his chapter of this volume, the number of conflicts, the number of battle deaths, and the ancillary consequences of conflict all fell precipitously over the next two decades. There are currently a couple of dozen wars ongoing, all civil, but most recent wars have been smaller, less destructive and shorter in duration than those that preceded them. Indeed, the World Bank has found that mortality rates have been declining of late *even in states in conflict*. Improvements in health care and economic growth have combined to increase longevity in societies around the world, and the pace of this process now exceeds the contrary effects of armed conflict even in most societies experiencing undergoing civil wars.[6] Andrew Mack's *Human Security Report* for 2009/10 comments on this counterintuitive phenomenon, noting that "the reality is simply that today's armed conflicts rarely generate enough fatalities to reverse the long-term downward trend in peacetime mortality that has become the norm for most of the developing world."

Given the growth in global population and the decline in armed conflict, it seems probable that a smaller proportion of humanity is directly affected by warfare today than at any time in human history. This happy situation does not represent the perfection of human nature or even the slow march of civilization. The first half of the 20th

---

[5] Figures 10/1 and 10/6, *Human Security Report 2009/10*, Simon Fraser University, Canada.

[6] Syan Chen, Noran Loayza and Marta Reynal-Querol, *World Bank Economic Review*, 2008.

century was, after all, probably the most violent in recorded history. Today's comparatively tranquil international environment is the product of geopolitical circumstances which may not last forever, but show no sign of rapid erosion. All of the world's major powers suffered grievous losses during both World Wars, and became more risk adverse as a result. Nuclear deterrence helped prevent direct conflict between these major powers throughout the latter half of the 20th century, but only at the risk of mutual annihilation. Since the end of the Cold War, the major powers have also ceased to conduct proxy wars against each other. On the contrary, they have routinely collaborated, usually via the United Nations, in settling localized disputes and working to prevent their reoccurrence. Wars, almost all civil in nature, continue to break out, but they tend to be contained, short-lived and not repeated due to international support for conflict resolution , peacekeeping and peace building and a growing international willingness to isolate, suppress and punish the worst offenders.

During the Cold War, Americans and, to an even greater extent Europeans were insulated from much of the world's turbulence by the absence of direct conflict among the major powers. In the subsequent two decades, Americans and Europeans have become more exposed to violence elsewhere, at least in a virtual sense, because they have joined with the rest of the international community in trying to stop it. The level of conflict has fallen because the level of international involvement in trying to end such conflicts has risen. Since the early 1990s a new peacekeeping mission has been dispatched, on average, every six months. Cambodia, El Salvador, Namibia, Mozambique, Albania, Bosnia, Kosovo, Macedonia, Sierra Leone, Liberia and East Timor are at peace today, and most of these societies are currently ruled by freely elected governments because United Nations, NATO, European Union or nationally-led coalitions have intervened to separate the combatants, disarm and demobilize the contending factions, stimulate the economy, promote political and economic reform, oversee free elections and remain long enough to ensure that the resultant governments can take hold. The United States and Europe have paid at least half the costs for all these operations, contributed soldiers and police to many of them, and led several of the largest.

America's Role

As the world's predominant power for another generation at least the United States will continue to assume leadership responsibilities for protecting the global commons, to include freedom of the seas, space and cyberspace. Security challenges during this period will continue to come not from peer competitors, but from rogue regimes, fragile or failed states, and non-state actors.

While continuing to shoulder the burdens of leadership, the United States will seek to share these more broadly. Washington has already begun accommodating itself to the rise of China, India and others by deemphasizing the Eurocentric G-7/8 in favor of the G-20. Over the next decade other such adjustments will be in order. The UN Security Council is likely to be enlarged to include India as well as Japan and Brazil. Within limits, India can be seen as a valuable counterweight to growing Chinese power. Nevertheless, there is no inevitability to conflict with China, and no aspect of Chinese aspirations, as one currently understands them, that necessarily threaten such conflict. Facing no peer, or even near peer competitor well into the next decade, the United States will have no need to build a countervailing alliance, and it should, on the contrary, work to diminish anyone's incentive to form such blocs.

NATO's Future

The continued relevance of the Atlantic Alliance, and its inherent limitations were both reemphasized in the 2011 Libyan crisis. NATO represents the only institutional alternative to nationally led ad-hoc coalitions in conducting peace enforcement or humanitarian operations in non-permissive environments. On the other hand, the Alliance's exclusively trans-Atlantic membership limits its appeal to and entrée into other regions. Its requirement for unanimity, its tolerance for national caveats on the use of their forces and its inability to provide non-member co-combatants an effective voice in directing operations makes it both more cumbersome and more exclusionary than the United Nations, where only five, rather than twenty-five members can exercise veto rights, and all states have at least occasional seats on the Security Council as well as permanent seats in the General Assembly that controls the purse strings.

Libyan operations also highlight the continued run-down in European military capabilities. Despite that country's proximity to Europe, despite heavy American commitments in both Iraq and Afghanistan and despite everyone's agreement that Europe, rather than the United States should take the lead in this mission, it fell to Americans both to lead and provide the bulk of the forces through the early days. Europe thus remains fully as dependent on American military capabilities today is it did sixteen years ago in the Balkans, despite all of the intervening rhetoric and institutional innovation designed to strengthen Europe's capacity for independent expeditionary warfare.

The Iraqi and Afghan experiences have led to a "never again" reaction among American and European publics, much as Vietnam did nearly four decades ago. In the aftermath of that earlier war the American military consciously turned its back on counterinsurgency for thirty years. As a result, the United States and its allies have had to reacquire these skills belatedly and at great expense in blood and treasure. It will certainly be tempting, as the Iraqi and Afghan missions wind down, to again turn away from this form of warfare. Yet experience also shows that the cost of doing so could be very high, since it is quite impossible to predict where Western forces may become engaged five or ten years hence. Indeed, who would have predicted in January of 2011 that NATO would be fighting in Libya by March.

The recent string of popular uprisings in the Middle East, like the fall of the Berlin wall, the disintegration of the Soviet Union, the collapse of Yugoslavia and the attacks of 9/11 remind us how rapidly the global security environment can change. Yet one encouraging aspect of the changes underway in the Middle East has been the relatively concerted international response. The United States., Europe and Russia spent the first half of the 1990s at loggerheads over what to do about the Balkan wars. They and the rest of the international community agreed to launch (or in Russia and Germany's case not to block) an intervention in Libya within days of commencement of large scale fighting there.

The current upheaval throughout the Arab world could well change the nature of American and European interaction with the Arab world. Depending on the fate of democratization in Egypt and Tunisia and on the outcome of NATO's engagement in Libya, one may see the evolution toward a more collaborative relationship between Middle Eastern nations and the Atlantic Alliance. Possibilities might include a NATO role in helping preserve an Israeli-Palestinian peace, and in securing the Gulf states against a nuclearizing Iran.

Europe's Role

President Obama's insistence on *not* leading the Libyan campaign any longer than necessary could also presage some larger rebalancing of Western burdens for security. Certainly the Obama administration would seem to favor such a development. But such a move would require that European governments take advantage of the opportunity, halt the decline in their military capabilities and narrow their differences over the use of armed force as an instrument of policy. As of this writing, one would have to assess the chances of that happening over the next decade as less than even. France and Britain have demonstrated their continued willingness to project power and employ armed force, but they have found it easier to carry the United Nations Security Council with them than either NATO or the European Union. Certainly individual European nations will continue to play important roles throughout the Middle East, while the European Union may likely become a more significant partner for the emerging democracies of the region in the economic, political and social spheres. Within the domain of defense and security, however, the most important decisions will continue to be made by national governments even when collective action is taken via NATO, the UN or nationally led coalitions in most circumstances. The European Union seems likely to continue to limit its military expeditions to the least demanding of cases.

Interdependence and Vulnerability

Since the end of the Korean War there has been no armed conflict between any major powers. Since the end of the Cold War, the major powers have also ceased to fight proxy wars. On the contrary, they have collaborated with the broader international community to end such conflicts and prevent their reoccurrence. As a result the world has become more peaceful. It has also, as a result, become more interdependent. The prosperity, if not the physical safety of Americans and Europeans depends on what happens on the other side of the globe, and on the reliability of the links which deliver people, goods services and information from great distances. Small groups of individuals or otherwise weak and insignificant states can wreak disproportionate damage by attacking these links. Piracy at sea is hardly a new phenomenon, but its recent revival is a reminder of the cost the entire world economy bears when a small and desolate portion of the globe is left ungoverned for any length of time. Airplane hijacking is also a familiar threat, made more dangerous when the planes themselves are turned into weapons of mass destruction. The internet represents the latest frontier of interdependence and consequent vulnerability, an exposure to risk from which geography offers no safety whatsoever.

Interdependence also brings heightened vulnerability to natural phenomenon. In 2010 more people died in Haiti's earthquake than in all the worlds' wars put together, yet Haiti was not deeply embedded in the global economy and its catastrophe had little larger effect. The following year far fewer people were immediately affected by Japan's earthquake, yet factories in American and Europe almost immediately slowed as essential parts threatened to become scarce. Global warming will affect different parts of the world differently, but its costs will be distributed universally, if not uniformly. Societal resilience will emerge as an important component of long term security, offering recovery from disasters which cannot be prevented.

Assuming continued collective action to reduce the scope and frequency of armed conflict, most of the world's population will find the weather to be more of a threat than any foreign or domestic enemy. Collaboration to address these less traditional security challenges is likely to take place largely outside NATO or the UN Security Council and to involve elements of national governments other then foreign and defense ministries. It is in these non-traditional security spheres that the European Union has most to offer its members and its external partners and it is into these areas that transatlantic collaboration will be increasingly moving over the coming decade.

About the Authors

Daniel S. Hamilton is the Austrian Marshall Plan Foundation Professor and Director of the Center for Transatlantic Relations at the Paul H. Nitze School of Advanced International Studies (SAIS), Johns Hopkins University. He also serves as Executive Director of the American Consortium for EU Studies, designated by the European Commission as the EU Center of Excellence Washington, DC. He has served as Deputy Assistant Secretary of State for Europe; U.S. Special Coordinator for Southeast European Stabilization; and as Associate Director of the U.S. Secretary of State's Policy Planning Staff. In 2008 he served as the first Robert Bosch Foundation Senior Diplomatic Fellow in the German Foreign Office. He hosted *The Washington Post/Newsweek International*'s online discussion feature *Next Europe*, serves as a consultant to Microsoft; and is a member of academic and advisory boards for the Robert Bosch Stiftung; the Stiftung Wissenschaft und Politik (SWP); the European-American Business Council; the Center for European Policy Analysis; the Prague Center for Transatlantic Relations; the Danish Institute for International Studies; and the Council on European Studies. He has also taught graduate courses in U.S. foreign policy and U.S.-European relations at the University of Innsbruck, the Hertie School of Governance in Berlin, and the Free University of Berlin. He has a Ph.D from Johns Hopkins University. Recent publications include *Europe 2020: Competitive or Complacent?* (2011); *Shoulder to Shoulder: Forging a Strategic U.S.-EU Partnership* (2010); *Alliance Reborn: An Atlantic Compact for the 21st Century* (2009) by the Washington NATO Project; The *Transatlantic Economy* (annual editions, 2004-2011); *Europe and Globalization* (2008); and *The Wider Black Sea Region: Strategic, Economic and Energy Perspectives* (2008).

Kurt Volker is Senior Fellow and Managing Director of the Center on Transatlantic Relations at the Paul H. Nitze School of Advanced International Studies (SAIS), Johns Hopkins University. He is also Managing Director, International, for BGR Group and a Senior Advisor at the Atlantic Council of the United States and a member of its Strategic Advisory Group. Prior to joining SAIS, Ambassador Volker was a career member of the United States Senior Foreign Service, with over 23 years of experience working on European political and security issues under five U.S. Administrations. He served as Ambassador and the 19th U.S. Permanent Representative on the Council of the North Atlantic Treaty Organization (NATO); Principal Deputy Assistant Secretary for European and Eurasian Affairs; Acting Senior Director for European and Eurasian Affairs and Director for NATO and West Europe at the National Security Council (NSC); Deputy Director of the Private Office of then-NATO Secretary General Lord Robertson; First Secretary at the U.S. Mission to NATO from 1998 to 1999; and as a State Department Legislative Fellow in the office of U.S. Senator John McCain. He has a B.A. from Temple University and an M.A. in International Relations from the Elliott School of International Affairs at George Washington University.

James F. Dobbins directs RAND's International Security and Defense Policy Center. He has held State Department and White House posts including Assistant Secretary of State for Europe, Special Assistant to the President for the Western Hemisphere, Special Adviser to the President and Secretary of State for the Balkans, and Ambassador to the European Community. He has handled a variety of crisis management assignments as the Clinton Administration's special envoy for Somalia, Haiti, Bosnia, and Kosovo, and the Bush Administration's first special envoy for Afghanistan. He is lead author of the three volume *RAND History of Nation Building* and *Occupying Iraq: A History of the Coalition Provisional Authority.* In the wake of Sept 11, 2001, Dobbins was designated as the Bush Administration's representative to the Afghan opposition. Dobbins helped organize and then represented the United States at the Bonn Conference where a new Afghan government was formed. On Dec. 16, 2001, he raised the flag over the newly reopened U.S. Embassy. Dobbins graduated from the Georgetown School of Foreign Service and served 3 years in the U.S. Navy. He is married to Toril Kleivdal, and has two sons.

Giovanni Grevi is a senior researcher with FRIDE and head of FRIDE's Brussels office. Before joining FRIDE, Giovanni was a policy analyst (1998–2002) and associate director of studies (2002–2005) at the European Policy Centre and served as a senior research fellow at the EU Institute for Security Studies between 2005 and 2010. He has worked and published extensively on the development of the foreign and security policy of the European Union, EU institutional reform and global governance, and has co-directed major foresight projects on the future of Europe and of the international system. He holds an MSC from the London School of Economics and a Ph.D from the Université Libre de Bruxelles.

Carl Haub is a demographer and Senior Visiting Scholar at the Population Reference Bureau (PRB) in Washington, D.C. He is the author of numerous articles, demographic studies and publications on U.S. and global population trends. Since 1980 he has prepared the annual *World Population Data Sheet*, the most widely circulated world population data source in use. His recent publications include the Population Bulletins; *The Global Demographic Divide*; *India's Population Reality: Reconciling Change and Tradition*; and a series of long-range projections of the population of the states of India. His international experience includes work in Belarus, Germany, Honduras, India, Jamaica, Seychelles, Trinidad and Tobago, Vietnam and Zambia. The demography of India, where he has traveled frequently since 1994, is a specialty. He has produced projections of the school-age population in both Jamaica and Trinidad and Tobago for the Education Ministries of those countries during a project funded by the Inter-American Development Bank and district-level projections in Seychelles for the World Bank. He has also served on United Nations Expert Groups on a variety of demographic subjects, most recently on future global fertility trends in 2009. He has provided daily support to the media, writers and staff of nongovernmental organizations and to government on demographic subjects in addition to frequent public speaking activities and media interviews. He has also worked in the field of demography at the National Academy of Sciences, the World Bank, and the U.S. Bureau of the Census. He holds a B.A. degree in Political Science and a M.A. degree in Demography from Georgetown University.

Bruce Jentleson is Professor of Public Policy and Political Science at Duke University. From 2009-2011 he served on a consulting basis as Senior Advisor to the U.S. State Department Policy Planning Director. His most recent books are *The End of Arrogance: America in the Global Competition of Ideas*, co-authored with Steven Weber (Harvard University Press, 2010) and *American Foreign Policy: The Dynamics of Choice in the 21ˢᵗ Century*, now in its 4ᵗʰ edition (W.W. Norton, 2010).

Reiner Klingholz is Director of the Berlin Institute for Population and Development, a German think tank that produces studies on different aspects of demographic change. The Institute has recently published "The waning world power—the demographic future of Russia and the other Soviet successor states" (2011), available at www.berlin-institut.org.

Bengt-Åke Lundvall is Professor in Economics at the Department of Business Studies, Aalborg University, and at Sciences Po, Paris. He developed the concept 'national system of innovation' in close collaboration with Christopher Freeman in the 1980s and the concept 'the learning economy' in the 1990s. Since 2003 he has been coordinating the worldwide research network on innovation research called GLOBELICS. He served as Deputy Director at the OECD from 1992–1995 and in 2009 he was nominated Ambassador for the European Year of Creativity and Innovation. His current research links innovation to economic development and learning at the workplace to national systems of innovation.

Andrew Mack is Director of the Human Security Report Project and a member of the faculty of the School for International Studies at Simon Fraser University in Vancouver. He has held teaching and research positions in the UK, Denmark, Australia, the U.S. and Japan and from 1998 to 2001 was Director of the Strategic Planning Unit in Kofi Annan's Executive Office at the UN. He has authored or edited some 16 books and monographs on wide range of international security issues including the *Human Security Report* and *Human Security Brief* series.

Shakuntala Makhijani is a Research Associate at the Worldwatch Institute. She works on transatlantic energy and climate policy issues and low-carbon energy development strategies in India and the Caribbean. Prior to joining Worldwatch, she worked with the Center for Clean Air Policy on international climate negotiations. She holds an M.S. in Sustainable Systems from the University of Michigan's School of Natural Resources and Environment and a B.S.F.S. in Science, Technology and International Affairs from the Edmund Walsh School of Foreign Service at Georgetown University.

Hanns W. Maull holds the Chair for Foreign Policy and International Relations at the University of Trier in Germany and spent the academic year 2010/2011 as a Senior Fellow at the Transatlantic Academy in Washington, D.C. He previously taught at the universities of Munich and Eichstaett in Germany, as well as at the Bologna Center of Johns Hopkins University SAIS. He serves as chairman on the advisory board of the German Institute for International Security Studies of the Foundation for Science and Policy (SWP), Germany's foremost foreign policy think tank, in Berlin.

Alexander Ochs is Director of Climate and Energy at the Worldwatch Institute in Washington DC where he is also a member of the Institute's management team and chief editor of the renowned Re I Volt blog. Since 2007 he has served as President of the Forum for Atlantic Climate and Energy Talks (FACET). Currently a senior fellow at the American Institute for Contemporary German Studies and an adjunct professor in George Washington University's Sustainable Urban Planning Program, he has held senior research and teaching positions at the Center for Clean Air Policy, the German Institute for International and Security Affairs, CUNY, as well as Munich, Princeton, Free University and Humboldt universities. In 2011, he received the Sustainable Future Award of the Austrian Academic Forum for Foreign Affairs.

Michael F. Oppenheimer is Clinical Professor in the Global Affairs masters degree program at New York University. His courses include International Relations, International Political Economy, U.S. Foreign Policy, and Future International Systems. He is the originator and director of the Carnegie Corporation funded project on alternate futures for pivotal countries, which has published *China 2020, Russia 2020, Turkey 2020, Ukraine 2020*, and *Pakistan 2020*. He has done extensive consulting, specializing in futures-oriented policy analysis for the U.S. foreign policy and intelligence communities, and for think tanks. He is a life member of the Council on Foreign Relations, The Foreign Policy Roundtable at the Carnegie Council on Ethics and International Affairs, and the American Council on Germany.

Demetrios G. Papademetriou is President and Co-Founder of the Migration Policy Institute (MPI), a Washington-based think tank dedicated exclusively to the study of international migration. He is also the convener of the Transatlantic Council on Migration, which is composed of senior public figures, business leaders, and public intellectuals from Europe, the United States, and Canada. He is Co-Founder and International Chair *Emeritus* of *Metropolis: An International Forum for Research and Policy on Migration and Cities*. He also is Chair of the World Economic Forum's Global Agenda Council on Migration. He holds a Ph.D in Comparative Public Policy and International Relations (1976) and has taught at the universities of Maryland, Duke, American, and New School for Social Research. He has held a wide range of senior positions that include: Chair of the Migration Committee of the Organization for Economic Cooperation and Development (OECD); Director for Immigration Policy and Research at the U.S. Department of Labor and Chair of the Secretary of Labor's Immigration Policy Task Force; and Executive Editor of the *International Migration Review*. He has published more than 250 books, articles, monographs, and research reports on migration topics and advises senior government and political party officials in more than 20 countries, including numerous EU member states. His most recent books include *Immigration Policy in the Federal Republic of Germany: Negotiating Membership and Remaking the Nation* (co-author, 2010); *Gaining from Migration: Towards a New Mobility System*, OECD Development Center (co-author, 2007); *Immigration and America's Future: A New Chapter* (co-author, 2006); *Europe and its Immigrants in the 21st Century: A New Deal or a Continuing Dialogue of the Deaf?* (editor and author, 2006); and *Secure Borders, Open Doors: Visa Procedures in the Post-September 11 Era* (co-author, 2005).

Madeleine Sumption is a Policy Analyst at the Migration Policy Institute, where she works on the Labor Markets Initiative and the International Program. Her work focuses on labor migration, the role of immigrants in the labor market, and the impact of immigration policies in Europe, North America, and other OECD countries. Her recent publications include *Policies to Curb Illegal Employment* (Migration Policy Institute); *Aligning Temporary Immigration Visas with US Labor Market Needs* (Migration Policy Institute, co-author); *Migration and Immigrants Two Years After the Financial Collapse* (BBC World Service and Migration Policy Institute, co-editor and author); *Immigration and the Labor Market: Theory, Evidence and Policy* (Equality and Human Rights Commission, co-author); *Migration and the Economic Downturn: What to Expect in the European Union* (Migration Policy Institute, co-author); and *Social Networks and Polish Immigration to the UK* (Institute for Public Policy Research). She holds a Master's degree with honors from the University of Chicago's school of public policy. She also holds a First Class Degree in Russian and French from Oxford University.

Christof van Agt joined the International Energy Program of the Clingendael Institute for International Relations in January 2009 (www.clingendael.nl) as Senior Research Fellow on Eurasian energy sector affairs. From 2001 to 2007 he managed energy policy initiatives with Caspian and Central Asian States for the Office for Global Energy Dialogue of the International Energy Agency in Paris. This involved in-depth analysis of regional oil and gas market dynamics and coordination of stakeholder dialogue with IEA on Central Asia and the Caspian Sea region. From 1996 to 2001 he administered technical assistance projects in Central Asia and the South Caucasus on inter-state oil and gas networks for the European Commission and assisted in negotiations on the Energy Charter Treaty, Transit Protocol and Model Agreements on Cross Border Pipelines at the Energy Charter Secretariat in Brussels. He coordinated various projects on energy sector reform in the Newly Independent States working with the International Institute for Energy Law at the University of Leiden from 1992 to 1996. He studied Slavonic Languages and Sovietology in Leiden from 1986 to 1991.

Theo Veenkamp is retired and currently advising the Netherlands Supreme Court. He holds an M.A. in Political Science from the Free University of Amsterdam. He taught Public Administration at the Free University and worked with the municipal government of Amsterdam (urban renewal policy) and the Gadjah Mada University in Yogyakarta (integrated rural delopment oriented upgrading of teaching and research). He was head of the NUFFIC (Netherlands Organisation for International Cooperation in Higher Education), the EU TEMPUS Office (support for higher education in Central and Eastern Europe) in Brussels, the Netherlands Agency for the Reception of Asylum Seekers and the think tank of the Netherlands Ministry of

Justice. He is associate of Demos, the London think tank, and of the Van Vollenhoven Institute for Law, Government and Development, Leiden University. He was active in boards and committees for public housing, secundary education, research in developing countries, the treatment of war traumas and the professional training of judges and prosecutors. He has published in a variety of ways on topics directly or indirectly related to his professional activities.

Richard Youngs is director general of FRIDE. He is also assistant professor at the University of Warwick in the UK. Prior to joining FRIDE, he was EU Marie Curie research fellow at the Norwegian Institute for International Relations, Oslo (2001–2004), and senior research fellow at the UK Foreign and Commonwealth Office (1995–1998). He has written six books on different elements of European external policy, the most recent of which is *Europe's Decline and Fall: The Struggle Against Global Irrelevance* (Profile Books, 2010).